STRATFORD DE REDCLIFFE

PRINTED BY
SPOTTISWOODE AND CO., NEW-STREET SQUARE
LONDON

THE LIFE

OF

LORD STRATFORD DE REDCLIFFE

K. G.

BY

STANLEY LANE-POOLE

Popular Edition

WITH THREE PORTRAITS

LONDON

LONGMANS, GREEN, AND CO.

AND NEW YORK: 15 EAST 16th STREET

1890

Stratford Canning

ÆT. 29.

From a miniature by A. Robertson 1816. Engraved by G. J. Stodart.

London. Longmans. Green & Cº

ADVERTISEMENT

THE present Edition is condensed from the Library Edition, published in two volumes in 1888, chiefly by the omission of the longer dispatches and memoranda. While nothing of general interest has been sacrificed, reference must be made to the larger work for such detailed explanations and authenticating references as are necessarily excluded from a volume of this scope.

S. L.-P.

CONTENTS

—◆◇◆—

INTRODUCTION

CHAPTER I

CHAPTER II

CHAPTER III

CHAPTER IV

1812-14 TWO YEARS OF IDLENESS 57

CHAPTER V

1814-19 THE CONGRESS OF VIENNA . . . 69

CHAPTER VI

CHAPTER VII

CHAPTER VIII

CHAPTER IX

CHAPTER X

CHAPTER XI

CHAPTER XII

CHAPTER XIII

CHAPTER XIV

CHAPTER XV

CHAPTER XVI

CHAPTER XVII

CHAPTER XVIII

CHAPTER XIX

CHAPTER XX

a

CHAPTER XXI

CHAPTER XXII

CHAPTER XXIII

CHAPTER XXIV

CHAPTER XXV

PORTRAITS

LIFE

OF

STRATFORD CANNING,

VISCOUNT STRATFORD DE REDCLIFFE.

———•◇•———

INTRODUCTION.

EARLY YEARS.

1786-1807.

THREE statues stand side by side in Westminster Abbey:
they represent George Canning, the Minister, his son
Charles, Earl Canning, first Viceroy of India, and his cousin
Stratford Canning, Viscount Stratford de Redcliffe. The
dates on the first and last of these monuments indicate a
period of no less than one hundred and ten years. From the
birth of Mr. Canning in 1770 to the death of Lord Stratford
in 1880, at the advanced age of ninety-three, more than a century of the world's history had elapsed. For fifty years of
that time Lord Stratford was actively engaged in public life.
His ambition, never relinquished through life, was to serve
England in England. Fate sent him to the East, and he took
up the burden—for burden it was to the last—and did there
what he would fain have done at home : he made the name
of England great with a moral force emanating from the
strength of his own character ; he held the balance of power
between contending nations, and virtually ruled the country
in which he dwelt.

The Cannings from early times had been honourably
known among the merchant class of the West of England.
From Bishop's Canynge in Wiltshire, which appears to have

B

been their early home, they moved to Bristol, where they first
appear in the civic annals in the person of William Canynges,
who was bailiff in 1361, and was subsequently six times
mayor and thrice member of Parliament for the city. He was
a contemporary of Thomas Blanket, whose connexion with
the woollen trade has been immortalized in one of its pro-
ducts, and like him was a wealthy clothworker and shipowner.
With other members of his family he liberally contributed to
the building of the Church of St. Mary Redcliffe: Chatterton,
in the fictitious Rowley Manuscripts, referred to his father as

> Thys Morneynge Starre of Radcleves rysynge raie,
> A true manne, goode of mynde, and Canynge hyghte.

The connexion of the family with the civic offices of Bristol
did not end with this worthy merchant, round whose name
many local associations still linger. His son was also mayor,
and of his grandsons one followed in the same office and
another became lord mayor of London. The former, the
Sir William Canynges who lies buried in the Church of St.
Mary Redcliffe, was even more famous in the annals of his
native city, where he has always been regarded as a type of
the merchant princes of his age. He was four times mayor
of Bristol in the middle of the fifteenth century, and in that
capacity entertained successively Margaret of Anjou and
Edward IV. when they visited the West. The College of
Westbury-on-Trim was indebted to him for its restoration,
and here he ended his days, having exchanged the cares of
business for the repose of a monastery. Many members of
his family had formerly belonged to the Benedictine order,
and in that society he was enrolled in 1467, and, rapidly rising
to the dignity of dean of the college, died about 1474. With
this second and greater William the family disappears from
the municipal annals of Bristol.

His brother Thomas Canynges was sheriff of London in
1450, when he took an active part in the suppression of Jack
Cade's rebellion. He was elected lord mayor in 1456, and
exerted himself in preserving order in a time of riot and confusion. By his marriage with Agnes Salmon, heiress of
Foxcote, the seat of the Le Marshals in Warwickshire, his
posterity became possessed of a county position, in which they
lived in tranquil obscurity until the estate, in default of heirs
male, passed in the present century into the possession of
the Howards of Corby. The fact that they always re-

mained catholics may account for the small share they took in politics; but the ancient commercial instincts of the family were not quite extinct, for members of it continued to uphold the traditions of their forefathers as merchants of Bristol.

The family of Lord Stratford de Redcliffe is connected collaterally with that of Foxcote. It combines the blood of the West-country with the honest strain of Ulster. A certain George Canninge, descended in the fourth generation from Sir Thomas the lord mayor, obtained the grant of the manor of Garvagh in Derry from James I. in 1618, and there died in 1646. His son William was killed in O'Neill's rebellion, and his grandson was attainted in the Irish parliament of 1689, but two years later the attainder was reversed. From him descended the present Lord Garvagh as well as George and Stratford Canning. The last name was introduced by the marriage of Lord Stratford's great-grandfather with Abigail, daughter of Robert Stratford of Baltinglass, in 1662 member for Wicklow. The only son of this marriage was the first Stratford Canning, generally known in his later days as Counsellor Canning, on account of his legal training. Like his immediate predecessors he lived in retirement, though his marriage with Letitia Newburgh of Ballyhouse, co. Cavan, brought him a substantial addition to his moderate income. His tastes, however, were not sociable; in his family he bore a character of extreme austerity, and his children used to recall the terror with which they listened to the creaking of his shoes as he walked about the house. His habitual stern-ness found ample exercise in the repression of his three sons, and it is a question whether the world ought not to be more grateful for Counsellor Canning's severity than for the indul-gence of other parents. At least it is remarkable that the two sons he disowned were the fathers of the two most distinguished holders of the name. The stimulating influence of comparative poverty upon men of worth has seldom been better exemplified than in the disinherited offspring of the first Stratford Canning. Banished from their father's house, the sons were forced to face the world upon their own re-sources and to make their way upon their own merits. Both died in early manhood, but each left a son capable of imitating the spirited independence of his father, and able to make a name for himself in the great world of European politics.

Of the three sons of the Counsellor, George the eldest displeased his father by an imprudent attachment, broken off, but followed by an equally imprudent marriage, which was soon dissolved by his premature death, after his wife had given birth to the well-known minister and orator, the Rt. Hon. George Canning. The youngest, a second Stratford, and father of the third of that name, was, like his elder brother, turned adrift penniless and unforgiven to the last. Our knowledge of him rests chiefly on his letters, of which a good many have been preserved. They shew a sensitive sweet disposition, stronger in the affections than in the will, and confirm the impression produced by his portrait by Romney at Frant Court. The countenance is singularly refined, but the delicately moulded features, despite a strong family resemblance, lack the strength of his son's powerful face. The elder Stratford had, however, will enough to resist his father's veto and to marry the lady he loved—Mehitabel Patrick, the daughter of a well-to-do Dublin merchant. He made indeed one effort to renounce her, and went abroad with that object; but on his return an accidental encounter in the street convinced him that he was no longer master of his heart, and there was no more talk of renunciation. They had a very hard struggle during the early years of their married life, and it is a sure proof of the goodness of the man's nature that in the midst of his own troubles he never ceased to help and comfort the widow and children of his elder brother, George, who had died in destitution in 1771.

Unfortunately, just when his business was growing into a prosperous state, and his boys were becoming old enough to need a father's guidance, Stratford Canning died (1787). His wife was left with an infant of only six months—the future ambassador—besides four elder children.[1] To tell how she brought them up, how she sat at her husband's desk in Clement's Lane, and carried on his business till her eldest son could take it up; how she contrived to combine the functions of mother, tutor, and banker, and to do all this with infinite credit, would be to write the life of this remarkable woman, which is not the present purpose. She survived her husband nearly half a century, and to the last retained her

---

[1] Henry, the eldest, died at Hamburg, British consul-general and diplomatic resident in that city. William, the second, closed his days at Windsor a canon of the royal chapel. Charles, the third, fell at Waterloo, a lieutenant-colonel in the Guards, and one of the Duke of Wellington's aides-de-camp. The sister married the head partner in the old banking-house of Barnett, Hoare & Co., by whom she had a numerous family. Her eldest son inherited the estate of Glympton Park in Oxfordshire, and was member for Woodstock.

always my dearest Bradford's loving Mother McGenning

mental vigour and much of her unusual bodily energy. Her strong sense, her admirable combination of practical wisdom and earnest piety, her keen intellectual qualities, shine out from the long series of correspondence which she always kept up with her migratory son. Through all her troubles, her poverty, her dependence ; in the solitude which the marriage or death of children necessarily brought upon her; in the anxiety which she endured when they were exposed to the chances of war or the perils of the Plague—she always kept a brave heart and the bright spirits of that Irish nature ot which she was so proud. Her beauty and her character are alike luminous in Romney's delightful picture.

The Stratford Canning of this history was born at his father's house of business in St. Clement's Lane, in the heart of the city of London, November 4, 1786. In those days great people used to spend their evenings with merchants who were not ashamed to live over their offices, and Fox and Sheridan were among Mrs. Canning's visitors. When the father died she took a cottage at Wanstead, and there the children had their home until ready to take their own flight in life. Stratford was sent to a neighbouring dame's school at the age of four, and at about six went to Mr. Newcome's school at Hackney. His recollections of these early days are recorded in the autobiographical Memoirs which he wrote nearly fourscore years later.

MEMOIRS. Hard in those days were rudiments of instruction at any considerable school, and awfully rough the manners of the boys. The smaller ones were neither more nor less than slaves. Children of tender age were often sent on a cold November evening to pilfer turnips from a neighbouring field, and many were the logs of firewood or kettles of boiling water that I had to carry up the dark and winding staircase in winter time. Compared with one of us Caliban was a sybarite, and our Prosperos were ever ready with hand or stick in cases of disobedience or awkwardness. The Sabbath, though free from lessons, was a dismal day. The formal walk to church in a line of two abreast, headed by the master and closed by his usher, the droning organ, the long-drawn, spiritless sermon, the monotonous reading from the "Whole Duty of Man," all tended to more than drowsiness, which fear of detection and punishment could not entirely repress.

Our school was more a little world by itself than any school is now. Events in the great external circle had but slight interest for us. Its greatest explosions failed to disturb our secluded atmosphere. A single grand exception lives in my memory. It was ushered in by the clamours of a large sonorous dinner-bell paraded through the premises at an unusual hour. As soon as the boys within hearing were assembled, our pedagogue-in-chief made his appearance and, placing his hat upon the table with an air of lively importance, announced the great naval victory won by Lord Howe, June 1, 1794. Loud was the cheer which ensued, and louder still the second shout, when, as corollary to the joyful news, a holiday was proclaimed.

His holidays were spent at Wanstead, where the monotony of rural life was dissipated by visits from his first cousin, George Canning, from Hookham Frere, Professor Smythe, and a near neighbour, Richard Brinsley Sheridan, of whom Lord Stratford retained some interesting memories. One is thoroughly characteristic. One of the Canning boys had his head broken while playing at quoits with Tom Sheridan. Bleeding was considered essential, but the boy obstinately resisted the operation. Sheridan himself came to the bedside, and by the promise of a pony induced him to submit. " It was a great success. Resistance ceased: the arm was held out, phlebotomy triumphed.—Promise answered its purpose so completely that *performance would have been superfluous.*" The pony never appeared. Stratford once heard Sheridan speak in the Commons, and was deeply impressed by his commanding tones, though the composition of the speech was embarrassed. Many years afterwards, while he was conversing with his cousin George at the Board of Control, a note was brought in from Sheridan, then at death's door. It begged for the loan of 200*l*. and enclosed an I.O.U. for the amount, " as you know my delicacy in such matters." Canning wrote the cheque, and threw the I.O.U. into the fire. The last recollection of all is curious. Stratford was one day examining a collection of skulls in Deville's shop in the Strand. One skull struck him as familiar, and he exclaimed, "Surely that is Sheridan's!" —and it was.

The influence of his cousin, which afterwards to a large degree moulded his career, was already felt in these early days. The future premier had always found a home with his uncle while he lived, and he was a frequent guest with his widowed aunt.

MEMOIRS. At the time when Canning first takes up a place in my memory, I was a laughing riotous brat. He was then about twenty-five years old. His features, alternately expressive of deep thought and lively wit, his mild yet penetrating eyes, his full but rather scornful lip, the handsome contour of his thin and slightly freckled face, are still before me. His dark well-shorn chin bore witness to the colour of his hair, which before he wore powder a raven might have envied. He took me to Eton and placed me there in the summer of 1795, when I was within a few months of completing my ninth year. We started on a fine day in July from the Treasury building in St. James's Park, where he had an official room. All on the road was new to me, and in those days people did not pass from place to place with the ignorant speed of steam. On turning into the Eton road at Slough, where the colossal telescope of Sir William Herschel first caught my sight, I felt a sense of awe on finding myself thus suddenly so near the great public school which had loomed to me in the distance like a new world of unknown and questionable inhabitants. We were to drive at once to the Provost's Lodge. That dignitary had been described to me as the local sovereign, the king of Eton. He had been headmaster of the school when Canning was gathering his first laurels as a boy of distinguished talents, and the recollection of his merits gave him, and even his little cousin, a seat at the doctor's table, who shrouded his local royalty under the simpler appellation of " Stentorian " Davies, as he was styled in the *Pursuits of Literature.* Next day I was presented to Dr. Langford, master of the lower school, and I should blush to relate that my starting point was settled to be [below] the form called " Nonsense," were I not at liberty to attribute that location to the scanty number of my years. Let me add that by the name of " Nonsense " was meant that form in which the metrical composition of Latin verse was taught by the selection of unconnected words having syllabic quantities. The next form upward was that of " Sense," so called because the exercises in verse were expected to have meaning as well as metre, and from this double source proceeded whatever additions to classical poetry are to be found in the *Musae Etoncnses.*

One more day, and I was left to my own resources in a strange country. My childhood, fraught with health and spirits, recommended me to the notice of some older boys, and the masters were indulgent, so that I went home for the holidays with a cheerful impression of my new community. At the end of a year I was invested with the college gown, and exchanged the comparative quiet of my dame's boarding house for the roystering publicity of a chamber containing fifty beds. Rough was the life I had then to endure. Fagging was in force, a custom having a strong family likeness to slavery, and tending greatly to substitute acts of servitude for habits of study. It is not wholly destitute of advantage, but the evils which result from it greatly preponderate; and if it cannot be made to undergo the fate of Montem, that long-favoured relic of medieval fancies, a judicious limitation of the practice would do no harm to the best of our public schools.

In the days of our good old king George III. much royal favour was bestowed upon the Eton boys. Large numbers of them were invited to the *fêtes* at Windsor and Frogmore, and the king never failed to notice some of them who in summer on Sundays joined the company on the terrace of the Castle. On one occasion his Majesty honoured me with a passing word. He asked me what part of the school I was in, and upon my replying in the sixth form, he said—" A much greater man than I can ever make you." Some of us were invited on another occasion to an oratorio at the Castle, and there I remember to have seen Pitt and Addington in the new court uniform, of which scarlet breeches were a conspicuous portion. The King was a regular patron of Montem, and it was my lot to flourish the college flag in his presence. On recovering from his last illness but one he returned to Windsor through Eton. The boys flocked out into the road and cheered him heartily. He stopped his carriage, and as he shewed himself at the window I saw the tears trickling down his kind and honest countenance.

A greater man even than the sovereign visited Eton while I was there. Who at that time could it be but Nelson, with all his wounds and all his honours? He came with Lady Hamilton under his arm, and made amends for that weakness by obtaining a holiday for the school.

Though but a schoolboy when it was sometimes my fortune to hear a debate in the House of Commons, I was old enough to listen with awed attention to a speech delivered by William Pitt. There was something singularly consistent in the principal qualities which combined to form his character as the minister of a constitutional monarch and the leader of a representative assembly. His features though plain were imposing; there was an air of natural command in his person; his voice was sonorous; he was at once without effort master of his subject, his language, and his arguments. From a window in Fleet Street I saw him go to St. Paul's with the grand procession of King, Lords, and Commons, which went to return thanks for the great naval victories of the time. He was more admired than popular, and his reception by the public partook of both sentiments. At one moment he might be seen bowing to a chorus of cheers and a display of waving handkerchiefs; at another, he slunk out of sight while the dense air of London seethed with hisses, groans, and reproaches.

Conceive him once more in the House of Commons, as my own sight beheld him not long before his death. The House was crowded; all the chief leaders of opposition were in their places; the Minister rose to speak; he was greeted with that sort of insulting noise from the opposite benches which boys at Eton sometimes make for the annoyance of their master. Mr. Pitt, without more change of posture than was necessary to place his hands upon the table before him in support of his tall advancing form, looked for a few seconds in silence into the noisy ranks, and said, in tones of resistless power, "Am I to be interrupted by clamour?" The effect was complete, and an impartial spectator might have perceived in it the triumph of a supremacy sustained on the whole during twenty years.

Once, and only once, I saw the great debater [Fox]. It was in the field of his glory. He was walking up the House to his seat. Dark but open features, beetling eyebrows, short stout legs, and a broad expanse of waistcoat composed the figure which still lives in my memory. I never heard him speak at any length. He appears to have been more or less intimate with my parents, and a brother of mine who fell at Waterloo was his godson.

He was at this time fond of athletic exercises, and played against Byron in the first Eton and Harrow cricket match; he acted in the " Heir-at-Law " in 1802 or 1803, and wrote the prologue; he edited and wrote for a school magazine, the *Miniature*, which ran for a year, and went to two editions in book form; and in due time, under the tutorship of the future Archbishop Sumner, he became captain of the school, and was duly elected scholar of King's College, Cambridge, in July 1806.

In his later years, when Lord Stratford could afford to look back with a critical eye upon his boyhood, he was wont to confess that he must have been something of a " prig " ; and if he was not, it was for no lack of encouragement. His schoolfellows wrote to him with an air of deference which was enough to make any boy conceited, and the flattery was the more dangerous because wholly unsolicited. He was fond of his own thoughts, and loved to indulge his romantic imagination in solitary musings. He was very sensitive to the influence of nature and the charm of association, whether in history or legend, and somewhat intolerant of those who could not see these things with his own eyes : and this intellectual barrier was widened by another quality which distinguished him from the generality of schoolboys. If he was impatient of a dull soul, he was at least equally fastidious about his friends' moral qualities. There are rare and refined natures in whom the inspirations of romance and enthusiasm suffice to fill the place which in others is held by the passions. The letters of boys to boys are an almost infallible test of such moral tone, and boys who were more than his equals in such mental feats as came within the range of Etonian studies wrote to him as to a critic and a superior.

The reason is found in the ascendency of a strong purposeful character, in which the imperious will was softened and beautified by a romantic sensibility and by a purity of thought and speech which seldom fails to have its effect in school or college.

MEMOIRS.   My college life was a short one.   The scholars of King's enjoyed the questionable privilege of drifting into their degrees without examination.   Lectures and rare compositions in Latin were the only demands upon their time.   I was one of those who were volunteers in the study of mathematics. My teacher was a member of Trinity.   He did his best to make me a worthy disciple of Newton, but I very much doubt my aptitude for solving the mysteries of Euclid.   I was sorely puzzled by some of them, and once left my tutor's room in an agony of despair which might have proved fatal to further progress, had I not chanced to meet Professor Smythe, who, on learning my distress, explained the point of difficulty in popular terms so clearly that I went to work again with fresh zeal.   Even in classics I had little to boast of.   Though a charitable friend might suggest that the shortness of my stay at the university shut me out from the chance of obtaining any academical honour, candour requires that I should acknowledge the failure of my only attempt in that line. Rennell, who stood so high at Eton, lost his footing, I know not how, at Cambridge.   Our common friend Lonsdale, the late respected Bishop of Lichfield, was more successful.   In mathematics Pollock was the most distinguished, in classics Blomfield, the former in after-life attaining the dignity of Chief Baron of the Exchequer, the latter closing his days in the lawn sleeves of London. They were both members of a spouting club, to which I also belonged, and where Lord Palmerston had made his first flights in oratory, and where Ellenborough, future governor of India, laid the foundation of his parliamentary fame.   Two famous men of a preceding generation, Porson, the Grecian, and Simeon, the Methodist, came within my sight, but nothing more, while I was at the university.   They were both remarkable for their appearance, and on that account their portraits are still, as it were, before me in the mind's eye.   Porson, when I saw him, was in cap and gown, a thin middle-sized figure, with lank black hair and cheeks of the palest cast.   He walked at a stealthy pace, and seemed to have a book which he hugged parentally under his arm. Simeon I saw in the pulpit.   He was seated in some way which kept him out of sight till he rose to preach.   His hands, with fingers flattened against each other and pointing upwards, played the part of dawn to his countenance, which came slowly into view, the eyes turned up, and mouth invested with a smile of sweet complacent piety.   The church was crowded, and a strong religious feeling seemed to prevail throughout the congregation.

He had only kept a couple of terms when he was called away to the Foreign Office.

MEMOIRS.　　In the spring of 1807, George Canning was placed for the first time at the head of the foreign department. Pitt had died the year before, while I was still at Eton, and I can never forget the impression made on the whole school—masters and boys—by the announcement of his death. A passage in Virgil in the lesson of that day struck me as singularly applicable to the event:

> Utcunque ferent ea facta minores,
> Vincet amor patriae, laudumque immensa cupido.
> *Æn.* vi. 823-4

Fox, his chief ministerial successor, had followed to Westminster Abbey in the autumn of the same year. The Grey and Grenville administration, known popularly as that of "all the talents," had flourished and given way, after a six months' tenure of office, to the Duke of Portland and his cabinet, of which Mr. Canning became a prominent member. To him I owe my first step in public life. The duties I had to perform were those of précis-writer at the Foreign Office. They were more interesting than onerous, more instructive than brilliant. They consisted principally in making summaries of the official correspondence carried on between the secretary of state and the diplomatic agents employed under his direction abroad. I had also to assist occasionally in writing out fair the drafts of instructions from the same source. The confidential nature of these duties gave a precarious character to my position. A change of ministry was sure to be as fatal to the précis-writer as to the minister himself; but this air of fellowship with a great man made up, as some might think, for the uncertainty of the tenure.

The interest of my employment was greatly enhanced by the opportunities it afforded of bringing me into closer communication with my illustrious cousin. Having a room in his house and a place at his table whenever he dined at home, I saw more of him than I was otherwise entitled to expect. I saw him in the free play of his genius and in the full enjoyment of success. I cannot easily forget the first diplomatic dinner at which I was present under his auspices, and still less the composition, which I took down as he uttered it, of his once celebrated reply to the Emperor Alexander's offer of mediation for peace between England and France. At dinner I sat at the foot of the table opposite to him, and my curiosity was not a little excited when I looked round the company and wondered which of the guests was the Austrian ambassador, or which the representative of some other Great Power.

In spite of these new duties, however, he contrived to come up for the Easter and summer terms, 1807, when a more

serious break took place in his university career, and he was sent
as second secretary with Mr. Merry's mission to Copenhagen.[1]
Even then he still hoped to complete his residence at Cambridge.
On his return he again went up to college, until Easter 1808,
and then a new diplomatic appointment terminated his
undergraduate life. It had been sufficiently difficult to keep
his place and rooms for him while absent at Copenhagen.
Other Etonians naturally wanted to step into his shoes, and
the Provost of King's had some trouble in calming their
jealousy. When his appointment as secretary to Mr. Adair's
mission to Constantinople was made, it was evident that he
could no longer retain his post as a scholar, and he accordingly resigned, and contented himself with the position of a
fellow commoner, with every hope of speedily returning to his
academical studies. His protracted detention at the Porte
frustrated this hope. He held, however, strong views as to
the possibility of effecting almost anything by influence, and
we learn from a letter of Rennell's that the youthful diplomatist actually contemplated keeping terms *at Constantinople,*
on the ground that an undergraduate " *regiis intentus negotiis* "
was by university statute entitled to wide geographical
latitude. It is difficult to imagine the feelings of a modern
Head of a House at such a suggestion, and even in 1810 the
proposal was negatived. The university, however, was proud
of its son's successes in the East, and in 1812 granted him
the degree of master of arts by a royal mandamus, which
passed the Senate without a dissentient voice, in virtue of his
absence " occupied in the king's affairs."

[1] It is unnecessary here to describe this fruitless attempt to conciliate the
justly offended Danes. Canning's part was naturally quite subordinate, and
had no direct bearing on his subsequent career. Some of his letters from
Copenhagen and Helsingborg will be found in the Library Edition, i. pp. 31–36.

CHAPTER I.

IN May, 1808, Stratford Canning unknowingly committed himself to a career for which he had no desire, and to a post which ever after was pre-eminently distasteful. He was appointed First Secretary to Robert Adair's mission to Turkey. He little knew, when he accepted the—for so young a man—very flattering offer, that he was forging for himself a chain which he would never be able to loose, and which would continue to gall his limbs to the very close of his public career. It is singular that the man who stands in the very foremost rank of English diplomatists hated diplomacy; and that the statesman who is most closely associated with Turkish history during the present century abhorred his Turkish exile. Such, however, was the case. He accepted his appointment merely as a temporary experience—an experience, as he said, " alluring for youth ; " his hopes and ambitions were centred in English public life ; yet he found himself forced to spend the greater part of his days abroad, and chiefly in a country which was the least hopeful, the most exasperating, in Europe. Duty, always a stern mistress, found in him an unflinching slave. Six times he shook off the dust of Stambol with the firm resolve never to return to the hated spot ; six times duty and the compelling desire to serve his country drove him back ; and his last farewell to Constantinople was uttered at the age of seventy-three.

The object of the mission was to restore peace between Great Britain and Turkey. In 1807 England was at war with the Porte in the interests of our then ally, Russia. Later in the same year the *raison d'être* of the estrange-

ment disappeared, for Russia had allied herself with Napoleon
in the famous—or infamous—engagement of Tilsit, and
England forthwith became at war with the Czar.   It was of
importance to induce Turkey to return to her former amity
with England, and the Porte, divining somewhat of the
treachery which had been planned between the two Emperors
at Tilsit, was not unwilling to be friends.   Adair, when at
Vienna, had been made aware of certain feelers which both
sides had cautiously thrown out, and, strongly encouraged by
Austria, who was burning to retrieve the disaster at Ulm, he
reported favourably to George Canning on the feasibility of
the reconciliation.   The result was his mission to the
Dardanelles.

In those days the voyage to Constantinople, three thousand
miles long, and necessarily by sea the whole way, was no light
undertaking.   The mission embarked in July, 1808, on board
H.M.S. *Hyperion*, 30 guns, and arrived off the Spanish coast
after a narrow escape from going ashore on the dangerous
Berling rocks.   Off Cadiz they held communications with
Collingwood's fleet, and heard of the preparations for what
was afterwards to be famous as the Peninsular war.   At
Gibraltar they met the governor, Sir Hew Dalrymple, and
learned the plans of the Spanish insurgents.   Canning's patriotic fervour was strongly moved by what he saw, and he
longed to bear a hand in the good cause, instead of wasting his
energies upon Turkish diplomacy.   He found, however, some
compensation in the classic spots of Sicily and Greece.   No
better moment could be chosen to visit the scenes immortalized
by Homer and endeared to us by Virgil than now, when the
young man was fresh from his studies at Eton and Cambridge,
and had his mind well stored with the legends and scenery of
the classical writers. It was the age of quotation, and Canning
and his friends seldom wrote a letter without a few lines of
Virgil or Horace to point an argument or illustrate a scene.
His reminiscences are full of such references, and his memory
of his favourite poets remained vivid and clear down to the
day of his death.

Writing, " Off Tenedos, 19 Oct. 1808 " to his school friend,
Richard Wellesley, a natural son of the Marquis, he gives full
vent to the enthusiastic feelings inspired by all he has seen:—

Dear Wellesley,—The news of our late victories in Portugal
arrived here yesterday, and if anything could add to the excessive

pleasure which such glorious events have given me, it is that we
are indebted to your gallant uncle for them.   I really feel a sincere
admiration for that man (*hero* let me call him), and think that I
cannot too often congratulate you upon being related to him.   How
fortunate he is to have such an opportunity of distinguishing himself—the cause so important—his opponents so strong—his rivals
so few.   I am the more pleased at his success, as it proves, what I
have always expected, that the hour of trial would produce as many
soldiers and generals as it has already produced sailors and
admirals.   It is, thank God! the same British stuff, whether in a
blue jacket cr a red coat.

Our little fleet, which consists of a frigate and two brigs, did
honour to the occasion by making as much noise as their guns
would permit, and so much was my patriotic ardour inflamed that
I volunteered, in spite of wind, rain, thunder and lightning, to go
up to the Dardanelles and put the Pasha there in mind of our con-
quests in Egypt by telling him how the French, all terrible as they
are, had been drubbed in Portugal.   However, I did not enjoy this
satisfaction; the " malignant and turbaned Turk " was absent, and I
saw only his secretary.   Still, the secretary was a Greek, and I
knew that he understood Homer; therefore, thinks I, he must have
something like a soul capable of enjoying such news.   Conceive my
disappointment and the dullness of the beast!   When I told him
what your uncle had done, his eyes did not sparkle, he said nothing,
he moved not a muscle, but stroked his beard.   I cursed him in my
heart, and told him that we were most probably in possession of the
Russian fleet in the Tagus.   Then, indeed, he was all joy and
ecstasy!   " Ma foi!   C'est très bon.   Oh! quel heureux événement! "
Yes, the animal, insensible as he was, hated the Russians, because
his masters the Turks hated them, and he had heard them dreaded
and abused at Constantinople, and though there was nobody, as
usual, standing by ready to bastinado him if his supple face did not
exactly express what his master expected, yet so strong was the
force of habit that he could not even in absence move a muscle
otherwise than he would have done at the feet of the Pasha.

I wish you could be, as you once gave me reason to hope, my
companion in this *arduous task*; but as that cannot now be, I will
console myself for the disappointment by telling you how much you
have lost.   Portugal, Spain, Gibraltar, Africa, Balearic Islands, Sardinia, Maretimo, Sicily, Malta, Peloponnesus, Attica, Greek Islands,
not to mention the ancient temples of Segesta and Girgenti, the
ruins of Drepanum and Agrigentum, &c. &c., temple of Minerva
at Colonna—not to mention the opportunities of seeing the different
manners and customs and productions of almost innumerable
countries ! ! !   Add to these treasures that while I am now writing
my eye is either traversing the waters of the Archipelago, whose
every wave is immortalized by some celebrated exploit, or resting
with awful reverence upon the summit of Athos or the snowy

ridges of Rhodope, or scanning with amazement the dark forests of Ida *with many fountains,* and the fertile declivities of the Gargara (*ipsa suas mirantur Gargara messes*), or tracing the course of the Simois and Scamander *with many whirlpools,* or gazing upon Tenedos—*notissima famâ insula, dives opum*—or expatiating in the vast expanse of the Trojan plain, where nothing remains to mark the situation of Troy, once so great and powerful, but the tombs of her destroyers.

But whither does the enchantment of the scene lead me ? The above detail will shew you what you have lost, and now that you have read it you will be *surprised* to know that I almost envy you for being in England at such a moment as this. I assure you I long to be with you, that I may more closely partake in the enthusiasm excited by the revolution in Spain and the joy of our common successes against France. In passing through the bay of Lagos we had the pleasure of subscribing a mite to the assistance of *the righteous cause* by giving a supply of arms to the Portuguese ; and when at Algeciras I may *boast* of having been one of the first Englishmen who shook hands with the Spanish patriots. My interest is so strongly excited that I cannot express to you how much I desire to have it in my power to assist them *personally.* I never before felt so deeply the misery of insignificance.

Arrived off the Dardanelles, the question arose whether the Turks were really disposed to make peace or not. The usual delays of oriental diplomacy ensued, and for a long time the *Sea Horse,* in which the mission had sailed from Sicily, had to make the best of an exposed position outside the Straits. To Canning, however, there were compensations even in this unpleasant situation.

MEMOIRS.   We were surrounded by classical inspirations, and great was the enjoyment derived from that abundant source. Without an effort, from the deck of the *Sea Horse* we could survey the plain of Troy, with Ida and Gargara in the background. The tomb of Antilochus rose from the fine coast which terminated in the Chanak castles and entrance of the Hellespont. Tenedos, with its far-seen hill, lay astern of us ; Imbros and Samothrace were on our starboard bow, and sometimes at sunset we could descry the broken outline of Lemnos and the still more distant peak of towering Athos. These objects of our early study operated strongly on the imagination at a time when steam, as applied to locomotion, was unknown, and a voyage to Constantinople had not the everyday aspect which it has since acquired. We felt what a beautiful and accomplished ambassadress had felt a century before, when she invested " the immortal islands and the well-known seas " with a new charm—the charm of her own delightful genius.

The process of cooling our heels could only be relieved by shooting over the deserted vineyards of Tenedos, which had been taken and abandoned by the Russians some months before, and by questioning for news the merchant vessels which had to pass up or down within hail of the *Sea Horse*. Supplies of excellent grapes were obtained at no cost and with little exertion from the unoccupied vineyards, and we revelled in floods of capital spring water, until we had the ill luck to discover a dead Turk at the bottom of the principal well.

At length, after many weeks of detention and every possible variety of vexation, we learnt that a plenipotentiary was to be sent from Constantinople, that the British dragoman was to be recalled from exile, and that a house would be assigned for our residence on shore during the future negotiation. Finally, on 11 November we were at liberty to proceed, and early in that day, befriended by a strong south wind, the *Sea Horse* stemmed the fierce current of the Dardanelles, and cast anchor within the straits about a mile or more below the inner Asiatic castle. A sad disappointment was at hand. The house, on which we had fed our expectations of escaping from cabin-life and sea-fare, vanished into space on our approach. The farmhouse, or *chiftlik* as it was called, had no accommodation of any kind, and could only be used for an occasional conference. Our prospect was that of an immediate return to the prison afloat, with winter coming on, and no small difficulty in communicating with the shore. The conferences were to be held at intervals. The plenipotentiaries had far to go. Their meetings depended on weather and instructions from Constantinople. The Turks seemed bent on delay. We were to be worried into certain concessions: the French were to be mystified by doubtful appearances.

At length Mr. Adair sent in his ultimatum, and prepared the *Sea Horse* for instant departure in case of any further demur. The picturesque attitude of the ship with its sails loose and its anchor a-peak, accomplished the work of twenty conferences. Mohammed Emin Vahid Efendi, so was the Ottoman plenipotentiary called, gave in, and the Treaty of the Dardanelles was signed on 5 January, 1809 [19 Zu-l-ka'da 1223], while the French consul's express, announcing our supposed failure, was on its way to Napoleon's embassy at Stambol.

When an English ambassador once more took up his residence at Constantinople, Napoleon was in the glow of his second great military passion. Foiled by England in his eastern schemes by the destruction of his fleet at Abukir and the consequent imprisonment of his army in Egypt and Syria; foiled again by England in his naval combination with Spain by the splendid triumph of Nelson at Trafalgar; foiled once again by England in his last attempt to raise a fleet, by Mr. Canning's seizure of the Danish ships: his invincible resolution

C

to humble the island empire burned hotter than ever; but the means of realising the resolve were changed. On the seas, England remained unassailable ; France could muster no fleet to cope with her. The attack must therefore be by land ; and Napoleon was now carrying out that policy which Mr. Seeley has tersely expressed as " conquering Europe in order to conquer England." He was creating that universal blockade of English trade, that general " boycotting," known as the Continental System, by which he hoped at last to bring the pride of the stubborn islanders to the dust. The surrender at Ulm and the battle of Austerlitz in 1805 had broken the German coalition ; Jena had reduced Prussia (1806) to despair ; Friedland (1807) had completed the work of Austerlitz in Russia ; and the treaty of Tilsit had united for the moment all the great powers of Europe in a general conspiracy against Great Britain. England held important posts in the Mediterranean, and had a grip on Portugal and Sicily : and that was all. Turkey was the only neutral power, and would not long remain so if Napoleon could have his will.

MEMOIRS. The state of Turkey itself was anything but satisfactory in view of those powers who did not wish the Porte to become the prey either of Russia or of France. The throne of the empire was filled by a young Sultan, who had recently succeeded to his brother Mustafa, whose immediate predecessor, their cousin Selim, had fallen a sacrifice to the mutinous spirit of the Janissaries. Mahmud, the reigning sovereign, was for some time the last of his race. Young, ignorant, and inexperienced, he had everything to apprehend from the circumstances in which he was placed. Both morally and materially his empire was bordering on decrepitude. The old political system of Turkey had worn itself out. The population was not yet prepared for a new order of things. A depreciated currency, a disordered revenue, a mutinous militia, dilapidated fortresses, a decreasing population, a stagnant industry, and general misrule, were the monuments which time had left of Ottoman domination in the second capital of the Roman empire and throughout those extensive regions which had been the successive seats of civilization, ever varying, generally advancing, from the earliest periods of social settlement and historical tradition. A continual and often a sanguinary antagonism of creeds, of races, of districts and authorities within the frontier, and frequent wars of little glory and much loss with the neighbouring powers, had formed of late the normal condition of the Porte's dominions.

Russia, France, Austria, and even Persia had by turns contracted the area and drained the resources of the empire. From

the corrupt monotony of his seraglio the Sultan had to send forth
his firmans, his emissaries, his bands of irregular soldiery, or, it
might be, his naval armaments, against an invading enemy, a
rebellious chief, or an armed insurrection. Several great families,
several unsubdued tribes, and here and there an over-powerful
pasha had succeeded in braving and circumscribing the imperial
authority. The Mamluks still prevailed in Egypt. The most important part of Syria was under the sway of a Christian Emir. Ali
Pasha of Janina exercised royal power in the provinces bordering
on Greece, and Greece itself, excited by Russia, was preparing to
burst the fetters which had so long bound her to the Ottoman
throne. Servia, Montenegro, and the Danubian Principalities were
all more or less in league with Russia, and the Porte, at war with
that formidable power, had everything to apprehend from the Russian forces concentrated upon her northern frontier. The Sultan's
fleet was manned with Christian Greeks from the island population
of the Archipelago ; the Barbary powers were scarcely even in
nominal dependence on the Porte ; and a sect of Mohammedans,
called the Wahhabis, and having a kind of analogy with our Puri-
tans, had hoisted a separate standard of religious belief in parts of
Egypt and Arabia.

It is interesting to learn what were the earliest impressions
made by the Turks upon one who was destined in after-years
to hold a predominant place in their councils. In the spring
of 1809 Canning wrote of them thus :—

> Very false notions are entertained in England of the Turkish
> nation. You know much better than I do the mighty resources and
> native wealth which this enormous empire possesses. I am myself
> a daily witness of the personal qualities of the inhabitants, qualities
> which if properly directed are capable of sustaining them against
> a world of enemies. But the government is radically bad, and its
> members, who are all alive to its defects, have neither the wisdom
> nor the courage to reform it. The few who have courage equal to
> the task know not how to reconcile reformation with the prejudices
> of the people. And without this nothing can be effected.

We are not concerned to trace the various steps of Adair's
diplomatic work at Constantinople in 1809–10.[1] His object
was to keep Turkey out of the arms of France, and in this he
succeeded. More could not be expected in the existing state
of Europe, especially after the second disastrous overthrow of
Austria at Wagram. All that could be done was to wait and
watch for an opportunity to draw the Porte closer to England.
Meanwhile Canning had little to do. As he says :—

[1] The details will be found in the Library Edition, i. 51–6, 81–82.

MEMOIRS.   The subordinates could not have much on their hands except time, when their chief was thus compelled to put his zeal and activity on half allowance. For my own part I had the lion's share of this unavoidable leisure. My share of business as secretary of embassy lay within narrow limits, capable indeed of development in special cases, but for the time of embryo dimensions and only eventual activity. My assistance was rarely wanted for copying, as the ambassador's staff was numerous for that service. He composed his own despatches. To draw up a report on some incidental matter, to convey an impressive message to some Turkish minister or other person of influence, and to take my place in public ceremonies, formed the whole round of my official occupations. I was at the same time allowed to read the public correspondence, and I had no reason to complain of any stint in the confidence and kindness with which I was treated by the ambassador. On one occasion, when his excellency was ill during several weeks, I had to write for him and to act under his directions.

We were thrown more than ever on local resources for our amusement and occupation. We had already slaked our curiosity, not only by visiting such objects and places of resort as every itinerant author has described, but also by attending official ceremonies and those occasional sports at which the Sultan presided in public, as well for his own diversion as for the gratification of his many-coloured and many-creeded subjects. We had ourselves figured conspicuously in the official audiences, to which the embassy had been admitted with customary forms of etiquette. We had also been present, under the rose, at some purely Turkish festivities whether of a religious or of a civil character. The splendid old costume, at once so appropriate and so diversified, shone out with Oriental brilliancy. The usage of centuries in dress and manners, associated with history and typical of the unchanging East, occupied even to rapture both sight and mind.

Of external events there was no lack. Before me lies a packet of papers docketed in Canning's hand " Bulletins. Pera, 1809." It consists of a series of broadsides printed by a Jew at a private press established by Adair in the British embassy. The object was to keep the Turks well informed of the successes of our armies in Portugal and Spain and of any other events which might serve to lessen the prestige of France. Side by side with these interesting documents are others printed by the French mission, and in these we see the reverse of the medal, and also read M. de Latour-Maubourg's indignant comments on the " insulting " bulletins which *somebody* had been issuing at Pera to the discredit of his imperial master. The two sets of papers form a chronicle of external events during a considerable part of

the year 1809, and shed a vivid light upon the anxious life of
the embassy at that time.   It is not easy to realize the eager
expectation with which the news was awaited which these
scraps of roughly printed paper disseminated in Pera.   How
those few Englishmen must have quivered when at long
intervals some vessel from Gibraltar or a courier from Austria
brought the last news from the seats of war!   One day they
were dispirited by a bulletin from the press of the French
mission containing Napoleon's inspiring address to his soldiers after the successes which had attended the beginning
of the contest with Austria :—" Soldats!   Vous avez justifié
mon attente : vous avez suppléé au nombre par votre bravoure ;
vous avez glorieusement marqué la différence qui existe entre
les soldats de César et les cohues armées de Xerxes. . . .
Avant un mois nous serons à Vienne."   Then they read the
Archduke Charles's vigorous exhortation to the armies of
Austria on 6 April, and hoped that his sanguine prophecies
would be realized.   In May they heard of his advance and the
triumphs which attended his arms, and on 23 June, the embassy press published the glorious news that the battle of
Aspern had been fought and won : " Bonaparte è stato total-
mente disfatto a Aspern i 21 e 22 Maggio da S. A. l' Archi-
duca Carlo ; questo principe ha fatto la sua entrata in Vienna
il 25 Maggio ; " and five days later this Italian bulletin was
followed by another in French : " Bonaparte est en pleine fuite.
Son armée, défaite successivement dans plusieurs combats
depuis le 26 jusqu'au 29 Mai, se trouve presqu'entièrement
anéantie.   Les débris n'ont pu qu'avec beaucoup de peine
gagner la Bavière."   We can imagine the enthusiasm with
which Canning copied out these joyful tidings for the com-
positor, and how eagerly he waited for the next news, and
read the Archduke's triumphant report of " that battle of
giants " at Aspern.   Alas! the news of Wagram soon cast
down all hopes of Napoleon's immediate destruction.

Meanwhile other events were keeping English eyes fixed
upon the west.   In March they learned that Moore had
defeated the French at Corunna.   Every month the slow
vessels of the time brought some few words to cheer them
with the hope that Wellesley would at last make head against
the foe.   On 16 Sept. the bulletin of the day promulgated the
news of the victory of Talavera, and once more the little
group of English at Constantinople held up their heads and
rejoiced that " the common enemy of Europe " had been beaten.

To turn over these bulletins is listening to the hopes and fears of a besieged garrison waiting to know their fate.

Fortunately, if there was little to do but wait, there was much to see. In the summer of 1809 Canning made a tour in Asia Minor, visited green-leafed Brusa and climbed Olympus; and with all the abandonment of youth enjoyed the rude experiences of Turkish travel— sleeping *sub Jove frigido* with a saddle for his pillow, and rising at the " sweet hour of prime " for an exhilarating canter over dewy herbage in the keen morning air. Everywhere he found relics of that classical past which possessed so deep an interest. At one time it was a truly Virgilian threshing-floor, with the *ingens farris acervus* ; at another the half-buried ruins of the temple of " Diana of the Ephesians ; " every spot had its associations, and he crossed the Caÿster with the Iliad in his hand, thinking of Καΰστρίου ἀμφὶ ῥεέθρα.

On his return from this interesting tour he found the embassy in the country :—

Memoirs.   Mr. Adair had rented a country house at Belgrade, and thither I went to resume my not very arduous duties. September was then in progress, and autumn is ever a delightful season at Constantinople,—almost a second spring. The scenery about Belgrade had much to remind an Englishman of his own country. The village, composed of two separate parts, was situated on a broken slope looking south. It was inhabited by native Greeks with the exception of a few houses occupied in summer by diplomatic or other foreign families. It was surrounded by forests of oak, beech, and Spanish chestnut, covering to a wide extent both hill and valley, though frequently cleared into grassy glades, meadows, and gardens, and vineyards, with large sheets of water, formed by damming up the brooks, and destined to supply the city and its suburbs with that necessary element by means of locks and aqueducts. From some higher points the Black Sea came into sight, and game was said to abound in the woods. My own experience confirmed this report, though not to its full extent. Of the larger kind, stag, boar, and roebuck were indeed to be found, but sparingly, and not without many a weary search. Woodcock and quail were the staple. Other kinds, the usual tenants of preserves, were far more rare. Still there was something of each, and more than could be expected in lands so partially cultivated, where birds of prey abounded and game laws were unknown. With a double-barrelled gun, which I owed to Mr. Adair's generosity, and a horse, which his Ottoman colleague at the Dardanelles had given me, I took my share of the sport. At times we went by moonlight to watch for wild boars in some lonely dell where they were supposed

to resort. Now and then a grand battue was got up in some
remoter part of the forest. In most cases the interest was greater
than the success. But even a complete failure would find some
atonement in the vicissitudes of an animating pursuit, when other
distractions, including the field of diplomacy, were at zero.

These out-of-door recreations, abundant as they were, derived
an additional zest from the desultory business with which they
were connected. I could not wait upon a Turkish minister, or
perform any current act of diplomacy on the ambassador's account,
without impressions reminding me of some chapter in Gibbon or
some tale of wonder in the *Arabian Nights*. They were the
more precious as our indoor comforts and social amusements
were curtailed not a little by the nature of the place and the
character of the times. With Turks, Greeks and Armenians there
was no society in the ways of Europe. The diplomatic circle was
at zero. Owing to various causes, entirely political, the only house
of that class in which we could pass an evening was the residence
of the Swedish mission.

To one who like myself had been placed more by accident than
choice on so vast and attractive a theatre with ample leisure for
looking round and some special facilities for moving about, the
interest of the situation was naturally exciting. I must, nevertheless, acknowledge the truth. My heart was not there. I had no
predilection for diplomacy. My tastes, my hopes, my prospects
were at home, in my native land, in its gigantic metropolis, the
seat of enlightened legislation, of civilizing power, and of honourable
contention for the greatest results of thought and the noblest prizes
of ambition. I was pleased with being brought so soon into
immediate though partial contact with great public events of the
day; I was far from being insensible to the striking objects and
various scenes around me; I was neither blind to the beauties of
nature nor deaf to the voice of ages; but all these appeals to my
attention, however forcible, however seductive, possessed in my
view but a passing interest. They would at times, in spite of
myself, contract an obstructive appearance, an air of something
which kept me away from pursuits more congenial to my real
inclinations and inherent cast of character.

The bloom of the peach was already rubbed off. Canning
had seen Constantinople, and was tired of it. No one could
have been more fascinated with its picturesque beauty at first,
but we may judge from the following letter to Richard
Wellesley, 9 November, 1809, how completely the glamour
had faded away :—

Upon our arrival here I was much struck with the strangeness
of everything around me. The grandeur of the city as we approached it, the variety of dresses, and the tones of so many

different languages, that each person seemed to have some twenty or thirty of those tongues and voices which Homer and Virgil talk about—all roused my curiosity. Above all the hearty welcome that the people seemed to give us made me regard everything in a favourable point of view. I thought my attention could never be wearied ; the time that I expected to stay seemed too short for all I wanted to see ; and even the dark, narrow, muddy, stinking streets, choked up with dead cats and mangy dogs, appeared by no means intolerable. The manners of the inhabitants, their way of living, the shops, the markets, the mosques and dismal burying-grounds, put me in mind of the Arabian tales, and I found that in reading them I had already been among the Turks. This resemblance gave me as much pleasure as if I had met with the lineal descendants of Hector and Aeneas at Bunarbashi, dressed in the armour of their ancestors, and anxious to carry the war into the country of their invaders. I scarcely dared to stamp upon the ground lest a genie should make his appearance. I expected to hear of the neighbourhood being infested by more than one band of Forty Thieves, and as for little Mustafa the tailor I saw him upon every shop-board in the town. How pleasant and how short is the reign of the imagination ! A few months have passed away—my curiosity is satisfied—the novelty is gone. I have seen all that is to be seen, and wish only to see it no more.

He was already weary of exile, though, little as he thought it, the term of banishment had in reality scarcely begun. He had confidently expected to return home " at the end of the long vacation " in 1808, and as another year wore on he grew more and more impatient of his enforced detention at a spot which despite its natural beauty had few charms for him. He longed for the companionship of his old schoolfellows, he missed his family, to which he was bound by very tender links, he pined for the intellectual and social energy of London and the keen contest for fame in politics and literature. He professed himself indeed " comfortable " with his companions; the kindly disposition of Adair warmed towards him, and in David Morier, the second secretary, he made a friend for life. But still he was lonely, and the monotonous life at Constantinople was stagnation to his vigorous and ambitious nature. In a word, he was young and restless, and needed more variety and interests in his life.

His chief happiness was in the letters of his friends. He must have possessed a curious power of fascination over his contemporaries, if these letters are sufficient evidence. The affection of his Eton companions lasted through their lives, and the brightest moments of his exile were the days which brought long chatty epistles from his special "chums," Gally Knight, Wellesley, and Rennell. Those were the days of real correspondence, and eight or twelve sides of close writing were no unusual feats of penmanship at a time when a two months' voyage was a rapid mail to Constantinople. Home politics, the news of the war, the doings of their small circle—for his friendships were close rather than many—fill page after page of this ample correspondence, which after three-quarters of a century retains an interest and vitality that constantly invite quotation. The triumvirate of special school friends was now largely increased by a circle of Foreign Office colleagues, among whom none was more devoted than Joseph Planta, who held the post of précis-writer during his friend's absence and eventually rose to be permanent Under-Secretary of State for Foreign Affairs. He wrote to Constantinople by every mail, collected huge bags of letters from all the family and friends, kept Canning *au courant* with whatever was going on at home, arranged his money affairs—and was constantly blaming himself for not doing more.

The news of his cousin's duel with Lord Castlereagh naturally increased his desire to be off. He wished to resign the service of a Ministry which his cousin had left. But Mr. Canning knew that his own return to power was uncertain, and he laboured to dissuade his cousin from abandoning a promising opening in the hope of possible promotion at home. He wanted to make him independent of the chances of party influence. It was with this aim that he sent his "most positive injunctions," on 9 October, 1809, just after his duel and resignation, and added, " I may or may not have it in my power at some future time to take you by the hand again. If not, you have a profession in which you may be useful to your country and do credit to your friends and to yourself, and you must not lightly abandon it."

There was no denying the wisdom of this advice, and Stratford reluctantly gave way. He yielded to the entreaties of his relations, but to his sister he confessed the pain it cost him (12 Jan. 1810):—

How unfortunate it is that our interests should sometimes be independent of our happiness! Yet this I am told is the case, though I am yet too young to comprehend the doctrine. However, there are duties the results of faith as well as of conviction. In this world we are often called upon to obey without knowing why, and to give up the exercise of our own reason to the advice of others.

This is at present my condition—no very pleasant one, you will allow, and doubly hard, as one has not even the consolation of complaint. For in the sort of willing yet forced submission that one's reason must sometimes yield to the united claims of gratitude, affection and respect, who can complain? It is thought for my interest to remain here; my friends I am sure advise me to do so even against their own wishes. I think differently on the subject, but respect for the friendly opinion of others offered upon such kind and generous grounds leads me equally against my judgment and my inclination.

It is not without great pain and difficulty that I act thus—but in such matters the approbation of those whom I love is paramount to every other consideration, at the same time that I trust that the same regard will be paid to my feelings and opinions as I pay to theirs. . . . In spite of the Devil and Dr. Faustus it must not be long before we meet.

He little knew that more than two weary years were to roll by before that wish could be fulfilled: the Devil and Doctor Faustus were too strong for him. He was obliged to follow Planta's advice, and to remember his own family motto: *Tu ne cede malis, sed contra audentior ito.* (*Aen.* vi. 95.)

The time was approaching for Adair's departure. His health had given way (though he lived to be ninety-two), and the harassing duties of his difficult post had told upon his spirits. His successor was not yet chosen, but Canning had long before been appointed *interim* Minister Plenipotentiary pending the arrival of a new ambassador. The appointment was made against his own wishes. Adair had sounded him on the subject, and had been answered that his Secretary had no desire for any but home service. Nevertheless, the dormant commission had been duly sent out, with a letter from George Canning, in which the Foreign Minister said, " Mr. Adair's reports of you and yours of him lead me to wish that he may continue where he is, and you with him; at the same time I feel myself justified on public grounds in doing what, on private grounds *alone*, you know me well enough to know I would *not* do, in your favour, in the event of his coming away."

There is one aspect of the question which perhaps would not naturally occur to anyone at the time, and this is the effect of so early and rapid an advancement upon character. In after years one who knew Lord Stratford intimately remarked that much of his exceeding masterfulness was due to the misfortune of having had things made too easy for him in early life. Leaving school as he did, the centre of an admiring circle, what he needed was a few years of real struggle with the world, to enable him to find out the limits of his own powers, and to master the art of getting on with others. But he was pushed up the easiest possible incline to almost the top of the ladder of diplomatic rank before he was twenty-four, and to this premature elevation must be traced in a large degree the faults which have been remarked by his contemporaries. Had he been compelled to work under taskmasters in youth, he would probably have learned the lesson of submission. He was impatient, because he had never known what it was to have to wait in despair of advancement; he was disposed to be suspicious because he spent his early manhood in a nest of intrigue. Of all schools for his nature, Constantinople was certainly the very worst. There he was compelled to deal in menace and high-handed authority, and the necessity created a habit. Circumstances strengthened the natural bent, which might have been softened and diverted by a different fortune. But had things been different, we might never have had a "Great Elchi."

In a letter to Morier, who was then at Tebriz, Canning humorously described his anxieties about his new duties :—

I have already ten wrinkles on my forehead, and feel so *responsible* that I dare not take up my tweezers to pluck a hair out of my cheek without due anticipation of results and consequences. The other day Bidwell was putting some mutton into his mouth rather eagerly, and I could not help exclaiming, "Good God! Bidwell, how thoughtlessly you eat, as if a man could swallow a mouthful of mutton without its consequences!"

On the eve of the great change in his responsibility he wrote thus to his old friend Richard Wellesley, who was just taking his seat in the House of Commons :—

I too, after four months of anxiety and putting off, am in the act of passing into a state of responsibility, which one can hardly do in times like these without certain feelings of apprehension. Mr. Adair has been detained here since the end of February, when he meant to have left us, by several unexpected events. His departure is now fixed for the middle of next week, and then my diplomatic labours will begin in good earnest. How long they are to last, I know not : that depends upon the noble Marquis your father. But I most sincerely hope not very long, at least in this part of the world. . . . However, the most distant chance of being able to serve one's country honourably, though humbly, goes a

great way towards enabling one to bear a thousand such evils and
inconveniences. I thank you for your wish that I should meet
you in the House of Commons; perhaps the day may come; I
am disposed to hope it. At all events, in parliament or out, I
trust we shall always be found among the number of those who
" dare be honest in the worst of times."

MEMOIRS.   By the *Salsette* [in May, 1810] two young travellers, both of distinguished merit, and one of world-wide renown,
appeared within our horizon. Lord Byron and his friend Mr.
Hobhouse, afterwards Lord Broughton, were the luminaries in
question. They formed together a most interesting addition to our
society. I had already seen the poet at a cricket match between
the boys of Eton and those of Harrow; we had both played in
the respective elevens, and I had not forgotten the impression then
made upon me by Lord Byron's appearance in his flannel jacket
with bat over his shoulder. The pleasure of making his acquaintance was reserved for me in the land of " the citron and vine."
He was then engaged, as I learnt afterwards, in the composition of
his *Childe Harold*. His *Poems of a Minor* were already eclipsed
by the success of his tilt against the *Edinburgh Review*. We took
several rides together, and I still retain a most agreeable recollection of his good nature and varied conversation.

Meanwhile the preparations for our ambassador's departure
were gradually maturing. His health was so far restored that he
could venture to apply for the customary audiences of leave.
Those cumbrous ceremonies were not yet divested of their antique
forms. A long procession on horseback, interrupted by a row
across the harbour in boats of Turkish fashion, led to the Porte
or to the Seraglio, according as the Grand Vezir or the Grand
Signior was to receive the embassy. The pageant began at a very
early hour, and took up the greater part of a day. The ceremonial
of the Sultan's audience included a dinner given by the Vezir, or
Sadr Azam, in the same hall where he had previously disposed of
a pile of money-bags in payment of the Janissaries, and decided
some questions respecting the fisc. The Christian guests were to
be clothed as well as fed before they entered the presence chamber.
and consequently every one from the ambassador downwards was
invested with a pelisse or robe of some kind according to his rank.

The Sultan's throne, which resembled a four-post bedstead,
hung with cloth and studded with jewels, almost filled the small
dark room in which he received us. He sat in the ordinary posture
of the west, his feet supported by a step. Near him at one side
was a rich casket and at the other a scimitar half-drawn. The
chief officers of state in their splendid costumes, invented from a
dream by Suleyman the Magnificent, were ranged on his right.
The ambassador, secretary, and suite, stood opposite. His excellency delivered a short address; the Sultan, or his Vezir, replied.

The two speeches were successively interpreted, and thus the audience concluded. In aid of the effect, the dead silence was broken only by the speeches, a lighted lamp glimmered, a small fountain trickled, in their respective corners, and two spare turbans of imperial shape surmounted with plumes from the bird of paradise, appeared in a recess near the throne. My thoughts went back to the time when a Christian emperor sat enthroned on the same spot. Now, if I were to revisit that scene of grandeur, I should look in vain for the Turkish pageant and find only a half-burnt ruin amidst the deserted groves of the seraglio.

On the occasion of these audiences an incident took place so amazingly characteristic of our noble bard that I cannot forbear to record it. We had assembled for the first of them in the hall of our so called palace when Lord Byron arrived in scarlet regimentals, topped by a profusely feathered cocked hat, and coming up to me asked what his place, as a peer of the realm, was to be in the procession. I referred him to Mr. Adair, who had not yet left his room, and the upshot of their private interview was that as the Turks ignored all but officials, any amateur, though a peer, must be content to follow in the wake of the embassy. His lordship thereupon walked away with that look of scornful indignation which so well became his fine imperious features. Next day the ambassador, having consulted the Austrian internuncio and received a confirmation of his own opinion, wrote to apprize Lord Byron. The reply gave assurance of the fullest satisfaction, and ended with a declaration that the illustrious penitent would, if permitted, attend the next audience in his excellency's train, and humbly follow "his ox, or his ass, or anything that was his." In due time he redeemed his pledge by joining the procession as a simple individual, and delighting those who were nearest to him by his well-bred cheerfulness and good-humoured wit.

Little now remained for Mr. Adair to do; his departure was fixed for July 12. On the appointed day I attended him to the water's edge, and took my leave with a deep sense of his invariable kindness, and with a feeling of bereavement which for a time overpowered every other consideration. With him departed the last of those who had been more or less my daily companions from the beginning, and few are insensible to the void which occurs when a society founded on similar pursuits and cemented by habitual intercourse finally breaks up. In the present case there was one important exception. My functions required that I should have an assistant worthy of my confidence and fully qualified to perform the duties of an official secretary. The gentleman assigned to me in that capacity was my friend Mr. David Morier, whom I had already learned to esteem not more on the ground of his moral character than by reason of his talents and literary attainments. He was my constant associate, my never-failing resource during the two eventful years which ensued.

The ambassador's parting letter is worth quoting :—

My dear Canning,—I could not read your letter without those strong emotions which the hurry of departure suspended in me for a moment yesterday, or rather helped me to disguise. Believe me that my regard for you is by [no] means the result of facility of temper, or of a loose and indiscriminating philanthropy. I esteem you for the powers of your mind, and I love you for your many virtues: among the first of which I class a proud and independent spirit which I remarked in you from our earliest acquaintance. This spirit is to me so sacred, wherever I find it, that I cannot bear to check even its faults ; for its faults are parts of its virtues, all *and the whole* of which we shall want in the adverse hour that awaits us. When these are accompanied with a warm and kind heart, which I know yours to be in an extreme degree, I say in two words that I am content with the man formed of such materials. He is good enough for me, and I am happy when I can call him my friend. Fare you well! and assure yourself that such I am to you, affectionately and invariably,

ROBERT ADAIR.

CHAPTER II.

MINISTER PLENIPOTENTIARY.

1810–12.

STRATFORD CANNING was only in his twenty-fourth year when he found himself placed in the responsible position of minister plenipotentiary at the Sublime Porte. He could not of course be blind to the honour which was thus early thrust upon him : yet the post was intensely distasteful. Adair had found in diplomatic intercourse with the Divan a resemblance to " cutting into dead flesh ; " but Adair was by choice a diplomatist, and did not quarrel with the profession in the abstract. His successor on the contrary, whatever gifts he had for diplomacy, had no liking for it, but longed for a career at home, among his friends, and in the midst of all those intellectual and political movements in which he took a lively interest. He had expressly stated his objection to the honour designed for him ; but in spite of this the commission arrived and he found himself forced to remain in exile. His sense of duty, strong as it was, could not reconcile him to his position, and his first act was to lock his door and burst into tears. Regrets, however, soon gave way to anticipations. He began to look round and estimate the work to be done and the resources at his command.

He had no instructions beyond the general policy laid down for Adair's guidance ; but he was at no loss to understand the duties of his position. His first object was to counteract the machinations of the French at the Porte and keep Turkey neutral in the European struggle, as she could not reasonably be expected to join what had not been so far the winning side ; his second object was to bring about a peace between Russia and Turkey, so as to leave the Czar a free hand in the event of his being won over to the English alliance. His principal weapons were the persistent tenacity of Wellington in the Peninsula and the undisputed supremacy of England on the seas. The Turks should at least be convinced that we were not beaten.

It was uphill work in those days at Constantinople. England was isolated by land, and it was often difficult to find a cruiser to carry despatches to or from Malta, which was the nearest British station. Besides such irregular communications, Canning had to maintain touch with all the consuls in the Levant, every one of whom was dependent upon the embassy. The British ambassador in Persia was trying to influence the Court of Teheran much as Canning was trying to influence the Porte, and the two embassies exchanged mutual support. Ali Pasha of Janina was an ally to be kept in good humour. Intelligence had to be communicated to our commanders in the Ionian Islands and Malta, and our admirals in the Mediterranean ; and there was a perpetual secret correspondence with confidants at Vienna and Petersburg which demanded the greatest care and precaution.

What, however, stood foremost, and required his urgent attention, was the continued reception given in Turkish ports to English merchant vessels captured by French privateers. Although the imperial flag of France had disappeared from the Turkish seas, the privateers of that nation were active and enterprising. They sailed boldly into the Archipelago, eluded our cruisers, and not unfrequently made our merchant vessels their prey. It was their business to find immediate shelter for the prizes from recapture, and on that account they did not hesitate to take them into the nearest Turkish port. The practice was manifestly inconsistent with the law of nations. The Porte was a neutral power with respect to France and

England, and it was not to be borne that depredations made
by our enemy on British trade should be encouraged and assisted, as in fact was virtually the case, by her connivance. In
proportion as instances multiplied Canning renewed his remonstrances by the various diplomatic means in usage, but the
French piracies continued to be a perpetual source of annoyance during the whole of his mission, and the relations between
the embassy and the Porte were in consequence frequently
strained. The Archipelago was a convenient warren for the
privateers, and no month passed without fresh additions to
the stock of grievances which the Porte, in dread of Napoleon's
wrath, endeavoured to stifle. It became a duel between the
English and French representatives. Canning was relentless
in besieging the Foreign Minister with demands for redress,
which M. de Latour-Maubourg sought to postpone or evade.
The following may serve as an example of the British Minister's written remonstrances : he seldom minced words with
the Porte :—

> With respect to the *Active*, you will tell the Reis Efendi that I
> can regard his demand of proofs for the identification of the vessel
> only as a pretext whereby to elude what I require, and I am sorry to
> add that I can attribute such conduct only to the deference paid by
> the Porte to His Majesty's enemies . . . In short, I demand most
> solemnly that the vessel in question shall be sequestered. I repeat
> that the manner in which that vessel is brought to this capital, under
> the very windows of my house, *is a direct insult to the King my
> master* ; and the Reis Efendi cannot be ignorant of what my duty
> will inevitably prescribe to me if he persists in refusing my demand,
> *especially at a moment when I see so much to excite my suspicion.*[1]
> I have borne a good deal with patience. But an insult to my
> sovereign I cannot and will not bear.

One is inclined to suspect that the bland interpreter
softened these incisive communications, but he could not do
away with their substance, which was stern enough to cause
the Turkish minister considerable uneasiness.

It must not, however, be supposed that the message quoted
above is typical of the general tone of his communications with
the Reis Efendi. Many such menacing words were certainly
addressed to that obstinate functionary, but a close study of
the whole series of instructions to the interpreter of the embassy proves that the general tone of Canning's intercourse

[1] Referring to the French proposal of alliance : see below, p. 51.

with the Porte was singularly patient and conciliatory. Much as there was in the interminable delays and vacillations of the Turkish ministers to irritate a temper naturally impatient, he kept a stern rule over himself, and again and again restored by some conciliatory act or word the amicable relations which the shifty policy of the Turks perpetually interrupted. He never wearied of dwelling—perhaps in a tone hardly flattering to Turkish vanity—upon the essential good-will of England towards the Porte. He constantly offered his services in effecting an understanding with Russia, even when serious grievances strained to the utmost his relations with the Divan ; no coldness, no insolence, could make him forget that the prime consideration was to keep the Porte true to England and prevent it from being drawn into Napoleon's " continental system." He never tired in his effort to convince the Turks that England, and England alone, was their friend, and in this he undoubtedly succeeded.

But while constantly recommending this policy of friendship with England to the Sultan's advisers, he was fully aware that such friendship would possess little effective value in Turkish eyes unless accompanied by respect and even fear. It was all very well for England to have the interests of the Porte at heart, but there must be a reciprocal good feeling on the side of Turkey. Such, he was frequently assured, was the case : but how could this be credited in face of the many outrages upon the British flag at which the Porte connived or which at least it did not redress or avenge ? Good-will accompanied by such insults was worse than contempt. It was essential to make the Porte observe the laws of neutrality, and, with or without good-will, to respect the power of England.

The Turkish Foreign Minister was shrewd enough to perceive the conflict which existed between Canning's desire to act a friendly part, especially with a view to keeping Turkey out of the arms of France, and his duty, as the representative of England, to protect British interests in the Archipelago. An attempt was made to work upon him on these lines. We quote from the Memoirs :—

One day our head-interpreter brought me a monster note from the Reis Efendi. It was written in Turkish, and, when translated, filled a quire of foolscap. A message was sent with it assuring me that the Porte had regard for my youth and did not wish to injure me. The note, it was stated, explained the Porte's views ; it was

D

sent to me confidentially in the first instance, and would be put into
a formal shape only in the event of my continuing to give trouble
by unseasonable remonstrances. On reading the note I found no
reason to change my course. There was much complaint of me,
but nothing to weaken the arguments I had employed. The Porte,
I declared, might do as it pleased with its note, but I should infallibly submit it to my Government, and unless I were instructed to
the contrary, should not desist from pushing my claims as before.
It was then whispered with affected regard that I was losing my
time about trifles, that the Porte was inclined to give me its confidence in higher matters, and in short, that I might help essentially
to bring about peace between Turkey and Russia. I knew all the
importance of this overture, but felt at the same time that I could
not hope to remove the obstacles to success, unless I previously
carried my point as to what concerned our trade, our right, and our
honour. I therefore replied that with every wish to promote the
Porte's legitimate interests, I could not yield to my inclination, so
long as the just demands and rights of my Government were disregarded : when satisfied in that respect, and not till then, I should
be free to act as the Porte might desire.

With this view of his duty, Canning persistently urged
the redress of the various grievances due to the Porte's
neglect of its duties as a neutral power. "All was to no
purpose," however, he wrote ; " our merchants suffered, our
enemies were emboldened." It was then, when all ordinary,
and even extraordinary, diplomatic pressure had failed, when
conciliation and threats had equally proved unavailing, that
he determined upon taking an " act of decision " which made
the Reis Efendi " furious." It was a bold hazard, for it might
end in a total rupture between England and the Porte. But
peace, he held, with any power could only be valuable " so
long as it is consistent with honour and the maintenance of
our rights." Moreover he knew his men. He had already
acquired something of that insight into the Turkish character
which served the Great Elchi so well in later years, and he
knew that a Reis Efendi might be " furious," and fume and
bluster, but that in the end he would give in. A display of
determination by one decisive act would do more, he felt,
than another year of diplomatic conference. Accordingly he
called upon our commander in the Archipelago to take the law
in his own hands (Nov. 1811). Captain Hope, like a gallant
seaman, was nothing loth. He entered the port of Napoli di
Romania (Nauplia) and demanded the restitution of the prizes
detained by a French privateer under the guns of that fortress. The privateer captain ran his prizes ashore and burned

them ; several shots were fired by our corvette ; the fortress was mute ; and now it remained to be seen how the lesson would be taken at Constantinople.

Canning justified the somewhat high-handed action which Captain Hope had taken under his express orders, on the reasonable ground that the custom of neutral states prohibiting the reception of prizes in neutral ports was based upon the principle that such reception gave the captor an unfair advantage over the opposing belligerent by preventing the chance of recapture by the latter's cruisers ; and that therefore if a neutral port in contravention of this principle gave shelter to the privateers and prizes of one belligerent, the other belligerent had a right to enter the port and recapture the prizes if she could, just as though they were in convoy on the high seas.

The steady purpose of the British minister, emphasized by this final demonstration at Napoli di Romania, carried the day. At first indeed matters seemed to be going from bad to worse. The Reis Efendi refused to do or say anything until satisfaction had been given for the violation of a Turkish port. He even threatened to set the English minister aside and complain direct to the British Government. Three weeks of suspense ensued ; but at last the Porte gave way. A special reason influenced the Divan in effecting a reconciliation with the young minister who had bearded them with so little awe for many months. His mediation was sorely needed to smooth away the obstacles that had arisen to the conclusion of peace with Russia. He had long endeavoured unofficially to heal the breach by his correspondence with St. Petersburg, with which the Turkish ministers were acquainted ; but now he was formally invited to write direct to the plenipotentiaries at Bucharest. He accepted the overture on condition that the piracy firmans were first granted. This was at last done. The firmans which had been promised for more than a year were finally issued, and he was able to turn his whole energies to the negotiation for peace. It would require, no doubt, constant vigilance and pressure to induce the Porte to put its own enactments into effect ; but the enactments had been made, and that was the first and vital point.

Before we enter upon the intricate course of negotiation which ended in the Treaty of Bucharest, it will be well to complete the picture of the ordinary work and occupations of

D 2

the British mission at Constantinople. The long struggle
with the Porte for the protection of English merchants in
the Archipelago was indeed the chief and all-absorbing
business of the two years during which Stratford Canning
held the post of minister. Scarcely a day passed without
some official communication passing between him and the
Porte on this thorny subject, and it is interesting to find that
he used the aegis of England to protect the then budding
commerce of the United States in the Levant. But matters
of considerable importance, besides the usual correspondence
with the consuls in the Levant, came up for consideration.
The other embassies required to be vigilantly watched, for
there was hardly one of them that did not try its hand at
some intrigue against the interests of England. At one time
it leaks out that the French chargé d'affaires has had a secret
interview by night with the Reis Efendi ; or a carriage has
been seen suspiciously waiting at the door of a great personage ; or the internuncio of Austria has had a post from
Vienna and gone with it straight to the Porte. The meaning
of all such occurrences had to be interrogated.

There was little time for relaxation. He took less
exercise than ever, though he still made frequent journeys to
and fro between Pera and Therapia or Buyukderé, where he
could for a brief season enjoy the cool breeze from the Black
Sea and escape from the heat and dirt and worries of the
capital. He had no country house, and it was only at long
intervals that he could with propriety pass a few days with his
friend Count Ludolf, the minister of the deposed Neapolitan
Court, at Buyukderé. In May and June the spacious well-
watered Valley of the Sweet Waters formed a delightful
breathing-place, but the enjoyment of it was not free from
annoyance, and a shot fired from a distance when he was riding
home one evening served to remind him that human life had
not the same value in Turkey as in Christendom.

Travellers, especially if they were " something companion-
able," were a godsend to one who was pining for the social
and intellectual pleasures of London. Not many came so far
in those days, nor was the passage of the Aegean absolutely
safe so long as French privateers were about. But in 1810–11
a series of visitors arrived to cheer the solitude of the British
palace. Among them were Lady Hester Stanhope, who
with all her eccentricity was never dull company ; Mr. North,
afterwards Lord Guilford, and his nephew Douglas ; the well-

known Pozzo di Borgo of Corsica ; Galt, a rather popular
novelist of the time : and above all a batch of Etonians,
including Gally Knight. Of most of these visitors, whose
arrival made a bright spot in his monotonous life, Lord Stratford's memory retained some characteristic trait when he wrote
his Memoirs after an interval of more than half a century.

MEMOIRS.   My brief intercourse with Mr. North atoned for
many privations. His conversation was delightful, he had much
varied knowledge in all branches of literature, a lively manner of expressing himself, a never-failing good-humoured cheerfulness, and a
large share of the family wit. It had been his lot to represent his
sovereign at Rome on behalf of Corsica, recently taken by a British
force. His arrival there, he said, was preceded by a very good-
looking secretary, who was mistaken for the ambassador on shewing
himself on the balcony of the hotel where the embassy was to
lodge. It so happened that a lady of high rank and equal susceptibility saw him from an opposite window, and caught by his
appearance, sent his excellency an invitation for the same evening.
Mr. North, much flattered by the impression he seemed to have
made, and wholly unsuspicious of any mistake, went gaily to the
rendezvous, and, after traversing a long suite of apartments, found
the fair expectant in a boudoir luxuriously furnished and evidently
arranged for the occasion. Imagine her disappointment and alarm
when, raising her eyes, she beheld a plain elderly gentleman, little
favoured by nature, and somewhat the worse for Indian wear, in
place of the blooming Adonis at whom her shaft had been so
unluckily aimed. A moment's silence was followed by a faint
scream, and the application of two most delicate hands to the fairest
of faces, not in the first bloom of youth, but still quite young, and
slightly disordered in its features by sudden emotion. Her power
of articulation came back in a single noun substantive forcibly
expressive, it must be allowed, of the deep contrast in her mind
between a pleasing illusion and a distressing reality. Scarcely had
the word *Diavolo !* passed her lips, than the intelligent object of
her ejaculation took the hint, and, more amused than mortified,
retreated backwards with many bows towards his hotel. He
delighted to tell this anecdote of himself.

His nephew Fred. S. North Douglas was also a trump, especially
at table. He shared in equal proportions the humour and plain
features of his family. Young as he was, he shewed bright rudiments of talents in more than one department and his jovial good-
natured vanity gave a special zest to the display. In talking with
him one day I asked whether Mr. North had ever committed himself to a printed composition. " Yes, once he had." " And was it
very clever ? " I asked again. " To say the truth," he replied, " I
never got to that part." I could cite other instances of his ready
playfulness, but my heart fails me when I recollect how soon the

fair promise was blighted by sickness and a premature death. I joined with other friends the sad procession of his funeral, and long felt the blank which he had left among his youthful contemporaries. His wife survived: but three generations of his blood—grandmother, father, and child—disappeared almost at once !

Lady Hester Stanhope brought with her all the interest which attaches to a person of her sex remarkable for talent and nearly connected with a great public character. Not only was she the niece of Mr. Pitt, but she had lived for a time under the same roof with that unspotted minister in the full intimacy of close relationship and daily intercourse. She had known many whose names were familiar to me, and some with whom I was personally acquainted. She had seen much of Mr. Canning. On these several accounts her conversation had strong attractions for me, notwithstanding its measureless exuberance and the not unfrequent singularities it displayed. Her travelling staff was composed of Michael Bruce, who acquired no little celebrity by the generous part he took in promoting the escape of M. Lavalette; of Mr. Pearse, the reputed son of Fox's friend Hare; and her physician Dr. Merriman, who subsequently published a sketch of her life. She hired a house at Therapia and passed the winter there.

She told me sundry curious anecdotes of her uncle and others—too many in fact to be remembered at this distance of time. Speaking of Mr. Pitt, she said that during his retreat from office he shewed no signs of discontent or restlessness; that, although she had slept under his bedroom at Walmer, she never heard the sound of his footfall after the hour—an early one—at which he had retired. She told me that he always expressed the highest admiration of his father, taking for himself, comparatively, a more humble position than she was inclined to admit. She spoke of the carelessness with which he often left his papers, either scattered about the room, or, at best, stowed away under the cushions of his sofa. General Moore appeared to be her idol, and she took an evident pleasure in talking of him. In proof of his truthfulness and sagacity she said that on taking leave of his minister, [Lord Castlereagh,] under whose instructions he was to act in the command of our army in Spain, he declared with his hand upon the lock of the door, that he had no faith in the expedition, and apprehended a failure. She added that General Phipps had made a call one day, and the conversation turning upon Sir John Moore, that he had sought to disparage that officer in Mr. Pitt's estimation, and that she perceiving his design, had said, " You imagine, General, that Mr. Pitt does not greatly value Sir John's abilities, but learn from me, you nasty kangaroo "—alluding to General Phipps' paralytic infirmity and imitating his manner of holding his hands —" that there is no one in the King's army whose services he appreciates more highly." " Lady Hester ! Lady Hester ! what are you saying ? " exclaimed Mr. Pitt, with an ill-suppressed smile which betrayed his secret enjoyment of the scene.

It is almost unnecessary to say that her eccentric ladyship got herself into trouble during her stay at Constantinople. She was dying to see Napoleon, and with that view held various private interviews with M. de Maubourg. To Canning any friendly relations with the agent of " the common enemy of Europe " bore the character of high treason, and he did not scruple to remonstrate tolerably plainly with Lady Hester. This drew forth a very characteristic and malicious epistle from the lady, nominally addressed to the Foreign Secretary, Lord Wellesley, (though it was probably never dispatched,) in which she taxed the young minister, with considerable satirical skill, for his prudery and fanaticism. For his years he was doubtless inclined to be over-dogmatic, and his singularly refined nature revolted from the looseness of morals and conversation which has always been characteristic of Pera ; moreover, in regard to Buonaparte he was unquestionably a fanatic, as every true Englishman at that period ought to be. But Lady Hester must have known that he was right about the interviews with Maubourg; and that she did not really mean half what she said is shewn by a subsequent letter, when the squall had blown over, in which, referring to Canning's successor at the embassy, she said : " It is little probable that he will shew me more kindness and attention than you have done—which, though I do quiz you sometimes, I am perfectly sensible of and shall ever acknowledge with gratitude. Quiz me in return, and take one good lesson before you go. When you are no longer a great man I shall speak to you with more confidence. You may think me a strange, but I hope always a very honourable, being. Now don't crack your brain. The wise man speaketh in parables, so may therefore a silly woman. . . Let me hear that you look well and in good spirits. You ought to see this beautiful place, but when no longer a great man you might fall in love with some of these very beautiful Turkish women, and that would be a great sin." Lady Hester evidently delighted in teasing the young man, but it is clear she really liked and respected him. She wrote again from Damascus, in October 1812, " I have laughed at you and scolded you, but I must ever wish you well, because I believe you to be an *honest man*, a rare thing in these times."

To return to his recollections of old friends :—

MEMOIRS.　　Count Pozzo di Borgo, who arrived in the spring of 1811, was recommended to me, not only by his friendship with

Mr. Adair, but also by his personal qualities and political opinions. He was an accomplished scholar, possessing marked talents for business of the highest kind, and gifted moreover with eloquence, fancy, and wit. He had been secretary of state in his native island, and Russian plenipotentiary in 1807 on board the Czar's squadron under Seniavin. He could not remain at Vienna, where he had largely contributed the year before to the declaration of war by Austria against France. Napoleon required his dismissal. He determined to take refuge in England, and so complete was our separation from the Continent that the Hanoverian minister at Vienna was obliged to apply to me in order to obtain his remittances from London! Count Pozzo had therefore no choice but to make a circuit through Turkey on horseback. When quite a stripling he had been intimate with the hero of Lodi, if not his fellow-student. He told me that, strolling one day with Buonaparte along the sea-beach, his companion, who as well as himself had sat down to rest awhile, suddenly turned to him and pointing in the direction of Italy exclaimed, " Sais-tu, mon ami, qu'avec dix mille hommes on pourrait se faire maître de ce pays-la ? " To his remark that the inhabitants had not spirit enough to rise, the other retorted— " Comment ! est-ce que l'esprit leur manquent ? et les muscles ? " —striking ideas, to be sure, for one so young, and strongly characteristic of the future conqueror.

On another occasion, when we were talking of the future prospects of Europe and the dark shadow cast upon them by the towering ascendency of France with its spirit of conquest and military despotism, he said, " Come what will, England has no choice but to resist. If she made peace with Napoleon, she would soon, as before, be compelled to begin again with all the disadvantages resulting from relaxation of purpose and the acknowledgment of a usurped empire. After all," he added, " the genius of the man is rather to pull down than to build up. Il est comme un géant qui est entré dans une forêt et qui a lié ensemble par la simple force de ses bras plusieurs des grandes arbres qui s'y trouvent. Eh bien ! le temps passe, n'importe que ce soit, la foudre du ciel ou la hache du bûcheron, le lien se détache et les arbres reprennent leur ancienne position." Such were his very words, and considering the time they were spoken, it must be allowed that they were more than remarkable, almost prophetic. On other subjects too, his expressions were often singularly effective. Some one called the Bosphorus by its French name—Le Canal de Constantinople. " Yes : " he said, " a canal, but a canal of the Almighty's workmanship."

Pozzo di Borgo never forgot his friend. They met frequently in later years, when he was Russian ambassador at Paris, and one of his letters tells Canning : " Vous êtes dans le petit nombre d'hommes envers lesquels il ne me serait jamais permis d'avoir tort, et je n'aurais pas de repos si vous pouviez

m'en supposer . . . Je vous jure que je sens pour vous la
même amitié [celle d'un frère]."

MEMOIRS.   It may well be conceived how I revelled in the
society of my late schoolfellows Knight and Fazakerley.   Years
have passed since the grave closed over them : but as long as
they lived our friendly intercourse continued in spite of my frequent
absences from England.   They still hold and will continue to hold
a living place in my recollection,

Dum memor ipse mei, dum spiritus hos regit artus.—*Acn.* iv. 336.

One can conjure up in fancy a picture of the symposia of
the old Etonians thus happily reunited in the autumn of
1810, but it would have been far more interesting to have
had their own recollections of them.   Unfortunately their
letters contain hardly anything bearing upon their stay
at Constantinople, or the numerous excursions and entertainments which their host arranged for their amusement.   Their
talk was largely political, we may be sure, and the one
reminiscence which Canning has put on record respecting
their visit shews the direction in which their thoughts were
travelling.   He and Fazakerley were of opposite schools of
politics, but he says :—

We agreed in deploring the lengths to which party spirit was
then carried at home, and the unhappy influence it exercised on
English society.   In talking over the subject we hit upon a
notion which we thought might be used with advantage as tending to allay in some degree the evil effects of this malady.   It was
the formation of a club adapted to the tastes of good society
and destined to unite its members round the same dinner-table,
without reference to their political opinions, during each session
of Parliament.   Fazakerley, who had gathered a numerous circle
of friends around him [at the old Christ Church Club] at Oxford, succeeded on his return to England in carrying out the
idea ; and when I reached home myself a year or two later I
found the Grillion Club in full existence and my own name in
the list of its original members.   [There were nineteen of them
(1813) ; and among the names we find those of Gally Knight,
Fazakerley, Stratford Canning, Richard Wellesley, F. S. N. Douglas,
Thomas Dyke Acland, R. J. Wilmot Horton, R. H. Inglis, Charles
Grant (Lord Glenelg), and Lords Dartmouth and Desart.]   The
list was gradually increased to fifty, with which number it celebrated its jubilee in 1863.   The members, or some of them, met at
dinner every Wednesday, while Parliament was sitting, at Grillion's
Hotel in Albemarle Street, whence the club was known as
" Grillion's."   Never was there a more simple institution or one

which has answered its purpose more effectually. Two years ago from the time I am now writing its fiftieth anniversary was celebrated by a grand jubilee; and it continues to flourish not only with unabated but with increasing vigour. In its catalogue of names are many of the highest distinction in the literary, professional, and parliamentary walks of life.

CHAPTER III.

THE TREATY OF BUCHAREST.

1810-12.

THE time had come for Canning to win his spurs in a contest of European importance. In defending the rights of English commerce in the Levant he was perhaps doing no more than any other representative of his Majesty's Government would have been bound to attempt. On the other hand, the work upon which he was throughout engaged *pari passu* was one to test his powers to the utmost; it demanded so rare a combination of caution and prompt decision, of cool judgment and rapid seizure of opportunities; it was hedged about with so many thorny obstacles, and surrounded by such perilous and unsuspected pitfalls, that no impartial spectator could have hesitated to predict catastrophe to the inexperienced young Englishman who had dared to attempt it. This work was nothing less than to defeat the Eastern policy of Napoleon by binding Turkey and Russia to the interests of England; and the first step towards that end was the conclusion of a peace between the belligerents on the Danube.

The situation was dramatic. On the one side was the French Empire, in other words almost all Europe: after the peace of Schönbrunn, Austria dared not lift a finger against Buonaparte; Prussia was his thrall; Alexander of Russia remained at present friendly with the despot, with whom he was bartering schemes of partition. Against this overwhelming coalition England stood alone, supported indeed so far as their power went by the Spaniards, but practically isolated in her strenuous and protracted defiance of France. Turkey remained neutral—the only neutral state in Europe—and in Turkey the diplomatic battle was to be fought which supported and completed the effects of the war of arms.

More than one covetous eye was at that time turned upon
the Ottoman empire. Friendly as were the outward relations
between France and Russia, Napoleon was step by step alienating his ally. In his zeal for a naval opposition to England
he was making a series of annexations on the northern coasts
of Europe—Holland and the Elbe and Oldenburg—which
were certain to rouse the jealousy of Russia. The preference
of an Austrian archduchess over a Romanov was another
slight, and the scheme of a resuscitated Poland struck home.
War was indeed foreseen as inevitable long before it actually
broke out. Hardly was Austria bound at Schönbrunn when
Napoleon was already meditating a Russian campaign, and
was looking about for weapons to aid his purpose. Austria
was bribed by a promise of a share in the partition of Turkey
which would follow necessarily upon the success of the emperor's Eastern projects. Persia was flattered and assured
of Napoleon's devotion, and urged to pursue with added vigour
the war against the Czar. Turkey, ignorant to some extent of
the various plans of partition which were being arranged at the
Tuileries, was by turns threatened and cajoled :—threatened,
in order that the Porte might not, by refusing provisions, destroy the hopes of the French in the Adriatic, where they
intended to make Corfu the first step in a general advance
towards a maritime empire in the Levant ;—cajoled by promises of perpetual alliance if the Sultan would prosecute the
war against Russia with resolution. The grand scheme was so
to use Austria, Turkey, and Persia against Russia that the Czar
must either submit unreservedly to Napoleon's dictation, or
else embark in a general and apparently hopeless war with all
his neighbours at once. In either case, Turkey was to be the
victim, and the only question was one of detail—how much
of the Ottoman territory should be given in compensation to
Austria or to Russia, and how much seized by France.

To defeat this vast scheme of spoliation was now the master passion of Stratford Canning. The policy of maintaining
a hold upon Turkey and restraining her from a French alliance
had been enunciated by Adair and endorsed by George Canning and the English cabinet. The general instructions
pointed to a vigorous effort in this direction, and prescribed
the furtherance of peace between Russia and the Porte. The
great object was to break up the formidable combination which
had been founded at Tilsit by the alliance of Russia with
France, and if possible to create a new coalition against

Napoleon. Adair's first plan was to form a triple alliance between England, Austria, and Turkey, to which Russia might eventually be added if a suitable peace were arranged on the Danube. The overthrow of Austria at Wagram defeated this project; but to detach Russia from the continental system remained a possibility, and, since Napoleon's Polish designs had matured, had even become a probability. Foreseeing this, France at first naturally pretended to use her own good offices for peace between the Czar and the Sultan, with the object of securing the Turks as allies in the event of war with Russia. It then became Adair's prime duty to keep the French out of the transaction and to secure for England the advantageous position of having acted as the Porte's best friend. Very little, however, had been accomplished; Adair gave up the task in despair; and his secretary was left to carry it out alone. Where a tried diplomatist had failed, it was hardly likely that an undergraduate of twenty-three would succeed. The attempt must have been regarded as hopeless by the home government, or they would scarcely have risked entrusting so responsible a post to such youthful hands. It is probable that no ambassador of standing would have cared to imperil his reputation by adventuring himself at the Porte at so critical and desperate a moment. To beard Napoleon in his dreams of universal empire was a task most men would think twice about. To withstand him alone, without a single adviser, and on one's own responsibility, must appear downright madness.

Yet this was precisely what Canning did. There was no one at Constantinople on whom he could rely for advice. Morier was indeed a trusty friend, but he was younger than his chief; Count Ludolf was loyal and useful—many years later he was remembered as "my chief and almost only comfort in the way of society"—but he had not the mental ability or the authority which was required in a counsellor; the Prussian and Austrian ministers were not to be trusted for an instant, and in the existing state of foreign relations it was in any case impossible to take them into his counsels. But, it will be said, he had no doubt ample instructions from the Foreign Secretary, and what more support or advice did he need? The fact seems incredible, nevertheless it is true, that not a word of political instructions did Canning receive during the two years in which he represented England at the Porte. From the summer of 1810 to the spring of 1812

the Marquis Wellesley and his under-secretary honoured his
Majesty's minister plenipotentiary at Constantinople with
sixteen despatches, and not one of these valuable documents
had any bearing upon the intricate and momentous negotiations which Canning was then conducting at the Porte.
Seven of the sixteen merely acknowledge the receipt of
despatches ; others announce public events, such as the death
of the Princess Amelia, or the blockade of the Guadalquivir,
or caution him about some impostor or adventurer who is
suspected of an intended visit to Turkey ; and one conveys
the order of government that ambassadors shall use thicker
envelopes to enclose their despatches ! One would imagine
that the Foreign Secretary was writing to a vice-consul at
some secluded spot in a time of absolute stagnation.

During these two years of suspense reasons more and
more urgent had called for some definite word from home.
The French were pressing every point that could estrange
the Porte from England ; France and Austria were both intriguing to defeat the negotiations for peace with Russia ; those
negotiations were in a strained condition which demanded
special activity on the part of the English minister and (as he
thought) of the English fleet, and his action needed the
strongest possible support from his government to enable
him to impress his views upon the incredulous advisers of the
Sultan.   As late as 12 April, 1812, he was still absolutely
ignorant of the intentions of the government, and wrote in
despair : " Without direct orders from England there is no
reason to expect any military or naval aid in case of emergency from H.M. forces in the Mediterranean, and without
fresh instructions and the more immediate countenance of
H.M. Government it is next to impossible for this mission to
struggle successfully with the many and formidable enemies
now united against it."   Again and again did he thus remonstrate " at the risk of importunity " with the indifference and
neglect of the home authorities.

Left to his own resources, he had first to discover what
those resources were.   There was no hope of armed support,
for in reply to his repeated inquiries whether any diversion
in the Black Sea on the part of the Mediterranean squadron
were practicable, the answer from the admiral was, as we have
seen, decisively negative.   The weapons to be used were
therefore purely diplomatic—seemingly a poor guard to set
up against Napoleon's victorious legions, and especially weak

when known to be entirely personal and unauthorised by the British government. Moreover in mere diplomacy Canning had a formidable antagonist in the representative of the Emperor of the French. Monsieur Just-Pons-Florimond de Fay de Latour-Maubourg, though a young man and only a chargé d'affaires, was a clever diplomatist, and neglected no move in the intricate game which he played for two years with his even younger but not less wary opponent. He resisted Canning's claims in favour of English commercial rights with every argument within his reach ; he insinuated doubts of the English minister's honesty and loyalty into the minds of the Turkish statesmen ; he left no stone unturned to stimulate the warlike feeling in Turkey and obstruct in every possible way the prospect of peace between the two belligerents on the Danube. Nor had M. de Maubourg the disadvantage of speaking without his book. Napoleon never left his representative at the Porte without precise instructions on every point; and while month after month the Englishman was forced to admit, in reply to the frequent and puzzled inquiries of the Turkish minsters, that he had no commands from London, the couriers of France were constantly arriving with full bags at the French palace at Pera.

Had the statesmen of Turkey been anything but Turks it would still have been hard to convince them of the preferableness of the English alliance to the French under such circumstances as these : but being what they were, the task must have appeared hopeless. Canning had formed his opinion of the Divan at an early period of his residence at Constantinople. Whilst still secretary of legation he wrote during Adair's illness to Lord Wellesley of the Turkish government " in whose conception political measures are best matured by procrastination, and which therefore imagines that peace can as well be made to-morrow as to-day, and that it is always time enough to assume the tone of conciliation when that of defiance has failed." As time went on, his estimate did not improve. " Pride, ignorance, and obstinacy," he said, " are the most prominent features of the Turkish character ; " Buyuklu Oglu Mustafa, the Reis Efendi, or foreign minister, was equally " obstinate and ignorant " and sometimes " insolent." The Porte still affected the dignity which appertained to her most glorious days. She forgot that Suleyman the Magnificent was no longer before the walls of Vienna ; and her ministers seemed to imagine that the dignity of the Köprilis and

Damad Ali the "dauntless vizier" was still theirs. When Canning offered a " protest " against the protection which the Porte afforded to French privateers, the Reis Efendi pretended not to understand the word, and said it did not exist in the Turkish language ; and when it was explained to him he declared that " whatever might be the consequences, the Porte would never suffer her subjects to be domineered over by England, and that whatever Heaven might have decreed, that should be abided by."

With such instruments to play upon, the task of harmony he had set before him may well have seemed hopeless. But Canning never fully realised the influence he exercised over others. Impervious as the Turkish ministers appeared to reason, the ardent young minister was already a power at the Porte. They recognized his intellectual ability, they had proof enough of his immovable resolution. and in spite of their incurable suspicion they could not help perceiving that he was loyal and straightforward. On the other hand, they did not believe in the assurances of France, and this was Canning's best weapon. " The Porte had too often been deceived by France," said the Reis Efendi, " ever to trust her again."

The first object was to increase this distrust of France and to diminish this fear of her overwhelming power. The secret article of the Treaty of Tilsit formed a strong argument, and the Turks had never forgotten that single act of treachery. Napoleon's injudicious speech to the French senate at the beginning of 1810 had also been carefully reported to the Sultan, and its effect was not lessened when it was discovered that the French mission was foisting a garbled version of it upon the Divan, where the passages offensive to Turkey were omitted. To diminish the dread of the French arms, the successes of Wellington in the Peninsula were Canning's chief resource, and bulletins were printed at the embassy press and given to the Divan and other persons of consequence with this object. The English minister made the most of these points in the game, but nothing short of Napoleon's own treachery could have sufficed to convince the Turks of the wisdom of his advice. The rounding off of kingdoms by unscrupulous partition of neighbouring states was among the traditions which Napoleon inherited from the *ancien régime*. As one scheme of partition after another came to light, the Porte could no longer refuse to believe the Englishman's voice when he warned her that, whether France made war with

Russia or not, Turkey would inevitably pay the cost of victory or the bribe of coalition. " The silence of Buonaparte," he said, " is more to be dreaded than his threats " : for silence meant secret treachery. By degrees the battle was won, but how and after what delays and alternations of hope and despair Lord Stratford's own Memoirs, printed in the large edition of his *Life*,[1] must tell. He wrote with the calm judgment of extreme age ; but we must not forget that, when the events he described were taking place, more than sixty years before, he was in the turmoil of the fight, alone and without instructions, leading a forlorn hope against overwhelming odds, and feeling his responsibility and isolation with an acuteness which the burden of every day only rendered more sharp and intense, till " the bitterness of the draught" became poisonous to his health and spirits. A very brief outline of these transactions will here suffice.

The situation was in the highest degree embarrassing, and it was difficult to discover arguments sufficiently cogent to induce either of the belligerents to come to terms. On the one hand Russia was beginning to suffer severely from the financial pressure of the war, and conscious of the instability of her compact with Buonaparte was already viewing with anxiety the prospect of having an army of twenty thousand men locked up on the Danube at a time when every soldier might be needed to resist the threatened advance of the Emperor. On these grounds the Czar was eager for peace, if only he could obtain it on such terms as might soothe his wounded self-respect, in other words if he could obtain some substantial territorial acquisitions on the Danube. Turkey for her part was conscious of her weakness, and stood in considerable dread of the enemy ; nor were her finances in better plight than his. Nevertheless, the Turks were proud and vainglorious ; a small success on the Danube was enough to restore all their ebbing confidence ; and above all they were animated by a rigid determination never to part with " an inch of land." In support of this resolve, they had the strenuous encouragement of France, of whom they stood in greater awe than ever, since the late annexation of Holland, which seemed to shew that the great emperor was as invincible as of old. The policy of France was obvious enough : Buonaparte wanted to have Turkey on his side in the event of hostilities with Russia ; and, should an accom-

[1] Vol. i. pp. 133-176.

modation be arrived at with the Czar, Turkey, successfully duped, and alienated from England, her only genuine friend, would serve as a useful weight to throw into the scale of negotiation.

Canning's own position was one of unexampled perplexity. He was perfectly clear as to the course to be pursued; he knew that no more important object existed at the moment than to release Russia from the burden of the Turkish war, so as to leave her free to turn her whole resources against Buonaparte. But he had nothing but his personal credit to bring to the support of his representations. The Porte was perfectly aware that he had received no instructions from home. Besides, the very policy which he urged was in itself liable to arouse the mistrust of the Turkish ministers. He perceived that nothing less than some sacrifice of territory would satisfy Russia, and in pressing the inevitable condition upon the Porte he laid himself open to the suspicion of being in the interests of Russia, with whom he was known to be in correspondence. And this very correspondence was an anomaly. It was a singular position for an English envoy to find himself in ; to act as go-between from the Sultan to the Czar (with whom England was technically at war), and to send his messages by the hands of a representative of an extinct Court (Count Ludolf of Naples), who had not even the advantage of being acknowledged by the Sultan, whose messages, in effect, he was often conveying to the emperor of Russia, the said Sultan's open foe ; and all this without the authority of the British government. Of course the paramount importance of the end justified such strange and roundabout routes ; but this did not render the position less invidious.

Events came to his assistance. The proud complacency of the Turks was severely shaken by considerable reverses on the Danube in the summer of 1810, and still more by the fall of Rustchuk and Giorgevo in October ; but, although the Czar encouraged by Canning's reports, had at the close of the year sent Italinski as plenipotentiary to negotiate a peace at Bucharest, Turkey still held out, and doggedly refused to take part in any conferences which might include the mere idea of cession of territory. It seemed as if there were nothing for it but *la guerre à outrance* ; when again the successes of the Russians came to the aid of diplomacy. The Grand Vezir was utterly defeated in the autumn of 1811, and the dis-

E

heartened soldiery clamoured for peace. The Janissaries, ever " ripe for revolt," if not this time " ready for revenge," refused to advance at their general's bidding. The crisis had come.

The terrible impression produced in Constantinople by these reverses may be divined from the following despatch which Canning sent in cipher on 9 November by the uncertain but rapid route of Vienna. The terse vigour of the description conveys a good notion of the state of things and the writer's sense of their importance.

My Lord,—The Turkish army is in the greatest distress. The troops cry out for peace. The Grand Vezir has been forced by them to sign preliminaries of peace on the basis of ceding all the Turkish territory between the Danube and the Sereth. The government is much agitated. A Grand Council of more than seventy persons was assembled yesterday to deliberate upon the ratification of the preliminaries. The decision rests with the Sultan. It has not yet transpired. A few days will most probably settle the matter. As the Vienna post goes out to-night, and as my means of communication with England by sea are uncertain, I hasten to send your lordship these few words ; to which my duty obliges me to add that the want of instructions and my uncertainty about Mr. Liston make my situation here every day more embarrassing. I can no longer hope to prevail upon the Porte to maintain its neutrality against the violence of the French without the direct interference of H.M. government.

The Sultan's ratification, after some delay and much discussion, in spite of these clamours and the general wishes of the people at Constantinople, was refused.

Canning was not blinded by this apparent resolution of purpose ; he knew that the Porte must yield before long, and he never for a moment relaxed his efforts to work upon the apprehensions and the hopes of both parties. With Russia he was so far successful that she agreed to an armistice—the Danube dividing the hostile camps. The Turks accepted his good offices still further. In February 1812, he was definitely requested by the Porte to mediate, by writing to the Russian plenipotentiary at Bucharest. He did more than this. First he wrote (19 February) to Italinski, sounding him as to the acceptability of this mediation, and representing that " the conclusion of peace between Russia and the Porte would be one obstacle the less to peace between Russia and England, and consequently to that peace which alone could assure the true repose of the universe," an argument to which Russia, on the eve of hostilities with France, was keenly alive. He wrote to Ghalib Pasha, the Ottoman plenipotentiary, informing him of the recent intrigues of France; advising him that peace between Russia and Turkey would remove the last chance of a reconciliation between Russia and France, and drawing a pleasing picture of the satisfaction with which the Porte might look on while her two most formidable foes mutually exhausted themselves. Finally he wrote to the Duke of Sierra Capriola, his correspondent at Petersburg, urging moderation in the terms of peace, lest Turkey should throw herself into the arms of France, whose insidious designs were plainly laid bare. These letters were laid before the Sultan and approved. The Porte promised exclusive confidence in England during the coming negotiations.

There was not an instant to be lost. The battle was not yet won. The French were leaving no stone unturned to secure the adhesion of Turkey to their plan of a triple alliance. De Maubourg offered all sorts of tempting proposals of support and concerted action against Russia. Napoleon himself wrote a letter " to the Great Emperor of the Musulmans." There seemed to be a near prospect of Turkey being drawn into the French system, and Canning wrote to the Marquis Wellesley in desperate terms (21 April, 1812) :—

> The conclusion of peace with Russia is the first remedy. I am doing all I can to bring it about; but my means are very scanty, and although I have not lost all hope, yet the chances are very much against that event. Both parties are obstinate. I am very much in want of instructions. Even the smallest communication direct from H.M. government, if greater means cannot be employed, would be of great service. The French are making every possible exertion. Courier upon courier arrives from Paris.

It was necessary to convince the Sultan that whether France or Russia came off victorious in the expected war, or if a reconciliation were effected between those two powers, the Porte would in any case be in a worse position for negotiating a peace than she was at that moment, when Russia was beyond all things anxious to get Turkey off her hands before the " common enemy of Europe " was upon her. France triumphant would doubtless share the Turkish provinces with Austria, in return for Galicia. If Russia were the victor, it was not to be expected that the Czar would

offer better terms or terms half as good as he offered in the
hour of anxiety. Russia and France reconciled—the only
other alternative—meant the partition of Turkey as already
proposed by Buonaparte. The peace must be now or never ;
and every possible argument must daily be brought to bear
upon the Turks to induce them to make a step in concession
which the Russians might meet half-way.

MEMOIRS. The time was now come for using an expedient
which I had long kept in reserve. Mr. Adair had obtained from
a secret source and consigned to my hands when he went
away a plan for invading Turkey, which had been prepared
at Vienna prospectively, in reliance no doubt on the French
emperor's concurrence, and with a view to partition at the first
convenient juncture. This alarming and unprincipled paper I
conveyed in the most impressive manner to the Reis Efendi, and
the effect it produced on that minister was fully equal to my
expectation. He had previously told me what shewed me that his
suspicions were at work in the right direction. He said that he
had embarrassed the internuncio, by asking how Austria was to be
indemnified for the part of Galicia which in virtue of her new
connexions she would have to make over to the kingdom of Poland
whenever Napoleon proceeded to restore that power, as the language
of M. de Maubourg held out in immediate prospect.

Austria too must needs help to do the dirty work for
Napoleon. The internuncio admitted that his government
was now in strict alliance with France, and proposed concerted action with Turkey against their common foe the Czar
of Russia. Canning's indignation at the perfidy of Austria
found vent in a vigorous despatch (25 April) :—

Your lordship will perceive by this with what blind and earnest
alacrity Austria is pressing on to the work of her own destruction,
as if the past were swept from her memory, and as if she thought
herself not deep enough in shame and bondage until she had signed
and sealed away every worthy feeling, every remnant of honour
and independence which had survived the last unfortunate war . . .
Though the crimes of the present government of France are permitted to succeed for a season, yet surely it may be hoped, my
lord, that Providence will not allow the example of profligacy thus
exhibited by Austria to pass with impunity. It will rather go forth
to future ages as an object of warning no less than of indignation.

The revelations, however, which he had already made to
the Porte of Austria's double-dealing completely counteracted
any effect which the internuncio's communication might

have had. Still in the face of such opposition, and considering that he was himself still regarded almost as a Russian agent, the prospects of a peaceful arrangement seemed as far off as ever. In this emergency, the young minister despatched a secret messenger to the Russian plenipotentiary at Bucharest to inform him of the latest intrigues of France and Austria against his master, and drawing a clear picture of the tremendous dangers which now menaced the Russian empire. This last message was perhaps the turning-point in the negotiations. Russia, who had hitherto stood out for the Sereth as the European boundary between the two empires, now agreed to accept the Pruth.

The effect of this communication indeed was to strengthen the good impression which Canning's correspondence had already made upon the Russian government. The Duke de Sierra Capriola had already written on 2 April to Count Ludolf, announcing " the excellent result which Mr. Canning's letter of 19 February had produced ; " and expressed sanguine expectations of a speedy peace : " Mon cher ami,—Le moment si désiré est enfin arrivé, et Mr. Canning reçoit en réponse tout ce que l'on désirera de son gouvernement et de lui : c'est à dire, que la paix avec la Porte, et avec les Persans, se fasse par l'intervention du ministre anglais : tout ce qui se traitera sur cet objet pourra être convenu entre Mr. Canning et Mr. Italinski, celui-ci ayant reçu la permission, même l'ordre, de continuer la correspondance avec Mr. Canning pour parvenir à cette paix si désirée." The letter goes on to say that " la modération et la conduite sage " of the English minister will have the grand result of bringing about not only the peace with the Porte but another between Russia and England, and concludes, " J'attends donc les résultats les plus heureux, parceque je me repose sur votre zèle et sur les talents de Mr. Canning."

The duke wrote in similar terms to Canning direct, for the first time, and, in a message to the Reis Efendi on 18 May, the English minister commented on the contents of letters just received from Sierra Capriola and from Italinski, in these words : " I most heartily congratulate the Porte, and particularly his Excellency the Reis Efendi, on the success of my letters to Russia. They have been laid before the emperor, who has expressed his satisfaction at my intelligence. Our correspondent has had two conferences with Count Rumiant-zov on their contents. In consequence M. Italinski is ordered to continue his correspondence with me, and I am invited to do the same."

The report which was brought back from the Russian camp went to the same effect. Italinski had received instructions from Rumiantzov to " cultivate and continue the correspondence which the minister of his Britannic Majesty at Constantinople had opened with him," for which "the Russian Court was very grateful." They regarded the English minister as united with them in a common cause, and begged him to use his good offices to accelerate the negotiations. The Russian plenipotentiary admitted that the reason why Russia was so anxious for peace was that she had at least twenty-two thousand good troops locked up on the Danube which might be much better employed elsewhere.

These letters shew clearly enough the share which Canning took in bringing about the peace. The communication made to Italinski overcame the last scruples of the Russians, who were now willing to stretch almost any point in order to keep Turkey out of the proposed connexion with France, and to free their own troops in readiness for the approaching struggle with Napoleon. The real difficulty now lay with the Turks themselves.

The truth was that the Porte had got into its head a not altogether unreasonable suspicion that England, in her zeal for a combination against Napoleon, was striving to force an unfavourable peace upon the Sultan in order to secure the free action of Russia against the famous " continental system." There can be no doubt that such a combination was the prime object of Canning's mediation, and had been the chief motive that inspired Adair's original efforts at the Porte ; but at the same time it would be unjust to conclude that such a design involved any disloyalty to the Turkish interests. Canning believed rightly that no more favourable time and no more favourable terms were likely to occur than those which were to be obtained in the spring of 1812, and the Porte had not only fully endorsed his opinions, but had authorized him to mediate with Russia. As a matter of fact one after the other of the Russian demands had been withdrawn at his representation, and the final treaty included a modicum of cession which the Turks would never have obtained if they had been left to negotiate by themselves.

Nevertheless nothing would convince the Reis Efendi that better terms might not have been secured by procrastination, and the Turkish ministers never ceased to bear a grudge against the mediator whom they had themselves nominated, for acceding, as they thought, to the demands of Russia. Remembering as we do the later policy of Lord Stratford de Redcliffe towards Russia, it is amusing to find him in these early days suspected of Muscovite proclivities. The Turks were wrong in their suspicions, for he had laboured hard to secure for them the most favourable terms possible, but some excuse may be found for them when it is remembered that they had already had more than enough of French, Russian, and Austrian intrigue, and it was but natural to suppose that now it was the turn of England. The situation was certainly peculiar : when England and Russia were still formally at war, Admiral Chichagov wrote to Canning " by the express order of the emperor " to inform him that Italinski was ordered to proceed to Constantinople to arrange an alliance with the Porte in concert with the British ambassador!

Fortunately it was not the Reis Efendi who had to conduct the negotiations at Bucharest. Ghalib Pasha was a wiser man, and while his colleague at Constantinople was doing his best to destroy a well-built edifice, the plenipotentiary was placing the coping-stone on the building. It was arranged that Russia should accept the boundary of the Pruth, and abandon most of her Asiatic claims. Servia was to be restored to Turkey. The Treaty of Bucharest was signed by the plenipotentiaries on 28 May, 1812. The Sultan's ratification was despatched on 20 June, and eight days later Canning joyfully delivered to his successor Mr. Robert Liston the charge of a mission which had throughout been to the last degree irksome and embarrassing. Mr. Liston brought with him an official intimation of the Prince Regent's "entire approbation of the industry, zeal, and ability" with which the duties of his post had been discharged, and these empty forms read even more foolishly than usual when we remember how the Regent's government had neglected the duties of responsible ministers towards their representative. The skilful manner in which he had, by indomitable patience and clear foresight, brought about the end so sincerely desired by all the enemies of France, was not at once understood. The new Foreign Secretary, Lord Castlereagh, however, from a study of the despatches, had formed a very high opinion of Canning's merits in the matter, and he took an early opportunity of shewing his approbation in the most substantial manner possible, by giving the young minister a high and responsible post. The Emperor of Russia instructed Count Nesselrode to convey to Lord Castlereagh his sense of the effectual manner in which " M. de Canning " had contributed to accelerate the last peace with Turkey, " cet événement si important par les conséquences qu'il devait avoir," and supplemented this communication with the present of a snuff-box, with the Czar's portrait set in diamonds.

But one whose opinion Canning valued infinitely more than that of the Foreign Secretary or the Emperor of Russia gave his conclusive testimony to the value of the work which had been achieved in the face of so many difficulties. The Duke of Wellington, in his important memorandum on Napoleon's disastrous Russian campaign in 1812 (in the 4th volume of the Supplement to his Correspondence), speaks of the effective resistance offered by the Russian army of the Danube under Chichagov to the French when the latter in their retreat from Moscow reached the banks of the Berezina. He adds :—

> In respect to the Porte, the British government seized the earliest opportunity of exerting their influence, and succeeded in inducing the Porte to make peace with Russia, thus relieving his Imperial Majesty from the contest with the Porte, and from the necessity of defending himself on his south-east frontier. If the great statesman who at that period conducted the foreign affairs of Great Britain had never rendered to his own country or the world any other service than those above noticed, his name would have gone down to posterity as the man who had foreseen and had afterwards seized the opportunity of rendering to the world the most important service that ever fell to the lot of any individual to perform.

The Duke of Wellington little suspected that his brother the Marquis had never moved a finger in this "most important service that ever fell to the lot of any individual to perform." The passage came, however, under the eye of Canning's old colleague, David Morier, in 1869, and he wrote as follows :

> Now this great service was effected by Stratford Canning, then plenipotentiary at Constantinople, without one word of instruction or even of notice, and still less of encouragement, from the Foreign Office, then fast asleep under the Marquis of Wellesley. It was to secure the result so justly appreciated by the Duke that our *Elchi*, with no assistance and no means but what his own ability and superior sagacity supplied, took upon himself to undertake the task,

beset as it was with difficulties and obstacles of every shape and
colour, of negotiating and effecting the peace between the Porte and
the Russian Government just in time to release Chichagov's army
. . . *Quod ego attestor.*

CHAPTER IV.

TWO YEARS OF IDLENESS.

1812–1814.

AFTER more than four years' absence Canning was once
more in England, and the first sight of his own country, of
her thriving towns and cheerful villages, and her many
wooded seats, was "one continued feast to sight and thought."
However much desired, the change was a violent one. Between the Bosphorus and London Bridge there was indeed a
contrast.

MEMOIRS. The romance of picturesque diplomacy, in a region
as classical as Greek and Arabian literature could make it, had
come to an end. Blue skies were exchanged for the fog and
smoke of London ; the Bosphorus was represented by the Thames ;
the stern realities of life and its ever-shifting quicksands were in
front of me. I was too young to estimate the difficulties of my
position, too sanguine to be disheartened, too fond of distinction to
abandon my hold on public employment. Mr. Canning was at
Liverpool, invited by Mr. John Gladstone and his party to represent that great commercial town in parliament, and having for his
principal opponent no less a person than Brougham, supported by
Mr. Roscoe and the Whig interest. He asked me to join him there,
and I made the journey with another first cousin, another George
Canning, who had married one of Lord Castlereagh's sisters, and
who afterwards became an Irish peer under the title of Lord
Garvagh.

On reaching Liverpool we found the town in an uproar. Party
ran high ; bitter speeches were exchanged on the hustings, and
mobs were violent in the streets. Windows were broken, candidates pelted, and for more effective missiles resort was had without
ceremony to the pavement and the area rails. Fortune declared
finally in favour of Mr. Canning, who was cheered, chaired, and
feasted to the top of his bent. I cannot venture to say how many
dinners were given to him and his friends by the Tory capitalists

of Liverpool. I know that they were enough, with the help of turtle and punch, to imperil health far more than any riotous assaults in the streets. It was an uninterrupted jubilee of two or three weeks, succeeded by a shorter but not less convivial ovation at Manchester, which as yet had neither a member of parliament to plead its interests, nor a bishop to watch over its morals. At the house of our host, a wealthy manufacturer, we sat down to dinner soon after six, and remained at the table till midnight in right of the sabbath which offered no other amusement. Port was the only wine in circulation on the well-polished mahogany, claret as a French wine being deemed inconsistent in our host's estimation with British loyalty. When at length we returned to the drawing-room we found the lady of the house reclining over a tepid coffee-pot in the last stage of exhausted wakefulness, and imagining, no doubt, her future lot in the event of Manchester becoming a theatre of parliamentary contest.

At a great entertainment given next day at the Town Hall there was, of course, no lack of toasts and speeches. The new member for Liverpool found a suitable occasion for the display of his eloquence and wit, nor were his friends allowed to shelter themselves from public notice under his overshadowing oratory. Each in turn was called upon to acknowledge the compliment of a toast to his health. To me the ordeal was terrible; and when after the dreaded plunge I landed nearly out of breath, a few good-natured cheers sounded like the huzzahs of a multitude when some unfortunate criminal recommended to mercy is snatched on the drop itself from the grasp of Jack Ketch. A neighbour of much better promise than myself had the ambition to begin with a dative case, which so embarrassed him that he lost his presence of mind and was obliged to sit down without completing his first sentence. He could not by any exertion and with every encouragement from his party get further than "To you, gentlemen, who——," and as he was known to have designs on the representation of the county, there was no help for it but to order post-horses and leave the town at daylight next morning. He was, nevertheless, a man of ability, a good scholar, ready and agreeable in conversation. The example is a pregnant one.

I accompanied Mr. Canning to his friend Lord Granville's in Staffordshire, and thence to Hinckley, where Mrs. Canning was residing for a time. Another day's journey took me back to London. There I found Pozzo di Borgo, whom I had already seen at Tixall. He was living in a small lodging at the back of Portman Square. When I entered his room he was standing at a tall desk which supported a huge folio, one of the volumes of Fra Paolo's *Council of Trent*—a great work of a great writer, well worthy of the large and acute mind which had taken refuge in its pages from the buffets of adverse fortune and the stings of a suspended ambition. He lived, as the world knows, to see more prosperous days, to witness the defeat of his imperial competitor at Waterloo, to point the intrigues of Russia at Paris during many years, and at the last to enrich his nephew with the spoils of a money-market open to the ever-shifting impression of a revolutionary period.

The question of how the ex-minister was to live was soon settled by the usual assignment of a diplomatic pension, thus announced by Lord Castlereagh, 12 January, 1813 :—

I am commanded to acquaint you that H.R.H. is fully sensible of the zeal and ability with which you discharged the difficult duties of your mission in a very important and critical period, and that in consideration of your services he has been graciously pleased to confer upon you a yearly allowance of 1,200l., upon the terms which are usually annexed to allowances in similar cases. You will permit me to add the personal satisfaction I feel in conveying to you these sentiments and this decision of H.R.H.

The " terms usually annexed " meant that the recipient of the pension was expected to accept the next diplomatic post offered him by government, and that in the meanwhile he could not enter the House of Commons. These conditions considerably diminished the value of the allowance in Canning's eyes, and there is no doubt that had he been in a position of independence, with a small income and no relations in need of assistance, he would have declined the pension. To be tied to diplomacy and barred from a parliamentary career were precisely the two things most disagreeable to him : but his circumstances made the acceptance of the conditions imperative, and he submitted with the best grace he could.

How he was received in England, what he did, and where he went, we are for the most part left to imagine, since the voluminous correspondence which his friends poured upon the distant representative of his Majesty at the Sublime Porte naturally came to an end or shrank into very exiguous proportions when " his Excellency " was once more to be met in Bond Street or Piccadilly, at Wellesley's rooms in the Albany, or his own lodgings in Cleveland Row, almost any day of the week. One thing, however, is clear. Like most active-minded men he found that having nothing to do was not so delightful as he had anticipated. He did not know how to occupy the leisure to which he had so joyfully looked forward, and an active part in public life was denied him, though it is evident that the politics of the day engrossed his interest.

Memoirs. The metropolitan life which now awaited me was by no means destitute of enlivening interests, but the share I took in it was coloured by my tastes, and limited by the circumstances in which I found myself. I cared very little for that kind of society whose principal features are morning gossip and evening pressure. Dances were thrown away upon me. Dinners, where good conversation was to be enjoyed, those in particular at "Grillion's," a play, an opera, a debate, were the recreations which most attracted me. Even for these objects it was my lot to move in a circumscribed area. My family connexions were greatly dispersed; I had been long separated by distance from those with whom I had formed intimacies at school and college; a new generation had sprung up during my protracted residence in the East. In more than one respect my position was little better than that of a foreigner. I read, but my readings were desultory, and an occasional dalliance with the muse shook many a precious grain out of my hour-glass. The *Quarterly Review* was open to me through the good-will of Mr. Gifford, its accomplished editor, and I contributed two or three articles to its pages. It so happened indeed that the existence of that periodical was in part due to me. I was walking one day in 1808 in Pall Mall with two of my Eton friends, Richard Wellesley and Gally Knight, when our conversation turned upon the *Edinburgh Review*, which was then in the first blossom of its long and well-sustained reputation. One of us exclaimed, What a pity that London has not a publication of the same kind but of other politics! The idea was at once caught up by all, and I undertook to propose it to Mr. Canning, who referred me with evident satisfaction to Mr. Gifford, who in his turn approved the proposal. The name as well as the idea originated with us, and I drew up the sketch of a prospectus. The first number of the *Quarterly* did not make its appearance till some time after I left England, and it owed its successful reception to abler and more experienced hands—to Southey, Scott, George Ellis, Barrow and others.

In later years Canning was an occasional contributor to the *Quarterly*, and exercised a species of editorial function in relation to articles on Greece and Turkey. Lockhart was ready to alter all such papers in accordance with the Elchi's judgment.

In the spring of 1813 Madame de Staël paid a visit to England. She took a house in Argyll Street, and drew a considerable portion of the London society about her. She aimed at giving an interesting character to her evening parties, and her dinners attracted many among the male celebrities of the day. At her table I met Lord Erskine for the first and only time. She conversed with the same animated flow of thought and language which characterizes her published writings. She admired Lord Byron, who was then mounting towards his zenith, not only for his splendid poetry, but, as she said, for the softness of voice with which he uttered the strongest thoughts.

Invited to dine at Kensington Palace with the Princess of Wales I had the honour of sitting next to her at table. During an interval of silence on her part, I ventured to remark that Her Royal Highness appeared to have given up the theatres of late. " In truth I never go to them," she said. " I do not like the plays, I have seen too much of them in real life. I began with the Fatal Marriage, and I suppose it will end with Queen Catherine." Ominous words, it must be allowed, though lightly spoken at the time.

The central figure in his world of politics was still his brilliant cousin. George Canning was then in a period of occultation. He had " buried his political allegiance in the grave of Pitt," and after his quarrel with Lord Castlereagh he could not be induced to join in any of the several schemes for the formation of a united ministry, which from time to time were attempted. He would not serve under Perceval, and when the latter came by his death in the spring of 1812, Canning found insuperable objections to accepting the Foreign Office while Castlereagh—with whom, however, he was now on amicable terms—had the leadership of the House of Commons. For the time, at least, his ambition had led to his retirement from public life ; he would be nothing less than first, and consequently for four years he was obliged to remain a private member of parliament. One advantage of this was that he had the more leisure to spare for his friends, and to none was his time given with greater freedom than to the young cousin whom he had set on the first rung of the ladder to fame. " In those days," writes the younger man, " he lived at Brompton, and his house, called Gloucester Lodge, was about two miles out of town. At the entrance of Piccadilly stood a turnpike, and his coachman had orders to wait for him on the country side of that annoyance, supported, as Sheridan used to say, by *in*voluntary contributions. It became almost a habit for me to accompany him to Hyde Park Corner, and he would often detain his carriage and walk to and fro on the Park side of Piccadilly going over the ground of some political argument, or relating passages of bygone interest in his public life. He talked as well as he spoke, and every conversation with him was to me a lesson of precious information and judicious management. I never met anyone who entertained so delicate a perception of the properties belonging respectively

to the art of speaking, talking, writing, and reading. He frequently employed with striking effect our short vernacular
terms of Saxon origin, but he steered between vulgarity and
affectation with never-failing tact."

In the late summer Canning paid his first visit to the Lake
districts, where his love of nature found ample exercise. " I
am as happy as the day is long," he wrote in rapturous words
to Fazakerley (26 August) from a cottage at Ambleside :—

I did not leave Hinckley till Tuesday week, and taking it for
granted that you had left Prescot, *cum penatibus et magnis diis*,
long before, I took the direct road through Leicester, Ashbourne,
and Manchester. I was tempted by the beauty of the place to pass
a whole day at Lancaster. Have you ever been there ? If not,
you would be delighted with it. The prospect combines the beauties
of England and Turkey. The cleanest town, the neatest cottages,
and the most cultivated hills, bounded on one side by a range of
rugged mountains, on another by the sea, watered by a noble
stream, and enriched with a bridge, a castle, and an aqueduct. Add
to all this that I saw it under as clear a sky as ever looked down
upon the Mediterranean or the shores of Greece. The greenness of
the meadows throughout Lancashire and Westmoreland is something quite exquisite. Or perhaps the sober verdure of the Hinckley
pastures has disposed me to look at everything of a livelier nature
with eyes of wonder. Conceive (" for thou canst ") my raptures at
discovering a fountain by the roadside near Lancaster, just the sort
of thing that the Surijis used to stop at in a long stage—but alas !
I looked in vain for the old plane-tree, the green platform, and the
turban making its bows to Mecca !

At Kendal also I was tempted to spend a couple of days—the
country there too is pretty, and there is a delightful little romantic
river, full of rocks and woods and waterfalls, and coolness and
retirement. But the weather was almost too cold for transports and
ecstasies. On Monday morning I got to the queen of romantic
places—and here I mean to stay for the next ten days or fortnight.
The weather continues delicious—quite un-English. If you have
anything like it at Cowes I shall expect to hear no more of pitch-
plaisters and travels in Italy. I am living in a decentish sort of
cottage in the village of Ambleside, which consists almost entirely
of detached houses. The said cottage in any other place, or temper
of mind, would hardly be called comfortable. It has little or no
prospect, and is made most dreadfully cheerful by the noise of some
dozens of children, who afford a most provoking specimen of the
happiness of the place. Then one is within a stone's throw of the
most delightful walks that can be imagined. Without exaggeration
it is impossible to conceive anything more perfectly beautiful than
it is in every direction. There is all the boldness of nature and the
neatness of art, and each sets off the other. One cannot expect the

grar.deur and wildness of Alps and Apennines, nor the vigorous, shining, gigantic vegetation of warmer climates.

> At latis otia fundis,
> Speluncae, vivique lacus, at frigida Tempe,
> Mugitusque boum, mollesque sub arbore somni,
> Non absunt, &c. &c. *Georg.* ii. 468 ff.

You must forgive me the luxury of quoting your favourite passage, and will do so the more readily as it brings me to the end of my sentimental effusion. . . . Sweet Sir ! I do admire Lord Wellington's last achievement with all possible wonder and admiration, and not the less because he recommended my brother for a lieut.-colonelcy, the which lieut.-colonelcy he is to have, or rather I *believe* he has it already.—But how do you think the campaign will end ? Sebastian and Pampluna not yet taken—our late losses between 8,000 and 10,000 men, and the French so near their own resources. If anyone is capable of fixing our triumphs it is Lord Wellington. So Allah kerim ! and the devil take the hindmost. Good-night, most serene owl.

Writing to the same on his return to London in February, 1814, he says :

You are most lucky in having escaped our English winter. It has been unusually severe, and it is only now that we are beginning to revive a little under the milder breath of a south-west wind. The roads have been impassable in many places, and the Thames, to the consternation of the excise and to the delight of gin-sellers, has been frozen over. The state of the streets here is still quite formidable. The motion of a hackney coach is exactly that of a boat at sea. These inconveniences and the late meeting of Parliament prevent the town from filling ; and if they do not diminish, confine the gossip of fashion to smaller circles. The Staël, I am willing to believe, is the most fashionable thing at present on its legs, because it is the only gay place at which I have been since my return to town. The dinner was pretty much like other dinners, and the rout that succeeded it was pretty much like other routs. To you who are a philosopher this will not appear strange. Lord Erskine signalized himself by quoting at the Duchess of Devonshire, who sat opposite to him, Milton's description of old age, with a most cruel exactness of memory. Do you remember it ?

> But then thou must outlive
> Thy youth, thy strength, thy beauty, which will change
> To wither'd, weak, and gray ; thy senses then
> Obtuse, all taste of pleasure must forego, &c. &c.
> *Paradise Lost*, xi. 538 ff.

The poor Duchess looked so exactly the picture of all this that the quotation was quite superfluous. Mr. Rogers the poet decided that lines of ten syllables are harder to compose than lines of eight, and that the former in rhyme ought not to be called exclusively heroic, inasmuch as those out of rhyme of the same length are equally entitled to that epithet. The Duke of Gloucester talked profusely to a Swedish officer upon various matters of military science, such as the age of Count Meerfeldt, the rank of Schwarzenberg, in such a year, &c. &c. But all I could distinguish was a rapid and continual repetition of " l'an quatre-vingt quatorze," to which the Swede always returned a " Monseigneur " that, to judge by the tone, must be French in Sweden for " point du tout." The heroine herself was rather *agreeable* than *grand*. Once she soared into eloquence upon the impossibility of admitting blank verse into French poetry—and only once. At times she is equally eloquent upon another impossibility equally important, that of admitting the Allies into France. The rout was a conversazione *anglaise à la française*, comprising all that is distinguished either *per se*, or *per alios*, in politics, literature, *esprit*, fashion, dress, beauty, rank, &c. &c. It was not a little amusing to observe how proud the noble peers seemed to be of being admitted into the pale of wit and learning, and *en revanche* how proud were the learned and the witty of being admitted into the presence of so much star and garter. How much entertainment one might find, my dear Faz, in this metropolis of absurdity, by going about with a little common sense, which I believe to be the true invisible ring of fairyland !

Apropos of fairyland—Lord Byron has just let out another new tale upon the admiring world. It is called *The Corsair*, and is in many parts eminently beautiful, shewing a great genius for poetry, a strong conception, a rich imagination, and a great deal of dramatic power—with a considerable alloy of slovenliness and a most lordly disdain of what is usually thought requisite for the structure of a story of any sort. In the midst of the finest bursts of poetry, but more especially where he tries to develop the workings of passion or to give particular form to his characters, one occasionally meets with obscure lines, sometimes with one wholly unintelligible. The Corsair is represented as penetrating in disguise into the chamber of a hostile Pasha without any reasonable object, and one of the Pasha's female slaves is represented with still greater improbability as gaining over his guard and with their assistance stabbing Pasha, delivering imprisoned Corsair, and escaping with the whole establishment. To conclude, of the three chief persons, one goes through an oubliette without a word of direction to say what is become of her—another dies, God knows how—and the third is returned *missing*. He is seen one day, missed the next, and given up for lost ever since. The poem does not sell a bit the less for all this—the rapidity of the sale indeed is only to be equalled, I understand, by that with which the noble bard composes. He says in his preface that he does not mean to publish again for some time to come, so that we may hope that his next work will be *quite worthy* of his really great genius.

As bread to his lordship's butter the female author of prose stories, Miss Edgeworth, has opened the press campaign with a novel in 4 vols. called *Patronage*. It is very clever, and very bitter, full of her characteristic beauties, but not without several faults of lengthiness, improbability, bad taste, &c., which she has hitherto avoided. Her satire is chiefly directed against diplomacy and fashion—the duplicity of office and the display of London life, as contrasted with the simplicity of country gentlemen, and the peaceful virtues of exertion guided by principles, and ambition checked by strong sense and a good education. You will easily guess from this that whoever thinks himself connected either with fashion or office thinks himself at the same time bound to revenge their cause upon Miss Edgeworth's novel, and therefore none but those who like myself happened to read it in the country would venture to mention its name in *polite* society.

To you who are (are you not ?) an admirer of Southey, I say nothing of his *Carmen Triumphale*. I keep a copy of it by me to send to any correspondent who may happen to incur my resentment, and I assure you it would be difficult to find a more complete revenge. It is indeed most woeful stuff.

I had a very fresh letter from David Morier [1] the other day, in which he sends his love to you. He talks of being likely to return to England very soon, which means I suppose that Lord Aberdeen is likely to do the same. It is asserted indeed that his lordship is recalled on account of his unfortunate speech to Baron St. Aignan. Recalled or not, public opinion seems determined to pass sentence upon him at once, and I have only to thank my stars that I did not go with him. Morier speaks with great confidence of the ease with which Buonaparte may be disposed of if the Allies push on to Paris. He writes from Basle on the 21st ult. The next day the corps diplomatique was to move forward into France. Lord Castlereagh had arrived, and to all appearance his object seems rather to urge the vigorous continuance of hostilities than to preside at a negotiation. Nothing, I hear, can be more warlike than the exterior of the mission. Planta does nothing but flourish about with a long sword and a military cloak, while the noble Viscount himself presses the war in a pair of red breeches and jockey boots amerced of their tops. Buonaparte certainly accepted the offer made through St. Aignan by the Allies. But the latter, thinking that policy is the best honesty, very naturally, if not very righteously, wish to get better terms now that they have found out his weakness. It was reported yesterday that the Emperor of Austria had given Monsieur passports to go to headquarters. This looks

---

[1] David Morier was attached to Lord Aberdeen's mission—a post declined by Canning—and sent home some very interesting accounts of the progress of the Allied armies.

F

something like throwing away the scabbard with respect to Buonaparte.

At home, except the state of the roads, nothing is talked of but what the Allies will do next, or what will become of Buonaparte. Even Doctor Drumgoolie is without an audience. The Prince, it is said, is strongly persuaded that he, and he alone, has done everything, whether it be Russian, Prussian, Spanish, or Dutch, and the Princess Charlotte wishes very innocently that her marriage (with the Prince of Orange) were *over*. These are all the home politics I can hear, and these will probably last till the next meeting of Parliament.

And now, worthy sir, I think I have given you letter enough for one dose. Of my own concerns, about which you deign to inquire, I have nothing to say. I am established, probably for the next five months, at No. 5 Cleveland Row, where I can soothe the sorrows of an ex-official life by gazing at St. James's Palace, and read the victories of the Allies to the tune of " God save the King " twice a day. I saw Lord Castlereagh before I left town in December, and made a general offer of service for abroad. His lordship was as gracious and smiling as diplomat could wish. I feel that this was right, but like other right things it will probably leave me just where I am. But what signifies ? I am a philosopher, or if not that, an owl, and care not a *damn* for anything— tol de rol lol. The *other affair* lies dormant until the campaign can open. It is likely to be late, as the Princess Nonparelia [Miss Milbanke, afterwards Lady Byron] has been ill, though now recovered. God bless you, dear Faz, write soon and often, come back to me the moment your health will permit.

29 March.—Kean's acting and Madame d'Arblay's new novel are the only admissible topics in this grave metropolis. The former is really very good and ought to supply you with an additional reason for coming home; and as for the latter I know nothing about it and care less. The Staël continues her gaieties, and has played her cards, or rather given her dinners, so judiciously that one rarely hears her abused. I dined with her the other day, and nothing certainly since Noah's Ark ever presented a more singular mixture—William Spencer, Baron Jacobi, Gell, Madame Catalani and her spouse, Viotti the fiddler, Count Palmella, M. Dumond, M. Rocas, the Baronne's reputed Cicisbeo, who picks his teeth with a fork and assists mastication with his forefinger and thumb. Mademoiselle hacked fish and roast veal at the bottom of the table. These were the *characteristics* of a dinner, even at Corinna's. *O quantum est in rebus inane !* The Staël herself is abundantly good-natured, and very delightful, when she is not too eloquent to be understood by ordinary persons. Mr. Spencer hazarded a joke in French at dinner ; it met with no better reception from his hostess than " Voilà M. Spencer qui vient de dire une chose qui n'a pas le sens commun,"—and she was perfectly right.

The horse-laugh with which she received Sir Jemmy Macintosh, who arrived in a court dress from the Speaker's, was amongst the most diverting incidents of the evening.

At the end of April he left London to see Paris, at last in the hands of the Allies. " I am so be-bothered," he told his mother, " with the noise that the King of France and the Prince Regent are making in the neighbourhood that I have scarcely brains (even if I had time) to scribble a second page. I am setting off this very night for Paris—not on any mission—but to employ this period of bustle in what promises most satisfaction."

Writing home of the impressions of his journey, he said :

The eye could nowhere perceive any traces of the late destructive war, and except that now and then one met a few foreign troops, or descried a Cossack riding quietly over the corn-fields, or a Russian proclamation stuck up at the post-house, a *deaf* man might have passed with a full conviction of living in the golden age. Ears were better informants. One heard everywhere of the devastations committed in other parts of the country—houses destroyed, fields left uncultivated, people half-starving—and those who had anything left them by the Cossacks, pillaged by the French soldiery. The Allies, however, seem to have done all in their power to keep their troops in good discipline. In one place I was told that a soldier had been whipped round the town for attempting to ill-treat a poor woman. The conscription was the great object of complaint. An innkeeper's wife told me, with the tears running down her face, that she had been forced to pay 20,000 francs to save her three sons from it. One of our postilions said he had just escaped from the army. Another man told us he had been concealed for several weeks to escape the conscription. Others again had had all their sons torn from them one after the other. The common observation was that the male youth was quite exhausted. Men of sixty were forced into the ranks when younger ones failed. Peace, peace, is the general cry. The Bourbons are the restorers of that blessing, and therefore they are received, and therefore their government is likely to last in spite of any discontent (and I believe there is a good deal) still lurking in the army.

Within the last few days a better spirit is visible among the public. The Senate is the most unpopular part of the new constitution ; and by the King's last declaration one is led to suppose that he means to take advantage of this in order to bring it more under his authority and to render its composition less objectionable than it is at present. Nothing could be more magnificent than his entrance into Paris. A Parisian mob is certainly a much more orderly and seemly sort of thing than a London one. There was not much acclamation near the spot where I was stationed, but a most loyal

display of white drapery, fleurs-de-lys, and fair faces. Happily for
the King there was so much dust and heat as to leave little room for
sentimental reflection ; otherwise what a strange succession of
thoughts must have crowded into his mind ! And the Duchesse
d'Angoulême ! What must have been her sensations ! I happened
to witness a very affecting sight the other day at the Tuileries.
The King was giving audience to several deputations. One of the
deputies spoke so feelingly in reference to the long exile and late
recall of the emigrants, that the old courtiers about the King, the
companions of his misfortunes, burst into tears. *Messieurs les
maréchaux de l'empire* looked sternly on. Whole shoals of
Englishmen were presented first to the King and then to the
Duchess in separate apartments. She was particularly gracious,
but she must take some lessons in dignity. Poor old Louis received
everyone sitting, his gouty legs well wrapped up in black velvet, and
the Order of the Garter to keep all tight. . . .

The Great Man's [Wellington's] reception here has been most
gratifying. People of all ranks crowded to see him. His presence
seemed for a time to eclipse everything else. The most delightful
sight I ever witnessed was his introduction to his fellow-heroes of
the Continent, Blücher, and Platov, and Wrede, &c. &c. It took
place at a ball given by Sir Charles Stewart, at which the Emperor
of Russia was present.

A few days ago I went to Versailles and St. Cloud : the one just
as it was left at the Revolution, entirely stripped of its furniture,
and scarcely a remnant to be seen but the dozens of looking-glasses
still remaining in Marie Antoinette's boudoir ;—the other with all
the emblems of Buonaparte's presumption as fresh as if he was
expected to return the next moment. *There* are materials for
moralizing ! The pains he took to surround himself with objects
that fed his pride and vanity are inconceivable. Not a room but
contains some memorial of his victories that seems to say, " Ah !
combien Monseigneur doit être content de lui-même ! " There is
no end to his eagles and ciphers. In every corner of the palace,
on every article of furniture, in every architectural ornament, one
is sure to find a great N, or an eagle, or a figure—sometimes
naked,—of the conqueror himself. A good number of these are
already effaced, but it will take a long time to get rid of them all.
The person who shewed St. Cloud confirmed the accounts of his
outrageous temper. When he was in a passion there was nothing
for it but to run away. The storm passed over with the object of
it, and, like other violent people, it seems he was not apt to bear
malice. The same person told me that he seemed fond of his
young wife, and often played with her in the gallery and about the
grounds *like a child*. His favourite antic was carrying her either
on his shoulders or in his arms, I forget which. They always slept
together. An aide-de-camp slept between the double doors of a
chamber leading to one side of his bedroom, and Rustem, his

Mamluk, did the same on the other. It is striking that both Rustem and his favourite valet refused to go with him to Elba. One still meets with people—particularly soldiers—who regret him and take his part. But this is very far from being general. Everyone, however, says that he did a great deal for the city, and so he did, but at whose expense? His designs, of which many remain to be finished, are very grand and in excellent taste. The historical pillar in the Place Vendôme is a magnificent thing. Still he is a wretch, and the basest of wretches. I believe I told Bessy in my last letter of his having requested an asylum in England, with many compliments to the nation. In passing through Avignon the other day he was pelted, and, to avoid a repetition of the salute, changed coats with Colonel Campbell, and cried *Vive le Roi* most loyally.

Canning was present at a fête given by Prince Schwarzenberg at St. Cloud : " and there I saw, and never saw again, the handsome youth, who was destined to hold the reins of empire in Russia, to keep all Europe in alarm for thirty years, and to close a proud career under the pressure of a disastrous war. His brother, the reigning emperor, sent for me, and by way of expressing thanks for my exertions in favour of peace at Constantinople, offered me the decoration of one of his orders, which I could not accept, and then a diamond box with his picture, which I was expected not to refuse." The Czar Alexander was pleasantly impressed by Canning, who little imagined that in his younger brother Nicholas—then seen for the first and last time—he would find a lifelong enemy.

CHAPTER V.

THE CONGRESS OF VIENNA.

1814-19.

AMONG the statesmen assembled at Paris was the English Secretary of State for Foreign Affairs. Canning had sought an interview with him some months before without definite result ; but from Paris he wrote to his sister (27 April) : " On calling on Lord Castlereagh, as I was bound to do on my arrival here, I was not a little surprized to hear him say, ' I

am very glad to see you, Mr. Canning, as I have something
to say to you about yourself'—in short, after a very kind
and flattering flourish, he offered me a foreign mission,
which I have accepted. It is indeed an unexceptionable one.
I cannot say more about it at present, except that I hope and
believe I shall be able to return to England before I set out."
The mission was that of Envoy Extraordinary and Minister
Plenipotentiary to Switzerland, and Lord Castlereagh's
"handsome" manner of conferring it, together with the
pleasant impression produced by his two interviews with the
Foreign Secretary, considerably modified Canning's opinion
of one whom he had hitherto regarded chiefly in the disagreeable character of his cousin's opponent in the duel on Putney
Heath. He was surprised to find Lord Castlereagh possessed
of so much good feeling and kindly manner, and was particularly pleased when he told him that he offered him the post
because it involved plenty of hard work, which he knew Canning liked.

After a brief stay in England, the new Minister set out for
Switzerland, by way of Paris.[1] His first impressions were
decidedly *en couleur de rose*.

Put on your spurs [he wrote to J. N. Fazakerley, Zürich, 5 July],
mount your yacht, and come the shortest possible way to this delicious country. When once here, you will acknowledge that you
have spent twenty years of your life most unprofitably. In short
you are, and must be, an owl, till you set foot in this land of liberty
and cocked hats. The finest mountains—the greenest hills—the
richest plains—the neatest houses—the best inns—the most limpid
streams, and for aught I know the most delightful fair ones, ever
yet beheld in this transitory sphere! Elysium and Mahomet's
seventh heaven are mere jokes to this earthly anticipation of Paradise! You will be particularly happy too to know, *for my sake*,
that ceremony is a plant unknown to these simple regions. I am
established at the Hôtel de l'Epée—in a single room, which serves
me "for parlour and kitchen and all," surrounded by deputies and

---

[1] Before he left England he had published anonymously a poem called
Buonaparte (in heroic couplets), which, though it achieved no great success
with the public, attracted the admiration of no less a critic than Byron, who
wrote two letters on the subject to the publisher Murray. In the first he said
"I have no guess at your author, but it is a noble poem, and worth a thousand
odes of anybody's. . . . After reading it I really regret having written my own.
I say this very sincerely, albeit unused to think humbly of myself." The second
letter was written after Byron had learnt the author's name. "I do not think
less of *Buonaparte* for knowing the author. I was aware that he was a man of
talent but did not suspect him of possessing *all* the family talents in such
perfection."

illustrious travellers, who turn out of the neighbouring rooms, in swords and cocked hats, to pay me *leurs devoirs*. About five minutes afterwards I go out of my room, take a turn in the passage hat in hand, and return the visit as if I had just arrived from the other side of the mountains.

The grand event of to-day is my visit to his Excellency the President of the Extraordinary Diet, a very respectable gentleman, verging upon fifty, reading English, and wearing a black coat and a pigtail. We exchanged speeches, in presence of sundry deputies and a general. Guards presented arms, and my procession, consisting of a coach and pair, seemed to produce no small sensation. You must prepare your stomach for dining at twelve, which is the usual hour. I have not yet seen any visible marks of society here; but I am told that at Bern the people are more sociable. As far as I can learn we are not likely to be kept in this town more than three weeks or a month; and I already anticipate the horror of being torn away from one of the most beautiful scenes in the world—which at this very instant of time I am enjoying from a window that looks out upon the lake and across it to the Lagerberg, the Albis, the crags of Schwytz, the snowy ridges of Glarus, and the glaciers of the Alps beyond ! Ye gods ! am I not to be envied ? —Come, come with speed ! *Per amicitiam nostram, per communem nostram twadlationem*, I entreat and implore; come and soften that dreadfully aristocratic and artificial digestion of yours among the children of freedom and simplicity ! Seriously, old owl, do write to me forthwith and fix the time of your arrival either here or at Bern—and I will engage to scramble upon any rocks you please with you. I am sure you will be delighted with the country. I greet the club. Remember me to old friends.

The most beautiful scenery in the world, however, and a people simple and idyllic enough to inspire a Theocritus, would not have satisfied Canning unless accompanied by real and responsible work. Fortunately, at the time when he entered upon his duties at Zürich, the affairs of the Swiss cantons were in a complicated state, which called forth his best energies to disentangle. He had been chosen for the mission because he was known to like work, and he soon found that there was plenty to be done before the tranquillity of Switzerland could be even temporarily secured.

MEMOIRS. The Helvetic Confederacy was at that time in a very disjointed condition. So long as Buonaparte's Act of Mediation was in force, the old and the new cantons we e sensible of a compression which more or less effectively held them together in spite of themselves. It is but justice to say that the act in question derived strength not only from the power of its author but in some measure from its intrinsic merit. The Allies deemed it a part of sound policy in the change of circumstances to untie a cord which attached the Alpine republics to France. By giving the Swiss a new political existence dating from their triumph in the cause of national independence, they hoped to establish a barrier favourable to their views in the centre of Europe. They imagined that the neutrality of a newly constituted Switzerland might be brought to operate as a check upon the normal tendency of France to extend its power beyond the Alps and to create aggressive dependencies in Italy and Germany, on the Po, or on the Danube. The Emperor of Russia, in particular, aimed at succeeding to that influence which Napoleon's abdication had left open to the most persuasive or the most commanding suitor. For this purpose he had found an able and zealous agent in Count Capodistrias, who in concert with Lebzeltern, an Austrian diplomatist, had already sounded the respective cantons and prepared them for a reconstruction of the federal act intended to be the result of their free consent, though fashioned under the impress of foreign influence.

It was a curious coincidence that Capodistrias happened to be with the Russian army on the Danube at the very time that Canning was bringing about the Treaty of Bucharest which (as Capefigue said) "broke the luck of Napoleon." The association was renewed not only in Switzerland and at the Congress of Vienna, but in Greece. In 1828 Canning had to negotiate the terms of the liberation of Greece with Capodistrias, then her President; and in 1831 the English ambassador was preparing for the mission to the Porte which terminated those long discussions, when Capodistrias met his death at the church of St. Spiridion at Nauplia.

MEMOIRS.　　Our duties in common were of two kinds. We had to bring the component parts of the Helvetic Diet into unison on the subject of their Federal Compact, and we had also to assist the cantonal authorities in framing their separate conditions in such manner as to make them harmonize with that instrument, and give satisfaction to the contending parties in each independent legislature. It must be confessed that there was plenty to do: much to adjust, much to amend, and, for us foreigners, much to learn. [There was also much to leave alone. Lord Castlereagh's despatches form one long panegyric of non-intervention.] Every form of republican constitution, from the purest democracy to the highest aristocratic rule, came under our inspection. At Neuchâtel there was even an infusion of royalty.

Notwithstanding these many difficulties the common sense of the nation and a just perception of its essential interests, to say nothing of a steady moral pressure, benevolent on the whole, from without, prevailed sooner than we had dared to expect. Before the plenipotentiaries of the Allied Powers could assemble at Vienna, the great majority of the cantons agreed to an act of federation capable of being presented to the Congress whenever it should open its negotiations. Some liberal parties, as we should call them now, had, however, given their assent to the act with the mental reservation of obtaining a revision at Vienna, and they reckoned, not without reason, on being supported in the attainment of their purpose by Capodistrias and his government.

Canning's poetic disposition was strongly moved by the associations awakened by the famous scenes of Swiss history, which he was able to visit during the recess of the Diet. His own intense patriotism found a sympathetic delight in retracing the course of the heroic struggle for liberty which is mapped out by such names as Sempach, Morgarten, Morat, and Granson. His Austrian colleague Baron Schraut, in a fit of asthma and choler, told the deputies that their favourite Tell was an assassin. Canning, troubled by no historical doubts, held him to be a hero, and every step in the fight against tyranny won his unbounded admiration. The spirit moved him to pour out such feelings in verse, and half-a-dozen stanzas, dedicated " to the Swiss, 1814," testify to the enthusiasm with which he revered the heroic traditions of their past. His poems, whatever may be said of their absolute merits, possess a relative value which cannot be neglected in estimating his character. They are throughout inspired by a romantic spirit which never deserted him. No touch of cynicism can be traced in a single line. Sadness, regret that so many dear and lovely things must change and pass away, sorrow for human sufferings and brief life's uncertainty—all these are there : but with them we find everywhere, even in poems written after the age of ninety, a young fresh spirit of belief in all that is true and beautiful—of faith in those " unrivalled images, those imperishable examples," which change and death cannot efface from the world's history. He was a great dreamer and passed much of his life in an ideal universe of golden deeds ; and to this he owed the marvellous elasticity and spiritual elevation which marked even the latest year of his long life. Even then the recollection of heroic deeds and devotion to country or friends would bring the flush of enthusiasm to his cheek and the moisture to his eye ; and how much more powerful must have been this spirit of romance when he stood in the glow of youth on the very spots which had moved it, surrounded by the grandeur of Alpine scenery, and in that pure air which seems perforce to raise the thoughts to the height of inspiration.

At that time Switzerland was the vestibule of Europe. People were crowding to the scenes of the recent war, to Paris, to Vienna, and to Italy, and Switzerland generally formed part of the route. Canning was seldom without one or other of his old friends. Wellesley, Fazakerley, Douglas, Rennell, and Gally Knight, all visited him in his Swiss retreat—the two first were with him together in October 1814—and some came more than once to enjoy his cordial hospitality, tempered with an alarming amount of his own poetry, and flavoured with many a joke. But he was soon to witness a very different and singularly impressive scene.

Lord Castlereagh had not been long at Vienna, attending the famous Congress, when he wrote to order Canning's presence there, and the latter was naturally delighted to " exchange the dulness of a Swiss winter for the more active scenes of the Austrian capital at a moment when all the affairs of Europe were about to centre within its walls." On 23 October he started. His impressions of the crowded capital were confided to his mother, with whom he always kept up a regular and detailed correspondence, writing her long accounts of all he saw and did, in a careful clear hand very unlike the rapid scrawls with which he often favoured other correspondents. He wrote on 24 December :—

It is at all times difficult for a stranger to get into the society of Vienna. The fashionable people live very much in coteries, and are not too fond of seeing strange faces. Still it is no easy matter to be dull in a place which, in addition to the usual amusements of a capital, possesses so many persons with whom it is a matter at least of curiosity to be acquainted, and which may be called the metropolis of politics. Without any violent exertion, but that of occasional patience, one may pass from three or four o'clock till midnight in society—and in good society. And this is not quite so idle an employment as it appears. As Congress has not yet assumed all its formality, chit-chat and gossiping are the principal agents of negotiation, and an evening party is the scene where the destinies of kingdoms and empires are decided for ages (perhaps) to come. In the midst of even these mighty concerns, I assure you, the affairs of the little cantons of Switzerland cut no contemptible figure. They have a committee, in which I have the honour of sitting, all to themselves ; and certainly if their importance is to be measured by the trouble they give, they must be very important

indeed. They are drawing towards a conclusion, and I begin to
think that another month or five weeks will put me some miles on
the way back to Zürich.

Among the illustrious persons with whom I have had the
opportunity of making acquaintance since I have been here is
Prince Talleyrand the Reverend. He is the professor and protector of all that is sound in principle, pure in virtue, and venerable
in establishment. He can't bear Jacobins, and wonders what
people can mean by talking of anything but the indefeasible preroga-
tives of kings and the inalienable rights of nations. He quotes
learned books about right and justice ; looks back with horror on
the Revolution, and calls Buonaparte a coward. Some little time
ago he was inveighing with great vehemence against Jacobinism
and Jacobins, when I took the liberty of saying to him—" Votre
altesse en a connu quelques uns."   " Oui," said he, " je les ai tous
connus—il n'y avait entre eux que l'égoïsme et l'intérêt personnel—
pas le moindre sentiment pour la patrie ! "   Is not this a lesson
never to be forgotten? You shall now have another. Sir Humphry
Davy, whom I met at Zürich, told me he was present at that
famous conversation of the French legislative body when Buonaparte was forced to confess for the first time that, if he had been
victorious, he had at least not been successful. On that occasion he
saw the Prince of Beneventum, preceded by a page, bearing a
cushion, hobble slowly up the hall, stop before Buonaparte, and
upon the cushion being carefully arranged at his feet, kneel down
and embrace the knees of his emperor. And this, it seems, was a
gratuitous adoration. About the same time Sir Humphry dined
with one of the French ministers, where Talleyrand was of the
party. Talleyrand took an opportunity to introduce the name of
Buonaparte, and made a sort of speech which lasted half an hour,
in praise of him, and in support of his famous doctrine, that the
connexion between him and France was necessary, and that all the
obligation and dependence were on the side of the latter. At this
very time Talleyrand must have been either in actual correspondence
with the Allies, or in the intention of being so at the first favourable
moment :—or perhaps that is pressing too hard upon him. The
devil himself, as saith the proverb, must have justice. The prostra-
tion and panegyric took place in December, the first overt act of
treachery—or rather of repentance and grace—did not take place
till early in the spring. So that a decent interval for change of
mind upon fair grounds may be supposed. The first communication from Paris was sent, I think, to the Emperor of Russia, written
without signature on a piece of cloth, linen or muslin. Talleyrand,
it seems, dictated, but did not venture his handwriting. The Duke
Dalberg, who is at present a member of the Swiss Committee, was
the cat's-paw. His hand was known at head-quarters. The proposal was expressed concisely and mysteriously. The end of it ran
thus :—" Why do you walk on stilts, when you can use your legs ?

You don't yet know what friends you have at Paris." Think of the amazing effect these few words have produced!

Talleyrand's manner is pleasing and gentlemanlike. His voice is low and monotonous. His address is awkward from his lameness, but not embarrassed. His countenance is almost always the same; impassive, yet by no means wanting intelligence. It may be prejudice, but one fancies that a great deal may be seen working under the surface. It puts me in mind of a rapid stream, frozen over smoothly and transparently enough to show the current without discovering its bottom. If he were anyone else, one would believe him amiable; and if one had never seen him by the side of a pretty woman, one might fancy him a man of great insensibility or self-control. Even when he talked to his niece, who is called a beauty here, there is something, notwithstanding the placidity of his face, most wickedly searching and sensual in his eye. His thoughts seem always at his disposal. He enters readily and good-naturedly into any ordinary subject, makes commonplace remarks, generally with a moral tendency, tells a sober anecdote, and listens in his turn. His appearance is quizzical. Besides his spindle legs and twisted ankles, which oblige him to walk in semicircles, not unlike a bad skater, he wears a monstrous coat, and a wig of natural hair in proportion, frizzed with great care, discovering, rather coquettishly, a part of his forehead, descending solemnly and profusely over his ears, and terminating, I think, in a pigtail behind.

The Memoirs fill in the details of the picture :—

People were not slow to perceive that the amusements of society proceeded at a swifter pace than the adjustment of European differences. Brilliant entertainments at Court, diplomatic dinners, and evening assemblies followed each other in rapid succession. On Sunday evenings, a city ball, with or without masks, attracted natives and foreigners of every description. Even the Imperial Archdukes did not hesitate to mix with the motley crowd. I retain a vivid recollection of a mock tournament given in the Redouten Saal, where twenty-four knights, chosen for their youth and good looks from among the best families, tilted, in gorgeous armour, at termini surmounted by Turks' heads, and received the reward of their dexterity at the hands of an equal force of female beauties rivalling each other in the charm of their manners and the tasteful magnificence of their dresses. The balls were usually opened with a polonaise, in which the highest potentates as well as the greatest statesmen took part, without excluding their younger or more animated brethren from the waltzes and quadrilles which habitually followed. Among the latter no one figured more frequently or more effectively than the Emperor of Russia. His smiling countenance and well-polished head were seldom withheld from the festive circle, nor would his good-nature and unassuming demeanour have failed to win all hearts if a shade of intrigue and a suspicion of duplicity had not crossed the radiance they so largely diffused. The Court and the houses of ambassadors and other official personages filled so wide a space, that little room was left for private individuals, however distinguished by rank and fortune, to display their hospitality. The Maréchale Lubomirska was, perhaps, the one who did most for general society. Her spacious hotel was open to visitors of all kinds every night in the week, with now and then an exception occasioned by some accidental circumstance. Those who were once introduced had free access to her apartments without invitation. At ten, or about that hour, supper was laid for any number of guests. It was laid on separate tables of different sizes throughout the suite of rooms, and those who stayed to partake of it had only to choose the table they preferred. For this a special invitation was necessary. I was introduced to the old lady by her granddaughter Countess Waldstein, whose charming character and remarkable talents assured me a kind reception. The Prince de Ligne, so famous for his wit, was taken ill on the very day I had agreed to go with Madame de Waldstein to a party at his house. He died a few days later and I never saw him.

The Countess Waldstein exercised a strong fascination upon Canning. She was the wife of the Count whom Beethoven made immortal by the dedication of the "Waldstein Sonata," and when one reads her letters one wonders whether the great master did not really get his inspiration from the wife, though the husband received the overt homage. Certainly she was worthy of the devotion which so many of the Englishmen then gathered together at Vienna undisguisedly paid her, with the full consent and approbation of her adoring husband. Among them, Canning stood foremost in her regard. They had many tastes in common, though music was not one of them, for Canning always maintained that his ear was only just good enough to distinguish "God save the King" when he heard it, and his reminiscences do not contain a word about the great concert where Beethoven conducted the "Battle of Vittoria." But they were both ardent lovers of nature, and her fondness for sketching suggested the gift of a drawing-book, while he was made happy by one of her sketches, which he ever afterwards preserved with affectionate care. To the day of his death it hung on the wall by his bedside.

Isabelle Waldstein was not the only woman at that time who felt the charm of the poetic young Englishman, or for whom he entertained a tender sentiment. He exerted that sort of influence over women which a singularly handsome

mobile countenance, a stately manner, full of the courtesy of
the old world, joined to an inflexible will and a temper inclined to be despotic, are sure to produce. His very austerity
and coldness of temperament, " cet air sérieux, fier, froid—
glacial," as one lady described it, piqued the curiosity of those
who were accustomed to conquest and found the " orgueilleux
Anglais " a difficult quarry ; and his sensitiveness to the finer
impressions of nature and poetry, his idealism, and his earnest
warmth of conversation, far removed from the prosaic and the
commonplace, were singularly captivating. Even in Switzerland, the glaciers were not chilling enough to repress the
raptures of the ladies of Zürich and Bern, as Addington's
letters to his chief abundantly shew. But reserve, or a naturally self-contained nature, sufficed to render Canning proof
against their fascinations. He was besides too much wrapped
up in his career, and his mind was too full of dreams and
ideals, to leave space or inclination for any relations but such
romantic intercourse as that with the Countess Waldstein.

Early in 1815 Lord Castlereagh, who had been completely
outwitted by his colleagues in the Congress, was called away
to play his part in the House of Commons, and was succeeded
by the Duke of Wellington.

The town [wrote Canning, 1 Feb.] was yesterday electrified with
the news of Lord Wellington's intended arrival. He is expected to
be here either to-day or to-morrow, and already half Vienna is on
tiptoe to look out for the great man. What a magnificent position
is his ! Every work of peculiar difficulty and glory seems naturally
to belong to him. In negotiation as in war everyone anticipates
success the moment his name is mentioned. How my fate will be
affected by the great man's arrival I know not. As yet I see
nothing that need necessarily hasten my departure, and I may still
have to pass three or four weeks here, or even more. To say the
truth, I have a burning curiosity to see the hero a little closer than
I ever yet have had an opportunity of doing, and am therefore in
no hurry to go away. Notwithstanding Lord Castlereagh's great
merits, and the sense of his very particular kindness to me, it is
impossible not to feel a little pride in the approach of a man so
exclusively qualified to do honour to his country and to shame the
squabbling sovereigns into the performance of their duty.

12 Feb.—I have at last had the pleasure of being introduced to
the Duke of Wellington. I have had one (and only one) long *tête-
à-tête* with him, and I do not despair of having sundry others in
due course of time. Nothing can be more open and agreeable than
his manners. Straightforwardness, good sense, and simplicity seem

to be the principal ingredients of his quiescent character. I am told he *can* be in a tremendous passion occasionally—a failing for which I have the highest respect. He spoke to me very kindly about Charles [Stratford's brother, who had served as aide-de-camp in the Peninsula].

4 March.—Tell Charles that my admiration of his old master, the duke, is as great as his ever was. The more I see of him, and I lose no opportunity of doing so, the more I find to justify the public opinion and to explain the phenomenon of his astonishing success. It is almost impossible to pass half an hour in his society without being the better for it. What a lesson to see the man who is covered with honours and titles, who has always succeeded, who hears nothing but his own praises, as plain and simple in everything he does or thinks, as if he spent a calm uneventful life in retirement and reflection! Nor does the wonder stop here. The man by nature ardent and impetuous is in practice patient and even sometimes docile! The general, accustomed to command, submits his opinions to the wishes and convenience of others! The man who has gained everything is as attentive to his business as if the whole race of ambition were still before him! This is a prodigious merit, is it not?—But I must leave the subject, not for fear of wearying you, but lest I should get too soon to the bottom of my paper. You will be sure to have more of it at some future time. The Congress is at length beginning to show some symptoms of drawing towards a close. The Emperor of Russia talks of setting off on the 15th or 17th, and the other crowned heads will, I suppose, follow his example. He is to go to Munich and Berlin for a few days before he goes back for good to Petersburg. What a comfort it will be to see all these good people at home once more—and Heaven keep them there!

MEMOIRS. The duke had little in view but to follow on the line traced by his predecessor. His clear energetic capacity had, no doubt, its full effect in that direction, but there was nothing else to call it forth, and no change took place in the relative positions. His mere presence at Vienna, nevertheless, gave cheer and encouragement to the English collected there. I had an ample share of their feelings. The duke was to me the personification of British glory and of that triumphant cause which had brought all Europe together for the establishment of its peace on durable foundations. Parts of my correspondence from Zürich had fallen under his notice at Paris, and he had written to me in gratifying terms. He received me with kindness. Possibly he remembered that a brother of mine had served on his staff as aide-de-camp during the Peninsular campaigns. The first time I went to pay my respects I found him wretchedly lodged. Lord Castlereagh's hotel was not yet open to him, and I found him writing in a room so small that the door, when I opened it, almost struck against the back of his chair, seated as he was at a bureau which touched the opposite wall. On his first appearance in public I happened to be with him. He was recognised by the people and cheered. He drew himself up in a stately manner and received their cheers with the glasses of his carriage down. The scene went to my heart, and for once in my life I kissed a man's hand. On another occasion, when I was walking with him, he expressed his admiration of the Austrian troops, some of whom happened to pass by, and he also spoke of his own soldiers in Spain, with full reliance on their military qualities, but adding that they required to be well fed. "It is not enough," he said, "to provide them with ample supplies, but you must put the food into their mouths." Drink was a snare to them, and he instanced the case of a siege in the Peninsula, I think that of Badajos, where the soldiers got into the wine cellars, and were found in numbers dead drunk, some even in the vats. As soon as he was established in his official residence, he frequently gave suppers, which afforded me an opportunity of hearing him talk. On these occasions I remarked that he shewed signs of reading habitually most of the political publications of the day, and that his conversation, though by no means restricted, was to the last degree dry, plain matter of fact or opinion, without a trace of wit or the slightest play of imagination. At times he was kind enough to admit me, when work was over, into his cabinet, and I delighted to afford him opportunities of reverting to his campaigns and showing "how fields were won." I remember in particular his account of the battle of Salamanca. Marmont commanded the French. The duke gave him credit for being able to make a slip, and consequently drew up his troops in position without exposing them, and waited. His calculation was correct. Marmont extended a part of his force too much. His adversary marked the fault and attacked him instantaneously. "We beat him," said the duke, "in forty minutes—forty thousand men in forty minutes"—and he repeated the expression several times with a tone of natural delight, but without a shadow of self-applause.

I was present when the other plenipotentiaries had their first meeting on business with the duke. His Grace was occupied in adjusting some papers at the table near which they were all standing. His look was one of concentration : theirs expressed a thought of acting in concert with him. At last he squeezed the balance of his papers into an office box, and turned the key with so conclusive an energy that they had nothing for it but to retire. Lord Cathcart, like a good old courtier, took the lead, Lord Clancarty hesitated a moment and then followed ; Sir Charles Stewart winked at me with a good-natured smile, exchanged a word with his chief, who called after him—*Charles !*—on the threshold of the door, and disappeared in turn. I was so much amused with the scene that, when I remained alone with the duke, I could not help exclaiming rather emphatically—" They're gone, sir! "—the duke looked up but said nothing.

Prince Metternich was by no means the stiff, reserved, and somewhat cynical statesman which the character of his policy might have led one to suppose. He was formed for society, given to conversation, good-humoured and capable of adapting himself with ease to all varieties. These qualities, when brought freely into play, gave sometimes a tone of bonhomie to his language and manner. In middle life, unstarched by office, he might have been a boon companion, perhaps even what the French call a *bon diable.* Although my occasions of intercourse with him were almost entirely diplomatic, his natural turn of mind in these respects came frequently under my notice. His voice in stating or arguing was sometimes loud and consequential, but not I think from worse causes than the power of the organ and the satisfaction he derived from hearing its echoes. His accent was what Lord Dudley described as *Teutonic,* and therefore, when playful, he could not quite shake off a certain heaviness which might be likened to the hair on the heels of a cart-horse transferred to those of a hunter. There was some popular scandal on the subject of his veracity, which applied to his father as well as to himself, with this difference, that one was said to lie mechanically, and the other by design. This saying, which had more the character of an epigram than of a charge, may be taken as proof of the lighter qualities with which I have invested the effigy of the great Austrian Chancellor. His famous interview with Napoleon, which lasted the greater part of a day, and fairly tired out the most indefatigable of mankind, came into his head one day when I was with him, and he gave me a full account of the whole combat. His object was to resist and weary the emperor without committing himself, and he boasted that he had sent the great captain three times out of the room for relief. When Napoleon dropped his hat, accidentally or on purpose, it was in vain that he waited for Metternich to take it up ; he was obliged to stoop for it himself. There was courage in this conduct of the Prince, and it looked like an omen of that turn of fortune which ultimately landed the arbiter of Europe's destinies on the rock of St. Helena.

Time went on, and still the Congress " dragged its slow length along." People amused themselves, but negotiations stood still. " Le Congrès danse, mais n'avance pas." Canning never forgot the tremendous shock which dispersed that august assemblage of High Contracting Parties. His Memoirs, written more than half a century later, contain a vivid picture of the scene :—

We were in that part of March which has the credit of being more like the lamb than the tiger, when the lay-conclave at Vienna

G

was suddenly roused by " a rattling peal of thunder." Napoleon had escaped from Elba, had landed in France, and was marching on Paris. No change of scene on the stage was ever more complete. Amusement, negotiation, intrigue were brought all at once to a stop. The settlement of Europe was like a thing mislaid; no man could think of anything but war and its preparations. The common sentiment was that a great opportunity had been lost, and that a fresh series of conflicts, sacrifices, and disasters would have to be encountered. The pen gave way to the sword, the ink-bottle to the magazine. All eyes settled upon the Duke of Wellington, and to judge by the flash from his eyes, when I saw him coming downstairs after his first war conference with the sovereigns, he felt within himself that confidence which he had so justly and generally imparted to others. One might now imagine that he had already in vision anticipated the apotheosis of Waterloo.

Fifty years have passed away in ever-changing succession since this eventful period. All those who took a leading part in its transactions have finished their earthly career, and in all probability I stand without a colleague in the survivorship of that committee with which I was immediately connected. Although, as I have already stated, I had no place in the list of plenipotentiaries, and still less any voice in their official deliberations, I was twice invited to assist at the Board of General Conference, and on one of those occasions the discussion or rather the conversation which took place brought Prince Talleyrand to the foreground so strongly that the picture stands, as it were, before me even now. Napoleon's return from Elba was known. How were the Allies to deal with him ? Was he to be opposed as a legitimate enemy, or was he to be outlawed as one beyond the pale of humanity ? Talleyrand, as far as I can remember, took no part in the debate, if debate it could be called. He sat for some time absorbed in thought, and twisting a piece of sealing-wax with his fingers. He then rose slowly up, paused a moment at the table, let the wax drop dead from his hand upon it, and, with a countenance which seemed to say " It's all over," moved his chair aside and disappeared by the nearest door.

The time was fast approaching for my return to Switzerland. Our Committee had got through their work with fair success. They concluded by adopting an Act of Federation essentially the same as that presented by the Diet, but offering some supplementary decisions on points left open at Zürich, and accompanied with a promise of neutrality and guaranty as the price of acceptance. The benevolent feelings entertained by all the Great Powers for Switzerland were recorded in a preliminary exhortation to peace and mutual good-will which I had the happiness to draw up.

On Canning's return to Zürich in March he found the whole country in a state of the greatest anxiety and excitement. As he told his mother (21 April) : —

The storm excited by the return of Buonaparte is rising slowly and portentously on every side. A few more weeks and all will be again wrapped in smoke and flame. Adieu to the visions of repose and security! They may return again, but many a day must be lost and won, many a fair field drenched with blood, in the interval. The efforts made by the royalists in the south of France with the Duke of Angoulême at their head have been sadly unfortunate. For once the *Moniteur* has had but little to exaggerate. They sent here, among other places, for assistance, but nothing could be done. At Lyons and in its neighbourhood the atrocities and absurdities of 1793 are reappearing—women parading the streets with naked swords—houses plundered, priests insulted and even massacred, it is said, at the altar—the black flag hoisted, and the most impious mottoes stuck about the town : for instance, " *Vive l'enfer, la république, et la mort!* " To what a desperate state must that wretched ambitious man be reduced when he resorts to such means, he whose power in former times was established on the suppression of Jacobinism. There seems to be so much union, activity, and resolution among the Allies that everything may be hoped. But think with what misery even success must be attained! My Swiss are behaving well, and I trust with proper encouragement they will continue to do so.

The " hundred days " were a not less anxious period for Switzerland than for the rest of Europe : indeed their proximity to France, and their lying on the road to Austria, exposed the cantons to the perils of revived Jacobinism and Imperial aggression in a special degree. Buonaparte had not forgotten the Confederacy of which he had once been " Mediator," but the Swiss were not to be brought over to his cause. Their leaning indeed was always towards France, but they distrusted the Emperor, and the Diet was all on the side of Louis XVIII and the Allies. They were even induced to coöperate, in a cautious manner, in the military opposition to the resuscitated empire. They collected some 15,000 men for the defence of the cantons, and had they followed Canning's advice they might have struck a decisive blow upon the French *corps d'armée* near the Simplon.[1] The royalist movements on the Swiss border did not command his confidence, but he was instructed to assist them, and for that purpose 1,000*l.* passed from English resources into the treasury of Count Auguste Talleyrand, who represented the royalists in Switzerland. Whatever might have been the issue of this enterprize, the battle of Waterloo soon superseded the necessity for its continuance.

[1] See the Library Edition, i. 257-8.

The news of the famous 18 June reached Zürich in the following hasty note from Lord Stewart :—

My dear Canning,—Altho' I shall write by another courier, as I catch a Russian just going off here, I cannot resist sending you a few lines lest he should arrive before the one sent by the Austrians.

Lord Wellington has gained the most glorious and difficult victory he ever accomplished. Bonaparte committed no fault, but the superior genius of the other was everywhere triumphant.

The attack was made by the French on the 18th on the British army in position near Mt. St. Jean. It was assailed in every part, the left and centre in the commencement of the action, but every effort was vain. Towards the close Bonaparte collected 17,000 horse to attack the right. Lord Wellington saw, and was prepared for his movement. Our cavalry supported by columns of infantry repulsed this last desperate attack, and the rout of the enemy became universal. Marshal Blücher towards the evening appeared and attacked vigorously the rear and flank of the enemy retiring. The effect now was decisive. All the cannon, ammunition waggons, baggage, &c., were abandoned, and the number of prisoners are immense ; 300 pieces of artillery and Bonaparte's baggage remained in our hands. But he, it is said, has left his army and gone off. Lord Wellington moved forward to Mons from Braine-l'Aleude, where his hd.-qrs. were previous to the action, and Blücher to Charleroi, and both are in full pursuit. The Guards and Life Guards particularly distinguished themselves. Poor Uxbridge had his thigh shot off, and has suffered amputation. Sir Thos. Picton, Col. Delaney, Qr. M.-Gl., killed ; Fitzroy Somerset, Vincent, Pozzo di Borgo, in the immediate circle of Lord Wellington, wounded. Many of [the] French soldiers and officers came over after the action. When I have more official news you shall know.

Your activity will disseminate this news ; send it on to France and spread it in every direction.

Yrs ever, in haste,
Stewart.

Our loss is stated at 12,000.

The tidings were received in Switzerland " with unbounded demonstrations of joy." Guns were fired, and deputations waited upon the English envoy to congratulate him on the gallantry of the army and the genius of the duke. For Canning, however, the pride of the victory was mingled with personal grief. His brother Charles had fallen in the battle. Many letters which constantly passed between them shew how deep was their affection for each other, and the pang of sorrow was, if possible, sharpened by the long separation which their several duties had entailed : they had not met for years.

The duke himself wrote to Mrs. Canning on the loss of her son, from Paris, 19 July, 1815 :—

I assure you that there was no person felt more sincerely than myself the severe loss you sustained in your son. The glory of the occasion in which he fell can afford you no consolation, but it must to know that I had every reason to be satisfied with his conduct, and that he fell in the zealous performance of his duty.

Stratford's sorrow at his brother's death was tinged with characteristic pride :—

After a long and painful silence, I once more take up my pen, my dearest mother, not to condole with you upon our common loss, but to congratulate you upon having had a son who has honourably and gallantly discharged the severest of duties, and who has fallen at the side and with the approbation of his great master.

While such momentous transactions were afoot, no one had any leisure to spare for the affairs of Switzerland. Indeed there was little to attend to. The cantons were gradually becoming reconciled to the Federal Compact and the decisions of the Vienna Committee, and such outstanding differences as remained might be left to time to settle. Under the circumstances, Canning found relief from official ennui and private sorrow in a brief tour among the mountains.

In this little country [he told his sister, 28 Oct.] all is as quiet as if the name of revolution had never been heard. Even the spirit of party seems to have subsided, and if I were not cursed with the most unquiet nature that ever fell to the lot of a poor devil without fortune and with very little talent, I should pass the most agreeable of lives in contemplating the blessed effects of tranquillity and independence restored to a worthy nation. But you who know me too well to make confession a merit will not be surprized to learn that such tranquillity has but few charms for me. My reason approves and admires it; I can even sometimes feel a pleasure in the fancy of having possibly contributed—in some remote degree contributed—to it; but my turn is not that way, and often in my best and most philosophical moments, when ambition and all its vanities are puffed to the idle winds, I catch myself building castles which prove but too plainly that with me contentment is the dream, and passion—for what else is ambition?—the reality. There, dearest Bess, is a bit of my inside for you—to shew that I have not yet lost all reliance on my old confederate. And here let us leave the subject for the present, and believe me, that wherever I may be placed, high or low, in the storm or in the calm, my heart, with all its faults and follies, will ever have one warm and faithful corner for the most beloved of sisters.

In November he had moved to Bern, to be nearer the seat of government. Here, to judge from a letter to his mother, he found more distraction than at Zürich (16 Nov. 1815) :—

And now, my dearest Mother, a word for your private ear—a secret of the most interesting nature ! Don't be frightened—I am not going to be married, nor have I even fallen in love : it is simply this—I have nothing on earth to do, and as far as diplomacy is concerned, I might as well go to China with Lord Amherst. But hush ! not a word about it for your life. It is very comfortable, and I would not be disturbed for the world. In proportion as I get out of work, I become daily more expert in the lordly arts of twaddledom, politeness, and gaiety. We flirt with the ladies, madam—we deal much in small talk, we dance, we waltz, and even have given, and think again of giving, balls ourself. The fair ones of Zürich have not yet recovered from the despair of our departure, and the misses of Bern are already tearing caps for us. But three days ago we drove sixteen English miles out of town to a ball, and what is more improper still, to a wedding, where we flirted and danced till three or four in the morning, and made love, or something very like it, to the mistress of the house, one of the prettiest and most amiable little Frenchwomen I ever met in my life. There we had a play, very fairly acted, and a supper—*chose assez rare en Suisse*—very well served ; and all this at the house of a M. Pourtales, one of three brothers whose father is said to have died worth fifteen hundred thousand pounds—I put the sum in letters that you may not think I make a mistake. You will easily conceive that the third of such a sum is enough to make a Swiss richer than Croesus and Midas together. And considering that any one of the brothers could buy the whole Confederacy out and out, it is not the least singular part of the story that they are all remarkable for their moderation and patriotism.

In the spring of 1816 he enjoyed the change of a visit to England, where he accompanied George Canning to Liverpool, and also visited the latter's mother at Bath. He did not return to Switzerland till September. During his absence all the gossips of Bern had been giving him in marriage to persons unknown, but they were probably equally surprized and disappointed to find their predictions realized. He came back to his mission with a bride. He had married (3 August) Harriet Raikes, the youngest daughter of a governor of the Bank of England, with whose family the

Cannings had long been acquainted. They journeyed to Switzerland in September, but did not immediately commit themselves to the firs and gossips of Bern. While waiting for a house there, they spent a few weeks at a pretty villa near Lausanne, which they had selected as their residence for the summer of the following year, whither they migrated with the first spring weather, after a not very enlivening winter at Bern. Canning had taken " La Chablière " mainly for the pleasure of his young wife, who would soon need all the cheerfulness that beautiful landscape and the wide view over the lake to the mountains of Savoy could yield her. They were very happy together there, so far as a few letters enable one to tell. Later on, her mother and sister came to stay with her, and their presence still further brightened the lovely spot where her brief married life was passed. Her child was born dead, and in a few hours the mother followed (16 June). She was buried at Lausanne, and an elaborate monument to her memory by Canova stands in the cathedral.

Canning felt the death of his wife very bitterly ; " the fair vessel wherein he had embarked all his soul's affections was sunk, and he stood alone upon the strand—friendless in the midst of friends " :—but his letters of this time are too private and exclusively personal to be printed.

At first the melancholy seclusion of " the poor Chablière " was cheered by the presence of friends. His brother William joined him at once ; Fazakerley came over soon afterwards and stayed till the end of October ; and the well-known politician, Mr. Fischer of Bern, passed his vacation with him. After that he was left to himself for the winter, and settled down to books and retirement. He was re-reading Gibbon, in sight of the place where the *Decline and Fall* was written. The seclusion and quiet of La Chablière suited his mood at the moment ; but it was of course impossible that one " cursed with an unquiet nature," as he said of himself, should long remain content with the aimless life he was leading. Retirement he believed (but wrongly) he could enjoy, but the half-way condition of " rustic diplomacy," which was at once work and no-work, disgusted him. He had sounded Planta on the chances of home employment before his marriage in 1816, and his wife's death made him the more eager for a change. He told his mother (4 January, 1818) :—

What I least like in the state of my mind is that I am continually living in the future. I feel as if I was tolerating a state of sacrifice

and restraint for the sake of some ulterior object, and though I
have no such object in view with any degree of distinctness, I take
but little pleasure in anything that does not seem in my imagination to be connected with it. Something of this is naturally, I
think, in my disposition; but the loss of her who had fixed my
affections, and the necessity of remaining in a situation, where
there is office without business—*i.e.* restraint without occupation—
are admirably calculated to assist the tendency of nature.

What he was aiming at was, as of old, a seat in Parliament,
or, in default of that, a more active diplomatic post. In this
sense he had written to his faithful adviser Planta in September, and it is amusing to find from this letter that he had
completely forgotten his early enthusiasm for Switzerland,
his resolve to live and die there, and declared that he " had
never liked it." Whilst there was active responsible work
to be done his energy exhausted itself upon that work ; when
the toil and difficulty were over, he grew impatient of the
monotony of his post.

Planta's reply, coupled with the advice of others, convinced
him that his hopes of a speedy release were not to be gratified.
He submitted to 'Αναγκαίη μεγάλη Θεός, the " goddess, to whose
decrees, engraved on adamant, all human affairs, desires, and
passions must give way " :—

But of one thing be sure, my dear friend, that, if I can anyhow
help it, I will never consent to pass my life in a middle indefinite
state between something and nothing. A certain time, I well know,
must be allowed for seeing or rather feeling one's way ; but the
days of initiation once fairly over, none but weak minds will voluntarily submit to remain in a neutral state. Active life and retirement have both their peculiar advantages—it is the middle condition which, like Milton's gryphon, half wading and half flying, has
all the odium, the inconvenience of office, without either its interest
or its dignity, and all the insignificance of retreat, without either
its leisure, its serenity, or its independence. You seem to think
me exorbitant in looking to office and Parliament *at once*; but in
my view of the matter they go together like bread and butter. I
care little about income, and I give you my word that if what small
private means I have were at my own disposal, and were not in
part destined to other wants than my own, I would willingly take
the unproductive half alone, and never think of its less honourable
but unfortunately almost indispensable companion.

His mother was mainly dependent upon him, and his
eldest brother had failed so completely in his attempt to carry
on his father's old business that heavy drafts had to be made

upon Stratford's purse. It was the consideration of these
claims which compelled him to couple his desire for Parliament with a wish for office. An appeal to George Canning
only led to a "set down." The latter probably perceived
that his sensitive cousin was not made for the rubs and
assaults of political life at home, and he was too fond of
managing people for their own good to be able to comprehend
their own views of the subject. The time for proving his
aptitude for home office was evidently not yet come; and
meanwhile diplomacy must be endured. It was not a very
heavy yoke, for there was really nothing to be done at
Bern, and accordingly in October, 1818, Canning obtained
leave of absence, and started on a tour in Italy. He had an
interview with the king at Turin, whom he describes as "one
of the plainest and meanest looking persons one can well
conceive. His stature is very short, his complexion of the
worst sort of brown, and his teeth strikingly defective." The
traveller visited Milan, Florence, and Rome, among other
cities; and came back to England in March 1819. In June
he was at Paris, and about this time he seems to have visited
the field of Waterloo, returning to Bern in July, when he
immediately asked and obtained (16 Aug.) leave to resign his
mission. The Federal Directorate wrote him a very handsome letter, and spoke with "gratitude and sincere attachment" of what he had done for the country, "services they
could never forget." And so he turned his back, but not for
ever, on the cantons with which he had been connected for
five years.

CHAPTER VI.

THE UNITED STATES.

1819 –1824.

THE mission to Switzerland was given up on the understanding that one of two things would be done for the ex-minister :
either a post in the government at home would be found for
him, which would enable him at last to realize his ambition
of entering Parliament, or he would be promoted to a higher
mission. At the moment of his application for leave to resign

there was some probability of his being sent to Copenhagen; there was no mention of America as a possible alternative. Yet in September, scarcely a month after his return, the die was cast, and Canning had accepted the post of Envoy Extraordinary and Minister Plenipotentiary to the United States. He was fully aware of the difficulties and drawbacks of the situation. His former secretary, Henry Addington, in congratulating him on his appointment, characterized the mission to Washington as at that time " the most important, difficult, and dangerous, of all on the list, embassies not excepted "; and added, " If you can succeed in keeping those schoolboy Yankees quiet and saving us another hundred millions of debt, you will be England's Magnus Apollo, and come home in the course of five years (nice prospect!) a G.C.B. with a handle to your name." His old chief, Sir Robert Adair, wrote also of the importance of the post: " Most difficult indeed will be your task, difficult beyond that of any European mission, but I have the fullest confidence of your succeeding there." George Canning declared, " I was never more clear in any opinion in my life than that the appointment is precisely the most advantageous in point of credit as well as of interest (fair honourable interest) that could have been proposed to you."

The very difficulty of the post formed an attraction to Canning. He had accepted the mission to Switzerland because he liked hard work, and had resigned it when the work ceased to be hard. He accepted Washington for precisely the same reason which had recommended Switzerland to his eyes. But there was a further motive for his ready acquiescence in another period of exile from home. That motive was the hope that his experience of American affairs might serve him as a sort of apprenticeship for public duties in England. There was no opening for him in England at the moment, but a few years of hard work in the United States would make him the better fitted for and the more deserving of a home office when such an opening should occur. At the worst the mission would probably lead to further diplomatic promotion. Residence at Washington was considered so unpleasant that the man who endured it counted upon a speedy promotion on his return. The last minister, Sir C. Bagot, had gone on to the important embassy of St. Petersburg, and Canning might look forward to a similar step, if his home ambitions were not to be realized.

In his narrative of life at the Court of London, Richard Rush, the American Minister, describes an interview with Lord Castlereagh, at which he was informed of the appointment of the new minister to the States:—

In speaking more particularly of Mr. [Stratford] Canning he carried back his narrative to 1812. That year found him, he said. . . . at the head of the embassy [at Constantinople]. In this situation, important duties fell upon him, which he performed in a manner highly satisfactory; but he attracted the favourable notice of the government chiefly by services which he rendered as auxiliary to the conclusion of a treaty between the Ottoman Porte and Russia, accomplishing an object dear at that time to Great Britain. He was soon afterwards appointed minister to Switzerland. This, although not generally a leading station, was converted by events into a conspicuous theatre for the display of his fitness for high diplomatic trust. . . . Mr. C. was requested to give his attendance at the Congress [of Vienna] . . . and from the usefulness of his information and discretion of his counsels left upon all minds the best impressions. Returning to his station he remained until a few months ago faithfully and ably discharging his duties.

Canning did not set out for America till August, 1820. The year's interval was spent chiefly in London, where he resumed the quiet enjoyment of intellectual society, which he had not tasted since 1814. He went very little into general society, but dined frequently at the Travellers' Club, of which he was an original member, and spent many evenings listening to debates in the House of Commons.[1] His long residence abroad had no doubt made him somewhat of a stranger in town, and his tastes pointed rather to intellectual intercourse with such men as he met at the Travellers' or Grillion's than to the indiscriminate chatter of crowded routs and the formal dulness of dinner parties. His old Constantinople ally Count Ludolf was minister for the Two Sicilies in London, and they met now and then at dinner. Inglis, Wilmot Horton, Planta, Morier, and T. D. Acland were the friends he saw most of, and at Mr. Canning's table he met such celebrities as Walter Scott and Hookham Frere. One incident may be quoted from his diary :

6 June, 1820.—I left the House at six, and at seven, from the balcony of the Travellers' Club I saw the Queen arrive with Alderman Wood by her side, in an open carriage, attended by a crowd of a hundred or two persons, partly on foot and partly on horseback.

---

[1] See the fragment of a Diary in the Library Edition, i. 290–6.

They shouted as they passed Carlton House, and the alderman
stood up in the carriage and waved his hat, and seemed to thank
and encourage the mob. I found afterwards that Ld. Castlereagh
had been with the King, as the cavalcade went by. Towards dusk
I penetrated the crowd which had collected opposite Alderman
Wood's house in South Audley Street, where the Queen had
alighted. The people were not very numerous, and extremely
good-humoured, confining themselves to crying out occasionally
for the Queen or her host and obliging the servants on such carriages
as passed by to take off their hats. God grant that this may not
prove a disastrous day for the British Monarchy—

> Ilion, Ilion
> Fatalis incestusque judex
> Et mulier peregrina vertit
> In pulverem!   Hor., *Carm.* iii. 3.

As the spring of 1820 wore on to summer he found himself more and more absorbed in the troublesome operation of
preparing for a three years' residence on the other side of
the Atlantic. In the present day little is thought of so
trifling a voyage, and one may safely reckon upon procuring
whatever is wanted on the American side. In 1820, however,
the transit lasted from six weeks to two months, according to
the state of the wind and water, and we learn incidentally
that Canning's return voyage, when he travelled almost alone,
cost 300*l.* in passage money. What the expense of setting out
must have been, with two secretaries and eleven servants, and
seventy tons measurement of baggage, we are left to imagine.
In those days the British minister had to take all his furniture
with him, as well as his French cook, his cabriolet, " a sort
of one-horse carriage which in less refined times was called
a *whiskey*," stores of all descriptions, wine and ale—in short
everything was sent out from England. It took four days, in
an epoch when the steam crane was unknown, to put the
baggage on board.

On 11 August he sailed in H.M.S. *Spartan*, touching at
Madeira, and arrived at Annapolis, the port of Washington,
in less than six weeks. Years afterwards he recalled in
his Memoirs the unprepossessing aspect of the American
capital :—

I know not what appearance the grand seat of government,
with its Capitol and the celebrated White House, presents at this
period, but when I first saw it forty-eight years ago, the Pennsyl-
vanian Avenue extending from the one to the other, or nearly so,

was the only thing approaching our notion of a street, and that for the most part rather prospectively than in actual existence. A low flat space of considerable extent, having for its southern boundary the Potomac, and to the north a low dwarf range of hills surmounted with a row of detached villas, formed the site of the embryo metropolis of the Union. The greater part of this platform was occupied by brushwood and swamps, with here and there a sprinkling of shabby trees, and intersected by two or three roads with several tracings of future streets, towards which its inhabited portion was gradually throwing out signs of intended growth in a straggling sporadic sort of way.

The letters and reminiscences of this period present an interesting picture of the United States seventy years ago. He was not indeed a sympathetic observer ; his character and training were alike antagonistic to the free-spoken independent habits of young America, and that lack of " reverence " which he held with Shakspere to be " the angel of the world." Americans were then shaking themselves into shape, and their angularities were not yet rubbed off by the long process of education to which they have zealously submitted since 1820. Canning was ready enough to admire the marvellous energy and industry with which they were creating out of trackless forests and poisonous swamps what he foresaw would become a great empire ; and his criticisms are directed rather against their social qualities and the conceit of a very young nation than against their moral and physical virtues, which he was quick to recognize. And even in American society, of which he expressed a by no means complimentary opinion, he enjoyed some very pleasant acquaintance. His description of the country life of the well-known Carroll of Carrolton, the last survivor of those who signed the Declaration of Independence, and the grandfather of the beautiful Miss Catons, one of whom (Mrs. Patterson) became the second wife of the Marquis Wellesley, is a charming picture of the best side of American society ; and in General Macomb, Mrs. Decatur, and a few more, he found congenial friends. He certainly did not allow his dislike of the general public to appear, for the newspapers extolled his " remarkable urbanity," and Henry Addington told him, after his departure, that he was more popular even than his predecessor, the genial Sir Charles Bagot.

Conciliation was then the policy of the British Government. England had learnt by more than one experience that the temper of the States was not to be rashly trifled with, and she was determined not to allow the many trivial points of dispute which still existed to draw her into further hostilities.   The animosity of the Americans at that time waxed warm against the mother country and it needed very little to fan the kindling spark into a flame.   " Sir," said Mr. Adams one day to Canning, " it took us of late several years to go to war with you for the redress of our grievances : renew these subjects of complaint, and it will not take as many weeks to produce the same effect."   The threat was unnecessary, for the daily press was proof enough of the inflammable spirit of the time ; but the minister was careful not to give the Secretary of State occasion for carrying the menace into action.   Under such circumstances he could hardly be expected to achieve any brilliant diplomatic triumph : his success consisted in an improved relation between the two countries.   " With respect to business of a diplomatic character," he wrote, " *stagnation* would perhaps be the most suitable word to express my share of it.   The duty imposed upon me by the authorities in Downing Street was principally to keep the peace between mother and daughter."

It was not very easy to keep the peace, when the daughter had but lately " come out," and was as vain and sensitive as new-fledged independence could make her.   A more patient nature than Canning's might have found it a hard task to soothe American susceptibilities, and it speaks much for his self-command that he had but one serious dispute with the Secretary of State.   " The feelings of the nation," he wrote, " are as pacific as they are ever capable of being—but so is gunpowder till the spark touches it."   To avoid communicating this spark was the difficulty, especially as the minister was expected to talk—a branch of business which was all the worse because it had to be " transacted interminably.'   " The diplomatic body at Washington," he said, " ought really to be reckoned amongst the labouring classes " ; and a foreign minister, " like a candidate at a popular election, must have his hand out for everyone, and a never-ebbing smile on his face."

The following letter to George Canning shews the opinions which the English minister had formed of the United States after a year's residence at Washington.   They are not complimentary, but Americans themselves will admit that there was a good deal in those early days to excite the disapprobation of so sturdy a Briton.   Public feeling on both sides has happily

changed materially as the recollection of the great struggle
has faded away. After referring to the unpromising financial
condition of the States, he says :—

These are no doubt evils for the time ; but I question whether
the country will not be all the better for them in the end. One of
their first effects is to sober down some of those brilliant fancies
with which the good people, one and all, have been possessed since
the pleasant days of neutral trade and the glories of Perry and
Jackson. Jonathan is still on horseback, but not quite so " high in
his stirrups " as of yore. The steed which he bestrides is the same
prancing kicking beast, but not being so well fed, it occasionally
hangs its ears and falls into a shuffling pace when not looked at.
Several of the newspapers continue to deal largely in coarseness
and invective, but that tone on the whole is decidedly softened. I
have met with few instances of impertinence, and more general
civility than I had been led to expect. Chewing and smoking
appear on the decline ; indoor spitting is also less common ;
breeches and silk stockings are not unfrequently worn of an evening ; but these innovations are perhaps confined to the courtly
regions of Washington. Even here the true republican virtues have
found a refuge at the Foreign Office : trousers, worsted stockings,
and gaiters for winter ; a white roundabout, i.e. a cotton jacket
without skirts, for summer wear, sans neckcloth, sans stockings, and
sometimes sans waistcoat. . . .

I have but few opportunities of seeing the President ; but he
really seems to be an amiable and upright man. While he remains
in office the chances of a fresh quarrel, as far as anything in this
country depends upon personal character, are certainly much diminished. It is but just to say that among the officers of the army and
navy I have met with considerable candour and good will. . . .

These are called quiet times ; yet the events of the year have
been enough to make an *annus mirabilis*, and one that has been
dwelt upon the least is perhaps the most striking : I mean Buonaparte's death. You are probably not aware that he died poisoned.
My authorities for this appalling charge are the *Washington
Gazette* and the *Aurora* of Philadelphia. Unhappily for the success of their lie, the same country which has furnished the venom
has also furnished an antidote. Some time before Buonaparte's
death was known, his brother Joseph, feeling himself unwell, sent
for Dr. Chapman, a physician of Philadelphia, and in the course of
consultation, after several anxious inquiries respecting the signs
and symptoms of a cancer in the stomach, confessed that he apprehended an attack in that shape, his father and someone else of the
family, he said, having died of the same disease. The fact is un-
doubted, and must surely be taken as a strong corroboration of
what Buonaparte is himself reported to have thought and said of
the nature of his last illness.

The only very pressing subject of speculation that we enjoy is the interchange of massacres between the Turks and the Greeks. As far as the Americans are concerned a damp is thrown upon the inquiry by recollecting that the Sultan plants his own tobacco, and that the Pasha of Egypt grinds corn for the consumption of both parties. To me, as an ancient sojourner at Constantinople, the struggle is full of interest : but I have not yet succeeded in persuading myself that the Greeks have a chance of recovering their freedom. Can they hope for success without the aid of Russia, and what would they become when delivered by that aid ? If Russia takes up the cudgels for them, can the Porte be mad enough to refuse such terms as the principal powers of Europe, unfavourable to Russian aggrandisement, would consider reasonable ? Without the sanction of such a refusal is it likely that the Emperor Alexander, engaged as he is in the great system of continental politics, would plunge into a war which in proportion to its success would bring half Europe on his back ? And are terms of accommodation recommended by other powers likely to embrace the independence of the Greeks, which could never be wrung from the Porte without a war, and which it would be impossible to undertake without risking the very result most certain to be deprecated ?

I speak of probabilities—as a matter of humanity I wish with all my soul that the Greeks were put in possession of their whole patrimony and that the Sultan were driven, bag and baggage, into the heart of Asia, or as a provisional measure that the divided empire which existed four centuries ago could be restored.

The last paragraph is particularly interesting when it is remembered that, on leaving America, one of Canning's next duties was to mediate between Turkey and the Greeks. Many of his letters refer to the death of Napoleon, and in one he quotes with his usual felicity the lines :—

> Demens ! qui nimbos et non imitabile fulmen
> Aere et cornipedum pulsu simularat equorum.

In the Memoirs, this part of which was written after Lord Stratford had entered his ninety-third year, he gives the following character of John Quincy Adams, the Secretary of State :—

He was more commanding than attractive in personal appearance, much above par in general ability, but having the air of a scholar rather than a statesman, a very uneven temper, a disposition at times well-meaning, a manner somewhat too often domineering, and an ambition causing unsteadiness in his political career. My private intercourse with him was not wanting in kindness on either side. The rougher road was that of discussion on matters of

business. The irritation of a sensitive temper had much to excuse
it in the climate.

Adams's opinion of Canning is also recorded.[1] " He is a
proud high-tempered Englishman . . . . with a disposition
to be overbearing, which I have often been compelled to
check in its own way. He is, of all the foreign ministers
with whom I have had occasion to treat, the man who has
most tried my temper. . . . He has a great respect for his
word, and there is nothing false about him. . . . Mr. Canning
is a man of forms, studious of courtesy, and tenacious of
private morals. As a diplomatic man his great want is
suppleness, and his great virtue is sincerity." For an
opponent the judgment is singularly just and clear-sighted.

The last time I saw Adams [wrote Canning to Planta, 3 April],
he expatiated largely upon the great advantages of temper,
acknowledging with candour that he had much to contend with
himself on that score. He never spoke a truer word. . . . Government and citizens, one and all, are very proud of the pending
measure for acknowledging the independence of South America,
though it is quite clear that they are not disposed to incur any
real risk for the sake of this favourite object. Adams confessed
to me that he regarded Spain as a man under the pressure of a
nightmare, longing to raise his arm, but unable to stir a muscle.
I had previously accosted him by saying, " So, Mr. Adams, you are
going to make honest people of them ? " " Yes, Sir," was his
answer; " we proposed to your government to join us some time
ago, but they would not, and now we shall see whether you will be
content to *follow* us." This was a cut in his old style, before he
had discovered the advantages of an unruffled temper, and I was
obliged for my consolation to think of the old lines in *Madame
Blaise,*

> The King himself has followed her
> When she did go before.

5 Nov.—On returning from my excursion to the North, I
found him civil and almost cordial, rather disposed to deal in
protestations of his love for peace, and inquisitive on the subject of
the new Secretary's personal dispositions and foreign policy, with
an evident leaning to the idea that G. C.'s accession to office is
likely to introduce a more liberal and vigorous system into the
cabinet.

It is needless to say much of the various matters which
came up for discussion between the minister and the Secretary

[1] J. Q. Adams, *Memoirs*, vi. 157.

of State. Very little was actually settled during Canning's
residence at Washington: his task was rather to prepare
matters for the several commissioners and arbitrators who
afterwards decided or failed to decide the points at issue.
Among these the chief was the means to be adopted for the
suppression of the slave trade; but an agreement could
not be come to, and the subject was relegated to a
conference to be held in London, in which the ex-Minister
acted as joint-plenipotentiary with Huskisson in 1824. A
great many minor questions came up for settlement, every
one of which demanded patience and temper in the irritable
state of the country, and especially of the press. One of
these was the cession of the islands in the Detroit river,
which gave great satisfaction to Mr. Adams. Another, which
threatened to be serious, was a dispute about the interpretation of the first article of the Treaty of Ghent (1818),
relating to the indemnity to be paid for slaves captured by
England in the late war with the States. The matter was
said to turn upon a comma, and, on the arbitration of the
Emperor of Russia, the comma cost England 100,000*l.*

Of the foreign ministers, Canning came into relations
chiefly with those of Russia and France. The former [to
quote the Memoirs], "M. Poletica, a clever man of Greek
extraction, had a curious way of opening conversation with
any new acquaintance of the native population. He used
the form of a triple interrogation—'Do you smoke? Do you
snuff? Do you chew?' An affirmative reply to these
searching questions might rouse a sympathy pregnant with
the elements of future intimacy. My friendly relations with
the French minister came to an untimely end. He took
offence at some undeclared alteration of sentiment towards
him in my manner; and after making an offensive display,
which I might have justly resented, he sent me a challenge,
accepted at once, though without the approval of my conscience, from a weak apprehension of being thought backward in matters of personal hazard. I laid down at night
under an engagement to exchange shots next morning with
my colleague, but before daylight an arrangement, volunteered
by friends, who saw the matter as it really was, and capable
of being honourably accepted by me, was made to my great
relief. I now perceive on looking back that I should have
acted with more true courage if I had declined the challenge
as resting on no warrantable grounds."

The social advantages of Washington were few, and were confined to the session of Congress, when the President held a drawing-room once a fortnight, and Mrs. Adams gave a weekly party. The members of the legislature seldom brought their wives, and there were few resident families of position. Now and then, however, a ball was got up, and dinners and routs were not unfrequent. On one of these occasions a trifling incident threatened to destroy Canning's peace of mind. A young lady gave him a flower, and he accepted it, and thought it a very pretty proceeding. To his dismay, one of his friends, doubtless a practical joker, informed him that this was the recognized form of betrothal at Washington. His Excellency, in a terrible state of consternation, rushed to his room, and addressed a despatch to the girl, disclaiming any particular signification that might be attached to the simple operation of placing a flower, given by her fair hands, in his button-hole, and requesting her to reply in similar terms. A regular convention was signed, and Canning got out of the scrape like a good diplomatist without cession or indemnity.

His own dinner parties called forth all his powers of self-protection :—

MEMOIRS.   When Congress was in session I had to entertain all its members in succession. I invited them by scores at a time, at the risk of overcrowding my table. Many of them still retained a sufficient recollection of the old country to look for an invitation to drink a glass of wine with their host. Wishing to encourage this point of sympathy and also to shelter my brains from excess, I ordered a bottle of toast and water to be placed by my plate with the exact resemblance as to colour of sherry or madeira. One day while I was talking to the left-hand guest, the gentleman on my right helped himself to a glass of my sham wine, and I had the luck of turning round towards him at the very moment when he had discovered his mistake. The unguarded impulsiveness and outspoken freedom of citizens proud of their independence deprived conversation in company of its usual ease. In my position it was advisable to narrow the openings for that inconvenience. I met the case by having a large basket of flowers, natural or artificial according to the season, placed opposite to my seat at table, and making the most of my two immediate neighbours. The device, simple as it was, carried me well through a succession of three seasons. Improvement was nevertheless in progress. My predecessor had greatly the advantage over me in his collection of good stories. I record one of them to serve as a pattern of the rest. He was Sir Charles Bagot, a man of very attractive manners, intelligent, witty and kind. An American minister and his wife dining with him one day, he heard Lady Bagot, who was at some distance, say rather quickly, "My dear Mrs. S ——, what can you be doing?" The salad-bowl had been offered to Mrs. S —— and her arm was lost in it up to the elbow. Her reply was prompt: "Only rollicking for an onion, my lady."

He was interested in the debates in Congress, and frequently attended the sittings. The following letter to Fazakerley (14 November, 1820) describes his first visit :—

I am just come back for the first time from the House of Representatives, where I left the members proceeding to ballot the fourteenth time for a Speaker, thirteen previous ballotings having failed in producing a decisive result. The successful candidate must have a majority of all the members present, and therefore there is no visible reason, except the weariness of the parties, why the balloting should not continue to the end of the session. No debate can take place till after the election of a Speaker, and as there was therefore no food for the ears I could only observe the scenery and the dramatis personae. First, it will surprize you to learn that instead of the venerable simplicity which *reigns* in St. Stephen's chapel, the H. of Representatives, besides being stoved, carpeted, desked, and sofaed in the most luxurious style, rivals and indeed surpasses the Legislature of Paris in decoration and drapery. The Speaker, though wigless and ungowned, presides under a silk canopy surmounted with a gilt eagle ; the independent representatives of Kentucky and Tennessee have the best Brussels carpeting to spit upon ; the citizens of Washington, arranged in the gallery, look down from beneath a festooned curtain of silk and gold ; and the foreign minister, admitted to survey these splendours, reposes meanwhile on a settee of real damask. Secondly, it may edify you to know that the general appearance of the members is considerably more respectable than one had been led to imagine. I observed several of them quite as well dressed as Morton Pitt ; the Quakers struck me as being particularly attentive to their persons, their chins close shaved and their hats of the very best beaver. Two or three, whom I took for representatives of the new States, were indeed in perfect costume of look and dress. They may be capable of making the very best laws, but I should not like to meet them in a lone place. The room in which the House assembles is semicircular, like the two legislative chambers at Paris, and supported by large columns of Potomac marble with white Corinthian capitals. It is very spacious, and would be really handsome if it were not for the bad taste of the decorations, but there is such an echo that although the members are generally far more quiet than our noisy senators at Westminster, it is very difficult, I am told, to hear a speech distinctly, if the orator

happens to be at a little distance from you. Under any circumstances a popular assembly must always be an object of interest,
and I intend being a pretty regular attendant at the debates during
this winter. The hours of meeting are sufficiently convenient for a
stranger, the doors being open at twelve, and generally closed at
three, the hour of dinner. They have also a very convenient
custom, which would hardly suit the atmosphere of London—it
is to hoist a flag on the roof of the *Capitol* during the sittings of
the Houses. This flag being visible from my windows, I run but
little danger of having to walk up and down the Pennsylvania
Avenue—no trifling distance, I can tell you—to no purpose.

When the legislative bodies were in recess, the ministers,
almost to a man, went to their respective States, and diplomacy, with rare exceptions, had little to transact or report.
This sort of lengthened holiday was the more precious as it
included the period of greatest heat, when it was occupation
enough to keep oneself alive. The thermometer ranged from
six degrees below zero to 101° Fahr., and when it was hot,
there was no mistaking it. Canning wrote thus, 30 July, to
his old ally :—

Hot ! hot ! hot ! my dear Planta, most horribly hot ! It is come
at last with a vengeance ; and such nights ! But it was my own
act, and I must bear it, and so must my liver, and so must my
secretaries, and so must my servants ! But you must not expect
me to write at any length till it gets cooler.

The worst part about the climate was not its heat or its
cold but its rapid alternations of both. As Talleyrand said,
" nothing was settled in America, not even the climate ! "

MEMOIRS. I sat down to dinner on one occasion towards the
end of March with Fahrenheit's thermometer at 73 : when I got
up next morning the mercury was at 18—fourteen degrees of frost
and long icicles were hanging from the eaves of the houses. This
extreme change had in all probability taken place in a much shorter
time, for a friend who left me after dinner, was nearly lost in the
snow on his way home. He had come on foot, and was too modest
to request the use of a carriage. During my stay at Washington
the Potomac was frozen every winter to the degree of bearing carts,
and, by way of contrast, even in the month of May there was at
times heat enough to make the nights severely oppressive. The
strongest effects of climate were produced by the north-west winds
which at times sweep violently the whole of Canada and the United
States, even as far south as the Gulf of Mexico. I took occasion to
ask one of the American ministers how, if at all, he contrived to get

through the hot summer nights without a total loss of sleep. " Sir ! "
he said, " I will tell you in confidence, hoping that you may turn
my example to account for your own comfort. My bedroom has
four windows, two on each side opposite to each other. Free from
all clothing I lie down on a hard mattress between and on a level
with the windows, and even then esteem it good luck to obtain a
doze or two as the night comes round." The Secretary of State
was seen one morning at an early hour floating down the Potomac,
with a black cap on his head and a pair of green goggles on his
eyes.

For twenty-two months Canning stayed almost uninter-
ruptedly at Washington. During session of Congress there
was plenty of society, but not of the kind he liked. In summer and autumn there was nothing to do and hardly anybody
to see.

With respect to *happiness* [he told his sister, 24 April, 1821], you
know, my love, that it is very much like the tail of a soaped pig, and
therefore might easily elude a more skilful grasp than mine. In the
present imperfect state of this celebrated metropolis, the life of a
foreigner at Washington must ever be one of privation and restraint.
The city, for so I must call it, possesses neither the elegant resources
of a large town, nor the tranquil charms of the country. But I consider that I am only a sojourner in the land ; I look forward ; I try
to make the best of my bargain ; I swear occasionally—you women
cannot conceive the comfort of swearing—and I occasionally repeat
to myself old saws and fag-ends of verses about patience. The mercury will sometimes go down in spite of me, and then, if I cannot
get the last new novel, I shut myself up and wait for better times.
My prime consolation is that whatever I feel, I feel it alone ;—if I
have no fair partner to share the gloomy hour with me, neither
have I one to reproach me with having brought her hither. But
while I thus lay my mind open to you let me not be unjust. Things,
upon the whole, go on more smoothly than I had expected. I have
met with a very fair quantity of goodwill and civility, earned indeed
with the sweat of one's brow, but still not to be despised. My servants have behaved uniformly well, and the accomplishment of
chewing tobacco has not yet been fatal to my carpets. . . . I am
seldom incommoded with visits ; and I know two young ladies who
can play " God Save the King" on the harp, and who do occasionally play it, on the condition prescribed by their papa, of playing
" Yankee Doodle " immediately afterwards. . . . My books—I must
not be so ungrateful as to omit them—are of the greatest comfort
to me ; and in the catalogue of consoling circumstances it would
be worse than ingratitude to pass over the *ragoûts* of Monsieur
Bernay.
Since the weather has become warmer [he wrote to his mother,

23 April], I get up between six and seven, breakfast and pass
the morning alone, dine at five when there is company or at six
when we are alone, sometimes gossip and tea-sip with a neighbour
for an hour or two in the evening, and to bed by half-past ten—
Mr. Keating the major-domo going round the house at the same
time with a lantern to shut doors and extinguish lights.—On Sundays we attend the Episcopalian Church, where I have a pew, and
where the Reverend Mr. Hawley prays for the *President*, and
assures us in his sermons that the devil (with his horns and tail)
is really and truly—all in short but visibly—at our elbows. The
Church service is the same as ours, with the exception of a few
judicious omissions, and the clergymen are mostly, I believe, Wes-
leyan Methodists, more remarkable for their whining tone, and the
severity of their creed, than for any very formidable deviation from
the doctrines of the Church of England.

   With one exception I have now sat down to dinner day after
day for more than a month with my two secretaries, who, I take it
for granted, have found the task to the full as painful as myself.
The *best of tempers* will be at times disturbed ; and for a few days
during the extreme heat we threatened one and all to become as
snappish as a pack of hounds just before the hydrophobia declares
itself.

   In spite of the monotony and listlessness of such a life
and the recurrence of " occasional blue devils," his letters
home during this period are unusually cheerful—surprizingly
so when it is remembered that he seldom wrote them till the
messenger was knocking at the door, and that he generally
heard the cocks crowing before he finished them. He had " a
mortal repugnance to compose a letter several days before it
had to set out on its voyage."

   His mother's vivacity and brightness, which came over
the sea " redolent with joy, I had almost said with youth,"
whilst they refreshed him like " a breeze from the ocean," are
a perpetual puzzle to his understanding :—

   Here am I but half your age, and still by courtesy a young man,
and yet I cannot boast, except on occasions for an hour at a time,
a tenth part of the alacrity and cheerfulness which you possess.
If the state of your mind were one only of calm and serenity—a
still, clear, sky—I should ascribe the advantage to conscious virtue
and the retrospect of a well-spent life ;—but all is animation and
gaiety with you, " nods and becks and wreathed smiles," while I,
poor devil that I am ! can scarcely command enough of animal
spirits to carry me with an air of decent composure through the
sociable part of the four-and-twenty hours. Near-sighted people
are consoled under their misfortune when young by the prospect of

having their eyes rather improved than impaired by the lapse of
years. In like manner I am content to hope that there is some
advantage in reversion for those who have to endure the pressure
of gloomy spirits before their time. I do not despair of being a very
merry fellow some fifty years hence.

He maintained his resolution of staying out his time at
Washington. His complaints were few, though he was generally more or less miserable ; he was gradually learning the
lesson of endurance which his favourite motto taught him :—

> Tu ne cede malis, sed contra audentior ito
> Qua tua te fortuna sinet :—*Aen.* vi. 95.

and he was beginning to outgrow the ill-effects of too rapid
promotion, and to realize that the discipline of discomfort was
a valuable part of education. His early experiences at Constantinople had not sufficed to teach him this, and Switzerland and Vienna were not calculated to supply the want. In
America he learned the lesson of patience and self-control in
a degree which he had never understood before, and he came
home all the better for the rough experience. That he recognized this may be seen from the following beautiful letter to
his mother :—

Though I have no " epistle " to thank you for, dear Mother, subsequent to number eleven, the receipt of which was duly acknowledged about three weeks ago, the 4th of November is not a day that
I can allow to slip by us unnoticed and in silence. I do not mean
that every gentleman, unless indeed he wears a crown on his head,
would be expected to celebrate his own birthday ; but here, among
strangers, in a distant land, I may perhaps be allowed to exchange
a few natural feelings with a loved and honoured parent, whose
thoughts, I am persuaded, are at this moment dwelling with fondness on the two unworthy children to whom, under Providence, she
gave being—we will not say how many fourths of November ago.
A strange and anxious gift it is, this life which I have received from
you, my dearest Mother, of precarious tenure and most uncertain
issue ; yet would it be the height of ingratitude not to acknowledge
that hitherto the good has greatly preponderated—that with some
struggles and some sorrows I have found abundant sources of
comfort and enjoyment. Washington is not the Island of Calypso,
nor is it the most delightful thing in the world to live far away from
one's country and all that the name comprehends, amongst those to
whom the hatred of that country is at once a passion and a principle. Yet in spite of all this, when I pause to reflect on the difference between my present situation and what I was but the other
day when I started in the race with no greater fortune than that of

an honest descent and a tolerable education, I am lost in feelings of
surprize and gratitude. These are flattering sensations, but they
do not pass away without awaking others of a more painful and
also of a more useful description. Heavens! what a wretch I am
to lag so far behind my fortunes! I find myself in a station worthy
of first-rate abilities and of first-rate acquirements; yet the utmost
that I can recognize at my command is no more than a faint glim-
mering of comprehension and knowledge, a disposition indeed and
desire to improve and to proceed in well-doing, but an indolent and
wayward temper, that is for ever at variance with the efforts of my
mind and the movements of my heart. These are subjects of real
and deep dissatisfaction to me; but fortunately Hope does not
abandon me at thirty-four, and I still live on in hope of becoming,
if my life be spared, a somewhat less worthless member of society.
I consider my residence in America as a second and rougher period
of education; one's passage through it is not unattended with the
privations and annoyances of school, but I do not quite despair of
being able at some future period to look back upon it as I now do
with thankfulness on the restraints and discipline of Eton. Come
what will of it, I cannot conceal from myself that, under Him to
whom all praise is due, I owe to a certain venerable lady the
greatest portion of the little good that I have in my character, and
by consequence of the worldly advantages which I am permitted to
enjoy—to myself alone nearly the whole of what I fall short in.—
So you see the birthday is celebrated not indeed with presents and
bumpers, but with confession and thankfulness.

It was no small sacrifice to Canning to keep himself a
prisoner at Washington for nearly two years. The heavy expenses of outfit and passage, furniture and servants, prescribed
a course of economy, while he longed for the free air and scenes
of the country. " My passion for the country," he wrote to his
sister (7 November, 1822), " like yours, has undergone no
diminution. In leaving town I always experience a sensation
of escape, and I feel that my home, my natural home, is in
the field and the forest." His long restraint in the city made
the few excursions he was able to take in 1821 doubly delightful. The first was only as far as Mount Vernon; but in the
autumn he spent some very enjoyable days in Maryland at the
country house of Mr. Carroll, a splendid old gentleman (born
in 1737), who had survived the title of rebel for nearly fifty
years; and in 1822 he made a three months' tour in the
northern States and Canada, again visiting Mr. Carroll on the
way.

The addition [he wrote] of another year to Mr. Carroll's advanced age does not appear to have made him an older man in any

point of consequence. He rises as he used to do at four in the
morning, throws himself head foremost into a cold bath, breakfasts
at half-past eight with his long white locks streaming over his
shoulders, transacts business, rides out to his farm, and drinks his
glass of champagne after dinner with as much alacrity and enjoyment as most young men of twenty or thirty. With all this he has
candour enough to groan under the heat to one's heart's content,
and avows with the most creditable liberality that the climate of
North America is more than a match for the patience of Job or the
constitution of Samson. At his house we stayed ten days, and experienced the utmost kindness from the whole family.

[At Ballston] we had an opportunity of seeing a member of that
famous and ill-omened family of whom we have all heard so much
during the last twenty years—Joseph Buonaparte, the *quondam* King
of Spain, with his daughter and two or three persons who formed
his suite. He dined in a private room, but joined the society of the
place at other times in the public apartments. There was no difficulty in recognizing his features as a member of the once Imperial
family. His countenance and general appearance seem to indicate
good health and good humour; and I was informed that, in memory
of his departed greatness, he continues to receive from his servants
the titles of Majesty &c. to which his ears were so long accustomed.
One of his attendants was overheard asking for something on behalf
of *the Princess* his daughter, who, in spite of her title, is as ugly
and as deformed as if she had never received a drop of Imperial
blood into her veins. On the same story in which they slept, slept
also the minister and representative of his present Catholic Majesty,
and the intermediate apartments, separating the rival dignitaries,
were occupied by myself and Mr. Wilmot. Diplomacy, as well as
poverty, may be said to make us acquainted with strange bed-
fellows.

Near Niagara Canning found the British lieutenant-gover-
nor, Sir Peregrine Maitland, and was delighted to find himself " once more under the old flag."   No one was ever more
intensely and enthusiastically an Englishman.   On leaving
Niagara, he went down Lake Ontario in a steamboat to Kings-
ton, thence in an open boat rowed by four Canadian *voyageurs*
down the St. Lawrence to Montreal.   Lord Dalhousie was
absent at Sorel, and thither he invited his colleague, who was
charmed with this " most amiable and worthy man."   Quebec
was full of scenes moving enough to the imagination.   " I
visited the river Montmorenci, where Wolfe made his first
attempt to force the French lines ; the cove, which bears his
gallant name, where he succeeded in landing and leading his
men up a steep and almost precipitous acclivity ; the plains of

Abraham, where he prevailed over an enemy worthy of contending with him ; and lastly the very place where he is said
to have died.   I know of no event in our history which takes
so deep a hold of the imagination, and I question whether I
experienced a stronger emotion of national pride in walking
over the field of Waterloo than in thus finding myself amidst
the rocks and towers of Quebec.   In the Governor's house,
the Château de St. Louis, where I am lodging, there is a good
bust of Wolfe, and underneath it are the following lines :—

> Let no sad tear upon his tomb be shed,
> A common tribute to the common dead ;
> But let the Great, the Generous, and the Brave
> With godlike envy sigh for such a grave ! "

At Boston he received the news of Lord Londonderry's, or,
to call him by his more familiar name, Castlereagh's, suicide.
It was a very real grief to him, for he had felt deeply the
Foreign Secretary's constant kindness towards himself, and
admired the virtues of the man more than the talents of the
minister.   To see Castlereagh prime minister would, he
thought, be a misfortune ; but as a hard-working, capable,
and considerate secretary of state, and an amiable and kind-
hearted man, he was much to be regretted.

The remainder of his residence at Washington passed very
quietly.   He was in better health and spirits, and his old secretary of Swiss days, Henry Addington, who was now attached
to the mission, joined him in December, to his chief's satisfaction.   The season was a dull one, and nothing was stirring in
Congress to excite the smallest interest.   In March Congress
was over, and nothing remained to be done.   Having obtained
leave of absence, Canning handed over the archives and
ciphers to Addington in June, and in the following August
sailed from New York for England, and arrived at Falmouth
8 September, 1823.

On his return to England his first impulse was to be idle—
to see his family and friends, and in their society to shake off
the ill-effects of the Washington climate.   He found his relations in more prosperous circumstances than when he left for
the States.   His brother William had been appointed to the
rectory of Heslerton near Scarborough, and was married.   His
other brother, Henry, had been gazetted consul-general at
Hamburg.   Canning spent some weeks at Heslerton in October and November with infinite enjoyment.   " To me, who

have been so long tossed upon the wild waters or upon the
rougher ocean of American politics and American society, the
delights of a quiet rural life are inexpressible, and to enjoy
them not only in one's own country but under the roof of a
brother and a *sister* is more than enough to make up for the
vile crampings and joltings of the mail between London and
York. . . . The weather continues favourable, and I trust
that another fortnight of fresh air, hard exercise, and regular
hours, will set up my constitution for the winter." Returning
to London in November, Canning took a house in Berkeley
Square for the season, and made the most of his leisure in the
enjoyment of his friends' society. He saw a great deal of his
cousin, the Foreign Secretary, and also of Lord Ellenborough,
who then lived at Roehampton, whence Canning would sometimes drive across Richmond Park to his kinsman Raikes,
at Sudbrook, Petersham, and there " dine and sleep amidst
the portraits of forgotten generations of the Burleigh family,"
to say nothing of memories of *The Heart of Midlothian.*

Such relaxations were not uninterrupted by business. In
December he was nominated, conjointly with Huskisson, as
plenipotentiary to arrange with Rush the points in dispute
between the States and the mother country. Their discussions were on the whole harmonious, and they agreed on a
Convention, of which Mr. Canning both publicly and privately expressed his entire satisfaction. President Monroe
was prepared to ratify the instrument just as he received it ;
but the Senate insisted on striking out of the first article certain words which had been introduced in the *projet* actually
prepared by the American Government itself in Washington.
After this decided manifestation of a resolve to come to no
arrangement, it was considered useless to persist in the negotiation. Rush was as disappointed as anyone, and George
Canning, who had been rejoicing in the triumph of " sheer
straightforwardness " over that " scoundrel " Adams, had to
make the best of an unmerited rebuff. We were at that time
in such mortal dread of exciting the hostility of our kinsmen
over the Atlantic that, sooner than risk another war, we
pocketed affront after affront.

CHAPTER VII.

MISSION TO PETERSBURG.

1824-5.

WHEN Stratford Canning returned from the *far niente* of his American mission, he was entrusted with the most important diplomatic task then pending in Europe, and as fate would have it this task drew him once more to the east. In spite of an invincible repugnance, which grew stronger at each recurring experience, Constantinople, " that semi-barbarous capital which had left so painful an impression on his mind," drew him eastward again and again with the attraction of a magnet. When it is remembered how strenuously he sought home employment, and how devoutly he had resolved never to return to the detested circle of Turkish diplomacy, it must appear surprizing that he should so speedily have yielded to a destiny which was in all points so diametrically opposed to his wishes: but on this occasion public and private reasons conspired to recommend his acceptance of the embassy at the Porte with a force which prudence could not resist. He was contemplating a second marriage, and this rendered the certain income of the embassy preferable to the chances of office at home. He felt moreover that it would be a mistake to quit the diplomatic service until he had attained the highest rank—that of full ambassador. And he was lured to his ancient exile with the promise of a speedy return. The mission was distinctly stated to be temporary and for a limited purpose. Mr. Canning had already tried (in March 1824) to secure the Treasury secretaryship for his cousin, but the Prime Minister had other views. He now told him that he had obtained Lord Liverpool's assent to the plan of offering him the vice-presidentship of the Board of Trade on his return. Such an offer would constitute a fair opening to an official career in England, and with that promise he found less difficulty in reconciling his mind to a brief return to the "horrible hole" on which he had so thankfully turned his back twelve years before. He could not foresee the unhappy fatality which, in closing his cousin's career just when it was rising to its zenith, would also destroy for a while, perhaps for ever, his chance of a place in the government.

Yet the real attraction of his new mission to an ambitious man was its extreme difficulty. Momentous issues then hung upon the wise and prudent conduct of affairs in South-east Europe. The aftermath of the French Revolution was ready for the sickle in the countries bordering the Mediterranean. Spain, Naples, and Greece had in turn disturbed the " legitimate order of things " which the Congress of Vienna and the subsequent meetings at Paris and Aix had committed with much pomp and complacency to official paper. Much now depended on how the Greek insurrection was to be dealt with. As it happened, Russia and Turkey had been almost at blows again, and it was chiefly by the action of the British Government and its ambassador at the Porte, Lord Strangford, that peace had been preserved and terms of arrangement— rather vague terms—accepted by both parties. The greatest of all dangers had thus been for a while averted. Russia was prevented from using the Greek revolution as a pretext for strengthening and advancing her private designs upon the Ottoman empire. The risk of misunderstanding was not yet, however, entirely over ; the terms of arrangement were not yet wholly fulfilled ; and the presence of a Russian ambassador at the Porte was still needed to put the seal to the reconciliation.

Meanwhile, and before the outstanding disputes with Turkey had been finally set at rest, the Czar took upon himself to come forward as a mediator between the Greeks and their old masters. His reasons for this step were mixed : he was at first in some degree influenced by impulses of humanity and even sympathy for the Greek cause ; he was naturally anxious to arrange a reconstruction of the Greek provinces in such a way that an independent kingdom should be impossible, and that Russia might obtain some such protectorate over them as she already exercised over Servia and the Danubian provinces ; and he was specially eager to be the first in the field, and so to prevent England, where symptoms of enthusiastic sympathy with the sufferings of the Greeks were growing alarmingly apparent, from coming forward in the character of the champion of Christian liberty in the Ottoman empire.

With these views a Russian " Memoir " was drawn up, in which a plan of pacification and reconstruction of Greece, in three provinces, including Crete and Epirus, but retaining the sovereignty of the Porte, was set forth ; and the Powers were invited to meet in conference at St. Petersburg to carry this or some similar plan into effect. The Turks, it is true, were known to be strongly opposed to the mediation of the powers ; but the Turks, it was urged, were always opposed to everything, and it was resolved to disregard their wishes. The Greeks, it was argued, could hardly fail to welcome a mediation which must end in a real improvement of their former position, even if it could not realize the dreams of independence which they had long nursed but which their arms were not likely to accomplish. The Conference was agreed to by all the Great Powers ; even George Canning overcame his dislike to congresses in this instance, and what lent a peculiar importance to his cousin's appointment as ambassador to the Porte was the additional and preliminary mission now entrusted to him as plenipotentiary at the St. Petersburg Conference. In the summer of 1824 all was prepared for an autumnal visit to Russia in this character ; when a slight communication overturned the whole arrangement. The Russian " Memoir " or some parts of it had leaked out, and the Greeks had become aware of the benevolent intentions of the Czar in their behalf; but so far were they from being grateful for the proposed interposition that the Provisional Government in August despatched an indignant letter to the English Foreign Secretary, protesting against the Russian proposals as cruel and oppressive, and calling upon England to protect the Greeks in their struggle for liberty.

Under these circumstances the British cabinet had no alternative, or more accurately the Foreign Office guided by Mr. Canning on broad principles would allow no alternative, but to abstain from the intended Conference. So long as one of the belligerents was prepared to accept mediation, the Conference was possible ; but when both protested, it became evident not only that the Conference was futile, but that it was derogatory to the dignity of the powers to engage in a proceeding which from the outset must command no chance of success. On this ground we informed Prince Lieven that the English government could not enter the Conference. Such a consultation of the powers might be desirable later on : but for the present England could be no party to it. The Czar was indignant at the change of front, and sought for deeper motives than the ostensible ground of the Greek letter. He fancied himself suspected of selfish designs in his policy towards the Greeks; and in turn he accused

Mr. Canning of long-standing sympathy with the revolutionary spirit as manifested in the Hellenic movement.

Partly to remove any misconceptions of this character, and partly to invite an interchange of views upon the whole question, it was resolved not to cancel Stratford Canning's appointment as special ambassador to St. Petersburg. He was still to go; but he was not to enter the Conference, should it take place in spite of the refusal of England to join its councils. His duties would be of an explanatory and interrogatory kind, and he was also charged with the conclusion of a treaty defining the boundary between British and Russian territory in North-West America, upon which a dispute had long been pending; and on his way to Russia, he was to visit Vienna and enter into explanations with Prince Metternich on the Greek question. The delicate and momentous nature of these duties is a proof of the high estimation in which his abilities were held by the government, and especially by that most searching and impartial of critics, his cousin; but the reader will not be in a position to estimate the full difficulty and importance of these now remote negotiations without a few words on the position at that time taken up by England in her foreign relations.

George Canning's foreign policy was a new departure, and has won for him the admiration of Liberal politicians who have little sympathy with his opinions in general. That policy consisted simply in the substitution of England for Europe. Instead of mixing himself up in the sort of general committee of European affairs which was then the fashion, he resolved that England should act only when her own interests or honour—this last claim had not then been abandoned—required her interference. With the European congresses and the principles of the Holy Alliance he would have nothing to do. "No more congresses, thank God!" was his exclamation in 1820. He did not believe in the Austrian plan of an Imperial police for the suppression of whatever smelt of Jacobinism, and for the maintenance of that best of all possible conditions, "the established order of things." He saw that the time was gone by for this high-handed suppression of popular movements, and that there were contingencies where the Holy Alliance, with all its solemn professions, would prove nothing better than the jailor of the liberties of Europe. He determined that England at least should have neither part nor lot in such a policy, and the Greek question furnished

him with an occasion for taking up the independent position
which he believed to be the true attitude for his country. In
his instructions to his cousin for the mission to Petersburg
the following memorable definition of the foreign policy of
England occurs :—

To preserve the peace of the world is the leading object of the
policy of England. For this purpose it is necessary in the first place
to prevent to the utmost of our power the breaking out of new
quarrels ; in the second place, to compose, where it can be done by
friendly mediation, existing differences ; and thirdly, where that is
hopeless, to narrow as much as possible their range ; and fourthly,
to maintain for ourselves an imperturbable neutrality in all cases
where nothing occurs to affect injuriously our interests or our
honour.

In applying these principles to the insurgent Greeks, the
third contingency alone came into operation. We were
under no pledges of honour to interfere in the interests of
either party ; our interests were not directly affected, except
so far as any disturbance of tranquillity in the Levant must
injure our trade ; friendly mediation had been rejected by both
belligerents ; and it remained therefore only to narrow the
range of the existing differences. With this object, as well as
to clear the way to possible mediation in the future, Stratford
Canning was instructed to proceed to St. Petersburg by way
of Vienna.

" To narrow the range of differences " in the present
instance meant a definite aim : nothing was more probable
than that Russia would seize the first pretext for coercing
Turkey by force of arms, and that must at all hazards be prevented. The dangers of Russian aggrandizement at the
expense of Turkey were not so fully felt in England then as
they have been since ; Austria had been more formidable to
the Porte in the past than Russia ; but both England and
Austria—especially Austria—were alive to the natural tendencies of the Russians to a southern port, and were resolved
to foil them. The difference was in the means to be employed.
George Canning set forth his plan with his usual lucidity in
his instructions to his cousin. There were, he said, two
essential conditions which must be fulfilled before England
could join in any scheme of mediation, invited or voluntary.
The first was that the Russian ambassador, M. de Ribeaupierre
should have actually taken up his residence at the Porte - or
in other words that all outstanding disputes between the Czar

I

and the Sultan must thus openly have been cleared aside, and
Russia could thus appear exclusively in the character of a
friendly mediator, *puissance amie*, in which alone she had any
treaty right to interfere on behalf of the Christian subjects of
the Porte. The second was that the mediating powers must
definitely pledge themselves before going into conference that
in no extremity would they resort to force. This was of
course also designed to "narrow the range of differences" by
preventing Russia from using the Greeks as an excuse for
aggrandizement. On these two conditions Mr. Canning was
inexorable. In vain might Russia urge that she had a chargé
d'affaires at the Porte : the English Foreign Secretary would
have nothing short of a full ambassador, in pledge of perfect
reconciliation with Turkey ; nor would he allow the possibility
of a recourse to arms. "To forcible intervention England
could not be a party, nor by consequence, to councils that
might lead to it." All he could contemplate would be "an
intervention strictly amicable," without joining either party,
or holding out "a menace which we have no desire to carry
into execution." A "previous and public disavowal of force"
by all the powers was a necessary preliminary to England's
intervention. These conditions granted, England would
mediate on the request of either belligerent, or even possibly
might *volunteer* her mediation unasked, though it was not easy
to foresee the circumstances which would lead to such a
position ; but voluntary or invited, no mediation could have
England's adhesion unless force were abjured and the Russian
ambassador were in his palace at the Porte.

If we seek to know what scheme of pacification George
Canning had in view, supposing these conditions satisfied, we
shall find that so far as written documents, public or private,
are concerned, his plans were vague. Something "considerably within" the two extremes demanded respectively by
Turk and Greek, of "unconditional submission" and
"unqualified independence," would be the end in view. The
creation of an independent Greek kingdom he then regarded
as impracticable, and later, when the Greek delegates in
London sounded him as to the possibility of Prince Leopold
accepting the crown of Greece, he refused the consent of the
government. On the other hand, to restore the old tyranny
of the Turks was out of the question. But on the details
of the *via media* which he advocated, his despatches of 1824
are silent.

It is not essential, though always desirable, that an ambassador should personally be in accord with the instructions of his government ; but in this case there is no doubt that the two cousins were of one mind, and that the Greeks regarded Stratford Canning's appointment to the embassy at the Porte as a sign of England's interest in their cause. His letters from America during the early days of the struggle for independence are conclusive on this point. He actually professed a secret wish that the expulsion of the Turks " bag and baggage " from Europe might become a possibility, in terms identical with those used by Mr. Gladstone half a century later. " The poor Greeks ! " he wrote to Planta, 30 July 1821, " I have almost a mind to curse the balance of Europe for protecting those horrid Turks ; " and again, " I wish to God it were possible to wring a cession of territory for their separate and independent establishment out of the Porte. There are plenty of rogues among them, but they are entitled to our compassion, and I wish to heaven that the interests of Europe would allow of letting the Russians loose *tout bonnement* on the Sultan and his hordes. I cannot suspect the Emperor Alexander of having brought about the present struggle, whatever a certain Greek secretary [Capodistrias] at his elbow may have done ; but he is no true Russian if his mouth does not water at the game which circumstances seem to have thrown open to him." A very general feeling at the time was expressed in an eloquent letter by Lord Erskine to Lord Liverpool, in which it was maintained that the conduct of the Turks as rulers had put them out of the pale of civilized nations, and that the Greeks were not in the position of a conquered nation rebelling against properly constituted authority administered in accordance with civilized views ; to interfere on their behalf was not only no breach of the law of nations, but was an imperative moral duty. Whether Stratford Canning went this length we have no means of judging : but it is evident that his sympathy inclined him to Erskine's view, while his prudence compelled him to advocate less thoroughgoing measures than he would have preferred had there been no European complications at stake. A memorandum [1] which he drew up in 1824 at the request of his cousin gives, we must presume, his own opinions on the proposed pacification of Greece. It begins by admitting that the " British government would hail the complete indepen-

---

[1] See Lord Stratford de Redcliffe, *Eastern Question*, 160 ff.

dence of Greece, if effected by the Greeks themselves, as the best solution " of the problem, but allows that " sentiments of humanity and natural sympathy " must not be permitted to exclude considerations of the peace of Europe ; and the leading powers, having assented to a plan which would preserve the sovereignty of the Porte, there " could be no question of the complete independence of Greece " at the conferences of St. Petersburg, but only of her security " from the violence and misgovernment " of her former masters. He maintains that it would be " the height of injustice and cruelty " to deny the Greeks the right to judge for themselves as to accepting any arrangement that might be proposed, and that " the allies are bound to stop short of war." Yet " virtual compulsion " must be exerted upon the Porte. " War, though not actually menaced, with some of the principal powers of Europe, or at least with one of them, must be made to appear the probable consequence of protracted hostilities between the Porte and her Greek subjects."

The memorandum exposes the difficulties of bringing coercion to bear upon the Porte : if Russia were put forward alone, there was the risk of her coming into collision with the Turks (and no one could foresee the end of that) ; if the Allies acted jointly, England would perhaps appear to be committed to the Holy Alliance. Separate but identical notes are proposed, with the last resource of withdrawing the five ambassadors from the Porte. Such pressure could not indeed be brought to bear upon Greece, because there were then no diplomatic establishments at Athens ; but the Greeks might be made to understand that if they rejected the mediation of the powers they would have nothing further to expect from them and would receive no further countenance. Such were the views of the new ambassador who was now on his way to Russia to exchange opinions on the pacification of Greece.

He reached Vienna before Christmas 1824, and here in the persons of Metternich and his two shadows, the emperor and Gentz, he found himself confronted with the dogmatic assertion of the principles of the Holy Alliance, or rather of that Imperial police of Europe which inaccurately goes by the name of that curious compact. Metternich took the didactic tone of the " guardians of the peace of Europe ; " he regarded the Greek revolution as part of the Jacobinical movement which he imagined he had suppressed in common with the

other Allies in 1814–15 ; and he considered Mr. Canning, author
of the *Anti-Jacobin* though he was, as, in his sympathy
with the Greeks, little better than a Jacobin himself. He
condemned his change of front, and did not accept the Greek
Letter as in any way representative of the Hellenic people.
Intervention, however, whether the Greeks liked it or not, he
regarded as necessary, if only to tie Russia's hands. As for
the independence of the Greeks, he held it to be a mere
chimaera, though he was prepared to see their position
improved as far as might be compatible with the sovereignty
of the Sultan ; but the danger of Russia using the quarrel as
a pretext for her own aggrandizement was no chimaera at all,
and for this object alone Metternich regarded the proposed
Conference as necessary, as the best way of tying Russia's
hands by making her go along with her allies. To discourage
the Greeks in their dreams of independence, and to keep
Russia from isolated action, would be a sufficient recommendation for the Conference—that it would be accepted by either
party of the belligerents he did not expect. But the moment
was critical ; there was a strong war party in Russia, and
Alexander needed all the support he could get to restrain
it from an attack upon Turkey in aid of her co-religionists.
Therefore Austria would join the Conference, not for the
sake of the Greeks, but to keep Russia quiet, and preserve
the "legitimate order of Europe," as understood at Vienna,
from subversive changes in the East. Force would be avoided,
but there was no need to tell the belligerents so, and a pledge
on the subject was more than the Prince felt disposed to
grant.

The following passages are taken from a private letter to
George Canning, 30 Dec. :—

My intercourse on matters of business has been entirely, or
almost entirely, confined to the three puissant personages who, as
you well know, are all in all within the limits of this empire, and
one of whom may perhaps be suspected of an occasional aspiration
to be equally so beyond them. All three have expressed regret at
the late determination of the Cabinet; all three have betrayed a
lurking suspicion that there was more than accident in the critical
arrival of the letter from Greece ; all three have declared the same
determination to stand by Russia in the state of desertion with
which she is menaced. But if any distinction may be established
amongst the members of such a triumvirate, I should say that
of the three I had found Gentz the most reasonable, Metternich the

most polite, and the emperor the most sincere. The most striking proof which I have received of H.M.'s frankness is a declaration in plain terms that he had rather I had been sent to Petersburg— "saving my person"—by some other road. The minister was considerate enough to add that such had been his first impression, when he understood that I was going to attend the Conference, but now that the case was altered he rejoiced to have the dressing of me *en passant*.

But all this is nothing to what I am to expect at my journey's end. A sulky emperor and a furious Nesselrode are to be the least of my calamities. A population of fashionables, faithful to the signal of the Court, and fretting under the joint effects of a recent inundation and a sick empress, is to be turned loose upon me ; and the conferences—*à parti carré*—are to flourish, it is thought, under the nose of the British nonconformist. In sober seriousness I must make up my mind, from all that I hear, to meet with long faces and rough language in the Imperial precincts, and dispositions not very accommodating even on the North-West business ; unless you authorize me, of which I have no expectation whatever, to take part in the conferences on Greece. . . . I must do Prince Metternich the justice to say that, considering his belief that I was in habits of intimacy with his bitterest enemy, to say nothing of an old grudge, and the sin of relationship to you, he has treated me with civility, with good-nature, and even with some appearance of confidence. He is a sanguine man, and for some days after my arrival here appears to have entertained a hope that I had some discretionary powers with respect to the conferences, and that he might be able to convert me to his opinion. The endeavours which I made in that interval to gain his good-will have not, it seems, been thrown away, and from what he has said to Sir Henry Wellesley within this day or two, he seems inclined of his own accord to put me on friendly terms with his *âme damnée*— M. de Lebzeltern. The acquaintance may be useful, though not wholly without danger.

Prince Metternich in one of our conversations spoke personally of you—not much in praise—but so as to give me to understand that he regrets sincerely your present distance from him and from his system of policy. His text was, *le diable n'est pas si noir qu'il ne parait*. After entering into sundry details to shew that he was himself most cruelly aspersed, as a man incapable of allowing a constitution to exist on the same continent with him, and pro- ducing a packet of daggers, with Latin mottoes against kings on their blades, to prove how Jacobins were still at work in Europe, he assured me in candour that he did not consider you a very extra- vagant example of Liberalism, but only slightly dangerous as en- couraging, without meaning it, characters less favourable to order than yourself. He spoke with regret of old times—of the comfort and conveniency and efficacy of settling matters of state by con-

versation at a round table—falsely termed a conference—and by
the meeting of two prime ministers belonging to countries essentially
pacific and identified in their leading interests like Austria and
England. In a word I conceived that he would be delighted to
have you enter into the same sort of understanding with him that
your predecessor did; but I am much mistaken if he be not prepared to do you all the mischief in his power—whatever that may
be—as soon as he loses all hope of making a tolerable colleague
of you. Meanwhile he is very entertaining, and not the least so
when he describes Capodistrias as having produced the Circular of
Troppau by an ill-timed paper, full of ultra notions of his own, and
drawn up, says the man who overthrew him, in malice, against the
Alliance, and also when he attributes to Chateaubriand, another
object of his dislike, the having given occasion for the publication
of the Russian Memoir, by sending it to all the French consuls in
the Levant. He is shy of speaking of Pozzo, which looks as if he
thought that he was still to be tolerated. One of P. Metternich's
expressions was that he had regretted during the last three years to
look around and to find no England on the Continent. Her *power*
indeed remained, but her *influence* had disappeared.

I have made a point of occasionally visiting Gentz, who is
literally Metternich's right hand ; but with the exception of some
light shade of difference on the subject of the Greek Conference,
and a more decidedly red-hot zeal against constitutions, I have
found his opinion very much the same as his employer's. Sir H.
Wellesley (who, by the way, has behaved with great propriety and
kindness to me) thinks that he is not by any means with Metternich
on the chapter of Austrian subserviency to Russia. It is very probable that I have not seen enough of him to obtain any portion of
his confidence. He is a timid man, as you know, and would probably expect to find my opinions very different from his own. It
is in his declarations in favour of a pacific system that I conceive
P. Metternich to be most unquestionably sincere. When I read to
him the day before yesterday that paragraph in your instructions
to me which describes the pacific system of British policy, and the
determination of the government to maintain neutrality when
peace was not to be obtained between two contending parties, he
observed that it perfectly expressed his own ideas, and that he
would sign the whole passage with the exception of what concerns
neutrality, which he asserts that Great Britain understands in a
sense of her own.

I am now convinced that Prince Metternich's principal object in
pressing for conferences is to use—not indeed force, nor direct
menace of force—but the influence of the Allies to discourage, to
restrain, and to divide, the Greeks, and thus to weaken any chance
which the latter may have of establishing a complete independence.

If Stratford Canning had left England with any hope of

inducing the Austrian and Russian Courts to change their
minds about the conferences, his interviews with Metternich
undeceived him.   Austria would certainly join the Conference,
and *à fortiori* it was beyond reasonable expectation that the
czar would be shaken in his resolve.   The attempt must be
made, however ; or at least some interchange of views and
explanations must take place : and as nothing was to be
gained by a further stay at Vienna, marching orders were
issued for the journey to St. Petersburg.

The mission started from Vienna on 7 Jan., 1825.
Henry Parish, his old secretary of Washington, was with
him, and a connexion by marriage, Colonel Barnett, besides
messengers and servants.   They were twenty-two days on
the road, and suffered the usual casualties of the journey
through Poland.

With Canning's arrival at St. Petersburg the serious
duties of his mission began.   He had already, according to
his usual habit, drawn up the heads of his negotiation.   Before deciding on a policy, or holding an interview with a
sovereign or minister, before making a speech or writing a
despatch, he wrote out the sequence of the several parts of
his argument.   His mind was strictly logical, and he was
never satisfied till, pen in hand, he had put down the argument in its due order.   Thus prepared, he sought the presence
of the czar and his minister.

He had met Nesselrode at Vienna ten years before, but had
not become well acquainted with him.   To uncertainty as to
his personal manners and opinions was added the unpleasant
knowledge that the czar and his minister were both intensely
irate at England's recent conduct on the Greek question.   It
was therefore with no very agreeable anticipations that he
waited upon the Foreign Secretary and sought an audience of
the czar, and his first interviews confirmed all his fears.

The reception by the Emperor Alexander was marked by
every appearance of civility ; but the czar maintained a dead
silence on the subject of Greece.   Perceiving that there was
still much irritation at the recent change of policy in England,
the ambassador prudently abstained from pressing his Majesty,
and subsequently learnt that he had won Alexander's good
opinion by his reticence.   He found Nesselrode equally courteous, and equally reserved at first.   One might have imagined
that there was no such land as Greece in the world.   Presently
however the Foreign Secretary admitted, with much polite

regret, that he was not permitted to discuss the Greek question. A despatch had already been sent to London, suspending confidential communications on that subject with the British cabinet. Of course if England would join the conferences then on the point of opening at St. Petersburg, this reserve would be abandoned; otherwise any discussion must be " totally useless "—and he had no more to say about the matter.

There is no use in knocking at a barred door : so Canning dexterously dropped the subject pending instructions from home, and devoted his energies to the second part of his duty—the conclusion of a treaty relating to British and Russian territory in North-West America. The object of this instrument was a good deal more than a mere question of boundary, though the latter was made to cover and mask the larger design. A Russian ukaze of 1821 had advanced claims to exclusive maritime rights in the Pacific, and some public repudiation of this inadmissible pretence had to be made on the part of England. This was to be accomplished in a friendly and innocent manner by the first article of the new boundary treaty, in which our maritime and fishing rights in the Pacific were clearly maintained. The article was debated by the Russian plenipotentiaries, Nesselrode and Poletica, but the treaty was finally agreed to, 28 February, without any material concessions on the side of England.

This matter being satisfactorily arranged, Canning found the Russian government in a more friendly disposition towards him on general matters, and resolved to make another attempt to open discussions on the Greek question. The conferences were now proceeding, and he gathered that the difficulties which met the plenipotentiaries at every turn had rather tended to strengthen the position of England by verifying her predictions of failure.

It was on the question of using force that the coöperation of England really depended. Other difficulties might be overcome or waived, but on this point there could be no compromise. After five weeks of silence, Canning at last induced the Russian government to speak. The American treaty having been concluded, he informed Nesselrode that unless the Greek question were to be discussed his mission was ended, and he must ask for his audience of leave. The Foreign Secretary was evidently curious to learn what instructions he carried : it was possible that he had powers,

on certain conditions, to join the Conference. At all events
the threat of departure determined the czar to break his
long silence and if possible to penetrate the equal reserve
which the English plenipotentiary had studiously maintained.
In truth, the latter had mastered the position with consummate
skill. He possessed in reality no power whatever of joining
the Conference; his instructions, as has been shewn, were
purely of an explanatory character—he was to exchange
views with Nesselrode. But had he admitted that he was
armed with no definite plan of pacification, and had no
discretional power to enter the Conference, the matter would
have ended immediately, and he would have had no chance
of probing the Russian government's intentions. Someone
described him as "the most unpumpable of men." "Vous
nous tenez le bec dans l'eau trop longtemps," said M. de la
Ferronnays : as a matter of fact he held out not a moment
too long. He finished the American treaty, obtained all the
information he could get on the progress of the conferences—
which eventually ended in smoke—and then, when no more
was to be gained by delay, he proposed to leave with his secret
unrevealed. This was too much for the inquisitiveness of the
Russian Foreign Office. They must find out what lengths
England was prepared to go. Accordingly the gag was
removed, and in two long interviews on 13 and 19 March
Canning and Nesselrode exchanged views on the Greek
question. It needed some firmness to break down the czar's
reserve, but at last a free interchange of opinion took place
between the ministers ; and it was soon discovered that
England had no immediate solution to propose, and that
Russia held to all her previous resolutions. The ambassador
played his cards very skilfully ; he made the most of the
English argument and extorted all the information he could ;
but Nesselrode saw that there was no hope of agreement, and
when his antagonist reduced the whole matter to a single
point, and asked whether, if other differences were waived,
and England consented to join the conferences on the sole
condition of a disavowal of force, Russia and the Allies would
pledge themselves to this repudiation, Nesselrode replied without hesitation in the negative. The dispute had thus been
reduced to a simple issue, and with such success as he had
gained Canning was forced to be content. He had never
expected much result from his mission : he called it a
" forlorn hope" and told Planta that he " had laboured most

diligently to make something out of nothing": "I have worked like a horse, and hope I shall not be treated like a dog." Considering the weakness of his weapons, it is surprizing that he won even so much as he did from the astute adviser of the czar.

He had undoubtedly smoothed away much of the irritation which the czar had felt against England. He had also laid the foundation stone of the edifice of Greek freedom which he afterwards helped to rear. The Duke of Wellington's protocol of April 1826 is generally held to be the first step towards Greek independence, and the earlier labours of 1825 have been ignored. But it is not too much to say that these preliminary discussions cleared the way for the later agreement. Had they been guided with a less steady and skilful hand, the road might have been blocked for many years and a serious misunderstanding might have arisen with Russia. As it was, this danger was averted, and the two governments were put in full and unprejudiced possession of their respective views. Canning's last audience of the emperor shewed that he had made considerable progress in winning his confidence :—

His Imperial Majesty seemed chiefly to have at heart to impress upon me, first, that the policy of his government was directed to objects of general good and not to interests exclusively national ; secondly, that his views were decidedly and systematically pacific ; and thirdly, that he was bent on a strict adherence to the principles of the Grand Alliance.

Applying these rules of policy to the affairs of Turkey and of Greece, the emperor declared that throughout his late differences with the Porte he had laboured conscientiously to avoid the necessity of an appeal to arms, in spite of the many provocations offered by that power. He assured me that in proceeding to take measures for restoring tranquillity in the east, his only motives were those of humanity towards the Greeks, of concern in the general welfare of Europe, and anxiety to remove as far as possible all subjects of irritation between himself and the Sultan. His Imperial Majesty added that it was not as a single power having questions of national interests to discuss with the Porte, but as one of the states of Europe, and in concert with his allies—with England among the number, if England were so inclined—that Russia proposed to interfere in the affairs of Turkey. To offer an equitable arrangement between the contending parties, and to enforce their acceptance of it by means which would not put to hazard the peace of Europe, were the simple and unexceptionable intentions which the Emperor described himself as entertaining. "I am well aware," said his Imperial Majesty, " that the resources of Russia, great as they are, could scarcely be called into action without exciting, perhaps not unreasonably, the vigilance and solicitude of other sovereigns, and it is on this very account that I have made it a solemn duty, since the evacuation of France by the Allied forces, to keep my empire in an attitude of perfect repose."

During the two months occupied by the mission, Canning lost no opportunity of seeing the life and society of the Russian capital, which he found agreeable enough. With the people in general he was pleased : he found the official circle sociable and well-bred, the lower classes civil and obliging. The Russians, he said, " are a people of lively imagination and deep feeling. Many a page of history has yet to be filled with their exploits ! " How true was this prediction he was himself able to realize thirty years later. The royal family created him well. He was particularly charmed with the emperor's mother, widow of Paul, and with the clever and beautiful Grand Duchess Hélène—wife of Michael, who " did not enjoy the same popularity as his wife, but I found him sensible, friendly, and unassuming. His brother, the Grand Duke Nicholas, had the character of a martinet, but I had no opportunity of forming my own opinion of him." The last remark is important, as disproving the often repeated statement that Nicholas's dislike of Canning in later years arose out of a quarrel at Petersburg in 1825. The two only met once in their lives, and that was at a purely formal reception at Paris in 1814.

The following letter was written to his mother, 5 April :—

It was on Sunday that I had my audience of leave, first of the emperor, and then of his mother, the empress dowager. It is not the custom for foreign ministers to take leave of the other members of the imperial family. The emperor received me, as at first, in his private room. I found him alone, and during the conversation, which lasted about forty minutes, we both stood and stood so close to each other on account of his deafness in one ear, that a hand could scarcely have been passed between our respective persons. There had been a grand christening at Court in the morning, a most fatiguing ceremony, at which he had officiated as godfather, and he was to preside shortly after at an enormous public dinner to be given in the palace ;—for which reasons I was anxious to get him on political topics without loss of time. It was happily accomplished. The emperor spoke in French, and not, as when I saw him at Paris, in English. He spoke with fluency and warmth, agreeably and impressively, but rather as a sensible, quick, well-educated man than as a man of much genius or remarkable capacity. He listened fairly to my replies, and on dismissing me expressed himself in terms of personal kindness. But to give you an idea of his feelings towards the *enlightened* part of our Government, he never once inquired after G. C., whom he personally knows, and only once after some hesitation pronounced his name.

The empress mother, a sister of the late King of Würtemberg, is really a very fine old lady, quite as upright in her person as an old lady of our acquaintance, and possessing besides the *kindred* virtues of early-rising, activity, and benevolence. She also presided and officiated at the christening of her little granddaughter in the morning —officiating I may well say, for it was a part of her duty as well as of the emperor to walk three times round the font, she carrying the baby on a cushion, and he with two lighted tapers in his hand. The object of the ceremony was a small Grand Duchess that came into the world about a month ago, the offspring of the Grand Duke Michael, the emperor's third brother, and of the Grand Duchess Hélène, daughter of the King of Würtemberg's brother, and as young, as pretty, and as clever as one could wish a wife to be. The empress, though she had been busy the whole day, received me, and sustained a conversation of ten minutes without the least appearance of fatigue. I found her standing in the middle of the room, one of her ladies in waiting at a little distance behind, and the two masters of ceremony who introduced me also waiting at some distance behind me. Her conversation turned upon common topics, and had no interest in it beyond a general expression of good nature. I kissed her hand on entering according to custom, and I ought in truth to have bestowed two kisses, or one more than usually audible, to make up for the total omission of that duty which I had made through inadvertence at my first audience. The reigning empress was not to be kissed, or even to be seen. She had been ill for some time, and though now a great deal better, she does not yet expose herself to the fatigue of public presentations. The whole family have been united at St. Petersburg this year, and they really seem to live on the most amiable terms with each other. The Prince of Orange, you know, is married to one of the Emperor's sisters. Think of his travelling hither from Brussels in ten days. If the rapidity of his journey was meant as a compliment to his wife, it was really a flattering one. When I was presented to him last week, he mentioned poor Charles with kindness, and that too without knowing that I was related to him.

With respect to such sights as the Court affords, I have been exceedingly fortunate. I have been present at a *Te Deum* in the Court chapel, a ball, and a masquerade, besides the christening; and this, let me tell you, is a great deal, considering that Lent has occupied so much of the time, and considering still more that the emperor hates society and gives as few entertainments as he

possibly can. The Winter Palace, in which the grand entertainments are given, is an immense pile of buildings, but more remarkable for its extent than for the purity of its architecture. It contains, besides innumerable chambers, three or four magnificent
halls of very large dimensions. There is the *Salle Blanche*, and
the *Salle de St. George*, and the *Salle des Marbres*, each more
striking than the other. On the night of the ball there was dancing
in the first, card-playing in the second, and supper, served under
orange-trees, with a profusion of flowers on the tables, in the third.
At the masquerade the public was admitted to the number of
several thousands, and the whole suite of apartments was thrown
open. The sight of such a crowd and so strange a mixture of
dresses and of ranks was curious; but the gratification of one's
curiosity was dearly purchased by the heat and the noise and the
pressure, to say nothing of more serious inconveniences inseparable
from such a collection of all classes. The behaviour of the people
was very orderly, and there was no appearance of the police. The
emperor occasionally danced, or rather walked a dance, called the
Polonaise, which consists in nothing but a walk to music throughout the apartments, each gentleman holding a lady by the hand,
and the couples following each other in succession. The empress
played at cards in the middle of the throng. While playing, she
sent for the different members of the Diplomatic Body and conversed with them in turns. The French ambassador was the only
foreigner invited to play with her.

But I must hasten to say a word about the society of St.
Petersburg. I am sure "you have kept a corner for that"; it
must however be only a word, or a very few words. In this, as in
other respects, the Court is all in all. The society with which I
mingle is composed of the foreign ministers and a few of the
principal families, attached in some way or other to the emperor
or his family. The Russians are not a dinner-giving people, and
the greater part of my visit here has passed during Lent, which
they keep more strictly than the Catholics. Neither are they much
in the habit of giving regular entertainments of an evening. Once
introduced you may call when you please, on the gentlemen in the
morning, on the ladies in the early part of the evening, and in
some families who sup at home, or who have their regular receiving
evenings, you may look in uninvited about ten and pass the remainder of the day there. One generally finds a suite of apartments open, spacious and admirably well warmed. Conversation is
not much to be depended upon; as instruction of any extent is
rare, and the events of the day are not sufficient to supply fuel for
small talk, besides that the fear of Siberia has a wonderful effect in
restraining the tongue on the great chapter of politics. But you
have cards, and chess, and billiards, and you may go out without
ceremony, and sometimes without notice.

To leave St. Petersburg without giving a thought to Catherine seems almost unnatural. Yet the only trace of the great man-empress which came under my notice was a sad one. At the Hermitage I observed an old lady with her head pressed down on her bosom and wheeled about in a garden chair. I learned on inquiry that the poor decrepit invalid was Mademoiselle Dashkov, who had shared with Catherine the glory and the guilt of that adventure which gave to Russia the most triumphant of its sovereigns after the reign of Peter.

On his homeward journey he visited Moscow, and passed through Warsaw, where he communicated to the czar, who had preceded him, the instructions delivered by the English government to Sir C. Stuart in reference to the South American Republics, and saw the Duke of Cumberland. From Warsaw he went on to Berlin, where he was presented to the King of Prussia, and arrived in England in May.

CHAPTER VIII.

NAVARINO.

1825-1827.

THE mission to St. Petersburg was hardly over when Canning had to make his arrangements for another residence at the Porte. This time he did not go alone : he took his wife with him. The second Mrs. Canning was a daughter of Mr. Alexander of Somerhill near Tunbridge, and was nineteen years of age. On 3 September, 1825, they were married, and at the close of October they started for Stambol. They went overland by way of Paris and Switzerland and Florence. At Naples they found their official "family" waiting for them, and after a presentation to the King of the Two Sicilies they embarked with their suite on Admiral Sir Harry Neale's flagship the *Revenge*, 74, for Corfu. There they were detained for some weeks by the serious illness not only of several members of their household, but of Mrs. Canning herself. An epidemic of scarlet fever raged in the embassy, and the Lord High Commissioner's house became a temporary hospital. There was serious anxiety for a while, but fortunately all the invalids recovered, and at the begin-

ning of January 1826 the embassy was once more on its road
to the Porte. On the way Canning took steps through
Captain Hamilton to afford the Greek Provisional Government an opportunity of laying its views before him, and an
interview fraught with important results took place off Hydra
on 9 January. The Petersburg Protocol of 4 April was the
direct consequence of his report of the proposals here made
to him unofficially by the Greek deputies.

MEMOIRS.   Before entering the Archipelago we passed a
night at anchor in a small bay between Cerigo and the main,
almost at the foot of that dark frowning promontory which stands
sentry over the waters of Greece. We woke next morning under a
fine blue sky and lost no time in setting sail to a strong southerly
breeze which soon bore us up to the narrow channel having the
peninsula on one side and the grand little island of Hydra on the
other. There we anchored again, and before noon were boarded
by two of the Greek leaders [deputed by the Provisional Government of Greece] then at open war with the Ottoman government.
These patriotic gentlemen were [Prince Alexander] Mavrocordatos
and Zographos, both of distinguished position among the insurgents,
and thoroughly acquainted with the state of public affairs and the
prevailing current of opinion in Greece. I could only receive them
privately, with such reserve as my official character and due
respect for a friendly power imposed. Sad was the picture presented by Greece at that period. Resources all but exhausted—
counsels more than distracted—hopes daily declining within—only
barren sympathies without—discouragement approaching to despair—and hatred of the Turks unsoftened, nay, inextinguishable
like the Greek fire of old. Harassed by such adversities and disheartened by prospects all but hopeless, it was natural for the
leaders in Greece, however patriotic, to look for relief in terms of
accommodation with the Porte, and as a last resource to reckon
upon our mediation as offering the best chance of negotiating
successfully with that power. In reporting to my government, as
I was bound to do, the real state of affairs in Greece, I found some
consolation in being at liberty to declare that an opening for
negotiation capable of improvement appeared to exist, nor did I
fail to give as much encouragement as I could with prudence to the
pacific tendencies and reliance on England which Mavrocordatos
and his colleague had manifested to me. The intimation I received
from them was the possibility of an arrangement by which the
Morea should be separated from the Ottoman empire for the
purposes of internal administration, while its principal fortresses
should be occupied by Turkish garrisons.

The most important points gained at this interview were
two : first, that the Greeks were anxious for English media-

tion; and secondly, that they would consent to something
short of independence, which they had never admitted before.
They desired a total separation of the Greek and Turkish
population; did not object to paying tribute to the Sultan,
and perhaps to indemnifying the transplanted Turkish landholders; nor would they refuse the Porte some share in
appointing the local authorities. On the very day of his
interview with the Greek emissaries, news came of the decease of Alexander, the Emperor of Russia, at Taganrog.
On getting outside the channel the *Revenge* was caught in a
terrific hurricane, which tore her old sails to ribbons and thus
probably saved the vessel. A companion, the *Algeciras*, commanded by Captain Wemyss, went straight to the bottom;
and the two Greek deputies, after a perilous escape, got
to shore more dead than alive. Such was the dramatic
climax of the first step towards the liberation of Greece.

MEMOIRS.   In the port of Ipsera we gathered cruel evidence
of what war is when kindled by the antipathies of race and creed.
It was little more than dawn when we anchored before the town.
The houses had every appearance of undisturbed repose, and the
early hour sufficed to account for the want of movement in
the streets. The admiral's steward went ashore with the full
expectation of finding a market well stocked with all the
objects he required. Imagine his surprise when the truth
broke upon him. A death-silence indoors as well as without,
not a voice, not a footstep, not an inhabitant; the town a mere
shell, plausible to the eye, but utterly void of life. Later in the
day a party of us landed with our guns and strayed among the
vineyards in search of game. At one spot near the coast we came
upon a piteous sight, the bones of many who had preferred a
voluntary death to captivity, when their homes became the prey of
a Turkish squadron. Mothers in horror and despair had slaughtered
their children on the cliff, and thrown themselves over on their
bodies which had already found a resting place below. Scarcely
less horrible than this scene of death was the apparition of two
survivors from the interior of the island. Worn nearly to skeletons
by fear and anguish and famine, the very types of hopeless misery,
with haggard eyes and loathsome beards, and tattered rags by way
of clothing, they told without language the history of their sufferings. Heavens! how I longed to be the instrument of repairing
such calamities by carrying my mission of peace and deliverance to
a successful issue!

On arriving at the Dardanelles the embassy was transferred to H.M. sloop *Medina*, and the ambassador regretfully

K

bade farewell to the kindly admiral, while the band of the
Revenge sent the national anthem of Greece pealing mourn-
fully over the waters of her oppressors. He was easily
moved by impressions, and the trials of the voyage had
shaken his nerve. He was not ashamed to confess that he
went down the side of the flagship with moist eyes.

Thirteen years had passed since Canning had left the
tumble-down Palace of the British Embassy at Pera—as he
thought, for ever. Great changes had taken place in the
interval. The " common enemy of Europe " was dead, and
England was no longer fighting alone against an overwhelming tyranny. She was now rather struggling against the too
close embraces of her allies, who in their exceeding affection
were eager to tie her hands by a series of conferences, conventions, and concerts. It was no longer necessary to wage war
with the French mission, which had lost most of its ancient
influence at the Porte: the antagonist now was Prince
Metternich, or his representative Baron Ottenfels—the internuncio of 1812—who was ably and unscrupulously abetted
by the Prussian envoy in carrying out the plots of the
"Prince of Darkness," as the chancellor was called. Instead of counteracting the overpowering strength of the
French empire, now no more, the task of the British ambassador was to defeat the intrigues of the Austrian dictator,
the soul of the somewhat superannuated Holy Alliance, and
the upholder of all that was narrow, dogmatic, and unbending
in the policy of the Vienna Congress and its appendices. The
latter struggle was hardly less arduous than the former, for
whatever Austria suffered in point of prestige, in comparison
with the triumphant position of Buonaparte in 1810, was
balanced by her possession of the ear of the Porte and by the
unscrupulous ingenuity of her intrigues.

Canning's main object was to secure the pacification of
Greece. It was an object, as Sir Charles Bagot told him, of
the very first consequence—" the one point upon which the
peace of Europe depended ; " but it was also one which must
tax the resources of mere diplomacy to the utmost. It will
be remembered that the Petersburg mission had left the
Greek question open as far as England was concerned.
Our government would have nothing to say to force or
menace, and the other powers declined to commit themselves
to a formal disavowal of this engine of coercion. England
had therefore stood aside while the four powers discharged

their little popgun at the Porte. Their very innocent recommendation of an arrangement with Greece ended in
smoke. The Porte would not listen to the voice of the four
charmers, and the force which they had so doggedly refused
to disavow was, strange to tell, not brought into requisition.
It was suspected that the Austrian internuncio, under Prince
Metternich's instructions, had secretly opposed the policy
which his Court had ostensibly adopted. Metternich frankly
detested the Greeks, and had only joined the Petersburg
Conference to prevent Russia from going in single-handed.
His envoy at the Porte was, it is said, instructed to inform the Sultan that Austria was not in earnest. Whatever the cause, the four powers failed in their plan of
mediation.

There was now no competitor in the field, and England
was free to try her own plan. It was no longer a case of unsolicited interference, for deputies from the Greek Provisional
Government had waited upon George Canning in September
1825 to place their country under the protection of England.
The responsibility was too serious to be lightly accepted, but
the suggestion paved the way for the mediation which was
invited at the interview with Mavrocordatos off Hydra, and
formally solicited by the States-General of Greece on 19 April,
1826. England had thus become not only the sole but the
authorized pleader for the Greeks. She had various points
in her favour. One party of the belligerents had agreed to
terms : the Greeks would follow her counsels, and would
probably do something to put down the piracy which had
made the Archipelago a den of thieves for the last four years.
The Turks could at all events find no interested motive in her
mediation ; with England there was no risk of aggrandizement, as there would be in the case of Austria or Russia ;
and the death of the Czar Alexander was regarded as favourable to the chances of pacification.

It was very soon obvious, however, that measures more
than merely argumentative must be employed to extort concessions from the Sultan. The state of the war was such
that the advice of the British ambassador in favour of large
mercies must have appeared simply ludicrous to the Turks.
Their Egyptian vassal, the famous Mohammed Ali, and his
son Ibrahim, were doing most of the work, and the Porte had
little to lose and everything to gain by a vigorous prosecution
of the war. Never indeed, since the days of her military

glory, was Turkey so little disposed to concession ; never was her imperial master's position stronger.

What could friendly mediation accomplish in such circumstances ? What argument could be used to convince the Sultan that it was to his interest to let his rebellious subjects go free—practically free—just when their submission seemed inevitable ? Frankly, there was none. More than this, there was hardly a shadow of an excuse for mediation at all. Turkey did not interfere to obtain concessions for the Peterloo rioters, and why should she admit the right of England to meddle in her internal affairs ? The answer to this, as Lord Erskine said in his letter to Lord Liverpool, was that the Porte had brought the interference on herself by misgovernment ; but this was an argument beyond the ken of a Turkish despot, and one which, if pressed to its logical conclusion, would expose every State to the perpetual risk of officious and interested meddling on the part of the rest of the world. The subject of Greece was one, said the Turkish Foreign Secretary, "which never *could* become a proper subject for discussion on the part of the Sultan's servants." This position was resolutely maintained by Sultan Mahmud, in spite of the remonstrance of the four powers in 1825, in spite of the reasonings of the Cannings in 1826, in spite of the joint urgency of England and Russia in 1827, in spite of the Treaty of London in July and the battle of Navarino in October ; and it took two Russian campaigns to break it. Through all these transactions the Sultan never wavered once. The Greeks were his subjects ; they had rebelled and they must be brought to submission ; that was his policy, and by that he stood. It is impossible to refuse him our admiration, even while we must regret the desperate imprudence of his high spirit.

Europe, however, had resolved to free the Greeks. The statesmen indeed were not so much moved as the poets and enthusiasts, and Greece owed much to the circumstance that both the Cannings belonged to the second as well as the first category. It is true that George Canning was on his guard against laying too much stress upon the heroic past of Hellas ; he dreaded sentimental statecraft, and wished to find something which "had nothing to do with Epaminondas" as a ground for mediation. But, let the reason be what it might, Greece must never again be under the Turkish yoke. Stratford was sent out to secure that end ; and although from the first he saw that the odds were heavily against him, he took up the cause *con amore*.

The usual compliments had been exchanged between the embassy and the Porte ; the chief dragoman had brought forty-five trays of flowers, fruit, and sweetmeats, and had received a diamond snuff-box in return; jewels and other presents from the British Government were flying about Constantinople ; and then Canning pressed for a confidential interview with the Reis Efendi, which after the usual demurs was granted. On 15 March they had a conversation, which lasted five hours, and in which Canning used every peaceful argument that his experience could suggest to induce the Porte to come to favourable terms with the Greeks. He was heavily handicapped by Lord Strangford's blunders at Petersburg, of which the Turks were well informed ; and he had to convince the Reis that England was not committed to other powers, just when Strangford had said she was. He made the best of a bad brief, but all was of no avail. The Reis Efendi on this and on subsequent occasions turned a deaf ear to all remonstrances and reasonings, and declared that it was contrary to the " sovereign dignity and the holy religion " of the Sultan even to reply to the mere suggestion of foreign interference in what was a purely domestic matter. His manner and position were haughty and disdainful, and to every repeated attack he offered the same unshaken *non possumus*. At the official audience of the Sultan, when by some accident the ambassador was permitted the unprecedented privilege of entering the presence with his sword, Mahmud said not a word about Greece.

Whatever arguments might be brought to bear upon the Sultan, it was clear that they must be sought from other sources than the immediate interests of Turkey or friendly consideration for Christian powers. The first attack was to be upon philanthropic grounds. As George Canning had written in January, the " barbarization " of the Morea was a much higher ground of mediation than any that had before presented itself. It was rumoured that Ibrahim Pasha intended to exterminate the population, or at least to transplant and expatriate them, and fill the country with Egyptians and Arabs. This was something that might perhaps form a ground of remonstrance and even intervention ; but unfortunately it was not true, or if the idea had once been entertained, it had certainly been abandoned. Later on, the atrocities of the Egyptians in the Morea, the wholesale massacres and enslavings, the hundreds of pairs of ears nailed over the Seraglio gate as trophies of war, formed a new basis of remonstrance ; but when these enormities were urged, the Reis Efendi would shrug his shoulders, deny some reports, call others exaggerations, and finally retort that the Greeks were quite as bad themselves. This was unhappily true enough, as the fall of Navarino and Tripolitza had shewn ; the rebels took their full share of treachery and murder, and Canning himself was obliged to admit that, wishing well as he did to the Greeks, " there is no denying that with few exceptions they are a most rascally set."

Setting aside, then, philanthropic grounds, which were rather thrown away upon the Ottomans, and which admitted of the retort of provocation, a remonstrance might be made upon the piratical state of the Archipelago. George Canning, feeling perhaps that his " higher ground," for poor humanity's sake, might not prove a firm footing for negotiation, suggested that it might be well to press the more earthly policy of our " commercial grievances." " Take them up and press them hard. If we are to have a quarrel, we must have the mercantile interests with us : hitherto their claims have been somewhat postponed to Russian accommodation. Take them up now." The piracy had indeed gone to such lengths that it formed a proper subject of remonstrance on the part of a ship-holding nation ; but the worst of the matter was that the pirates were for the most part Greeks, and when pressed on the subject the Reis Efendi had the obvious reply, " Let us put down our rebellious rayas in Greece, without any more of this foreign meddling and disavowed support of the rebels, and you will soon hear no more of piracy." The answer was so true that it was hardly worth while provoking it ; but it took a longer experience than even Canning had yet had of the Porte to realize that Turks are not always quite such fools as they look. The experiment was tried and failed. It does not appear to have been tried again for some time.

What remained, when friendly mediation based upon presumed Turkish interests, upon humane grounds, and commercial considerations, in turn proved useless ? Mesolonghi had fallen in April and this success naturally increased the determination of the Turks not to listen to terms of dismemberment. There was not an arrow left in the quiver of diplomacy to let fly at the Sultan. Canning had seen from the beginning that force was the only remedy, and he had striven hard to lead his cousin to something "more or less coercive " but "just short of war." So far, however, he had not been able to obtain sufficiently forcible instructions.

Whatever the Foreign Secretary might think about employing an English menace, there could be no doubt about the policy of harping on the old Russian string, and holding before the eyes of Turkish ministers the chances of a war with the czar. But just at this moment a change came over the ostensible policy of Russia. Nicholas did not appear to have inherited his brother's Greek mantle; Alexander died with threats of war on his lips; but Nicholas delivered himself of pacific utterances, and a general impression prevailed that he would not lift a finger to help the Greeks, whatever he might do to settle the outstanding claims which still kept the Russian ambassador away from Constantinople. The Duke of Wellington, who had gone to St. Petersburg on a complimentary visit upon the Emperor's accession (and with some ulterior views), was completely deceived by these protestations, and wrote in sanguine terms to the ambassador at the Porte.

Canning, however, was not so easily converted; and his doubts of the correctness of the duke's impressions were confirmed on hearing that an ultimatum had just been presented to the Porte by the Russian chargé d'affaires demanding three specified points relating to the Danubian provinces, Servia, and some other unsettled matters, on pain of war. This ultimatum had been dispatched from St. Petersburg without Wellington's knowledge, and the circumstance did not tend to strengthen his Grace's opinion of Russian honesty. It is true Greece was not mentioned in the ultimatum; but the document was enough to raise up all the old Russian panic in Turkey, and to counteract any soothing effects which the previous pacific declarations of the czar might have produced. At all events it emphatically confirmed Stratford Canning's warnings, and his cousin was not slow to congratulate him as a true prophet :—

You have *beau jeu* now with your misbelievers.

They were convinced that the Emperor of Russia would not go to war. You told them that he would. Behold the verification of your warnings.

They believed that we and all Europe should oppose him if he did. You warned them not to trust to that expectation. Behold the war coming, and none stirs to avert it.

More recently all your colleagues told them that the emperor cared not about the Greeks. Somebody else will have told *you* so too and will perhaps have restrained you from contradicting your colleagues. Behold, you are now authorized to say that Russia joins with us as to the question of the Morea, and to insinuate that we may join with Russia hereafter if the Turks will not come to some understanding with us about the Greeks.

The last sentence refers to a very important step in the Greek question. By a Protocol signed at St. Petersburg on 4 April by Wellington, Nesselrode, and Lieven, Russia and England agreed to concert joint measures for the pacification of Greece. Stratford Canning's report of his interview off Hydra had done its work : his cousin told him

It is not only that the Protocol *defines* and limits the considerations, which had been always hitherto left indefinite and unlimited : but it is that, *but for* your conference with the Greeks on your way to Constantinople (the unofficial prelude to the official demand of our mediation) *there would have been no Protocol.*

The Turks meanwhile had agreed (4 May) to the three points of the Russian ultimatum ; their plenipotentiaries had set off to meet their antagonists at Akkerman. On the Greek question, however, they remained stubborn, and nothing could shake them. The single-handed mediation of England had been tried and had failed. That anyone could have supposed that it would succeed is the surprizing thing about it. The English ambassador had no effective weapon to strike down the Sultan's rigid guard ; and mere argument was so much wasted breath. " When I look back," wrote Lord Stratford, " after an interval of forty years, to the whole of the circumstances, it appears to me quite clear that the success I so ardently desired was a simple impossibility."

At this moment, whilst the Greek question remained a forbidden subject at the Porte, a new and tremendous change took place in the military organisation of Turkey. This was the celebrated massacre of the Janissaries.

MEMOIRS.   Much discontent had prevailed among the Janissaries for some time. They had shewn a great reluctance to take the field, and the Sultan was in consequence unable to count upon their fidelity. They apprehended a revival of the new organization which they had successfully resisted in the days of Sultan Selim, and Mahmud had strengthened their fears by making away in secret, one after another, with many of their number who were suspected of entertaining rebellious designs. I remember that in crossing the Golden Horn from time to time I had observed loose mats floating here and there upon the water, and that in answer to my inquiries I had been told in a mysterious manner that they had served for covering to bodies thrown after private execution into the harbour, and had risen to the surface when detached from their contents by the process of decomposition. It was in June, 1826, when the conspiracy, if such it was, assumed the character of an open revolt. I had sent off a messenger in the night, and had not been long in bed, when my sleep was interrupted by the sudden appearance of a dragoman, who announced that the Janissaries "were up." I asked whether the courier had actually set out, and being told that he was still within reach, I wrote a supplementary despatch to the Secretary of State, and proceeded to dress. Soon afterwards a message came in from some of the merchants requesting that I would obtain an extra guard for their protection. I lost no time in applying as they wished to the Janissary Aga, and I received for reply an assurance that he could not spare any of his soldiers until their safety was secured, but that he would then send as many as I liked, and that meanwhile there was nothing to fear. Later in the morning I walked out into the garden. I had not been long there, when I perceived that some one from behind was lifting the skirt of my coat. On turning I recognized the commander of our Turkish guard, himself a Janissary, almost on his knees in a posture of supplication. There was no need of language to tell me that the revolt had failed, and positive intelligence soon followed to confirm that impression. It became more and more manifest with every passing hour that the government had secured its authority, and we could do nothing better than to wait patiently for the final result. The weather was hot, and we dined at an early hour. My seat at table fronted the windows which commanded a view of Stambol beyond the Golden Horn, and I had scarcely taken my place when I observed two slender columns of smoke rising above the opposite horizon. What could they mean? I asked, and the reply informed me that the Sultan's people had fired the barracks of the Janissaries, who had no resource but to fly. To fly, if they could—but in truth they were hard pressed, numbers perished on the spot and those who got away found it very difficult, if not impossible, to evade the subsequent pursuit of justice.

The Sultan was determined to make the most of his victory. From the time of his cousin Selim's death, he had lived in dread of the Janissaries. A strong impression must have been made upon his mind by the personal danger which he had then encountered. It was said that he had escaped with his life by getting into an oven when the search for him was hottest. His duty as sovereign gave strength as well as dignity to his private resentment. That celebrated militia, which in earlier times had extended the bounds of the empire, and given the title of conqueror to so many of the Sultans, which had opened the walls of Constantinople itself to their triumphant leader, the second Mohammed, were now to be swept away with an unsparing hand and to make room for a new order of things, for a disciplined army, and a charter of reform. From these high claims to honour and confidence they had sadly declined. They had become the masters of the government, the butchers of their sovereigns, and a source of terror to all but the enemies of their country. Whatever compassion might be felt for individual sufferers, including as they did the innocent with the guilty, it could hardly be said that their punishment as a body was untimely or undeserved.

The complaints of those who were doomed to destruction found no echo in the bosoms of their conquerors. They were mostly citizens having their wives, their children, or their parents, to witness the calamity which they had brought in thunder on their necks. Many had fallen under the Sultan's artillery; many were fugitives and outlaws. The mere name of Janissary, compromised or not by an overt act, operated like a sentence of death. A special commission sat for the trial or rather for the condemnation of crowds. Every victim passed at once from the tribunal into the hands of the executioner. The bowstring and the scimitar were constantly in play. People could not stir from their houses without the risk of falling in with some horrible sight. The Sea of Marmora was mottled with dead bodies. Nor was the tragedy confined to Constantinople and its neighbourhood. Messengers were sent in haste to every provincial city where any considerable number of Janissaries existed, and the slightest tendency to insurrection was so promptly and effectually repressed, that no disquieting reports were conveyed to us from any quarter of the empire. Not a day passed without my receiving a requisition from the Porte, calling upon me to send thither immediately the officer and soldiers comprising my official guard. I had no reason to suppose that any of them had been concerned in the revolt, and I was pretty sure that they could not repair to the Porte without imminent danger of being sacrificed. I ventured therefore to detain them day after day, first on one pretext then on another, until, at the end of a week, the fever at head-quarters had so far subsided as to open a door for reflection and mercy. Relying on this abatement of wrath I complied, and the interpreter whom I directed to accompany them, gave every assurance on their behalf which I was entitled to offer. The men were banished from the capital but their lives were spared, and many years later I was much pleased by a visit from their officer, who displayed his gratitude by coming from a distance on foot to regale me with a bunch of dried grapes and a pitcher of choice water. Let me add that this instance of good feeling on the part of a Turk towards a Christian is only one of many which have come to my knowledge.

On 17 June the formal abolition of the corps of Janissaries was solemnly proclaimed by the Imam in the Mosque of Sultan Ahmed in the presence of Mahmud himself. The Holy Standard was taken within the Seraglio court, and thither all the official members of the government flocked for safety and council. On the 20th :—

> The Sultan's ministers are still encamped in the outer court of the Seraglio, and I grieve to add that frequent executions continue to take place under their very eyes. This afternoon, when the person, to whom I have already alluded, was standing near the Reis Efendi's tent, his attention was suddenly caught by the sound of drums and fifes, and on turning round he saw, to his utter astonishment, a body of Turks in various dresses, but armed with muskets and bayonets, arranged in European order, and going through the new form of exercise. He supposes the number to have been about two thousand, but never before having seen troops in line he may have been deceived in this particular. He says that the men acted by word of command, both in marching and in handling their arms. The Sultan, who was at first stationed at the window within sight, descended after a time, and passed the men in review. His Highness was dressed in the *Egyptian* fashion, armed with pistols and sabre, and on his head in place of the Imperial turban was a sort of Egyptian bonnet.
>
> Rank, poverty, age and numbers are alike impotent to shelter those who are known as culprits or marked as victims. It is confidently asserted that a register has been kept of all persons who since the accession of the Sultan have in any way shown a disposition to favour the designs of the Janissaries, and that all such individuals are diligently sought out and cut off as soon as discovered. Respectable persons are seized in the streets and hurried before the Seraskier or Grand Vezir for immediate judgment. There are instances of elderly men having pleaded a total ignorance of the late conspiracy, and being reminded of some petty incident which happened twenty years ago, in proof of their deserving condign punishment as abettors of the Janissaries. Whole companies of labouring men are seized and either executed or forcibly obliged to quit Constantinople. . . .
>
> The entrance to the Seraglio, the shore under the Sultan's windows, and the sea itself, are crowded with dead bodies—many of them torn and in part devoured by the dogs.

The many atrocities of this terrible time might, one would think, have produced a counter-revolution : but the people were numbed by the suddenness and severity of the blow, and any attempts at conspiracies against the Sultan were easily and summarily subdued. Canning looked on in amazement as he saw matters quieting down, and the Sultan's authority

growing daily more assured. The Janissaries were extermi-
nated ; the capital had been deluged with blood ; yet no one
raised a hand or uttered a protest.

MEMOIRS. The Janissaries had perished; a regular army
was to be created. The task was urgent, and the Sultan set about
it in good earnest. He shook off the habits of an indolent, luxurious
life. He took an active part in training the new battalions.
European officers were employed for their instruction. He assisted
in person at their exercises. Camps were formed around Constantinople. The foundations of vast barracks were laid on both
sides of the Bosphorus. In short, the old military genius of
Turkey seemed to have sprung into fresh life. The forms were
changed, the spirit was the same. The head of the nation was
once more a Sultan not only in title but in act and power. This
revival in the department of arms had very important consequences
in that of politics. Russia began to fear that the prey on which
her eyes has been so long fixed even to fascination would escape
her. Greece, palpitating under the pressure of superior forces, hoped
to obtain a breathing time, precious, though it might prove of short
duration. England felt a certain reluctance to take advantage of
the Sultan's precarious and unguarded position. In general
throughout Europe a mixed emotion of surprize and admiration
retarded for a time the flow of sentiments unfriendly to the Porte.
The Greeks, however, in their extremity had awakened sympathies
which were not slow to produce a counteracting effect. The fall of
Mesolonghi had been attended with such heroic actions and such
affecting circumstances that their partisans in every country
bestirred themselves to keep up their courage and to obtain assistance for them whether in money, or in arms, provisions and
clothing. Their present necessities and their prospective hopes
concurred to animate their zeal. They would not overlook the
importance of turning the momentary lull to account. It might
suit the interests of Russia, while going into conference with
Turkey for the purpose of settling her own affairs, to pretend indifference to those of Greece, but the Protocol signed at Petersburg
apart from Austria would hardly fail to germinate into a convention
between the two contracting parties and France, ever ready to
move in a generous purpose. I knew that Charles X. had declared
in private his willingness to place a French squadron under the
command of a British admiral for the sake of peace and humanity.
In a word delay, and not abandonment, was the policy of the
hour.

The position of affairs was so completely changed that
there was nothing to be done but wait. The Protocol of
4 April created a new departure in the Greek question ; it
was no longer a matter of single-handed mediation, but of

joint intervention by two, perhaps even concerted intervention by five, powers. Nothing could be attempted till the terms of the Protocol received more definite shape and practical application. No one could have predicted that more than a year would elapse before Canning could receive the necessary powers to act under the Treaty which grew out of the Protocol ; but he was prepared for some delay, and two circumstances so fully occupied the Turkish horizon that he saw that the time for reviving the question of Greece was not yet. One was the absorption of the Sultan in his military reforms, already described ; the other was the negotiation then going on at Akkerman. When a hitch occurred in these proceedings, Canning did not hesitate to throw his influence on the side of Russia, anticipating the instructions to that effect which distance from home frequently delayed beyond the time of their application. He could not but deplore the needlessly offensive tone taken by the Russian plenipotentiaries at Akkerman, and regret their design of raising new difficulties out of the Treaty of Bucharest. But the majority of the issues had already been decided, and the balance was not considerable enough to risk a war and overturn the Greek negotiations. The massing of Russian troops on the Turkish frontier in September settled the question. The Treaty of Akkerman was accordingly concluded on 7 October, 1826, and the road was clear for the Greek operations.

Still nothing was being done for Greece. The Petersburg Protocol seemed destined to lead to nothing, and Canning was sick of his compulsory inaction. As the year wore on, it need hardly be said that his spirits did not improve. Had he been still a widower, the troubles of his post would have almost overwhelmed him ; but fortunately in his wife he had a sure ark of refuge. Young and diffident as she was, she possessed, in her bright even spirits, her never-failing sympathy, and the tact which made her comprehend instinctively when and how to use it, the very qualities that are best calculated to soothe an impatient nature. With a charm of face and manner captivating even to strangers, she won an easy entrance into most hearts ; while to her husband, the brave, unselfish nature which was able to cheer and encourage him even in the darkest times was a constant source of strength and consolation. It was no wonder that her influence was soon felt not only by her husband but throughout the Embassy. The " Old Barrack," as it had been called, was transformed

by her ingenuity into a comfortable English home, where the
attachés found themselves always welcomed by one who was
ready to listen to their difficulties and if possible smooth
them away. There was not one of the staff who did not long
retain a grateful memory of the young ambassadress. She
joined her husband heartily in his hospitable system, and,
despite the novelty of the position, presided with equal grace
and dignity at the embassy dinners and receptions. Never
was there a more open house or a freer hand at the British
palace or at the picturesque house which Canning hired by
the water's edge at Therapia, from which the following letter
was written :—

Imagine a squarish wooden house, three stories high, the two
upper ones jutting out beyond the lowest, and the centre windows
advanced beyond the side : the whole edifice, except its tile roof,
painted a dingy black, and placed on a narrow stone quay, close on
the margin of the Bosphorus. The rooms are pretty and very
cheerful. The ground rises so abruptly behind the house that from
a window on the highest story we go out immediately on a terrace,
which in company with several of the same kind forms our garden.
The opposite coast of Asia is about a mile or a mile and a half from
us in a straight line, presenting a beautiful variety of hills and
mountains, and woods and vineyards, and from the hills above as
we look directly up the last reach of the Bosphorus into the Black
Sea. The constant passage of ships and boats is a never-failing
source of interest and amusement—but what a people to inhabit
such a country ! Within the last few days fresh horrors have
taken place in the city. It is said that a conspiracy has been discovered, and that armed parties of insurgents are in several parts
of Asia Minor. Executions and banishments are again therefore
resorted to by the Government. What are units and tens in other
countries on such occasions are here hundreds and thousands.

Of our society I have little to tell you. Our immediate neighbours are the French embassy. They are numerous, and Count
Guilleminot, the ambassador, with his wife and two daughters, all
in their different ways what the French call *aimables*. The young
ladies have formed quite an attachment to E. But we see each
other less frequently than might be expected under such circumstances. In good truth I am persuaded that the best way of
keeping well with French people is not to see them too often. The
rest of the diplomatic body live at another village, within sight,
but separated from us by a deep bay. Our own party consists
of six, since the departure of our much-valued Colonel [Barnett].
And such is the punctuality with which we meet to perform the
daily duties of breakfasting at nine and dining at six, that E. and I
have only once enjoyed the luxury of a *tête-à-tête* dinner since we
came into the country.

Three-quarters of the year 1827 passed in anxious waiting
for the effective interposition of the Allies. The record of
Canning's official life during this harassing period may be
summed up in the word *remonstrance.* His despatches are
one long series of appeals to the government to do something.
He brought the Greek question before the Porte again in
January and February, with the concurrence of the Russian
chargé d'affaires, but with no hope of producing any useful
impression. The Turks regarded England, and the two
Cannings in particular, as the main cause of the Greek agitation. The ambassador's " poor despatches announcing failure
upon failure " seemed to have no effect upon the government. Planta indeed assured him that the Office was extremely pleased with them, that his memoir on Greece was a
" most masterly performance," and George Canning publicly
and privately wrote handsomely about his cousin's proceedings. But no effectual step was taken, and the menace of
force, which the ambassador knew to be the only valid argument with Turks, was still withheld. Such instructions as
he had received had so far proved inadequate to their purpose.
The joint representations of England and Russia in pursuance
of the Protocol had been as fruitless as the single-handed
mediation. The Russian ambassador at last arrived, but
M. de Ribeaupierre's apparently loyal coöperation did not
answer the expectations of the two Courts, and the Sultan
remained inexorable. Meanwhile the Austrian and Prussian
missions had never ceased their jealous opposition and scan-
dalous intrigues against the Allies. In Greece itself matters
were in a suspended state. Church was planning vigorous
measures in Western Greece, but the other leaders were doing
little to the purpose. Mohammed Ali was cautiously feeling
his way, and was inclined to risk the wrath of his suzerain
the Sultan rather than lose the chance of a good understanding with the Western Courts. But for this, the struggle
might soon have been ended. The Greeks were at the last
gasp, and nothing but the interference of the powers could
save them.

On Mr. Canning's accession to the premiership, Lord
Dudley took the Foreign Office, which he retained after the
former's death in August of the same year, and to him the
Elchi wrote, 16 Sept., in urgent terms :—

Put your shoulder to the Greek treaty and enable us to carry it
through with acclamation. If not—good my Lord, pray let me go.

I have been leading a dog's life here for some time, but I do not wish to be treated like a dog. . . .

You will not go to war. The Chancellor of the Exchequer dares not; the Archbishop of Canterbury might, but Lord Stowell will not let him. War, then, will perhaps go to you. I thought so three weeks ago: but the Sultan appears to become cautious, and a cautious Turk is not easily caught warring. But he is very likely to let you go on excluding, intercepting, and pacifying.

This was written after he had received the news of the Treaty of London of 6 July, by which England, France, and Russia agreed to carry out the terms of the Protocol of St. Petersburg. His comment was: " the treaty is good, but it should have come sooner." He did not see how it could be used to bring the Sultan to terms, any more than the Protocol which preceded it. George Canning looked upon the " recognition of the independence " of Greece as the *ultima ratio*. He had never spoken of positive independence before. But his cousin doubted the efficacy of such a step, even when announced by ships of war. How was a naval demonstration to avail, without troops on land to support it ? He suggested the withdrawal of the embassies and a blockade of the Dardanelles, and recommended Lord Dudley to " change your present neutrality with folded arms into a French neutrality with both hands out." The latter position soon became a fact in the harbour of Navarino.

MEMOIRS. The summer was far advanced when a letter from Mr. Canning announced the conclusion of the long expected Treaty. The spirit of that agreement was peaceful interference recommended by a friendly demonstration of force. *Pacem duello miscuit.* Three squadrons, sent by the Allies, were to shelter Greece from invasion by sea. The three ambassadors at Constantinople were to press their offers of mediation on the Porte. The instructions were of course identical, and the squadrons, amounting each to four sail of the line, were to receive their ulterior directions from the respective embassies. Sir Edward Codrington no sooner reached his station off the Morea than he wrote privately to me professing an uncomfortable uncertainty as to what he was to do, and requesting some information which might help him to see his way more clearly. I answered :—

" I have considered and talked over with my colleagues, Ct. Guilleminot and M. de Ribeaupierre, the several questions mentioned in your letters. . . . On the subject of *collision*, for instance, we agree that, although the measures to be executed by you are not adopted in a hostile spirit, and although it is clearly the intention of the allied Governments to avoid, if possible, anything that may bring on war, yet the prevention of supplies, as stated in your instructions, is ultimately to be enforced, if necessary, and when all other means are exhausted, by cannon-shot.''

I should have avoided the expression " cannon-shot,'' and used, though writing privately, the more diplomatic phrase of coercion or forcible measures, had I received the slightest intimation of Sir Edward's fiery and enterprizing spirit. The joint official instructions addressed subsequently to the three admirals by me and my colleagues were in strict conformity with those under which we were ourselves to act, and nothing could be more satisfactory than the manner in which they were carried out when Ibrahim Pasha was intercepted by the combined squadrons in the vicinity of Patras, and turned away from the Gulf of Corinth by their judicious manœuvres. The object of the Alliance was attained without an act of hostility.

Such, however, was not the nature of the next important step. While the ambassadors were pressing upon the Porte the recommendations arising out of the Treaty of London, very different events were happening at Navarino.

MEMOIRS.   One Sunday afternoon I was on the point of going to our daily meeting at the French embassy, when a shabby bit of paper, like a note picked up in the street, was put into my hands. I opened it hastily and found that it contained intelligence of the deepest interest. Captain Cotton, in command of a cutter or small sloop, reported that he had been becalmed at a distance of several miles from the island of Cerigo, and in that position had heard a violent and protracted cannonade, attended from time to time with loud explosions. He had subsequently reached Smyrna, and the intelligence was forwarded to me forthwith. It could not be doubted that a general action had taken place, and that several ships on one side or the other had been blown up. I thrust it into my pocket, and went on to the Conference. Despatches from the squadrons were read over, and some ordinary business was transacted. The reports were quite satisfactory and M. de Ribeaupierre was about to retire with me, in compliment to General Guilleminot's dinner hour, when I begged a moment's pause in order to communicate a few lines which might prove of interest to all of us. So saying I drew the explosive note from my pocket and placed it quietly in the General's hands. As he read, the colour forsook his face, and presently turning to me, he said, " Trois têtes dans un bonnet—n'est-ce pas ? " I could have added, " et dans un panier, peut-être—qui sait ? " but I confined myself to a word of assent, and as we could only wait for further information, it was useless for the Russian and myself to keep our French colleague longer from his soup.

Despatches from the fleet appeared in due time, and it was some

L

relief to find that the first shot at Navarino 20 Oct. had been fired
from a Turkish ship. The ambassadors could allege in defence of
the admirals that they had not entered the harbour with any
hostile intentions, that they had transgressed no law or treaty by
taking that step for the convenience and eventual safety of their
ships, that they had not opened fire till after they had been fired
upon, and that if the Turkish fleet had suffered a heavy loss, the
responsibility rested with those who had ordered the attack. There
was much plausibility, not to say reason and truth, in this explanation. But it might fairly be said that to take so large a force without previous agreement into a port, which, though belonging to a
friendly government, was already occupied by a numerous fleet
bearing that government's flag, was in the first place a flagrant
breach of courtesy, and in the second a provocation to that very
natural impression which brought on the battle with all its
disastrous consequences. It was shrewdly remarked by one of
our officers that Sir Edward might as well have kept the tompion
in each of his guns, which would have looked like a denial of any
hostile intention without causing the slightest impediment to their
discharge in case of attack. One thing is certain that, whatever
justification the admirals might derive from local circumstances,
neither the letter nor the spirit of their instructions could be cited
to warrant their hazardous but effective decision. [The recommendation of cannon-shot applied only to the stoppage of warlike
supplies.]

There was much in all this to check the first sallies of resentment. But the Sultan, nevertheless, was furious, and his first
impulse, as we were afterwards informed, was to hold the
ambassadors responsible for what had occurred. Our persons
were respected, but at night our houses were surrounded by
military patrols. Not knowing what was to follow, I burnt that
same night a number of papers, which, although there was not a
syllable in them at variance with what we had declared in previous
communications, might have been misinterpreted by angry examiners
and perverted to our prejudice. Fortunately the Sultan was
brought into milder counsels by an old statesman, who, as Pasha
of Egypt, before the usurpation of Mohammed Ali, had acquired
a degree of experience which added to his natural prudence gave
him favour and influence with his imperial master. It was also
fortunate that the Musulman population viewed with indifference
an event which in earlier times might have roused them to acts of
sanguinary vengeance. As time passed away without the adoption
of any violent measure it was not unreasonable to hope that the
losses sustained by the Turks at Navarino would incline them from
a sense of weakness to listen more favourably to our proposals.
No such improvement, however, took place. *Manet alta in mente
repostum.* Negotiation had no longer a chance of success. In that
respect the embassies were at a dead-lock.

Numerous conferences indeed took place, and messages passed to and fro between the Porte and the embassies ; but nothing came of them.   The Reis Efendi at first adopted an apologetic air and tried to separate England from her allies by offering a new and close alliance if she would drop the terms of the treaty ; but finding this overture rejected, he presented the old stolid front of resistance to dismemberment, and declared that nothing but the absolute submission of the Greeks would meet the difficulty : the ambassadors might plead what positive instructions they pleased ; his were " from the Almighty " and could not be disobeyed.   As a matter of fact, it was known that Canning's arguments had convinced everyone but the Sultan ; but Mahmud was adamant, and his ministers were forced to hold out.   The Greeks should have a mild governor, and their grievances should be re-medied ; but they must first submit, and the powers must abandon the treaty.

MEMOIRS.   We came to the conclusion that the only course which offered a chance of our gaining the object of the treaty, with-out going to war, was a rupture of diplomatic relations and conse-quently the retirement of the three embassies.   In all likelihood the threat of such a measure would be sufficient to bring the Porte to terms, but of course, if menace failed, we should have to give it a real effect by our departure.   Fail it did ; and we had no alternative but to ask for our passports.   The Porte refused to grant them, and we were consequently obliged to run the risk of being stopped at the Dardanelles.

On 8 December, 1827, I embarked on board a small merchant vessel previously hired for the purpose.   My wife went with me. Our companions were numerous—secretaries, attachés, consuls, interpreters, followed by our respective servants.   We had to walk a considerable way through the town.   It was already dark when we started.   It blew hard from the north, and rained plentifully.   We had the streets in consequence to ourselves ; there was no hindrance to our exodus, and the wind, though strong, was favourable.   The French ambassador had weighed anchor an hour or two before us, but we passed him in the night and were the first to reach the Dardanelles.   On our way down the Straits our vessel grounded, although it was then broad daylight, but she was soon floated again, and we passed on gently towards the inner castles, one of which may be supposed to have replaced the tower whence Hero was wont to welcome her youthful swimmer.   Here we had to encounter the officers of the custom house, and here, if mischief was intended, we should have to undergo an awkward detention. It was desirable to keep the inspecting officer on deck, and with

L 2

that view, chairs were placed, and coffee prepared. While he was
thus amused, I got into a boat, and waited on the Pasha, who
treated me as a mere English traveller with becoming hospitality.
The windows of his Excellency's apartment looked out upon the
water, and when I saw that our vessel had cleared the line of his
guns, I told him who I was, and explained the circumstances under
which I had left Constantinople. He took my communication
with Turkish gravity, and personal good-humour. It looked as if
he had received orders to let us pass; but perhaps he had been
left in ignorance and only gave us the benefit of his government's
silence. We had scarcely cleared the Dardanelles when we were
told to be on our guard, as pirates were supposed to be in the
neighbourhood. The warning was thrown away upon us, for our
vessel was not armed, and I doubt whether there was a single gun,
pistol, or cutlass on board. Our business evidently was to push
on, and we were fortunate enough to reach the Gulf of Smyrna
without accident or alarm. A royal frigate was waiting for us
there.

The flags of the consuls were ordered to be struck, and
England, France, and Russia disappeared officially from the
Levant. On arriving at Corfu, Canning found that his conduct "during an eventful period," so far as known, had received "his Majesty's entire approbation." Every step he
had taken was fully endorsed by his government, although
the lamented death of Mr. Canning had deprived the Greeks
of their warmest advocate, and the ambassador of not only a
beloved kinsman but of a type of statesmanship which had
always impressed him with the deepest respect and admiration.
The only point to be ascertained was what view was taken of
the final rupture with the Porte, and to satisfy himself in this
respect he journeyed home from Ancona.

CHAPTER IX.

THE LIBERATION OF GREECE.

1828–1832.

ON reaching London, Canning found that there was no sign
of disapproval, either as to Navarino or the rupture of diplomatic relations with the Porte, on the part of King or
government. The Ministry of the day was a curious mixture
of Tories and Canningites, with Wellington at its head, and

like all coalitions was deplorably weak. The European situation was one of the utmost gravity; Russia had declared war against Turkey, upon no valid grounds whatever, and in defiance of the Treaty of London, which precluded separate action by any of the three contracting parties; yet the British government stirred never a finger. Lord Dudley, feeling the temporary nature of his position, shirked responsibility; and when Canning ventured to urge upon the Duke himself the absolute necessity of coercive measures, in the interests both of Greece and of Turkey, Wellington would not hear of such a policy. A French army and a British fleet would have brought the Porte to reason, and deprived Russia of any pretext for continuing the war; but the government objected to anything like strong measures.

English interest and credit, as well as the cause of Greece, had suffered a disastrous loss in the death of George Canning. The firm hand and clear eye had deserted the Foreign Office, and "the measures adopted to coerce the Sultan were timid, desultory, and dilatory. A bold and prompt declaration of the concessions which the Allies were determined to exact in favour of the Greeks would have been the most effectual mediation. When Russia declared war with Turkey, England ought instantly to have recognised the independence of Greece, and proceeded to carry the Treaty of 6 July into execution by force. As France would in all probability have acted in the same manner, the consent of the Sultan would have been gained, and a check might have been placed on the ambition of Russia by occupying the Black Sea with an English and French fleet." [1]

Some allowance must be made for the inevitable confusion of a period of transition, and there is no question that the Duke had a difficult task on his accession to office; but the real obstacle to an energetic policy in the East lay in the character of Wellington himself, and that of Lord Aberdeen, who succeeded Dudley at the Foreign Office when the "friends of Mr. Canning" went out in 1828. There is no need here to enlarge upon the defects of the Duke of Wellington as a statesman. The caution or timidity of his foreign policy was seen at its worst in connexion with the Greek question, and unfortunately in Lord Aberdeen he found a colleague at the Foreign Office only too ready to follow his hesitating steps.

[1] Finlay, vii. 25.

One of the first acts of the new government was to recall Admiral Codrington, not on account of any mismanagement at Navarino, but because he had allowed certain Egyptian ships to return to Alexandria with, it was alleged, a number of Greek slaves on board. Into the merits of the controversy it is not necessary to enter, but the effect upon the world in general and the Turks in particular was to declare that England would countenance no more exhibitions of force.

The change of policy which followed the death of George Canning is well marked in the words which occur in a letter from Lord Aberdeen to Stratford dated 20 December, 1828 :— " We may differ with respect to the Treaty of 6 July itself ; . . . but as the Government have honestly resolved to carry it into execution, *so far at least as they think the country is bound, and as may be consistent with its interest*" &c. Here we see the difference between the policy of Mr. Canning and that of Aberdeen. Canning went into the Greek question with enthusiastic zeal, and wished to carry out the July treaty, in its entirety and to the fullest extent, for the benefit of the Greeks : Aberdeen only thought of executing the treaty so far as he was absolutely bound, and sought to give it the smallest scope compatible with written engagements. The one took up the business with his whole heart, the other merely as an awkward inheritance from a previous government; the one resolved to make a working settlement of the question, the other only tried to get out of it as creditably as he could. How this change affected the pacification of Greece will be seen in the sequel. At present it is only necessary to remark that when the government abandoned George Canning's vigorous policy, they shewed a singular want of foresight in retaining the services of his cousin. It was not to be expected that the ambassador would at a word throw overboard all the convictions which he had learned by long experience in the east and close intercourse with his distinguished cousin ; and the result of employing a bold plenipotentiary to carry out a timid policy soon brought embarrassment upon the government. Had it rested with Lord Aberdeen alone, the Greek question might have long waited its solution. Fortunately for the Greeks, France decided to take action. Canning would greatly have preferred a joint expedition, but a French army in the Morea was better than nothing, and finally Marshal Maison was despatched to Greece with 20,000 men.

Meanwhile the three ambassadors were instructed to meet and draw up a plan for the settlement of Greece. Their instructions were of the vaguest possible description. They were to investigate and determine the various questions on the spot. The principal points to be settled were the tribute to be paid by the new Greek state to the Sultan, the compensation to be made to the ousted Turkish landholders, the amount of control to be exercised by the Porte over the appointment of the Greek government, and, most important of all, the delimitation of the frontier. On this last head the government gave no opinion ; four widely different frontiers were mentioned as having been put forward, one of which was drawn as far north as from the Gulf of Volo to the mouth of the Aspropotamos, while another limited the new Greece to the Morea, yet the Conference declared, with singular impartiality, that they all " in a considerable degree possess the requisite qualities," which they took to be that " the frontier should be clearly defined and easily defensible." A hint, however, of a boundary running through northern or continental Greece was to be traced in a reference to the facilities of delimitation afforded by " deep ravines " and "abrupt ridges of mountains." A " large proportion of the Greek Islands " were also probably to be included in the new state, but while fixing an arbitrary line of latitude and longitude within which the insular boundary (including chiefly the Cyclades) might be traced, it was allowed that "some deviation " might be necessary. The main point was to "include a fair proportion of the Greek population who have been in actual insurrection against the Porte." It will be seen presently that a good deal turned upon the interpretation of these instructions. Vague as they were, they were quite sufficient for the purpose that they were intended to effect—to obtain accurate information on the spot ; but if the British Government had meant them to include strict limitations capable of controlling the decisions of the plenipotentiaries, they should have worded them very differently.

On 8 July, 1828, Canning started alone for the scene of negotiation. He journeyed rapidly by Paris, the Simplon, and Ancona, to Corfu, where he spent a fortnight in collecting information and waiting for his French and Russian colleagues. He visited his old friend Sir Richard Church, the commander-in-chief of the Hellenes, at Mitica, opposite the island of Calamos, and anchored in the celebrated bay of Navarino.

I have just been making acquaintance with Ibrahim Pasha [he told his wife, 5 September]. Figure to yourself a fat short man, sitting like a Christian with his legs down, a large clear blue eye, a high forehead, a brownish-reddish beard straggling from beneath a face much marked with small-pox, and the whole appearance, in spite of shortness and corpulency, that of an active intelligent man, full of enterprize, subject to humours good and bad, and eager for instruction. Considering that he is on the point of being turned out of his province, bag and baggage, he was in excellent spirits. He shook me heartily by the hand, and *hobanobbed* with a glass of the admiral's Constantine. I left the admiral to settle all disagreeable business with him, before I made my appearance.

The ship is going round at this moment, and the rocks of Hydra are passing, as in a magic lantern, before the stern windows near which I am writing. Heavens! what a love must be that of liberty when it can be content to breathe on such a spot. Rock and houses, there is nothing else; not a blade of grass, not a spring of water; the wild Aegean at their doors, and a scorching sun, or the keen northern blast, tyrannizing by turns. Yet there is a worse tyranny, and that the freeman of Hydra avoids and defies.—This reflection brings me to the sense of an anxiety far greater than any which attends on sultry weather or greasy cutlets. Here is this poor country of Greece, mangled and panting, like a frog just torn from the jaws of a serpent, with scarce enough of life in its veins to make it capable of sustaining the preservation so miraculously offered to it. And there is Europe thrown out of its peaceful attitude by the effort of saving the poor victim, and exposed to chances which may prove fatal to its peace for years to come. And, further, there is the serpent, scotch'd but not slain, resigning its prey with sullen reluctance, while it grapples with one assailant and seeks to gain time from the others for scenting fresh means of resistance and oppression. Three ambassadors and the Greek President arrive to complete the picture! Four sapient noodles, duly instructed to cure the wounded, and to pacify the fighting parties.—Now would your Strat. give all that he possesses, save conscience and his E., to effect his share—which you see is a fourth—of this mighty work. But alas! it is to no purpose that he beats his brains below in the cabin, and wears out the quarter-deck with arguments and theories; a dark cloud rests on the horizon, and he can neither remove it nor see through it. It would be a comfort to him, to find other people more penetrating than himself; but no—everyone sees the necessity of going on, but no one can discover the end of the business. If he does not utterly despair, it is only that the case is every way so well worthy of a miracle that he may reasonably hope to see one wrought in its favour. Small comfort that the letter of his instructions may be speedily fulfilled, and he be at liberty to leave the scene of disaster. The mischief will in that case be too deep and too wide to admit of being counterbalanced by any selfish gratifica-

tion.—It is something to be sure that I have lived to see the starved
Egyptians crowding down to the beach for embarkation, and their
haughty chief endeavouring to drown the sense of humiliation in
wine and laughter. There is something also in seeing, what I see
at this instant, the rock of Hydra, stern and barren as it is, with
its opulent houses and busy population, surviving to bless the influence which has saved them from the destruction of Ipsera. I
thank God, dear E., for these events, and will endeavour to trust in
Him for the issue !

MEMOIRS. The task of laying the foundations of a new
Greece was rendered more difficult by the character and position, perhaps by the views also, of the man to whom we were
bound to look for information and assistance. Such as they were,
the powers of Greece were at that time centred in the person of
President Count Capodistrias. A Corfiote by birth, a Russian by
adoption, a liberal in politics, arbitrary by temperament, with much
to conciliate goodwill and much also to inspire mistrust, he stood
like a party-wall between the country he governed and those who
were commissioned to mature its independence. It was evident
that dislike to our interference overpowered his sense of its necessity and usefulness. The failure of our endeavours would have been
no disappointment to him. He let out occasional doubts of our
competency, and shewed a constant unwillingness to supply those
local statistics which he was best qualified to obtain and which we
required for the adoption of a sound and equitable opinion. It
became necessary to control the tendency of his mind by some
display of determination on our side. We gave a peremptory tone
to our requisitions, and for my part I did not hesitate to declare
that as Venice had been raised upon piles, so would we have papers
whereon to build the new state of Greece. Meanwhile the symptoms of returning peace grew stronger with every day, and it soon
became evident that a large portion of the French army could be
recalled without a shadow of imprudence. The remnant which
stayed in Greece after the retirement of Marshal Maison was quite
sufficient for any supposable contingency, and the confidence given
to France by her allies was fully justified.

One morning after a night of broken sleep I came to the resolution of calling upon my colleagues to give a formal character to
our repeated discussions and preparatory deliberations. Under the
pressure of this intention I rose from my cot, and sat down without
dressing to give it effect. I drew up a sketch in the form of articles
declaring our joint opinion on the several points which had to be
settled for the pacification of Greece. They were not many altogether, and those of most importance could be counted on the
fingers of the hand. It was clear that the relative situation of the
contending parties could only be one of total separation. The limits
of independent Greece and its form of government were the questions of most difficulty. The Greeks were comparatively few and

poor: how could they support a royal court with all its attendant circumstances? Yet they had need of an imposing authority,
of a government adapted to their wants, their weaknesses, their
passions, and their obligations, capable at once of fostering their
good and restraining their evil tendencies, of forming them into a
community progressive by means of industry and inoffensive on
principle. In their existing condition, democratic or republican
forms were little calculated to secure their internal peace, to conciliate the goodwill of their neighbours, or to win for them the
confidence of Europe. I did not therefore hesitate to recommend
a kingly form of government, subject of course to constitutional
limitations, not to be drawn too closely at first, but capable of a
generous though gradual enlargement—foreseeing, as no one could
fail to foresee, that the crown would have to descend on the brows
of a foreign prince to the extinction of all envenomed rivalries at
home.

The question of territorial extent was of necessity subject in a
greater degree to the will of that power from whom the sacrifice
would have to be exacted. Every state is naturally averse to any
curtailment of its dominions, and the Sultan was urged by a religious motive to maintain, if possible, the integrity of his. A
cession of territory would, moreover, be doubly repugnant to his
feelings when made in favour of subjects to be set up at his very
door in all the pride of triumphant rebellion and under the protection of Christian powers allied with his normal and ever-
encroaching enemy. If peace and a suspension of the Eastern
danger were the chief objects to be attained, we were bound in
reason to put some measure to our demands. We were not at
liberty to take for our only guides the admiration of Greek genius
and a sympathy compounded of religion and benevolence. Such, I
felt sure, were the sentiments prevailing in Downing Street, and
therefore both duty and prudence appeared to circumscribe my
sphere of action. In this way I came to the conclusion that if the
future territory of Greece included to the north the sites of Ther-
mopylae on one side, of Actium on the other, and to the south and
east the Morea together with those islands where a Greek population
abounded, as much would be obtained as the London Conference
was likely to approve, or the Ottoman authorities could be persuaded to accept.

The meeting I had proposed took place on an early day. My
initial sketch was taken as the groundwork of a more elaborate
arrangement. I agreed with my colleagues that we should each
endeavour to shape a portion of the articles, and meet again without
unnecessary delay in order to compare our respective labours and
mould them into one consistent form. This was not to be done in
a moment, but still it was done, with such variations as further
discussion eventually suggested. The idea of a kingdom maintained
its ground. And so did that of a total separation between the Greek

and Turkish populations. The territorial allotment on the contrary
underwent a considerable change. The French ambassador gave it
as his opinion that the northern line of frontier should be extended
to the mountain range which divides Thessaly from the district or
province of Zeitoun. His main argument in support of this proposition was geographical, and he was well entitled to attention by
his scientific and practical knowledge in that department. He had
published a map of Greece, and urged moreover that on the grounds
of resources and separation the further line of boundary was desirable. His reasons, I thought, deserved to prevail, and therefore
I consented to the amendment for which they pleaded. Such was
the conciliatory spirit which reigned in our counsels and finally
brought them to a harmonious and efficient close.

The various questions connected with the new state of
Greece had thus been settled by the Poros Conference, on the
whole, to the satisfaction of the Greeks, and the settlement
would, it was expected, be adopted by the superior Conference
in London. It remained to give effect to this decision by obtaining the assent of the Porte. Overtures had already been
made by the Reis Efendi and the Seraskier of Roumelia, and
letters had passed between them and the plenipotentiaries of
Poros, and also the Duke of Wellington. The Duke and Lord
Aberdeen were anxious to get the ambassadors back to Constantinople at almost any cost, in order to counteract the
effects of the Russian war. It was to the last degree important to prevent the czar from obtaining the advantages of a
predominant position in the mediation on behalf of Greece,
and nothing could be done till the English and French ambassadors had returned to their palaces at Pera. Canning
was waiting at Naples to learn the results of the communications then passing between the Porte and the allied courts.
Should the Sultan admit the mediation under the Treaty of
London, and proclaim an armistice—the necessary preliminary to pacification—a return to Constantinople would be the
consequence.

It was not however his fate to return immediately to
the Porte. A serious misunderstanding had arisen between
the ambassador and his chief, the Foreign Secretary. Lord
Aberdeen disapproved of the action of the three plenipotentiaries in prolonging the blockade of the island of Crete, and
was still more opposed to the boundary which they had recommended for the new kingdom of Greece. This was traced
from the Gulf of Volo to that of Arta, and this frontier
was approved by the French and Russian governments. The

British Cabinet however had made up its mind to limit the
new state to the Morea and the Cyclades. How or when
they came to this decision it is not easy to determine. The
joint instructions to the plenipotentiaries of Poros admit
several lines in Northern Greece, and by a reference to ranges
of mountains seem to encourage the adoption of a boundary
not very different from that recommended by the plenipotentiaries. From July to November, the public despatches
contain no modification of this instruction. The London
Conference very properly admitted that it was not in a position to form definite opinions on the matter until it received
the report of the Poros plenipotentiaries, and several points
of ignorance in the British memorandum attached to the
Protocol of 16 Nov. confirmed this admission. Lord Aberdeen, however, very soon began to cultivate doubts as to the
extension of Greece beyond the Morea. On 26 July he wrote
privately to Canning : " If after all we are compelled to give
up Athens, it will be a cruel sacrifice, but I foresee the possibility of such being the case," and on 18 November he
finally communicated the positive decision of the British
cabinet that Greece should comprize nothing north of the
isthmus of Corinth. It may well be asked what right the
English cabinet had to formulate decisions of this kind pending the sitting of conferences with allies on the very subject ;
and even if they had the right, what grounds had reached
them to modify the statement often repeated (even as late as
20 Dec.) that they could decide nothing till they had the report
from Poros. Whatever they had received in the way of
information from Canning tended in the opposite direction
from their verdict. What then was their reason ? The
answer is clear enough. Fear of Russia dominated their
actions, and they were convinced that the new Greece would
be, if not wholly under the influence of Russia, at least sufficiently so to be irrevocably hostile to England. They had no
intention of making a working state out of the new Greece ;
they wished barely to carry out the letter of the Treaty of
London, and were not inspired by the spirit which had created
it. To pacify Greece and put an end to the troubles of the
Levant in the cheapest and most perfunctory manner, so as
to curry favour with the Sultan and recover some of that
influence which the action of Russia threatened to destroy,
was all they would attempt. Lord Aberdeen considered the
separation of the Morea "a sufficient execution of the Treaty "

—he did not say a satisfactory execution, but merely a sufficient one, just enough to save appearances.

Under these circumstances Canning had to decide a serious
question. Could he continue to represent a government with
whose views he was at variance? Could he consent to undo
at Constantinople the work which he had done at Poros? It
was obvious that he could not use his personal influence to
this end without loss of character. The only possible terms
on which he could proceed to Constantinople to recommend
the decisions of his government would be these : That the
Allies should agree on a fixed settlement of the Greek question, with no latitude for separate influences, and that he
should be called upon merely to act with his colleagues of
France and Russia in placing before the Porte a decision on
which he had to express no opinion and for which he had to
employ no personal and separate pressure.

Lord Aberdeen's reply however to this suggestion left
Canning no alternative. The Foreign Secretary wrote :-

The two ambassadors are charged to make certain propositions
to the Porte, founded upon the terms agreed to at Poros; but with
an injunction to weigh and examine the objections which may be
urged by the Turkish government. No agreement whatever exists
between the three powers respecting the limits which they think
desirable for Greece, even if such limits could be obtained; while
the opinion of the British government is strongly expressed, and is
annexed to the same Protocol, that the terms proposed as the basis
of the negotiation are in the highest degree improper and unjust.
It is obvious, therefore, that any objections made by the Porte will
be admitted as valid by the British government; but it would
undoubtedly be too much to expect from you, that you should
labour with zeal to destroy at Constantinople, what you had constructed with so much pains at Poros. Yet this will be the main
object of the British minister, so far as the question of limits is concerned. . . . I therefore can entertain no doubt that, according to
the conditions specified in your letter, you would not feel yourself
disposed to attempt the performance of such a duty as would be imposed upon you at Constantinople. I have thus, in consequence,
considered your letter as a conditional resignation of your present
situation. It would have been much more agreeable to me to have
placed under your view the actual state of the affair, and to have
obtained, specifically and finally, your decision. But adverting to
the clear statement in your letter, and feeling the urgency of the
moment, especially with reference to the French government, I
have thought it best to decide at once, instead of incurring the
delay of six weeks, by waiting for answers from Naples before

anyone could be despatched from this country. My brother [Sir R. Gordon] will therefore leave London immediately and will proceed from Naples to Constantinople. I could certainly have wished that the whole of this question should have been concluded by yourself, and that you might have found it consistent with your own views, to have assisted in the execution of the wishes of the government, but I am perfectly willing to do justice to the motives by which you have been influenced. Although we have unfortunately differed in opinion upon some parts of this question, no man is more sensible of the great ability and indefatigable zeal which you have displayed.

Canning's reception of this curious epistle was characteristic. "When I had read half of it," he told a friend, "I threw it on the ground and stamped upon it. But I picked it up again and read the rest; and then I thanked my God that the government did not *dare* to ask me to do such work as they had given that fellow Gordon." His polite acquiescence in their decision followed as a matter of course. But the double policy of the Government caused him unbounded astonishment. Writing to Planta on 27 April, he said :—

The true object of regret is not that I escape returning to Constantinople to play a double part, to eat up my words, and afterwards either to take part in a wretched result, or to be suspected of not having been zealous enough in trying to bring it about, but that government takes such a line in the business as to make it impossible for me to continue the negotiation with tolerable consistency or a fair prospect of conducting it to any issue satisfactory at once to them and the public at large. I have already told you what I think of the course which they are adopting, but which they will find it difficult to adhere to—and I can only say that I see no reason to alter my opinions. I would at this moment most willingly go to Constantinople, if government were to find sufficient motives (as I cannot but think they will before long) for acting in a resolute straightforward manner.

The prophecy came true, but not of that government. It was not until Palmerston took over the command of the Foreign Office that Canning was sent to Constantinople to carry into effect the proposals which he had recommended all along. In the meanwhile, for nearly three years the Greek question knew him no more. On his return to England he was given the Grand Cross of the Bath, and disappeared for a while from the diplomatic world. Moreover, his long-desired opportunity for parliamentary work had come at last, and he exchanged the dignity and emoluments of an ambassador for the hazardous enjoyment of a seat in the House of Commons. What concerns this phase of his career must be reserved for the next chapter, and the Greek boundary question must be brought to an end—an end, by the way, which was really so far final, that it lasted unchanged for half a century by his special mission to Constantinople in 1831-2.

A very few words will explain what had happened in the interval. Sir Robert Gordon and General Guilleminot had presented to the Porte the proposals of the Protocol of the London Conference of 22 March 1829 with the result that Canning had anticipated. As it was known that England had her own views about the frontier, differing from those stated in the Protocol, the Porte of course insisted on a narrower boundary, and the Morea was agreed upon, as forming with the Cyclades a sufficient territory for Greece. Then followed exactly what any foreseeing statesman might have predicted. Russia, having brought Turkey to her knees at Adrianople, September 1829, insisted on the literal execution of the Protocol of March, or, in other words, of the Poros proposals, and thus acquired what she wanted, the leading position in behalf of Greek freedom. To this move the English and French Governments replied by a counter-effort at popularity—by proclaiming Greece independent and offering the crown to Prince Leopold, who accepted and afterwards declined it. A compromise of a very unsatisfactory nature was arrived at as to the boundary, and Greece meanwhile was torn in pieces by factions. Under these circumstances, in the autumn of 1831, Lord Palmerston proposed that Canning should go on a special mission to Constantinople, to obtain an additional extent of territory for the new and independent state of Greece. Being, however, in parliament at the time, and taking a lively interest in home politics, he was not inclined to embark in a distant and probably a lingering enterprize ; the chances of ultimate success were by no means promising, and he begged to be excused ; but friends were urgent that he should accept, and " my own conscience suggested that the cause of Greece had further claims on my exertions."

Canning proceeded by way of Corinth and Nauplia ; but he approached the shores of Greece in no very hopeful mood. He wrote to his wife from on board H.M.S. *Actæon* at sea, 17 December 1831 :—

It grieves me to the heart to say that I hear nothing good of the Greeks, as we approach their shores. No fresh crimes, and that is all. But disunion, and party hatred, and political intrigue carried to the worst extremes. The Scripture expression—" to the Greeks foolishness "—is for ever running in my head, and I am at times half-persuaded that they labour under a curse. Most certain it is that in spite of their heroic resistance to the Turks, their hairbreadth escape, and marvellous good fortune in establishing their independence, they do seem to want what is requisite to make a people and a government of them. And there are plenty of enemies of theirs and ours to note and to take advantage of their weakness. What, then, can I hope to do for them? Alas! I dare not trust myself with answering the question, and my only hope is that Providence may possibly choose to glorify itself by employing the weakest of its instruments in effecting the general good.

He was received with enthusiasm. The patriots one and all hailed him as the saviour of their country. Letters from Mavrocordatos, Tricoupis, Zographos, and others attest the delight which they felt at his arrival. He had not come a moment too soon. The dissensions among the leaders and the foreign residents threatened to overturn the new state which had been created after so much labour and so many expedients. It was doubtful whether the country would hold together till the king arrived to take possession of his thorny crown.

MEMOIRS. The War of Independence, which left such melancholy traces of its fury, had ceased. Turk and Greek were at peace with each other, but Greek was at war with Greek. The Morea freed from its turbaned oppressor was the scene of civil conflict. Two hostile parties were in presence, one composed of the local natives headed by Colettes, whose main strength lay in his mountain followers, of more than doubtful character ; the other having the prestige of government, but also more of the foreign and doctrinal element than suited the wild habits and lawless notions of the Pale-chairi and their chief. Colettes had served in the court of Ali Pasha of Janina, no very strict school of morality ; he was in high credit with the French, and a reputation by no means undeserved for bravery and intelligence gave him a plausible title to their support. The ruling President of Greece was Count Agostino Capodistrias, a younger brother of Count John, who had fallen not long before by the hand of an enthusiastic assassin. His abilities were not of a superior cast, and his leaning towards Russia, though it procured him the favour of that power, diminished what little claim he possessed to the confidence of his country. The influence of England was exerted to prevent a collision between the adverse forces, but it made no impression on the Government, and, right or wrong, the

insurgents held out for the redress of their grievances. Some skir-
mishing took place near Argos, and there was bloodshed, but not
enough to produce any positive result. Walking one day for exercise on the road to Argos I met a horseman with blood streaming
down his leg. "What has happened to you, my friend?" said I,
and his answer was "There is war, sir!"—and war indeed there was,
of that kind which checks all wholesome progress, without creating
any remedial energy. Very sad, I thought; but what could be
done? I added my efforts to those of Mr. Dawkins. All was unavailing. The Government, if it deserved that name, had no ears
for any suggestion coming from beyond its own restricted circle.
Finally, an appeal to the Conference in London was my only resource. I drew up a statement of what I had urged in vain upon
the President's consideration, and, after sending it to Lord Palmerston, resumed my journey to Constantinople.

A sentence from a letter from Lord Palmerston shews
that more had been accomplished by his mediation than he
thought :—" The Conference are delighted with what you did
in the Morea, and all agree how lucky it was that you should
have dropped down there at the moment you did."

Pursuing his journey by way of Athens he arrived at Constantinople on his third mission to the Porte, on 28 January,
1832. He found Stambol more tolerant of Christians than
of yore, and when he had his audience of the Sultan, he
was surprized to find the old humiliating etiquette abolished,
and various new and improved features introduced into the
ceremony. The guards presented arms to the Elchi for the
first time, the Sultan held a friendly conversation with him
instead of the old rule of set speeches, and even the
staff of the embassy came in for the imperial notice. Such
things had never before been known. "The ancient feeling
of affection towards Great Britain," reported the pleased ambassador, "has greatly revived in the Court and partly in
the Cabinet of Constantinople."

Agreeable as all this was, Canning did not see his way to
inducing the Turks to enlarge the boundaries of Greece. It is
a religious principle with them never to cede territory, except
under the pressure of positive necessity; the Greeks were the
last to whom they would willingly make a sacrifice of that
kind. To sell any portion of the land acquired by their
ancestors under the shade of the Prophet's banner is, in their
view, a shame and a sacrilege. Moreover, the amount of
purchase-money to be paid by Greece in return for the required
cession was limited, and of little value but what it derived

M

from the guaranty of the Allies. The only hope was to rouse
the fears of the Sultan in some other direction. It happened
that the ambitious career of the Egyptian Viceroy Mohammed
Ali was at that time exciting Mahmud's alarm and jealousy,
and Canning resolved to seize upon this means of influencing
his stubborn Majesty. To reach his private ear, he employed
a discreet, if not very honest, Greek, one Vogorides, who
afterwards rose to be governor of Samos, but who was happy
in these earlier days to be the channel of the Ambassador's
communications with the Sultan. The physician of the
embassy was employed as a secret go-between, and thus the
matter was kept entirely out of the ears of the regular interpreters. One of Canning's letters to Dr. MacGuffog (30 March)
is worth quoting, since we find in it for the first time an
expression of those hopes of Turkish reform which afterwards
became so prominent a part of the creed of the Great Elchi :—

Instead of having my feet in hot water, I am sitting up to the
chin in ink. A messenger came in from England this morning and
has given me as much to do as my ride hitherto enables me to
digest. It is now your turn to be tormented. Let our friend know
of the messenger, and tell him that I cannot give him a greater
proof of confidence than by sending him the enclosed bulletin.
Read it over to him, and if he wishes it, let him take notes of its
contents, but I should not like him to have a copy of it.

Your next object,—illustrious Plenipo. !—must be to learn the
impression made on our friend's mind by the conversation of yesterday, and to ascertain what he has done, or means to do in the way
of reporting. . . . I repeat that these delays are ruinous. Tell him it
is because I want to see the Porte more free to advance his present
system of improvement—favourable alike to the preservation of her
own power, and to the happiness of her Christian subjects,—that I
am anxious for her to lose no time in coming to an agreement with
us.—I want to see her in a situation to receive the full tide of European civilization, to enlist the whole force of the country in support of its independence, to take her proper place in the general
councils of Europe, and to base her military and financial systems
on the only true foundations of security for persons and property.
Beg of him to reverse this picture, and to imagine the Sultan wasting
the remains of his strength in civil war with Egypt, alienating himself from his natural and most tried friends by rejecting their proposals, making himself unpopular at home by half-measures of
innovation, without carrying them far enough to acquire confidence
and sympathy abroad, and left to struggle as best he may in the
toils which cunning aided by superior discipline has wound so
dexterously around him. I say that it would be better for him to
revive the Janissaries, to resume the turbans and pelisses of ancient

times, and to demand the restoration of Greece. The choice lies
between *fanaticism* and *discipline*; there is no middle line.

MEMOIRS.   The Sultan in his way fought as hard with me behind the scenes, as his ministers did with my colleagues and me in
front of them. An appearance at least of concession in some particulars became a necessity. I yielded to the pressure so far as to consent that the new frontier line of Greece should be shortened, without
receding, by having its termini east and west, at the respective
Gulfs of Volo and Arta ; the waters of both being thrown open to
the trade and vessels of either state. This arrangement, to speak
truly, involved a very small sacrifice, and with it the permanent
advantage of a more complete separation.

As soon as my understanding with the Sultan was complete,
there remained the task of making its result acceptable to my colleagues, and working it with their concurrence and with that of the
Turkish plenipotentiaries, into the form of a regular convention. To
accelerate these operations, a little innocent stage effect,—what the
French would call a ' coup de théâtre '—was brought into play.
In the midst of one of our joint conferences, a messenger direct
from the palace suddenly made his appearance, and announced the
Sultan's desire that we should agree to that conclusion, which
really seemed to promise satisfaction to all parties. Such an intimation could obviously have no binding effect on the representatives
of the Alliance, but it created a general inclination to seek the
solution of all remaining difficulties in a fair consideration of his
Majesty's wishes. Thus it was that we at length reached our goal.
The several points of agreement were thrown into a conventional
form, and a final meeting was appointed for signing the document.

We fondly imagined that the cup and lip were now brought
into contact, and that any apprehension of further disturbance
would be entirely misplaced. Our place of meeting was an Imperial kiosk on the European side of the Bosphorus, half way
between Therapia and Yeniköi. We entered upon business soon
after ten o'clock one morning, and broke up at three the next.
There was an interval for dinner, and no doubt the pipe as usual
played its part. The rest of the sixteen hours passed away on
wings laden with cavil, expostulation, and complaint. Our Musulman antagonist [Suleyman Nejib Efendi] began by opening a fire
of small shot upon our lines. From mere politeness we gave way
on matters of no essential consequence : he took courage, and
endeavoured to wring more serious concessions from us. Our
refusals provoked him ; he was reminded that we had met to sign
and not to dispute. He declared that he would rather cut off his
right hand than put his signature to such a convention. We took
the liberty of telling him that if he cut off one hand, he would still
have to sign with the other. At last it became necessary to threaten
him with the Sultan's indignation. Even the fear of that peril did

M 2

not immediately subdue him. Weariness and despair at length
came to our aid, and after sixteen hours' dispute the hateful convention received his signature, before the light of another sun had
fully risen upon its pages.

Such were the means, such were the slow and weary steps, by
which the new Hellas was lifted up to that great mountain ridge,
whence the eye of the traveller may range unchecked over the
pastures of Thessaly. Six and forty years have closed over that
memorable transaction. So long have the Greeks enjoyed the fertile
territory, which was then shaken out of the Sultan's grasp for their
benefit, and so long have they left the price of that cession a dead
weight on the resources of their confiding benefactors.

The main object of the mission was now accomplished, and
my thoughts were at liberty to prepare for an early departure, but
I could not of course embark without taking leave of the Sultan. I
I was given to understand that my final audience would be confidential, and that the occasion would be used to apprize me of his
Majesty's reliance on the good will of England, in case his relations
with Egypt should assume a hostile character. [In fact, direct proposals for a defensive alliance were mooted by the Sultan himself
in August.] I felt keenly the danger of saying too much or too
little. In one case, I might cause very serious embarrassment at
home; in the other, I might throw the Sultan at once into the
arms of Russia. Subsequently, when I had access to the Turkish
instructions, it relieved me from much anxiety to find that they
tallied entirely with the language I had held. Whatever pledge
was implied in that language, I amply redeemed, by submitting to
my chief the expediency of sending a small squadron to keep watch
over the ambitious movements of Mohammed Ali. That no such
course was taken may or may not be regretted; but the truth is
that Lord Grey, our then Prime Minister, having no ships to spare
on the existing establishment, could not make up his mind to apply
to Parliament for more.

The audience went off as I had been led to expect. It took
place in the Palace of Istavros Serai on the Asiatic side of the Bosphorus. The Caliph was extremely gracious. For the first time
he received me on his legs. None of his ministers was present.
At the close of our political conversation, he caused me to be invested with his Grand Order; the insignia being his portrait in
miniature, attached to a gold chain and set in diamonds. I never
saw him again, but the outlines of his character and person, as they
appeared to me in his life-time, may here find an appropriate place.
It may be said that a sovereign is always sitting for his picture.
From me Sultan Mahmud shall have neither malice or flattery.

Resolution and energy were the foremost qualities of his mind.
His natural abilities would hardly have distinguished him in
private life. In personal courage, if not deficient, he was by no

means superior. His morality, measured by the rules of the
Koran, was anything but exemplary. He had no scruple of taking
life at pleasure from motives of policy or interest. He was not
inattentive to changes of circumstance, or insensible to the requirements of time. There was even from early days a vein of of liberality
in his views, but either from want of foresight, or owing to a certain
rigidity of mind, he missed at critical times the precious opportunity
and incurred thereby an aggravated loss. His reign of more than
thirty years was marked by disastrous wars and compulsory
cessions. Greece, Egypt, and Algiers, escaped successively from
his rule. He had to lament the destruction of his fleet at Navarino.
On the other hand, he gathered up the reins of sovereign power,
which had fallen from the hands of his immediate predecessors;
he repressed rebellion in more than one of the provinces, and his
just resentment crushed the mutinous Janissaries once and for ever.
Checked no longer by them, he introduced a system of reforms,
which has tended greatly to renovate the Ottoman Empire and to
bring it into friendly communion with the Powers of Christendom.
To him, moreover, is due the formation of a regular and disciplined
army, in place of a factious fanatical militia, more dangerous to the
country than to its foes. Unfortunately his habits of self-indulgence
kept pace with the revival of his authority, and the premature close
of his life superseded for a while the progress of improvement.
Mahmud when young had rather an imposing countenance; his
dark beard set off the paleness of his face, but time added to its
expression. His stature was slightly below the average standard,
his countenance was healthy, he wrote well, he rode well, and acquired a reputation for skill in archery. It may be said with truth,
that whatever merit he possessed was his own, and that much of
what was wrong in his character and conduct resulted from circumstances beyond his control. Peace to his memory!

I turned my back once more on the city of Constantine,
Nauplia lay in our way, and we sailed up the gulf, but with
no intention of making any stay in its waters. A deputation
was sent off to me, headed by Colocotrones, and composed of other
notables, more or less distinguished by their conduct or position.
After the usual exchange of compliments and news, I was requested to state my opinion as to what should be the policy of
Greece, when left to the enjoyment of its newly acquired independence. My first reply was an expression of surprize, that having
worked out their freedom at so much cost, they should look to a
stranger, however desirous to help them, for advice as to their
future course. They were not discouraged by the evasion, but
returned more pressingly to the charge. Finding it useless to parry
their advances any further, I said, that since they appeared to
value my opinion in good earnest, I would not withhold it, more especially as it might be conveyed to them in half a dozen words.

Your immediate business, I continued, is to repair the ravages of
war, to plough your lands, to build ships, and above all to increase
your families. Material prosperity is the true basis of moral and
political advancement; institutional securities come in their turn.
A strong hand is your first need. They smiled and thanked me,
but I much doubt their having given much heed in practice to my
counsels, frank and simple as they were. The convictions which
then possessed me on this subject have never varied, but the Greeks
do not see with my spectacles. Their *grande idée* is a pernicious
illusion. The Turkish Empire is not yet weak enough to become
their prey, but it may be used as their garden and field of productive industry. Grant them a natural ambition—they must still
employ the means required for its success. Efforts beyond their
strength, immoral enterprizes, exaggerated pretensions, can only
end in failure and humiliation. They have to strike root into a
soil which many stubborn conditions of their present existence
concur to circumscribe. They have to gather strength from without as well as from within. Their true policy consists in merit-
ing the confidence of Europe, and cultivating the good-will or
their neighbours, at the same time that they give free play to the
springs of internal progress, and uphold for their protection, the
authority of law in all its departments.

On Sir Stratford's return to England in September he
was welcomed by his wife with a new-born son in her arms.
His labours were greeted with applause on all sides. Palmerston wrote, " I congratulate you with all my heart upon
your safe return from your successful and brilliant mission ; "
and presently sent him the following official letter of royal
approbation :—

Upon the termination of your Excellency's embassy to the Sublime Porte, I have received the King's especial commands to signify to your Excellency his Majesty's gracious approbation of the
whole of your conduct during your official residence at Constantinople, and particularly during the course of the very arduous
negotiation which was trusted to your Excellency in concert with
the representatives of France and Russia for the improvement of
the boundary of Greece. His Majesty considers the success with
which that important negotiation has been crowned, to be mainly
attributable to the distinguished ability which your Excellency
individually has displayed in the conduct of it; and to the spirit
of conciliation by which you have been able during the progress of
discussions of tedious duration to maintain the harmony of the
three Powers, parties to the treaty for the settlement of Greece, and
to preserve unimpaired the friendly disposition of the Sultan towards Great Britain, even whilst you were inducing his Highness
to acquiesce in arrangements to which, although they were really

advantageous to him, his first impressions and personal feelings were naturally repugnant. It is with great pleasure that I find myself the instrument of conveying these gracious sentiments of his Majesty to the knowledge of your Excellency.

Hardly less pleasant was the news he received from David Morier of Talleyrand's approval :—

Sitting next to old Talleyrand yesterday at dinner at Lord Granville's, in my new and to me most unexpected character of plenipot., he informed me of the news just received of your complete success at Stambol. I can't express with what sincere delight I heard this _Doyen_ of European diplomacy speak with admiration of my old master, and attribute to your sole management so great a triumph in the science of negotiation.

MEMOIRS. The joy of returning to a peaceful home was enhanced by the kind approval with which I was greeted by Palmerston. He placed his hand upon my shoulder, and, to use his own words, said, " Canning, you are the man." How could I be otherwise than flat-tered by so expressive a welcome ? Yet, strange to say, a few weeks later, while I was still but the length of a single street, and that a short one, from his abode in Great Stanhope Street, he never disclosed the slightest wish to learn what I thought of the Greeks in their actual condition, or of what remained to be done, in order to place the administration of their country on a firm and suitable footing. His choice of a Bavarian lad to wear the crown of Greece, had nothing but the rarity of candidates to recommend it. The Regency constructed under his auspices could hardly have been formed of elements more incongruous and unpromising. The character of Prince Otho, which in later years operated so fatally on the interests of Greece, might easily have been ascertained from the books of the Jesuits by whom he was brought up, and without pretending to any peculiar sagacity, I could have pointed out the danger of setting up three Regents invested with coördinate powers. The Greeks had already broken into three parties, and they would be sure to paralyze the action of the Government by sowing disunion among its directors, one of whom was to be the nominal chief, _primus inter pares_, an object of jealousy to his colleagues, and himself exposed to the temptation of coveting a more than equal share of authority. There may have been reasons for incurring the hazards of a dis-tracted Regency, but if the measure was unavoidable, the results of that necessity are not the less to be deplored. To say the least, we were unfortunate in what was done for Greece, at a time when its future destinies were in the mould : nor were we more happy in what we declined to do for Turkey at the same decisive period. It followed upon the Sultan's disappointment, that in despair of getting help from England he turned with open arms towards Russia, and, come what might, accepted the aid of a Russian army encamped within the forts of the Bosphorus, and also within sight of his capital. The ground we then lost was indeed recovered some ten years later, but at no small expense, in the very teeth of France, and even at the risk of a general war.

CHAPTER X.

THE HOUSE OF COMMONS.

1828—32.

THE official life of Stratford Canning falls into two well-marked divisions. From the age of twenty to forty-two he was with but one considerable interval almost continuously engaged in diplomatic service. Then from the early part of 1829 to the close of 1841, with the exception of two brief special missiohs, he disappeared from the world of embassies and despatches. Then again from the beginning of 1842 to 1858 he was seldom absent for many months from the Porte. The first diplomatic period, 1807 to 1828 (with an appendix in 1832), comprised miscellaneous missions in different parts of the globe, unconnected by any fixed purpose, unless it were that of being quit of diplomacy at the first honourable opportunity. During this period Canning felt no special tie, no compelling sense of duty, towards any one Court or State. It was different with the second period, when he returned again and again to the city he liked so little, drawn almost against his will by the feeling that he might perchance be able to save Turkey from herself. This feeling gradually grew upon him, however, and there is no reason to suppose that he felt any peculiar link with the country with which his name is inseparably connected during the interval of work and rest in England which divided the first half of his career from the second. He had not yet discovered that his presence was essential to the Porte; it may be questioned whether he ever fully realized his own power in the East.

For rather more than twelve years his chief public interest was centred in the House of Commons. Whilst still ambassador he was elected member for Old Sarum in the spring of 1828.

MEMOIRS.   I was indebted for the seat to my father-in-law, Mr. Alexander, who jointly with his brother, the East India director, possessed the nomination at Old Sarum.   I cannot say that I was much attracted by the honour of representing the rottenest borough on the list.   But several considerations pleaded in its favour.   The seat was free of expense; it had been occupied by the best of patriots, Lord Chatham; it bound me to no party; and, whether I was the member or not, it would still be a close borough.   Moreover, it gave me the true constitutional position, as I understand it, of a member free to act on his own judgment, though, what is not so constitutional, it also relieved me from all responsibility to the constituent body.   My constituents were eleven in number.   They voted in obedience to their landlord.   Not one of them did I ever see.   Their votes, however, served to gratify a long-cherished wish of my heart.   But did they enable me to attain the object of that wish?   No; I cannot say that they did.   I was kept back by something under the name of shyness or timidity, and penury, I fear, of spirit "repressed my noble rage and froze the genial current of my soul."   It cost me a good deal to walk up the House.   To go above the gangway was for some time simply impossible.   I screwed up my courage to the point of speaking once in my first session; but the sentiment which inspired left my judgment to shift for itself, and the few sentences I pronounced in favour of a pension to Mr. Canning's widow had little to recommend them but a certain proud earnestness and warm devotion to his memory.   At later periods I overcame this weakness in part; but to this hour the remains of it hang like a wet swab round my thoughts, and smother in speaking the better half of my natural faculties.

This frank admission of his want of oratorical powers does not wholly account for Canning's failure to achieve a prominent place in the House of Commons.   Bad speakers may make excellent ministers.   But there was a second and more formidable obstacle to his success.   He was what was then the most hopeless thing in politics, a Liberal-Tory or a Constitutional Liberal, according to the side of the House from which the phenomenon is regarded.   He was not even strictly what was known as a " Canningite."   He belonged to what George Canning himself told him was " your favourite sect of the independents," and an independent member, unless he possesses peculiar gifts both of oratory and self-propulsion, is seldom a popular character with ministries.   The result was that the man who perhaps knew more about foreign policy than any other member of the House of Commons saw others his inferiors in knowledge and experience walk into high office, while he remained a private member, respected indeed and consulted by many of the most distinguished leaders, such as Stanley, Graham, and Sir Robert Peel, but with no more hope of office than if he were still at Stambol.

On his return to England, after his disagreement with Lord Aberdeen about the Greek frontier in the spring of 1829, he divided his time between close attendance in Parliament and quiet country life at Mr. Alexander's house at Somerhill. " Even in our ungenial climate," he remarked, " there is a mild and cheerful zone of life between the extremes of fox-hunting and place-hunting, where one may re-enact the dreamy enjoyments of the Roman poet :—

> Nunc veterum libris, nunc somno et inertibus horis,
> Ducere sollicitae jucunda oblivia vitae."—Hor. *Sat.* II. 6, 61.

In the midst of his rural pleasures he was summoned to London, in July 1829, to be invested with the Grand Cross of the Bath—the least honour that Government could recommend after his long services and the singular manner in which they had, for the time, been terminated. Old Sarum was represented in 1830 by its owners, the Alexanders, and after one or two unsuccessful canvasses of parliamentary boroughs Canning stood for Stockbridge, upon the Reform Bill dissolution of 1831, as " a very moderate reformer indeed "—so said the Government—and he admitted to his friends that he dreaded " a flood of reforming opinion that will sweep everything before it." Yet he saw that opposition was useless, and his address to " the worthy and independent electors of Stockbridge " (who were about to pocket his thousand pounds) stated that he was " not unfriendly " to the principle of " safe and necessary reform " ; and in due course he voted for the Bill when the division was called. He was an eager attendant at the debates, though obliged sometimes to go to the House very early to secure a place. On 4 July he found 150 seats taken at 7 A.M. The crowd that thronged to hear the King's Speech on 21 June was dense :—

To his Wife, 21 June.

A line to you, dearest E., if I die for it, though it is within five minutes of the time when I must be in the House. *There* I have been already and was really squeezed to a mummy. Such a crowd ! and such a rush ! . . . My chief object in passing through so many dangers was to see, what is nowhere else to be seen but on a sign-post—a king with his crown on. Alas! I failed in my attempt.

I heard every word, or nearly every word, that his Majesty uttered ; but hearing was the only sense that was gratified. The Speech, too, sounded most dolorous—a series of disagreeable subjects, though the King pronounced it exceedingly well. How he was received by the populace I know not; but when I went out, after his departure, to thread the long string of carriages and passengers, I saw nothing but good-humoured faces, glowing under a sun which would have done honour to Stambol.

The month of July brought an event which to Canning was of even more moment than the passing of Lord John's Reform Bill by the Commons. His mother, his earliest and always constant friend, died on the 12th. His letters have shewn how deep was his love and reverence for her, and during the long correspondence which they maintained for a quarter of a century not a single word of discord can be traced. Mrs. Canning had seen much happiness since her early years of trouble were over. In her sons, one of whom she had often near her in the cloisters at Windsor, she had good reason to feel pride and satisfaction. The boys who had been left to her, with but doubtful prospects, had answered to her spirited call, and if one had died, it was on the most glorious of England's battle-fields. Her daughter-in-law, Lady Canning, to whom she was tenderly attached, was happily present to soothe her last moments. In spite of her advanced age—she was past 80—she retained her faculties to the end, and her loss was deeply mourned by all her children, but by none more than by her youngest and perhaps most beloved son Stratford. Some lines written long afterwards may come here, not because they display the writer's poetic powers at their best, but because they were written when the son was himself an old man of 90, and shew that nearly half a century of separation had not weakened his loving memory of his mother :—

> Dear saint, whose image, though long years have fled
> Since thou wast numbered with the viewless dead,
> Still with my heart's best treasures holds a place,
> Time fondly hallows, nor can e'er efface.
> I hail thee now, ere life quite ebbs away,
> And this last tribute to thy virtues pay,
>
> .   .   .   .   .
>
> For many a year one desolating trace
> Dimm'd the clear eye and marr'd the genial face ;
> For many a year the weeds of mourning told
> How love by sorrow harden'd grows not old.

But soon the tears not Heav'n itself could chide
And all foreboding cares were dash'd aside;
Thoughts nursed by hope thy bosom nobly stirr'd ;
What purpose flagg'd when Duty's call was heard ?

   .   .   .   .   .   .

Oh ! loved and honour'd ! to life's latest beat,
Dwell, e'en as now, in memory's faithful seat !
Oh ! type of those who most by worth excel—
In one dear word, my Mother, fare thee well !

While the member for Stockbridge was absent at Constantinople in 1832 his borough sank beneath his feet—in Schedule A of the Reform Bill. He had only spoken once in the House as its representative, and its loss did not affect him much. A very important event, however, had happened to him on his return from Constantinople : he was gazetted ambassador to the Emperor of All the Russias. The appointment gave the greatest pleasure to those who knew anything about foreign policy, but to the Court and Government of Russia the choice was exceedingly distasteful, and the Emperor took the unusual course of refusing to receive him. Various reasons were suggested for this embarrassing decision. It was said that Madame Lieven, the wife of the Russian ambassador in London, had taken some offence, and had revenged herself by intriguing against Sir Stratford's reception at Petersburg. We know that Canning's quick feelings and outspoken frankness were apt to make him enemies, and he was not a favourite of the lady who endeavoured to manage Russian affairs in England. Another ground was discovered in some alleged disrespect shewn by the ambassador to the Grand Duke Nicholas when at Petersburg in 1825, and this excuse was alleged by Count Nesselrode in an interview with Mr. Bligh, the English chargé d'affaires. There was only one objection to the plea, and that was the fact that the Grand Duke and the ambassador never met in 1825.

There was naturally considerable indignation, not only among Canning's friends, but in all who appreciated the depth and significance of the insult offered to England. It meant, first, that Russia thought fit to dictate to us what sort of ambassador we should send to Petersburg ; and, second, that the sort she would accept must not be one who knew too much about her proceedings in the East. The truth was that Sir Stratford's eye was much too keen to be suffered to explore the mysteries of the Russian Foreign

Office at headquarters: they were afraid of him, and with good reason. Still that was no argument for England to submit, and Palmerston stood to his guns for some time, declaring to Count Lieven that the Czar's conduct was " an outrageous piece of arrogance." However, it was finally decided to compromise the dispute by appointing no ambassador whatever, and thus to leave Russia in the humiliating position of receiving no more exalted representative of England than a chargé d'affaires (until 1835); a step which compelled the Czar to adopt a similar reduction in London, and to recall the Lievens. Canning naturally submitted to the decision of the Foreign Minister, but he demanded at the same time that his name and character should be vindicated, and that he should not be allowed to appear in the light of a discarded servant. Lord Palmerston recommended him for a peerage, but Lord Grey, while anxious to shew his thorough appreciation of the ex-ambassador's talents and services, had too many powerful claims on his hands to be able to entertain another; and from his successor, Lord Melbourne, Canning declined to accept any honour, though offered the governor-generalship of Canada. The peerage did not come till nearly twenty years later.

It was in the midst of the Russian *impasse* in 1832 that Lord Palmerston proposed that Canning should go to Madrid, and endeavour there or at Lisbon to make peace between the brothers Dom Pedro and Dom Miguel, who were then contending for the crown of Portugal, the former on behalf of his daughter Donna Maria. The mission was intended to be, as Palmerston phrased it, merely " an episode to Russia," and in Canning's letters of credence to the King and Queen of Spain he was styled "Ambassador to the Emperor of All the Russias." There is no need, however, to narrate in detail the negotiations which Canning conducted at Madrid; they were frustrated even before they had been begun. It appeared that Zea de Bermudez, who had been recalled from the Spanish Mission in London to preside over the Foreign Office at Madrid, had before leaving England made no secret of his intention to reject Lord Grey's proposals, and without Spain it was hopeless to influence the struggle in Portugal. It was also clear from the first audience that King Ferdinand did not believe a word of Lord Palmerston's assurances: his Majesty was pleased to regard the mission as an elaborate farce, and was obviously in sympathy with Dom Miguel;

while Queen Christina, inspired by more liberal views and moved by a feeling of interest for the young Portuguese princess whose situation bore so strange a resemblance to that of her own daughter, was all for Dom Pedro. On 5 May, 1833, the British proposals were definitely rejected, and the ambassador hastened to take leave. Palmerston, indeed, wholly satisfied with the way in which the negotiation had been conducted, offered him the ordinary embassy at Madrid, but neither the place nor the people he had to deal with had any attractions for him. He was not sorry to find himself back in England, though his position was singularly embarrassing. He had no seat in Parliament, and his appointment as ambassador to Russia was still an open question. In the absence of foreign employment, home politics engrossed a large part of his thoughts, and an unexpected invitation presently recalled him to public life.

MEMOIRS. The change of ministry which took place in the autumn of 1834 was followed by a dissolution of Parliament. Lord Althorp's elevation to the House of Peers on the decease of his father, Earl Spencer, had afforded the King an opportunity of substituting a Conservative for a Liberal government. The Duke of Wellington was first sent for, but subsequently Sir Robert Peel was charged with the construction of a new cabinet, and, until he could return from Italy, where he was travelling at the time, the seals of sundry chief departments were entrusted to the Duke, who paid a daily visit to the several offices, and exercised his judgment on the affairs which in each required immediate attention. Some little time before, Lord Melbourne's Cabinet had been weakened by the secession of four of its members, namely, the Duke of Richmond, the Earl of Ripon, Lord Stanley, and Sir James Graham. A question affecting Church property was the ostensible cause of their retirement from office. Their watchword and that of their friends at the election was *A fair trial for Peel*. I wished to obtain a seat in Parliament, but could hear of no suitable opening. . . . Judging from what passed at the famous Lichfield House meeting, I could anticipate no good from a government reconstructed by Lord Melbourne. I thought it would rest upon an unconstitutional basis, and that if I took part with an opposition capable of excluding it from power on principles of Liberal-Conservatism I should but perform my duty towards the public. As parties were likely to be almost balanced, an unusual value would necessarily attach to a single vote, and, oddly enough, though Peel on the meeting of Parliament was obliged to give way to superior numbers, Lord Melbourne in the end was in his turn upset by a majority of *one*.

We were then at Somerhill, and Lord George Bentinck was unexpectedly announced. The visit, I soon learnt, was to me; and when we were together alone, he told me that a seat was open at Lynn Regis, in Norfolk, which he had himself represented, and proposed that I should stand in concert with him as a candidate for that borough. We might have a contest, but he thought his friends were strong enough to carry my election as well as his own. There would be no bribery, the legal expenses would be small, I should be expected to support Lord Stanley, who was to act on the idea of giving Peel a fair trial, but in every other respect my votes would be free. The case was so clearly in accordance with my own views that I should have been justified in starting with him at once. I took, nevertheless, a few hours for consideration, and then, my first impression being fully confirmed, I set out with Lord George for Lynn. There we found a cordial welcome, and also an opponent in the person of Sir John Scott Lillie, a Middlesex magistrate of Radical politics. We had therefore to go through a regular canvass, calling personally on every one of our constituents, whose number amounted to more than eight hundred. Our party was a mixed combination of Liberal Tories and frightened Whigs. The most powerful interests opposed to us were those of Holkham, Lord Albemarle, and Sir William Fowkes. Our return was finally secured, and we were drawn triumphantly through the town with the usual display of flags and ribands.

When the session began I took my seat in the House near Lord Stanley below the gangway on the right of the Speaker's chair. On the first trial of strength, which was not long deferred, the new minister found himself in a minority, and was obliged to pass over to the Opposition benches. Lord Stanley and his friends retained their position, without making any nearer approach to the ministerial policy. As the debates proceeded it became more and more evident that there was no real difference between Lord Stanley's opinions and those of Sir Robert Peel, and it seemed to me that much and more than awkwardness would eventually arise from so marked a want of agreement between the appearance and the reality. Under this impression I wrote privately to Lord Stanley suggesting the advantages which he might derive from quitting an equivocal position and presenting to the public eye a party of Liberal constitutionists unmistakably united. He wrote me a friendly answer, but was not prepared to adopt my suggestion. It happened not long after that, in consequence of a taunting speech from O'Connell, he had to cross over to Peel's side while the House was sitting, and take his place among the Conservatives. The two distinguished statesmen had been brought together more by accident than by sympathy from opposite points of the political compass, and I have some reason to believe that they met for the first time in society at a dinner in my house in Grosvenor Square. With respect to Lord Stanley, I take this opportunity to remark that although he gave offence now and then by a sort of schoolboy recklessness of expression, sometimes even of conduct, his cheerful temper bore him out, and made him more popular than others who were always considerate but less frank. From the time when he made one with the Conservatives, Sir Robert took the lead at all their meetings, whether general or select. I was rarely absent from those of either kind, but I must in candour admit that I might as well have kept away. Though I took a lively interest in all that passed, and did not fail to form my own opinions, I never could overcome a certain diffidence as to taking part in any discussion, and consequently from first to last maintained an unbroken silence.

For seven years, 1835-42, Canning represented Lynn in the House of Commons. He was re-elected in 1837 after a close contest with Major Keppel, and for a third time in 1841, when he was unopposed. Now and then, rather against the grain, he was obliged to journey into Norfolk to take part in a loyal and constitutional dinner at which the members were expected to speak. As Lord George always spoke first there was not much for his colleague to add, and this was a relief to one who announced to his family that "the delivery of a speech is a most awful piece of business—depend upon it." This feeling too often prevailed in the House, where Canning would sometimes arrive armed with careful notes, and then retire without making the intended speech. He forced himself to speak now and then, however; asked questions, after the fashion of diffident members; and had the great satisfaction of calling O'Connell and Hume to order. Only four or five times in these seven years did he make any considerable oration. Twice he spoke at length (in 1836 and 1841) on the subject of the lawless occupation of Cracow, and his indignant protest brought a letter from Prince Czartoryski to thank him for the "noble zèle et l'habilité avec lesquels vous avez plaidé la cause de Cracovie." He attacked the Government roundly for their foreign policy, not only as regarded Cracow, but (in 1837) on the affairs of Spain. In 1838 he moved for a select committee on the seizure of the *Vixen* off the Circassian coast, and on a division was defeated by sixteen votes. But if he was not a shining light in debate, he could always be trusted to appear at a division. Four days in the week he refused all evening invitations in order to devote himself wholly to the business of the House. It is evident that his object, by this constant application to parliamentary work, was to fit himself for that employment at home which we have seen was his earliest desire and most constant ambition.

Society on a large scale had never any special attraction for
him, though the conversation of clever men and women was
a real enjoyment.

When Parliament rose he went into the country like the
rest of the world. We find him at one time living at Sutton
Place, a quaint old-fashioned house near Guildford ; at another
at Oxonhoth, a place belonging to Sir William Geary, which,
besides its own special merit of overlooking the Weald of
Kent, had the advantage of being only six miles distant from
Somerhill. A more lengthy expedition was made in 1836,
when, accompanied by his wife, Canning paid his first visit to
Scotland. This was before the days of railways, so that three
months were easily spent in moving leisurely from one country
house to another, sowing the seeds of many friendships which,
lasting through all the agitations and absences of the next
twenty years, blossomed again with renewed vigour when
Lord Stratford returned in his old age to settle at home.
He was one of the privy councillors who met on the eventful
20 June, 1837, and, like all who were present, was charmed
with the young queen's manner at her first council. He told
his brother :

I cannot better express my thanks for your bulletins about the
health of our good old departed King than by telling you that
nothing could be more satisfactory than the demeanour of our
young Queen at the Council this morning. She has really gained
everyone's good word by her modest self-possession and the excellent manner in which she delivered her declaration. I was present
and can honestly bear witness to the truth.

In 1839 he took his family abroad. He had now four
children, and the loss of his diplomatic pension—the necessary
consequence of holding a seat in parliament—made it desirable
to economize ; but there was another and a sadder reason
which led to this breaking up of the English home. Soon
after the return from Spain in 1834, while staying at Bognor,
the boy whose birth had crowned his happiness two years
before was taken suddenly ill, and, after struggling for many
days between life and death, recovered indeed, but only to be
a constant source of anxiety and care. The baths of Wildbad
in the Black Forest were recommended by the doctors, as well
as a subsequent residence in Italy ; but, though for a time the
change seemed to have a beneficial effect, gradually the bright
hopes faded away.

To have a son who, trained and modelled on his own ideal

N

of an English statesman, should perpetuate the name of the
man he honoured most—for in his boy he proudly hoped to
see a second George Canning—had always been his great ambition ; the prize seemed placed within his reach only to be
snatched away, for no other son came to fill the vacant place,
and none but the wife, whose patient faith helped him to bear
the burden, knew how heavy it was or how nobly it was borne.
Henceforth every fresh step in his career brought painfully
to his mind that he stood alone, and each time that he turned
from the busy public life to the quiet of private life it was
to miss more and more the son in whom all his chief interests
would naturally have centred.

The beginning of winter, 1839, saw them settled at Genoa,
where the best part of the next two years was spent by Lady
Canning, who found in the constant kindness of her many
Italian friends some compensation for her loneliness while her
husband was absent in London during the session of Parliament. A few extracts from his correspondence at this time
illustrate the political excitement of the time.

To his Wife, London, 4 May, 1841.

Our *crisis* here is more urgent than ever; and the votes of
Friday next will probably decide it. The Cabinet is beaten black
and blue, but life is not extinct, and Sandon, as Matador, is to give
the *coup de grâce*. Having been forced to give up their Irish Bill,
the Ministers presented their Budget, which we know they reckoned
upon as presenting something of a popular and saving character.
Out it came, and such a Budget was never yet seen ! Perhaps it
owes its singularity in part to the extraordinary circumstance of
its having been produced by a Chancellor of the Exchequer in the
middle of his honeymoon.

10 *May.*—These detestable Ministers, though killed in power
and character, still survive in place, and much do I grieve to say
that one, who ought by this time to have learnt better, is the principal cause of their tenacity. Yet do not think that they can escape.
At least, if they do, the country is doomed and they are immortal.
My belief is that they will be in a minority of from ten to twenty
on the next division—I mean the pending one relative to the sugar
duties, part of their Budget—and that they must then go, or dissolve, and that the latter alternative, though they still hesitate,
they will not venture upon. I may be deceived, but this is what I
expect. Their friends give them up.

ᴵ30 *Aug.*—Politically, all is right. The Ministers have resigned
gracefully, though late, and Peel has been to Windsor this morning.

From all that I can learn, there is every appearance of his acting judiciously and being able to justify the turn of public opinion in his favour. There is a good working majority of 80; and I really believe that the Queen, though regretting the chief at least of her late advisers, has made up her mind to act with fairness and sincerity towards their successors.

Personally, all is in the dark. I do indeed know some few of the forthcoming appointments; but in general Peel has kept his word of reserving himself till after his first interview with the Queen. I have been twitted with the tardiness of my arrival; but everyone admits that the diminution of such a majority by a single unit was of no consequence either to the state or to the party; and as for myself, I must have toiled and sacrificed to little purpose for the last six years if the present omission were to affect my interests.

His expectation of a place in the Conservative Government was doomed to disappointment. He had been passed over in 1834-5, when Peel formed his first short-lived administration, in which Canning had hoped to find office. Probably Lord Stanley's refusal to join the Government had something to do with this; but Sir Stratford's deficiency in debate might account for the omission. When Sir Robert came into power again in 1841 Canning's name did not appear in the list of ministerial appointments. They again offered him the Viceroyalty of Canada, which he did not want, and the Treasurership of the Queen's Household, which was not suited to his tastes and feelings of independence. He did not feel attracted by the routine of a Court appointment, and he did not wish to leave England. On the other hand, he was making no useful progress in the House of Commons, and his seat deprived him of his diplomatic pension. Under the circumstances he felt himself almost compelled to accept the offer of a return to his old embassy at Constantinople, and so in a doubting and not very hopeful frame of mind Sir Stratford Canning returned to Turkey, in the first month of the year 1842, there to make for himself a position, an influence, and a name, unparalleled in the annals of diplomacy.

CHAPTER XI.

THE GREAT ELCHI.

It was during his long reign at the Porte in the fifth and sixth decades of this century that Canning displayed those qualities and acquired that influence which have gained him the title of " the Great Elchi." It is only in England, however, that the words bear the special signification which Mr. Kinglake has made immortal. In Turkey every ambassador is styled *Buyuk Elchi*, or " great envoy," to distinguish him from an ordinary minister plenipotentiary. The Christians who dwelt under his protection used a much higher title when they spoke of their deliverer : they called him " the Padishah of the Padishah," the sultan of the sultan. But the term is nothing ; for the meaning is undisputed. What we understand in England by "the Great Elchi," what the Armenians and Nestorians and Maronites and other down-trodden sects meant by "the Padishah of the Padishah," what every victim of wrong or persecution in the most distant province of the Ottoman Empire appealed to when he used almost the only English name he had ever heard—in this there is no ambiguity. The various words were but synonyms to denote that unparalleled influence for right and even-handed justice which was exercised throughout every part of Turkey, in Asia as in Europe, by the Great Ambassador. An English nobleman who was journeying in the wildest parts of Asiatic Turkey in 1853 remarked how touching was the trustfulness with which people of all races and religions looked to the British palace at Pera for protection. Nestorians, Yezidis, Maronites, Druses, " and the dwellers in Mesopotamia, and in Judaea, Jews and proselytes, Cretes and Arabians," Christians and Musulmans, one and all turned for succour to the far-reaching arm of the British ambassador. From end to end of the Turkish dominions his power was felt ; and it is significant of the supreme position which he held, that when Lord Raglan arrived at the Bosphorus as commander-in-chief of the English expedition to the Crimea, one of his earliest charges to a chief of department was : " Lord Stratford wishes this ; and I would have you remember that *Lord Stratford's wishes are a law to me.*"

Years of patient labour were needed before this supreme influence was attained. In former pages we have seen something of the nature of Turkish government and the obstacles which the slow, crafty dilatoriness of the Ottoman ministers was able to throw in the path of the ambassador. To the last, even his authority was unequal to overcome this procrastinating quality, the *vis inertiae* of the Porte; and though he often won his point it was not without contesting it inch by inch.

No greater mistake can be made than to conceive of Stratford Canning as a simple ambassador—a mere mouthpiece of the decisions of the British Government. He belonged to a time when the foreign representatives of England were much more independent of the home authorities than they are now; and though he gradually passed into the new order of things, he never entirely submitted to it. When he began his diplomatic career his communications with the Secretary of State were slow and occasional. To receive an answer to a request for instructions involved a delay of four months, and by the time the instructions came, the crisis for which they were required would in all probability be past. The minister was thus compelled to act upon his own responsibility, and partly in consequence of the distance from home, partly because the Foreign Office chose to leave him unnoticed for nearly the whole of his earliest mission, when he was but a boy-minister, he acquired the habit of acting on his own responsibility to a degree which no modern ambassador could realize. To be hampered by frequent instructions from home was intolerable to one who had so long borne the weight of personal responsibility, and a study of the later correspondence shews that there was sometimes a touch of jealousy between the ambassador who had been accustomed to steer by his own chart and the Foreign Secretary who sought to bind him with the complicated knottings of official red tape. The latter did not always recognize the important fact that, while Canning, like other envoys, owed his official dignity to his government, he added thereto a personal ascendency which no Cabinet could command and which raised him into a peculiar and authoritative position wholly distinct from that of other ambassadors. On his side, Canning knew too much of departments, and could barely conceal his contempt for them. He made too little allowance for the difficulties of a Cabinet minister, and ascribed the timidity of one or the caution of another to mere weakness, when the cause should have been traced to considerations of expediency, for which, it may be added, he had no respect whatever: right and wrong he knew, but the expedient was a middle course which he refused to recognize.

In support of these independent views came a peculiarly exalted conception of the character of ambassador. A minister may be nothing more than the spokesman of his government, but an ambassador is the personal representative of his sovereign. To Canning this was a very real doctrine, and one that affected his conduct in many ways, both in relation to his government and in his bearing towards foreign Powers. He felt that it belonged to him to sustain the dignity of his Queen by his every act; that he was the embodiment of the English Crown in the eyes of the Court to which he was accredited; that a slight offered to him was an insult to his sovereign. This high and noble feeling had nothing personal in it. Those who knew him best at the epoch of his greatest renown agree in describing him as singularly unassuming, almost humble, in his private capacity; diffident as to his personal qualifications and glad to avail himself of others' knowledge. Self-absorbed he was, in a degree, —it was the natural result of his career, of his long solitudes, and his official supremacy—but he was far from overrating his personal attainments, and would converse as frankly and modestly on great matters of State with a youth fresh from the university as with a grey-headed statesman. To young men who came in contact with him during the critical period of the Crimean war his frank graciousness was captivating. Somehow, when engaged in intimate converse with the many strangers whom his lavish hospitality welcomed at the Embassy, he contrived to lay aside the awful majesty which made the Great Elchi a name of terror, and shewed only the aspect of the cultivated scholar of Eton and Cambridge, the simple-hearted gentleman, the poetic idealist, the man of high thoughts and glowing imagination. His conversation was brilliant. Persigny said that to talk with him on such things as literature or history was delightful; but once let a contested point of politics be raised and "immediately you heard the roar of the British lion." Canning, the man, with his perfect grace, his manners of the old school of courtesy, his tone of *preux chevalier*, possessed a charm which was felt by all who

were capable of appreciating so refined and exalted a nature :
but Canning the image of the Queen of England—the embodiment of the country he loved—was a majestic personage.
The thought of the Sovereignty which he had to impress
upon an ignorant nation—full of its own conceit and incredulous of the might of England—inspired him to an almost
heroic ideal of conduct. He was the sort of man to have
defended the divine right of kings in the seventeenth century;
and in the nineteenth, his enthusiastic loyalty and patriotism,
and his own responsibility for the worthy maintenance of
English honour, led him to a line of action which seemed
almost to embody a doctrine of the divine right of ambassadors.

Though cast in the diplomatic career, Canning was no
diplomatist in the common sense, of manœuvre ; statesman is
his true title, and his successes were gained by the simple expedient of being so straightforward that everyone suspected a
plot of more than Machiavellian craft.   To say that he did
not meet mine by countermine, and that he never had recourse
to secret interviews and private sources of information would
be to acknowledge that he was incompetent for his post; but
in no single instance did these confidential transactions approach the character which we reprobate in the term " plot."
To baffle an antagonist is one thing, to trick him is another ;
and while Canning was a master with the foils, and could turn
his opponent's guard with consummate skill, he never con-
descended to an unworthy expedient.   Above all he never
fought for himself: his country alone commanded his sword.
This honourable straightforwardness was perhaps the most
striking feature in his conduct as a statesman, and especially
in such a place as Constantinople.   The Turks were slow to
perceive it; but even they came by degrees to believe that
what Canning told them was true, and that he honestly meant
them well ; and that was a novel and reassuring thought in a
land of diplomatic mirage.

Yet there was one part of his statesmanship which impressed them even more than his veracity ; they never felt
sure that he had come to his last cartridge ; they could never
tell what weapon he held in reserve.   There is hardly an
instance, in his long career, of his exhausting his resources.
When he won his first and greatest diplomatic triumph in
the signature of the Treaty of Bucharest, he retained unex-

changed a secret article which would have cost England a third of a million of money; that *ultima ratio* was held in reserve. In his later missions to Turkey he acquired such a thorough confidence in a skilful use of peaceful methods that he was content with very limited credit. When he drew up his own instructions in 1853, at the critical time of the Menshikov negotiation, he gave himself no extraordinary powers; he merely assumed the discretion of requesting the English admiral to hold himself in readiness for sea; he did not take authority to call up the fleet : and had he been left without interference from home, the fleet might never have appeared in the Dardanelles. High words he spoke and often to the Porte; deep and ominous was his menace; but there was always something behind to be used in the last extremity; and above all other qualities, it was this suspicion of latent power that impressed the Turkish imagination.

A sincere friend is seldom a popular character. Canning found himself no exception to this rule. The Turks might respect his honest truthfulness, but when it took the form of plain-spoken, and sometimes very hotly-spoken, reprimand, they began to wish for a little polite insincerity. The British ambassador was a good doctor, the best of them allowed, but his physic was exceedingly disagreeable. Wholesome truths do not fit in well with Ottoman notions of government, and most of the pashas were out of sympathy with their physician's theories of Turkish reform. They had not forgotten the prominent part he had taken in the emancipation of Greece, the first serious step towards that partition of the Ottoman Empire into Christian States which has since taken so large a development; they knew that he had come to protect the despised rayas, and this was no title to their regard; they had no faith whatever in his scheme of equal citizenship for the Christians. Moreover if they were obliged to endure a mentor, they would at least prefer one who was a trifle less dictatorial. The ministers, except Reshid (and not always excepting him), lived in terror of a personal visit from the ambassador. When Pisani, or even Alison, made his appearance at the Porte, it was possible to shuffle and evade; but when the set face of the Elchi himself penetrated the Sublime Porte, panic seized upon every official, and the Grand Vezir himself would condescend to hasten in a tremor of anxiety to meet his inexorable visitor and learn his behests.

Personal interviews of this kind were rare and always

meant serious business. When Sir Lintorn Simmons, then
a young officer, was about to leave Constantinople on a
boundary commission, he found himself hindered by all kinds
of delays on the part of the Ottoman grandee who was to act
as his colleague. The Englishman was ready, but the Turk
was still peacefully engaged with his chibuk. At last Colonel
Simmons, in despair of ever getting off, ventured to apply to
the ambassador. "Why did you not come before?" asked
Canning, and forthwith ordered his horse. But even the
time needed for saddling was too much for his patience, and
he dashed off on foot, and breathlessly mounted the narrow
streets of Stambol till he reached the Porte. In a moment
the news had spread through every office in the building—
"the *Buyuk Elchi* is here"—and every man's heart dived
into his slippers. The Grand Vezir received his visitors with
precipitate politeness, and offered the customary pipes and
coffee. "I have not come here to smoke pipes, but to do
business," said the Elchi; "and I think it would be well if the
Sultan's servants smoked less and worked more. Why is not
the Turkish commissioner ready?" In a few minutes the
matter was settled, and by the following morning the dilatory
official was on his way to the scene of negotiation.

The clubs were once full of similar tales, often much
exaggerated; but that the Elchi had a quick temper is a
matter upon which there has never been the smallest controversy. Indeed, Mr. Kinglake has rightly discovered something of a virtue in this natural irascibility. "His fierce
temper," he writes, "being always under control when purposes
of State so required, was far from being an infirmity, and was
rather a weapon of exceeding sharpness, for it was so wielded
by him as to have more tendency to cause dread and surrender
than to generate resistance." In private his wrath was less
vigilantly guarded, but it is only fair to say that in most
cases it was rather the fiery indignation against wrong and
falsehood, the fierce scorn of baseness, than the petty irrita-
bility of small men. He hated what was mean and dishonourable with a living personal hatred, and could not suffer deceit
or insincerity.

Yet it were vain to pretend that the Elchi always "did
well to be angry." Little things would irritate his nervous and
overtaxed brain to fits of unnecessary passion, to which his
natural quickness of temper made him especially prone. The
many letters that have been quoted in earlier chapters of

this work reveal clearly enough that his nature was impatient; a small thing would "put him out," especially when the pressure of work was severe and matters were not going well at the Porte. Sometimes he would come in after a long and exasperating conference with a dilatory minister, and then nothing would satisfy him, and woe betide the attaché or servant whom he first encountered. Absolute meekness and silence were the only policy; opposition was out of the question. On one such occasion his *chef* sought vainly to please him; dish after dish was sent away in disgust, and finally down came the Elchi's fist on the too fragile table, and plates and glasses went crashing on the floor with the *disjecta membra* of the unoffending article of furniture. Battiste, an old courier of the first Napoleon, was waiting when this happened, and of course came in for his share of the storm; but next morning the ancient servant had some kind words from his master, who was never above tendering an apology to his subordinates, and would sometimes explain regretfully that "something at the Porte had upset him." His servants knew that there was a reason for his impatience, and the best proof of his essential kindness is that they remained with him year after year. One of them was with him nearly forty years, and death alone severed the connexion. In spite of his hasty temper, they knew how to appreciate him; and one reason of this was the brief endurance of his wrath. He did not bear malice, and his anger rarely lasted till the sun went down.

There can be no doubt that the Elchi was an exacting taskmaster to his attachés, but it was known that, hard as he worked his men, he worked harder himself. If Mr. Hay had to copy despatches for thirty hours, Sir Stratford was writing the drafts all the time. If on Mr. Odo Russell's arrival at Constantinople the ambassador, delighted to get a fresh, vigorous young hand, kept him imprisoned and hard at the grindstone for six weeks before he allowed him to satisfy his curiosity about the mosques and bazars of Stambol, he at least shared the imprisonment and worked unflinchingly at his side. It was no uncommon thing for an attaché to enter his Excellency's room in the early morning and find him still in his evening dress. No doubt the ambassador forgot that even youth might not possess his iron endurance and marvellous power of work. Few men could toil as he did. Rising at five or six every morning, and despatching a hasty

cup of tea, Canning sat down to the long file of petitions
which always lay on his table for immediate attention ; petitions from persons of all kinds, merchants who had claims
against the Porte, Ionian scoundrels who used the protection
of England to cover their crimes, Christians of every race
and form of creed who sought his protection against injustice
and persecution. These being duly docketed with instructions
to the consuls or other officials, the correspondence began, and
often lasted through a great part of the day, varied by much
pacing to and fro, as is the habit of thoughtful men. Sometimes the stress of business compelled him to postpone lun-
cheon till it was almost time for dinner. At ten he retired,
but retiring seldom meant immediate rest. Far into the night
his light was burning, and in times of great pressure, when the
courier was at the door, waiting for despatches, it was often
morning before the last signature was subscribed. Six o'clock
nevertheless saw him again at his work.

He was essentially a desk-negotiator. He reserved personal conferences for the last resource, and preferred to
transact all business by the pen. We have seen examples of
the memoranda he wrote for the dragomans to read to the
Turkish ministers and of the detailed plans of negotiation
which he drew up for his own guidance. All these involved
considerable manual labour, and the usual rule confining each
despatch to the Foreign Office to one subject greatly increased
the bulk of his official correspondence. Besides this, at the
time of the Crimean war, there was correspondence with
three generals, with heads of all the army departments, hospitals, transports, foreign colleagues, ambassadors at other
Courts, besides the routine business with consuls, pashas,
merchants, and in short with everybody who had something
to do or of whom something had to be obtained. His power
of continuous work was the more remarkable because Lord
Stratford led a sedentary life. Since he left school he had
never attempted athletic amusements. He rode, it is true,
whenever he could ; but he was not much of a sportsman,
and though he made an annual expedition to the forest of
Belgrade to shoot boars, he took care to keep a good marks-
man by his side. In short he spent most of his day at his
desk, and a by no means regular walk, ride or drive, was his
principal form of exercise.

The climate of Pera was hurtful to him, and Therapia
was his breathing place ; but even there, with incessant work

and little exercise, it needed great care and abstemiousness to ward off illness. In 1844 gout laid its hand upon him, and from that time forwards he was liable to its onslaughts. When the attack was sharp, and the heat was trying, and the business of the Embassy weighed heavily, Canning might vent his irritation in good, honest Saxon, but he never slacked speed at his desk, though it had to be placed on his bed. When the courier had departed, the ambassador alone appeared unmoved : there was " a general occultation of the minor luminaries." He was often surprized to observe how easily he bore fatigues which disabled the young men of his staff. On one occasion, when he made his annual excursion to the forest of Belgrade, accompanied by the attachés, the ambassador was the sole survivor at the dinner-table. The day had been long and fatiguing, and they had ridden from the early morning to 9 at night, when they returned to the palace to find some guests awaiting dinner. Lord Stratford was dressed and at table in ten minutes ; but not a single attaché appeared.

Naturally a man who at the age of seventy could endure fatigue such as this was not likely to be an easy taskmaster. The attachés complained that he worked them to death. Mr., now Sir John, Hay, told me that he was once very nearly killed by overwork ; and as Canning, immersed in business, had little time for studying the complexions of his staff, the Embassy doctor took upon himself to warn him that Mr. Hay must have rest. The Elchi was the last man to overlook such a hint : he put the attaché on board a man-of-war then lying in the Golden Horn and sent the vessel with despatches to Malta. The staff knew that if once a man found favour in the ambassador's eyes and did his work well, Canning would be staunch and loyal to him to the end. No one under his orders ever suffered for lack of his support. Whatever error there might be, Canning took the responsibility of his subordinate ; and each man, be he attaché or consul, knew that he could depend on his chief's support even against the Foreign Office itself. While thus just and staunch to all subordinates, he had his preferences. He was quick to form his impressions, and his first likings seldom changed. The ambassador's eye saw deeply into a man ; people used to say that he looked them through ; and Titov, the Russian minister, remarked that this eye was its owner's chief enemy. Instead of the easy, frank, unsuspicious air which a diplomatist should employ when he wishes to lure his antagonist on to compromising revelations, Canning, said Titov, appeared to be gazing right into your soul, where he evidently expected to find something very disagreeable. This is the criticism of a friend, and there is some truth in it. The Great Elchi was by nature or by force of circumstances over-apt to suspect insincerity and double-dealing, and his eye would sometimes betray him; but that he could suppress the penetration of his glance when occasion demanded was frequently shewn, and notably at the famous conferences with Prince Menshikov. When circumstances required it he could become blind; and when the Russian plenipotentiary once insulted him, he turned the matter over in his mind a moment, and, seeing that a quarrel was inexpedient, immediately *became deaf*.

Whatever the eccentricities of some of his assistants, few ambassadors have been served by an abler, one may even say a more brilliant circle of men. The Oriental secretary, Charles Alison, with many peculiarities, was not only a marvellous linguist, but a man of subtle and penetrating mind, and his services proved invaluable to his chief. He it was to whom Canning entrusted the most difficult negotiations, where a knowledge of Turkish was essential; he was more at home in Pera families than the ambassador could possibly be, and if there were an intrigue on foot Alison was tolerably sure to hear of it from his extensive Turkish and Greek acquaintance. The despatches are full of praises of his achievements, and, however little sympathy on most great questions there might be between the ambassador and his Voltairean *laissez-aller* secretary, the latter was a zealous and efficient instrument of his chief's designs, and Canning never failed to give him full credit for his success. A staff that included from time to time men of such varied attainments as Percy Smythe (afterwards Lord Strangford), Lord Stanley of Alderley, Lord Napier and Ettrick, Robert Curzon (Lord Zouche), Lord Cowley, Odo Russell (Lord Ampthill), Sir John Drummond Hay, and such outside assistants as Layard, Rawlinson, and Newton, can hardly be described as less than highly distinguished in many brilliant qualities of mind and learning. To their abilities much of the success that marked Canning's reign at Constantinople was undoubtedly due; but it may well be questioned whether without his firm hand and stern resolution, which some of them found hard to bear, all their combined intellects would have brought about the

diplomatic triumphs which he attained. His success at the
Porte was mainly one of character; and though he needed
clever supple minds to work out his measures, the ideas originated with him alone, and owed their effect mainly to his
rigid resolve and unflinching perseverance. His brain conceived the scheme, the heat of his enthusiasm forged and
welded the scattered links of Turkish reform; he alone dreamed
of a regenerated Turkey where Christian and Musulman
alike should resist in firm unity, shoulder to shoulder, the
insidious approach of Russia. Alison and others might help
him, and did help him, with infinite skill; but Alison, who
liked the Turks very well as they were, would have shrugged
his shoulders at reforms, and let them alone, had not the fiery
zeal of his chief set him to work. Whatever was great, whatever made for even justice and the protection of the oppressed,
whatever, a cynic may add, was Quixotic and impracticably
ideal, in the statesmanship of the British Palace at Pera, was
due to Canning alone. Others might trim the sails of his
vessel of state, others might load her guns and stand ready
with the fuse, but so long as he was captain of the ship no
hand but his touched the helm, no other voice rang out when
the broadside was to be fired.

Yet it is above all things noteworthy that with this
immense influence, with an authority which was as nearly
despotic as that of a Christian and a foreigner can ever be in
Turkey, he was not arbitrary. He used his power, not for
power's sake, but to attain a definite end. He entered upon
his dominion at Constantinople with a fixed purpose—to make
the continuance of the Ottoman Empire possible by making
it European. His policy was open, avowed, straightforward.
Private motives he had none. He would save Turkey in spite
of herself if she could be saved at all. Whatever made for
this goal found a firm advocate in Canning. An equitable
pasha, a wise minister, a just law, a single-minded colleague,
need fear no opposition from him; his voice was always ready
to be raised in their behalf. But let all take heed how they
thwart him in his *grande idée*. Should the French ambassador
seek to increase the prestige of his king or president or emperor by supporting the Turks in their opposition to reform,
or by any policy hostile to his great scheme, that ambassador
would probably be recalled. A Turkish minister who attempted
to return to the old Ottoman ways was doomed to fall. A
pasha who refused to execute the humane laws passed at

Canning's instigation lost his post. But all this was in pursuance of a fixed policy, a policy that never once wavered during sixteen years of sore trials and many reverses. He had laid out his road before him, and in that road he and the Sultan were to walk. If any man uprose in the way he must be made to stand aside ; if another would come and join in the procession, he was heartily welcome. But whether they stood in the road or followed in his train, one thing was plain, —he was going straight on. In spite of obstacles, and with or without assistance, he would pursue the path he had marked out for himself and for the empire which he dominated. To the Turks this immovable resolution carried with it some- thing of the air of destiny. " If what he directed was incon- sistent with the nature of things, then possibly the nature of things would be changed by the decree of Heaven, for there was no hope that the Great Elchi would relax his will. In the meantime, however, and by the blessing of God, the actual execution of the ambassador's painful mandates might perhaps be suffered to encounter a little delay." [1] This indeed was the one form of opposition which Canning found hardest to bear and to overcome. How he overcame it step by step, how he sought to impose upon the Sultan and his ministers his idea of a New Turkey, an empire worthy to take a place in the councils of European States ; what he achieved, and where he failed ;—this is what we must survey in the chapters to come. As the story wears on we shall often see a strong man in adversity, but we shall never be tempted to forget for a moment that the man is strong.

CHAPTER XII.

THE REFORMER OF TURKEY.

1842-56

WHEN for the fourth time Sir Stratford Canning went to take charge of the English Embassy at Constantinople in 1842, he found himself in almost a new Turkey. Outwardly, at least, everything appeared changed. Stambol, as he remembered

----

[1] Kinglake, *Invasion of the Crimea*, i. 120.

it in 1810, or even in 1826, was a different place from Constantinople in 1842. The mosques still crowned the Seven
Hills, the narrow, crowded streets and bazars climbed upwards from the Golden Horn, the " Bab-i-Humayun " itself—
the Sublime Porte—was still to be dutifully visited hard by
the ruined vestiges of Eski Serai ; but the character of
the place, of the people, of the Porte itself, was altered and
transformed. The day when Sultan Mahmud II. struck the
resolute blow which put an end at once and for ever to
the baneful tyranny of the Janissaries was the birthday of
modern Turkey. On that day an old system passed away
and a new one came into being. The paralysing panic of
military despotism was removed ; the royal power was restored ; and in the hands of Mahmud that power might be
exerted for great ends. He was the one ruler who in happier
conditions could have saved Turkey. He it was who saw the
needs of his country, formed his purpose, pursued it secretly
for twenty years, then dealt his sudden blow, and at once
inaugurated his reforms. Such resolution, such immovable
firmness, such patience, are rare among princes ; and though
strength of will in Mahmud carried with it an unpleasing
rigidity and in religious matters a quality of fanaticism, there
is no doubt that he had the ability as well as the desire to
revive the ancient lustre of his house by bringing to it some
glimmer of the light of Western civilization.

It is easy to look back now with a pitying smile over the
failures, the broken vows, the paper constitutions, of half a
century of Ottoman history, and to wonder why people
expected so much of Mahmud's reforms, why men hoped for
the regeneration of " the unspeakable Turk "—aye, and continued to hope for many years after the reforming Sultan had
been laid in his grave. But at the time there was something
touching in the strong, ignorant man's struggle against the
corruptions of his empire—his blind feeling after the best
means to raise his country to the level of a European State.
We picture to ourselves the Sultan casting aside the fond
traditions of the past, unlearning what he had been taught in
his youth, and groping blunderingly among new principles
and new customs. We do not imagine him an ideal reformer,
a man of broad views and the wisdom that comes from ripe
study ; his mind was built in a narrow and unbending mould,
and he did not dream of such a regeneration of Turkey as
Canning afterwards attempted. But he saw the first obvious

necessities of government and he made unhesitatingly in their direction. He knew that a strong ruler upheld by a loyal and disciplined army alone could rescue the empire and stem the tide of corruption and foreign aggrandizement, and he knew that an army such as he needed could only be formed on a European model. Hence we see him immersed in a French drill book ; hence he unlearns his old Turkish riding, and fearlessly mounts a barebacked horse till his long legs acquire the seat of an English dragoon ; hence he casts away the turban and kaftan, and assumes the European coat, trousers, and boots, and retains as a distinguishing mark only the red fez.

It was a brave effort, and the more astonishing since it was made in solitude and isolation. No one prompted Mahmud, no one man can be pointed out as having prominently and voluntarily assisted him ; what help he had he commanded and he rewarded. It was his misfortune as well as his glory to be before his age, to attempt reform, however crude and elementary, at a time when no one understood the necessity or believed in the policy. He began single-handed, and his greatest difficulty was to find a single capable instrument to carry out his designs. He failed to realize his ambition, not from lack of resolution, but because his countrymen were not prepared and because foreign powers left him unaided. England, France, and Russia were the foes that crushed Mahmud's wise projects. Russia perceived that her prey was escaping her, and determined to strike at once. Filled with a half-Christian, half-antiquarian enthusiasm, England and France joined in the Czar's designs and outraged the national feelings of the Ottoman Sultan by demanding the dismemberment of his empire for the sake of the Greeks. They allowed Russia to make a wanton war upon him just at the moment when they had so tied their hands by treaty that they could not defend him, and when they had seriously injured his chance of success by sending his fleet to the bottom of the bay of Navarino.

The loss of Greece and the humiliation of the Treaty of Adrianople destroyed much of the Sultan's spirit and prestige; and when, with an incredible lack of political capacity, and in disregard of the solemn warnings which Canning addressed to them, the English Government had succumbed to French ascendency and allowed Mohammed Ali to carry his triumphant standards across Syria and well-nigh to threaten the

o

sacred city of Constantinople itself—then broke the proud spirit of Mahmud, and the man who had so resolutely and so carefully planned a new era for his country, just lived to see his every hope extinguished, and closed his eyes in welcome death that he might not witness the dissolution of his empire.

Yet the end of Mahmud's reforms was not all failure. The improvements of Abdu-l-Mejid and his advisers were the fruit of his father's sowing. Above all it was Mahmud who first awoke Canning's interest in Turkish reform. During his earlier residences at the British palace at Pera it is not too much to say that the ambassador had hardly given a thought to the separate and independent interests of the Ottoman Empire. To Turkey as the barrier against Russia, the doorkeeper of the Dardanelles, he ever gave his hearty support; she was necessary to England, and that was enough. But to improve, to Europeanize, the vast, disjointed empire of the Grand Signior seems hardly to have occurred to him as a possibility in those early days. From 1810 to 1812 he was busy night and day in defending England's rights and resisting French influence. In 1826–27 his attention was again diverted from Turkey to an extraneous object. His mission was directed almost exclusively to mediation on behalf of the Greeks, and this alone was sufficient to extinguish every hope of sympathy between him and the Turkish government. In Mahmud he saw chiefly the relentless despot of Hellas; he had no time to view the other side of his character.

It was not much before 1832 that the ambassador whose name is now identified with the cause of reform in Turkey began to see clearly the vital need of radical changes in the administration of the empire. His intercourse in that year with the Sultan became suddenly more intimate and confidential. Mahmud perhaps began to perceive that if foreign aid were needed to realize his hopes, there was no man more fitted by nature to help him than the resolute ambassador who had so often defied him. Canning on his side felt more kindly and respectfully towards the Sultan; and with the growing esteem came a corresponding interest in the policy of internal reform. He began to approach nearer to confidential relations with the Turks, and with this came a more accurate insight into the position of affairs. He grasped the vital importance of the crisis; the time had come to choose between two courses: to leave the Turkish Empire to its inevitable fate or to try to save it by "an approach to the civilization of Christendom." He announced this conclusion at the close of a memorable despatch to Lord Palmerston (7 March, 1832)—almost the first hint of the policy to which he devoted the rest of his official career. We quote the concluding paragraphs:—

> The great question to be resolved is this : *How far is it possible to introduce into the present system of administration those improvements without which the army and finances of the country must be equally inefficient ?* . . . More than five years have elapsed since the Janissaries were destroyed, and although some regulations of a better kind have been adopted, and the Sultan's policy is in general of a milder and more protecting character, no beneficial results, except that of a diminished animosity between Turks and Christians, are yet visible. The regular army is not more numerous now and scarcely better disciplined than it was before the war with Russia. The financial embarrassments increase, and commerce is still depressed by a pernicious system of monopoly. . . . *I think the time is near at hand, or perhaps already come, when it is necessary that a decided line of policy should be adopted and steadily pursued with respect to this country. The Turkish Empire is evidently hastening to its dissolution, and an approach to the civilization of Christendom affords the only chance of keeping it together for any length of time.* That chance is a very precarious one at best, and should it unfortunately not be realized the dismemberment which would ensue could hardly fail of disturbing the peace of Europe through a long series of years.

In the words which I have italicized we find the germ of that policy of reform for which Canning laboured during sixteen years. He was not yet sure of Mahmud, as the tone of the despatch indicates ; but his opinion of him improved as the year 1832 wore on, and the final audience of leave—the last occasion on which he saw the Sultan—made a deep impression upon him. Then he returned to England and the House of Commons, and for almost ten years he had no voice in Turkish affairs, till at last in the fulness of time he went forth again to the Bosphorus, and now—not to hold the fort against the French, nor to mediate for insurrectionary Greeks —but to work for the Turkish Empire itself, to carry out that system of reform, that approach to the civilization of Christendom, which he had foreseen in 1832.

This was the keynote of his mission. The first "instruction" which he received from Lord Aberdeen, after the usual command to support the Sultan's authority and the integrity

of his empire, proceeds forthwith to the burning question :
he was to "impart stability to the Sultan's Government by
promoting judicious and well-considered reforms." He was
not, indeed, to meddle busily in the internal affairs of Turkey
—that was not within the province of an ambassador—but
he was to support and even to suggest such measures of
reform as were manifestly and imperatively called for. In
the list of pressing questions the reform of the army held
the first place : the Turkish forces required to be limited and
subject to better discipline. The whole administration and
police were to be improved for the better tranquillity of the
empire. Public officers were to be chosen with more care.
Christians were to be treated with humanity. The trade and
resources of Turkey, her mines and forests, should be developed by an enlarged system of roads and increased steam
communications. The chief cause of provincial discontent
was to be removed by a better system of collecting the taxes.
Such were the leading points in the outline of reform presented in the instruction of her Majesty's Government. In
addition Canning was to promote a good understanding between the Porte and the Pasha of Egypt, to endeavour to
settle the outstanding pecuniary and commercial difficulties
with Greece, to press upon the Porte the utmost indulgence
towards the Christians and Druses of the Lebanon, to soften
the animosities and allay the frontier disputes between Turkey
and Persia, and, in short, generally to use his every effort for
peace abroad and tranquillity and good government within the
borders of the Ottoman Empire.

Despite many outward changes, the state of affairs on his
arrival was by no means encouraging to the hopes of improvement with which he had left England. A strong
reaction against Western influence had set in. Fortunately
we are not here concerned with the management of diplomacy
in Turkey during Canning's absence ; otherwise it might be
necessary to enquire whether a firm, steady policy such as his
might not have saved the Porte from the many troubles which
encompassed and well-nigh overwhelmed her between 1833
and 1841. At least we may be sure that the Treaty of
Hunkiar Iskelesi would never have been signed had he
been at the British Embassy. The tardy though eventually
signal intervention of England between the Sultan and Mohammed Ali might also have been accelerated by a strong
ambassador. Lord Ponsonby, however, did his best, and the

settlement of the Egyptian question owed much to his exertions. But he left the Porte in very evil plight, and in no very grateful mood towards her lethargic allies. The war with Egypt, the temporary loss of Syria, numerous insurrections and defections had seriously impaired her strength and finances. Syria had indeed been restored to her by the allies, whose army and fleet had just been withdrawn ; Mohammed Ali had been reduced to what England considered his proper place ; the Turkish fleet had been surrendered by the Pasha of Egypt ; and the most dangerous article of the Treaty of Hunkiar Iskelesi had been repealed by the treaty of 1841, whereby the Bosphorus and Dardanelles were once more made Turkish and not Russian waters.

But Turkey had been alarmingly weakened by the attacks of the past fourteen years. Russia and Egypt between them had refused Mahmud that period of peace which alone could have rendered his reforming policy triumphant. Moreover the great Sultan was dead, and an amiable but irresolute youth reigned in his stead. How far the well-intentioned weakness of Abdu-l-Mejid was on the whole an advantage in the hands of such a tutor as Sir Stratford Canning we shall see as we go on ; but in the absence of some such controlling influence the change from a mind—narrow perhaps, but resolute, indefatigable, and commanding—like Mahmud's, to the mild intelligence of his son, must appear an incalculable calamity. Canning indeed presaged good results. He preferred a pupil to a rival, and wrote, after his first audience of the new sovereign, that " the graciousness of his manner and the intelligent, though gentle and even melancholy, expression of his countenance warrant a hope, perhaps a sanguine one, that with riper years and a more experienced judgment he may prove a real blessing and source of strength to his country."

Subsequent intercourse with the young Sultan confirmed this favourable opinion. On one occasion when the ambassador had a private audience of his Majesty, with no one present but Riza, the grand chamberlain, and the interpreter, the Sultan was unusually affable and encouraging. He spoke openly of his personal views, and said that " the great object of his policy was the happiness of his subjects ; he intended and had ordered the execution of those humane laws which had been promulgated at Gulhané and consigned to the reformed code ; he wished to maintain the relations of peace

with every European Power and those of confidence and intimacy with Great Britain." Reform, he protested, was dear
to him, and could he but find ten pashas to coöperate he
would feel sure of success; the difficulty was to find willing
instruments. Swayed as the young prince might be, to and
fro, by divergent counsels, at heart he was always true to
reform and staunch to its chief European advocate. " He
possessed," wrote Canning in later years, " a kindly disposition,
a sound understanding, a clear sense of duty, proper feelings
of dignity without pride, and a degree of humanity seldom, if
ever, exhibited by the best of his ancestors. The full development of these qualities found a check in the want of vigour
which dated from his birth and which his early accession to
the throne and consequent indulgence in youthful passions
served to increase. The bent of his mind inclined him to
reform conducted on mild and liberal principles. He had not
energy enough to originate measures of that kind, but he was
glad to sanction and promote their operation." What fitter
qualities could be desired in the royal pupil of the Great
Elchi ? The intimacy which gradually sprang up between
them was something unprecedented in the Turkish state, and
assumed by degrees the character of personal affection. At a
private audience one day Canning ventured to say that the
first time he had been presented to his Majesty his heart had
gone forth towards him. " And mine towards you," was the
Sultan's response. Without this intimate understanding the
ambassador's task would perhaps have been hopeless. His
intercourse with Abdu-l-Mejid, whether by audience public
and private, or by means of the secret agent who went between
them, was his final weapon when diplomacy had exhausted
its resources upon the Porte.

With the Turkish ministry he had far less cause to be
satisfied. Reshid Pasha, by his too rapid and sweeping
reforms, outlined in the famous Tanzimat or Hatti-Sherif of
Gulhané 1839,[1] had not only procured his own fall, but had

---

[1] This document, the Magna Charta of Turkey, provided for the security
of all subjects, without distinction of creed, in life, honour, and property; for
the equitable distribution and collection of the taxes; and for the systematic
recruiting of the army. It confirmed Mahmud's ordinance by which no one
could be executed without regular trial and sentence, and established the
principle of public trial for all accused parties; it asserted the right of all
persons, criminals included, to hold and devise property without let or hindrance; and appointed a council to elaborate the details of administrative
reform. See Sir E. Hertslet, *Map of Europe by Treaty*, ii. 1002.

created a dangerous reaction. The government manifested a
petulant impatience of European interference. Its policy was
reactionary, fanatical, and anti-Christian. It was mainly
composed of the old Turkish party, and aimed at a return to
the system overturned by Mahmud. Redress of any sort, if
granted at all, would be granted in its minimum. Least of
all would the government listen to the advice of one who had
so often offended its prejudices before.

The general state of the empire was such as might be
expected after the late troubles and under the existing rulers.
Disorder reigned in the provinces. The misgovernment of
Wallachia offered an opportunity for Russian intrigues;
Bulgaria had caught the fever of disquiet, Albania soon broke.
into revolt, and in 1843 Servia rose against her prince. The
local pashas did as they pleased. At Scutari three Christian
peasants were executed without trial ; at Trebizonde the pasha
cut the throats of two criminals in the public street; the
governor of Mosil rushed out one night, mad with drink, to
murder at pleasure ; two towns were razed to the ground by
the troops in Albania ; the soldiers mutinied for their pay at
Salonica, tried to kill their colonel, and then burnt the stores
in a caravanserai, while the pasha looked on ; unequal and
cruel taxation was driving the people to despair ; the ministers
of the Porte used their official authority in favour of their
private trading, and invited presents of hush-money from
offending pashas. Fanaticism against Christians was increasing, and Pera was placarded with threats of burning the Frank
quarter. "There is no such thing as system in Turkey,"
wrote the Elchi. "Every man according to his means and
opportunities gets what he can, commands when he dares,
and submits when he must." Financial embarrassment,
public and individual, prevailed to an alarming extent. The
only active trade was the traffic in lucrative posts in the public
service ; but salaries were in arrears ; commerce languished ;
the currency was ruinously debased ; forests and mines and
other resources were neglected ; communications were bad—
no roads or mere tracks ; good land on the coast within fifty
miles of Constantinople was to be bought for two shillings an
acre, while Russian grain was sold at a comfortable profit
hard by. Ignorance and corruption prevailed in every department of the state ; brutal violence and torture were employed
in the law courts ; Christian evidence was not accepted against
Muslims ; Christians were annoyed if they entered the Turkish

quarters of the capital ; constant cases occurred of fraud and
outrage against them : yet in spite of these disabilities the
rayas were slowly advancing in wealth, education, and independence, whilst the Turks were losing ground.

A drastic remedy was necessary ; but how was it to be
applied in face of the opposition displayed by the government
to all foreign interference ?   The intervention in Syria, though
in the interests of Turkey, had left a sore feeling at the Porte,
and foreign representatives, indeed foreigners of all grades,
barely maintained their positions.   If Lord Aberdeen wished
merely to stand well with the Turks, wrote Canning, he had
better not meddle at all, but let matters drift.   On the other
hand the rising importance of the rayas might end in revolution, and it would be impossible to uphold the Porte against
its progressive Christian subjects.   Popular sympathy, secret
societies, the power of the press, all would urge England in
the opposite direction.   What then could be done ?   He advised " an active but friendly interference," in the interests of
Turkey and Europe, with real, united action among all the
Great Powers, so that the Porte might have no opportunity,
as heretofore, of playing off one Power against another.   The
only alternative was " tacit acquiescence " in the reactionary
policy now pursued by the Turkish ministers ; to keep on
good terms, and " never mind the credit."   He perceived no
middle course.

With such an envoy it is needless to say that the former
alternative was adopted.   The Foreign Office indeed cautioned
the ambassador repeatedly to proceed gently ; but to proceed,
not to stand still, was the policy he was to choose.   Yet
" active but friendly intervention " was more easily conceived
than executed.   Canning was hampered by countless obstacles.
The relations of the Porte with Greece and Syria were a
source of obstruction ; the Turkish ministers, while accepting
his good offices in bringing the Greeks to reason, could not
forget the share he had taken in setting them free ; and Syria,
though restored to the Sultan mainly through the exertions
and arms of England, was a constant cause of suspicion and
jealousy.   And apart from these outside disturbances, there
were serious difficulties to overcome in his own relations with
the Turkish Government.   As ambassador, his first duty was
the protection of English interests.   Just as in 1812 he would
not move a step to help the Porte in its negotiations with
Russia until the commercial claims of England had been ad-

mitted ; so in 1842 it was impossible to stand forward as the friendly adviser of the Sultan in Turkish interests until the grievances of British subjects had been redressed. Moreover, a large class of " protected " subjects appealed to the British ambassador. These were natives of Malta and the Ionian Islands, who could claim the privileges of British citizens, though not subject to English laws ; and these formed by far the most troublesome branch of Canning's clients; for the system of consular jurisdiction was in a very unsatisfactory state. They were clever enough to absorb a large amount of the British trade in the Levant, and unprincipled enough to constitute the most conspicuous class of criminals. Constantinople itself was flooded with miscreants, who fought in the streets or stabbed in the dark and then fled to the Embassy for protection.

Besides, whatever might have been the legal bounds of British protection, Canning took a very elastic view of his responsibility. In places where there was no American consul he took upon himself to afford protection to citizens of the United States. Dutch Jews in Syria looked to him for satisfaction for their wrongs. Greek artisans in Pera owed their safety to his intervention. The long-continued persecution of the Armenians, which had burst forth with relentless severity after the battle of Navarino, was ended at his instance, and the Nestorians in Mesopotamia, victims of a cruel and bloody oppression, found an untiring advocate in the British ambassador.

In face of the reactionary attitude of the Turkish government, Canning found the position of adviser to the Sultan both trying and irksome. In 1843 an incident occurred which tested to the full his power of enforcing reforms. If he failed, the future was perhaps desperate ; if he succeeded, he might feel some confidence in his authority. The case involved much more than ordinary principles of justice and humanity; it required a reversal of a criminal law presumed to be based upon the Koran. A Christian who had embraced Islam had recanted, and by the law of Mohammed was executed. Could this law be repealed ? This was the problem to be solved, and Lord Stratford shall tell the solution in his own words.

MEMOIRS. A painful incident, the execution of an individual on religious grounds, brought on a most important change in the practice, if not in the principles, of the Sultan's government. A young Armenian, subject of the Porte, adopted the Musulman faith, or, to use a vulgar expression, "turned Turk." He soon repented of his apostasy, and returned to the church of Christ. A relapse of this kind drew down upon him the vengeance of Turkish authority. He was imprisoned, tried, and condemned to death. The case was brought to my attention by some of his nearest relatives, who intercepted my carriage one day on the road from Pera to Buyukderé, and throwing themselves before the wheels implored my interference on his behalf. A friendly intercession was all I could undertake, and my efforts at the Porte in that sense were unhappily attended with no success. The unfortunate renegade was executed. But his blood did not sink into the ground unfruitfully. My report to the Foreign Office and that of my French colleague to his government were followed by pregnant effects. I was armed with decided instructions by Lord Aberdeen. Baron Bourqueney was directed by M. Guizot, at that time Louis Philippe's chief minister, to act in concert with me. We were both authorized to require of the Porte that punishment should no longer be inflicted on persons who seceded from the Mohammedan religion. No precise form or limit was given by our instructions to what would be the consequence of refusal. It became our business to produce the strongest possible apprehension of eventual consequences in the minds of the Turkish ministers. My official note to the Porte was framed with that view. When I placed it in the hands of Mr. Frederick Pisani, our principal interpreter, he remarked with his habitual bluntness that it never would succeed. I looked him in the face with fixed determination, and said, "Mr. Pisani! *it shall.*" To say the truth, in using this curt phrase, I rather expressed my will than my conviction, and I felt moreover the necessity of conveying my own intense earnestness to the mind and manner of my agent and through him to the Turkish minister. Rif'at Pasha, who held the Foreign Office, received my missive with his natural courtesy, and a long negotiation, not of the most promising kind, ensued.

The details may be read in the *Correspondence relating to Executions in Turkey for Apostasy from Islamism,* laid before the House of Commons in 1844. It was clear from the first that the better minds among the Turkish ministers revolted from such sanguinary acts. Raûf, the Grand Vezir, said that personally he had not the heart to kill a fowl, and that his sentiments were entirely in accord with the ambassador's ; but the law of the Koran was inexorable, and the execution was "a misfortune for which there was no remedy." The Foreign Minister expressed equally humane and equally discouraging opinions. It appeared, however, that there were bigots in the Divan, notably, the President of the Council, who insisted on enforcing the law. The Grand Mufti was not one of these, for when consulted on a similar case he had advised the ministers "not to bring it under his notice, as he had no choice but to declare the law; and a charitable intimation was added that, where a State necessity existed, the Porte would herself be found the most competent judge." No one, however, doubted that the law was distinct and final; and all that Rif'at Pasha could suggest was to issue instructions by which future apostasies might be hushed up without capital punishment. The Porte, he said, not only could not alter a divine law, but could not risk her character as a Musulman Power even by a written reply to the remonstrances of the five Powers led by the British ambassador. A very deep and serious impression had indeed been made by the general feeling of indignation aroused in Europe; but no repeal of the law was so far considered possible. Meanwhile, another religious execution took place at Brusa, Dec. 1843, this time of a Greek, followed by similar protests from the five ambassadors. Lord Aberdeen supported Canning by an unusually vigorous despatch, which, when communicated with due solemnity by the ambassador, produced such an effect on Rif'at Pasha that he jumped up and left the room for some minutes. Still the Turkish minister maintained that "a law prescribed by God himself was not to be set aside by any human power." The Sultan, he said, might risk his throne in the attempt. Canning perceived that the only course that remained to be tried was to "search the scripture," the Koran itself; and the result of this search was the conclusion that no specific ordinance for the execution of apostates was to be found in the holy book.

This discovery increased the ambassador's confidence, and after a long controversy the Porte gave way so far as to exchange notes of agreement on the subject, and finally came an undertaking that such barbarities should not recur.

MEMOIRS. The answer to my note [wrote Canning], though virtually a surrender to our demand, required a supplement to make it permanently effective. The Sultan was to complete the engagement by an oral declaration to me; but a form so fugitive required some addition to fix it, and therefore I addressed another note to Rif'at Pasha expressing in distinct terms the construction to be put upon the whole concession. His silent reception of the note would be sufficient for my purpose. He had wit enough to perceive this consequence and struggled hard to escape. It was not till we met

for my audience at the imperial palace that I succeeded in forcing
the note upon him, and even then he only yielded to a threat of
my demanding his dismissal if he continued to resist. My audience
followed, and Abdu-l-Mejid performed his promise to the letter.
He added that he was the first Sultan who had ever made such a
concession, and was glad that the lot of receiving it had fallen to
me. I replied that I hoped he would allow me to be the first
Christian ambassador to kiss a Sultan's hand. " No—no— " he
exclaimed, and at the same time shook me by the hand most
cordially. Thus ended this redoubtable negotiation.

It was on occasions like this that Canning's fierce zeal
bore all before it. Nothing less than violence could have
taken that kingdom by storm.

One of the chief points in his programme of reform
was the removal of all the distinctive disabilities which oppressed the Christians ; he meant to make the rayas the best,
the most free and progressive, part of the Sultan's subjects.
To that end he was resolved to stand forth as their protector—
not because he would not protect Muslims, towards whom
he never failed in his duty—but because the Christians, after
centuries of practical outlawry, required more protection to
bring them up to a political level with their Musulman fellow-
subjects. This was his view, and he never swerved from it,
let the home Government "instruct" him never so wisely.
The abolition of religious executions was his first great step
in this direction, and it was completely successful. Of course
instances occurred where popular fanaticism brought lynch
law into operation, but the provincial governors, acting under
strict orders from the Porte, exerted themselves to save the
lives of renegades, and several instances of successful intervention occurred in the autumn of 1844.

Fortified by the "bloodless victory" which he had won
over the Porte, he proceeded to advocate reform after reform,
and to remove one disability after another. Two months had
not elapsed when he obtained a notable firman by which the
use of torture was formally abolished throughout the empire.
In September 1845 he gained a long contested point, the right
to establish a Protestant church at Jerusalem for British and
Prussian subjects—a success for which he received the cordial
thanks of the King of Prussia in an autograph letter, in which
his Majesty expressed his gratitude for the ambassador's able
and indefatigable efforts, and assured him of his personal
esteem. In 1846 he mediated on behalf of the newly declared

Protestant sect of Armenians, which was exposed alike to
the persecution of the Porte and the enmity of the leading
Armenian Church, and his efforts resulted in the complete
restoration of the sufferers to civil rights and religious toleration. He even removed so trifling a disability as a distinguishing flag by which the Christian ships of Turkey were
branded, and obtained a common mercantile ensign for all
vessels of the Porte irrespective of their owners' creeds. His
vigilant eye searched every corner of the empire, and when
persecution was discovered the offender was instantly reported.

While it is true that the ambassador's most signal victory
over Turkish prejudices, the abolition of capital punishment for
apostasy, was achieved without the help of any Turkish minister,
it is not less certain that Canning afterwards owed much to
the support and friendship of the most enlightened minister
of modern Turkey—Reshid Pasha—nor was he slow to admit
his indebtedness.

Among the ministers [he wrote in his Memoirs], whether in
office or expectant, Reshid Pasha was the one who in sentiment
and policy sympathized most with me. The Sultan seemed to be
jealous of our intimacy. Some intriguer had probably turned his
mind that way. " You are too fond of Reshid," he said to me one
day. " Fond, and not without reason," I replied, " for I find him
the most able and faithful of your Majesty's servants." By birth
and education a gentleman, by nature of a kind and liberal disposition, Reshid had more to engage my sympathies than any
other of his race and class. He was bred, if not born, in the Morea.
He lived for a time, I believe, in the family of Veli Pasha, son of
the famous Ali of Janina, and governor, either in whole or in part,
of that country. At an early age he began his official career at
Constantinople. When he first drew my attention he was one of
the under-secretaries of state at the Porte, and in that capacity
assisted at Therapia in giving the form of a convention to the
points of agreement settled in the summer of 1832 between the
Turkish government and the representatives of the three Allied
Powers, with a view to the territorial enlargement of Greece. His
features were cast in the Circassian mould, their expression was
lively and intelligent. In point of stature he was below the middle
height, and his general appearance conveyed the idea of a cheerful,
inquiring, sympathetic character. I saw but little of him at that
time. Subsequently he arrived in London as the Sultan's ambassador, and our acquaintance was then renewed. I remembered
that he opened himself to me on the subject of reforms in Turkey.
It was evident that he looked to taking an active part in the new
policy inaugurated by the overthrow of the Janissaries, and stimu-
lated by the example of Mohammed Ali in Egypt. He asked me

when and how the promoters of the system ought to begin. I replied, "*At the beginning*." "What do you mean by *the beginning*?" he said. "Security of life and property, of course," I
rejoined. "Would not you add the protection of honour?" he
asked. "No doubt," I said. But in truth I wondered what he
meant by honour among Turks, until I recollected their practice
of applying the bastinado without discrimination to persons of any
class or rank whatever. He was right, I thought, and so I told
him. Nor did the intention stop short of performance. Summary
inflictions of corporal punishment are excluded from the new code
of law in Turkey. In the days of M. Guizot's administration
Reshid was ambassador at Paris. [He returned to Constantinople
in March 1843 and was appointed governor of Adrianople; a favour
which he regarded as a sign of political ruin; and it was finally
arranged that he should return to his embassy in France in
November. Thence he was suddenly recalled towards the close of
1845 to assume the command of the Turkish Foreign Office.] A
weak constitution, the education of the Seraglio, and a total inexperience of state affairs consigned the young sultan to a condition
of helpless dependence on his ministers, whose titles to his Majesty's
confidence were none of the best. It was very desirable that he
should be in better hands, and I thought that Reshid restored to
office would prove a suitable keeper of the imperial conscience.
When he was at Balta Liman on the Bosphorus in 1843 we wished
mutually to meet; but in Turkey an unemployed minister has to
be constantly on his guard, as intercourse with a foreign ambassador lays him open to suspicion, and therefore we had to meet
in a third house and quite secretly. A change of ministers in due
season was the consequence of these meetings, and I found in
Reshid Pasha on many occasions a friendly and powerful auxiliary.
We agreed in principle on most questions of reform, but in point
of execution he was timid and tardy, not indeed so much from any
unwillingness to act as from the difficulty of bringing his colleagues
into accordance with his views.

Before Reshid's accession to power the two men had been
on unusually friendly terms. Reshid used to come to dine at
the Embassy and bring his children with him. When he
scented a plot, on his appointment to the government of
Adrianople, it was to the English ambassador that he applied
for advice and protection. In 1845, when Lady Canning
passed through Paris, Reshid told her that he knew her
husband to be "the most loyal, conscientious, and upright of
men and the truest friend to his sovereign and the Turkish
Empire," and hoped he would not leave Constantinople too
soon or for too long. Hardly had this conversation been reported when Reshid returned to the Ottoman Foreign Office,

October 1845. The change was no result of caprice or Court
intrigue, but of general conviction. His opponents had had
a fair trial, and they had by their maladministration reduced
the empire to the lowest pitch of anarchy and corruption.
The provinces were in revolt; the public service was openly
venal. People agreed in condemning the reactionaries, and
when they were replaced by a more moderate government
affairs were but slightly bettered. There was a general cry
for Reshid, as "the man of the crisis," and Reshid came.
Canning had worked hard in private to induce the Sultan to
recall him, and at last Rif'at Pasha, who had become president of the council, joined in the entreaty. One of the
most satisfactory circumstances in the manner of his recall
was a message which the Sultan simultaneously sent to the
English ambassador, in which he assured him that the appointment was not due to any wish to be agreeable to France,
but that "his sole motive was to give to all an undeniable
pledge of the policy which he had sincerely adopted and which
was to be invariably directed to the improvement of his empire, the relief of his people, and the cultivation of friendly
intercourse with the States of Christendom." And what surer
pledge could he give than by restoring to power the author
of the Constitution of Gulhané ? Canning regarded Reshid as
the last hope of salvation for the Ottoman Empire, and his
anxiety as to the future was proportionately intense. "If the
chosen instrument," he wrote, "of the Sultan's policy were
to fail in realizing the hopes which he has inspired, either by
introducing a wanton spirit of innovation or through inability
to cope with the difficulties of his station, I know not where
it would be possible to find another rallying point. The
various parts of this vast empire are too ill assorted and ill
balanced to preserve a state of repose by mere cohesion. The
old system of administration has caused that exhaustion for
which a remedy is wanted. If the principles now in requisition are found unequal to the process of restoration, what but
despair can ensue, what but indifference to all within the empire and a mistrustful apprehension of all without ?"

Reshid did not disappoint these high expectations, though
the difficulties which encompassed him retarded and sometimes prevented their entire realization. He did not rush
excitedly into innovations or, as Henry Addington said, "lay
on too much steam and blow up the engines." On the other
hand he steadily persevered in the course of reform which he

and Canning had marked out for the future. His coöperation
was invaluable if not essential to the ambassador's plans, and
though when we look upon Turkey as she is now we must
lament how much remains to be done, we must remember
that these reforms, however much they may be in abeyance,
have not been repealed, and that such internal improvement
as may be discovered in the Turkish Empire was mainly their
work.

CHAPTER XIII.

THE WORK OF THE EMBASSY.

1842-16.

THE most absorbing interest of Canning's mission from 1842
to 1846 was the question of internal reform. This was the
subject that engrossed his attention and commanded his energies day and night during those years. But it was far from
being the only troublesome problem to be solved. Never was
the ambassador confronted with a larger or more bewildering
forest of difficulties and complications. His letters to friends
commonly begin with some such phrase as "I have but a
moment to tell you," &c., and the state of his handwriting
renders the study of his hurried *brouillons* or draft despatches
a fit problem for a palæographer. It was often beyond the
skill of his attachés, and even of himself. On one occasion,
in order to save time, he proposed to read a draft despatch
aloud for an attaché to copy at dictation. The Elchi had not
proceeded very far when he stopped, and, after holding an
illegible word in various lights in the hope of deciphering it,
finally exclaimed in desperation, "Zounds! I can't make it
out. Here, *you* read it."

I may perhaps be excused for reproducing here a well-
known story which I heard from Sir John Drummond Hay,
till lately minister at the Court of Morocco. There had been
a very busy time at the Embassy, where Mr. Hay was then
the acting attaché. It was the time of the Apostasy question
and the disturbances at Mount Lebanon, and many despatches
had to be drawn up and copied for home. For more than
thirty hours the ambassador and his assistant sat at their

desks, with but brief intermissions for hurried meals. At last
the bag was sealed up for the messenger, and Canning observed that it might be as well to go to bed. It was an hour
or two after noon. As they were leaving the room, the
ambassador turned round and remarked that he expected a
special courier presently, and Mr. Hay would of course receive
and prepare the papers for his chief. Mr. Hay made no reply,
but inwardly resolved that after thirty hours' strain he would
not be baulked of his sleep. Accordingly on reaching his
bedroom he summoned his Greek servant and showing him a
loaded pistol informed him that if anybody opened his door
before six P.M. he would infallibly put a bullet into him, no
matter who he was. The servant retired in consternation and
in due course the special messenger arrived with despatches.
" Where is the acting attaché ? " was his first question. " In
bed." " Go and call him." " If you please, sir, he has a pistol
at his pillow and swears he will shoot the first person who
opens his door before six." Mr. Hay was naturally allowed
to repose in tranquillity. At six he dressed, and very soon
a message came that his Excellency commanded his presence.
He found Sir Stratford in no very amiable mood. " What is
the meaning of this, Mr. Hay ? " and the ambassador indig-
nantly recounted the messenger's story. The attaché explained
that after thirty hours of unremitting work he really could
not keep his eyes open. " D——n your eyes ! " burst from
the Elchi's lips before he could control himself. Mr. Hay
was not the man to be backward at such an invitation. Gracefully combining respect with the expletive, he replied " D——n
your Excellency's eyes ! ' Upon this Sir Stratford became suddenly very grave and stately. " I am sending off despatches
this evening, Mr. Hay," he remarked with studied politeness,
" and you shall convey them to England. I shall inform the
Foreign Secretary that I have no further need of your services." " With all my heart, sir," replied the attaché, in a
rage, and left the room. While he was hastily packing up for
his journey, Lady Canning, who ever acted the part of peace-
maker, came and besought him to apologize, or at least to go
and say good-bye to the ambassador. After much persuading,
he consented to bid his Excellency farewell. Hardly had he
entered the room when Sir Stratford had him by the hand,
saying " My dear Hay, this sort of thing will never do ; what
a devil of a temper you have ! " The two were firmer friends
than ever after this, and Sir John Hay now looks back with

P

pride and gratitude to the training he received at the hands of the kind if passionate ambassador.

Troubles with Greece, disputes with Persia, disturbances in Syria, such was the staple of the reports which poured in daily upon the Embassy. To relate a tenth of the negotiations, proposals and counter-proposals, intrigues, disputes, promises, and retractations that came at this time under supervision would demand a separate volume. The correspondence about Greece alone is enough to dismay the stoutest heart that even a biographer of a diplomatist can boast. Canning and Sir Edmund Lyons, then Minister at Athens, exchanged reams upon reams of closely written manuscript on this provoking subject, and never seemed to have approached a step nearer to a satisfactory solution. In those days Greece was the *bête noire* of politicians. Nothing could be made of her, and all the aspirations of the great and good men who had devoted their lives to her regeneration had crumbled to dust. King Otho and his German following seemed to invite deposition, and persisted in refusing the constitution which formed one of the conditions of the monarchy. Foreign despotism had reduced the country to a state of suppressed revolt little better than the anarchy which had preceded it, and such order as existed was only obtained by severe repression. Nothing appeared to grow towards settlement. This anarchic condition was a perpetual thorn in Canning's side. He felt a degree of responsibility towards the country which he had largely contributed to free; he knew that his influence there was considerable; and he resolved to use every endeavour to heal the wounds which an unwise government had rent in her polity.

Canning's despatch on Greek affairs written after his arrival at Constantinople draws a gloomy picture of the state of parties at Athens. The royal authority was degenerating into despotism; the better classes and working people were disgusted with their Bavarian Court; the country had not justice done to it, its resources remained undeveloped; and some constitutional check upon the crown, and some responsible form of administration, and above all a tribunal of public opinion were needed to appease the popular discontent and to give character and soundness to the Government. Any king of Greece, he admitted, must have a difficult part to play; but Otho was personally despised, lacked the qualities of mind and character which were essential to his position, and had no sufficiently capable council or minister to make up for royal deficiencies. Canning went so far as to tell King Otho that he must beware of the course he was pursuing; that " the throne of Greece had not been set up as an idle pageant, but for purposes which Europe had a right to expect that he should realize." Advice however sound was of small avail, and the ambassador foresaw that an internal explosion or interference from without would probably be necessary before a thorough change of system could be introduced. The former came in a calm and prudent form in the revolution of 14 September, 1843. The Greeks at Pera were enthusiastic over the new constitution, and when they met in the street, instead of using the usual " How d'ye do " and " Good morning," or their Hellenic equivalents, one would say Ζήτω, and the other reply Σύνταγμα : "Long live"—"the constitution!" The hopes of the English party were soon doomed to disappointment and none deplored the fall of Mavrocordatos and the accession of Colettes more grievously than Canning. His correspondence with Lyons and Church shews how keen was his interest in the shifting scene of Greek politics ; but he could do little at Constantinople to steer the ship, and while he never quite despaired of Greece his forebodings were at times far from cheerful. He often appealed to Addington, the Under-Secretary, to use more vigour, but the Foreign Office dared not risk war. " You ask how long we mean to allow King Otho to play his antics with Colettes and Piscatory," replied Addington. . . . " What can we do except by force ? but force is not lightly to be resorted to—besides two can play at it. . . . Is Greece worth such a stake ? A knife will walk into Otho, and Colettes too, one day if they don't take care. But a vacant throne would not suit us more than a perverse sovereign and minister." As ambassador at the Porte, Canning had to consider the Turkish aspect of the Greek question, and that there was danger to the Sultan in the rash and unscrupulous policy of the Greeks was beyond doubt. Their *grande idée*, which consisted in the foundation of a Greek empire on the ruins of Ottoman domination, was especially objectionable to him, and he did his best to repress it. Border disputes, moreover, were constantly occurring, and the Porte found it necessary to keep a considerable force on the frontier to guard against marauders. The violent language of the Greek press and Colettes' government encouraged systematic brigandage, and it needed all Canning's influence to soothe the irritation of the Porte, especially as the French representative strenuously defended the arbitrary and foolhardy action of the Greeks. The expropriation of the Turkish inhabitants, also, under the provisions of the Treaty of 1832, involved claims for compensation which were not honoured without vexatious contention, and which opened the door to more serious disagreements.

The Persian Frontier Commission was another constant source of anxiety. The two Mohammedan states were in imminent danger of war in June 1842, when the Persian Foreign Minister requested Canning to use his good offices in obtaining a reasonable settlement of the various matters in dispute. The obstacles were indeed formidable. To draw a boundary line through migratory tribes is an almost insoluble problem, as our Afghan frontier commissioners have more than once discovered. In the case of the Persian boundary there were also serious religious jealousies to be overcome. A massacre at Kerbela in 1843 had rekindled the old animosity of Shi'ite against Sunnite to a dangerous heat; protection for Persian pilgrims to holy shrines in Turkish territory was hard to ensure; there were difficulties about Persian marriages, judicial trials, and other matters on Turkish soil; and there was a claim on the side of the Porte to the town of Mohammara, which the Persians, supported by Russia, stoutly resisted.[1] Colonel Williams deluged the embassy with long rambling letters and despatches; the other agents in Persia, Colonels Sheil, Farrant, and Rawlinson, sent frequent communications; and endless interviews took place between the ambassador and his Russian colleague, who was now (1843) M. Titov. The home Government supported Canning with some vigour, thanks to a great extent to his old friend Addington, who became Under-Secretary for Foreign Affairs early in 1842, and endeavoured to put a backbone into Lord Aberdeen's policy. The latter was in perpetual dread that Sir Stratford would commit the Government by some too decided act, and frequently rejected Addington's draft despatches as being too vigorous.

The harmonious coöperation of Canning and his friend Titov effected an arrangement to which Turkey assented in 1846; but Persia threw it out, and the whole negotiation had

---

[1] Mr. A. H. Layard arrived at Constantinople in July 1842, and his knowledge of the Turco-Persian frontier proved very useful to the ambassador, who employed him in various confidential services, and endeavoured to reward him by a post at the Embassy, but was opposed by the Foreign Office. A good account of the Turco-Persian dispute is found in Sir A. H. Layard's *Early Adventures*, vol. ii. ch. xix. (1887).

to be recommenced *de novo*. At length the Treaty of Erzerum was concluded, as has been said, in October 1847, but was concluded in name alone. It soon appeared that the settlement was purely formal, and it was not till after the Crimean war that any approach to a final arrangement was arrived at.

Another subject involving infinite trouble was the unhappy condition of the Lebanon.

MEMOIRS.   Syria, after the expulsion of Ibrahim Pasha and his Egyptian troops, had remained in a very unsettled state, and the Allied Powers deemed it their vocation to take a leading part in restoring some kind of order amongst its discordant elements. The Porte had owed to all of them, except to France, who favoured Mohammed Ali, the restitution of that interesting province to its own immediate authority. It was natural, therefore, not to say necessary, for the Turkish Government to acquiesce in their interference. Their five respective representatives, the French ambassador being one of them, were charged with the task in question. We had numerous meetings, much correspondence with our consuls in Syria, much discussion among ourselves, and occasional communications with the Porte. We found no end of obstructions in the way. The Turkish ministers were averse to every limitation of the Porte's authority. The old Sheykh of Mount Lebanon wished to recover and fortify the former condition of approximative independence which he had contrived to maintain before the war. The Druses, half heathen and half Mohammedan, were ready to draw the sword at any moment upon their Christian neighbours. The respective populations, including patches of Greek, Armenian, and other races, were so intermingled as to make their political separation next to impossible, and the French had no mind to give up a tittle of their ancient pretensions, warranted in some degree by treaty, to the protection of the Roman Catholic mountaineers. The manner in which this complicated skein was finally unravelled has little interest now. The cordial desire of the powers to deal fairly by all parties, and the influence of such of them as had no immediate interest in the country, enabled us in the end to form a plan which placed the whole province under the paramount authority of the Sultan, but secured a separate administration, more or less independent, to each of the tribes distinct in race and religion. That all the parties under such circumstances should be completely satisfied was not to be expected, but we had reason to believe that our arrangement on the whole was generally acceptable, and in particular both M. Guizot and the French ambassador in London expressed to me their approval of it, though in truth the old pretensions of France with respect to Mount Lebanon were neither confirmed nor even recognized.

The progress of these various negotiations and the general character of the work accomplished in 1842–46 will best be seen in extracts from Canning's private letters. This source of information is, however, very irregular, and there are long intervals of silence. His most frequent correspondent, his mother, had ended her long and honourable life in 1831, and had been followed by his sister and eldest brother, while most of his old friends were either dead or in feeble health. The two chief aids to our knowledge of his daily life and work are several long letters to his only surviving brother William, then a canon of St. George's Chapel, Windsor, and the correspondence which he kept up with Lady Canning during their separation, in the summer of 1845 when she and her children returned to England. We can trace the gradual growth of hope and confidence as one measure of improvement after another was carried into effect, and we shall never again have so good an opportunity of witnessing his daily round of work and pleasure—much of the first and a little of the second—at Constantinople.

Towards the end of June 1842 Lady Canning joined her husband. He sent her a few words cf " welcome to old Stambol. You took rather a discourteous leave of it a few years ago [after Navarino], but we are on quite another footing now, and, please God! all will go well." It was characteristic of his devotion to duty that he did not go to meet her after a separation of six months. The courier was waiting for despatches, and no private interest could be allowed to interfere with his public duties. Accordingly Lady Canning and her children proceeded alone to the country house at Buyukderé, where the ambassador joined them in the evening. Though political matters had improved since their former visit, in the comforts of life they had much to desire. The palace at Pera had been burnt down some years before, and for the present, pending the erection of the new embassy, they had to accommodate themselves in town to an inconvenient temporary house; while the hired villa at Buyukderé, prettily situated on the water's edge, was hardly calculated to offer a firm resistance to the weather. Of society there was little to be enjoyed. Canning bewailed the change to his old friend Planta (31 Dec.) :—

You have written to me four times and, alas! I have not written to you once. In return for my gratitude you must give me your compassion. I have really no time to write to those of whom I most frequently think. My public duties absorb the whole of my day, and often cut deep into the night. This was always a busy place, but the labour which was formerly occasional is now become incessant. The worst of it is that, compared with former days, I have no house, less society, a diminished salary, and fifteen additional years. Yet somehow or other—I know not why, I know not how—the struggle goes on with more spirit than of yore, and neither health nor cheerfulness is wanting. . . .

Here as elsewhere the events of Kabul and Nankin have given a great impulse to our credit. We have also had our fingers in the pie of Eastern pacification. The Syrian question is settled, as far as diplomacy can settle it, and the Turks and Persians, instead of cutting each other's throats, are going to negotiate, with fair prospect of success, under the joint mediation of England and Russia. Old Turkey and her young Sultan do not make a very good match; but the latter means well, and I hope that Reshid Pasha, who is recalled on his own request from Paris, will help in time to put him more completely in the right way. Great changes have certainly taken place here within the last twelve years. But they are rather on the surface than at the bottom. On arriving I found a system of reaction established in spite of Syrian laurels and the Quixote who preceded me. It has cost me months to upset the private influence of the Seraglio and to turn out a President of the Council and a Grand Vezir. These things being happily accomplished, it remains to look out for the fruits thereof; but they are slow in coming.

I really believe [he wrote to his brother, 5 February, 1843] there is some truth in the old maxim, "A busy man has not time to be ill." What surprizes me is that I am sometimes kept indoors for ten days, and still not the worse for it. Perhaps we require less exercise as we get older. We certainly do with less sleep, and might I suspect get on better with less food. I rarely go to bed before twelve or half-past, and I am called at six, though I will not answer for being up every morning quite so early. I generally shave, however, by candle-light. The business of the Embassy is certainly immense, and, what is worse, it grows with success, and, what is still worse, buried affairs *walk*. A few weeks ago we flattered ourselves with having fairly and discreetly interred the *Syrian* question, and the King of France gave the world its epitaph in his last speech; but it has since " burst its cerements " and promises to become a most troublesome ghost. . . . Last week I sent off commissioners with about three reams of instructions to patch up peace between Persia and Turkey, and I have since heard of an incident at Bagdad [the Kerbela massacre], which threatens to blow up the whole negotiation.—Woe is me! Alhama! In spite of all this I work on as well as I can, grumbling and swearing—with an *r* or a *t* as you please. . . . The narrow, dark, close, muddy streets of this miserable suburb are odious; but we have fair views of the Bosphorus, and fine air on the hills. We mean to rush back into the country as soon as possible; but the amusement costs some 600*l.* or 700*l.* a year, Government not choosing to allow a country house, as France, Russia, and Austria do. Our opera, bad as it looks, is really very tolerable. But we do not go often, though we have a box, which is the envy of all the diplomatic body. We have boats, and carriages, and saddle-horses in abundance; but the difficulty is how to use them. When we do use our four greys and English postilions, half the town assembles to stare, though our Excellencies may go out on foot without drawing a look. E. gave a children's ball some days ago, and we succeeded in getting (for the first time in history) a dozen of Turkish boys and girls of good family to dance with the little Christians. I was glad to hear that the Sultan's prime favourite, who was present, regretted that he had not sent his children too. It is a small matter, dearest William, to read of in this scrawl of mine, but a great and a good deed was done in that hour, and the seed there sown shall be a tree, when I am in my grave. You have now reached the truth at the bottom of the well. It is this hope that sustains me through trouble, fatigues, and privations, not omitting the bitter feeling of disappointment under which I came here for the fourth time in my autumnal days.—God's will be done! I have *obeyed* and hope it may not be in vain.—But you need not be told it is uphill work. Such roguery, corruption, and falsehood and deep anti-social selfishness. Still, my influence strikes deep root, and I hope against hope.

In 1844 the renegade question, Syria, Persia, and a revolt in Albania fully occupied the Elchi's time, and when he wrote to friends he confined himself to the briefest possible bulletins. At the opening of the new year, 1845, he made amends to his brother in a long epistle, which contains some interesting retrospections :—

In politics, too, I have had very uphill work—that is, uphill for me, but down hill for this country. . . . At this moment the position is so far improved that I am fighting with all the weight of Government at my back. It is a last deadly struggle with corruption, and here on the spot I am alone, though in the light of a clear and resolute conscience. To you at a distance this may sound a little romantic, but there is in reality no exaggeration in it. Luckily for yourself you are too far off to provoke me to an explanation, and the newspapers will probably in due season give you the result *in shorts.* Our *last* result belongs to the deceased year. It was a great one, but little understood beyond the veil. It reads innocently—" Renegades from Islamism to be no more put to death." —Yet was it the first dagger thrust into the side of the false prophet

and his creed. Such wounds may widen, but they never close—
Which grave remark is not the worse For being, as you see, a verse.
Whenever we meet again, if it please God that we should do so,
and you rather like to be bored to death, I will tell you how
marvellously and providentially the whole affair was carried
through. In the meantime you may bear being told that we go to
town in two or three days, having already weathered half a winter
of cold winds and snow in the country. . . . Our large wooden
house on the river's edge with a large marble hall and a saloon to
match it overhead is so little suited to the season that we had
much difficulty in uniting our few half-frozen neighbours under a
magnificent bunch of *mistletoe* on Christmas Eve, which, on looking *afterwards* into the rubric, I blushed to find appropriated by
our Church to seriousness and not to revelry. Visitors, with one
rather peculiar exception, have long since left us, and we have been
obliged to make the most of our own resources. They, as you may
imagine, are rather monotonous, and at this season not a little
interrupted by the badness of the roads, which break up regularly
in autumn, as boys in England do for the holidays. As for me,
during a great part of most days and occasionally of the night also,
I am glued down to my writing-table, which is often a thankless
task separating me from those I love, and putting me in contra-
diction with the younger and more careless spirits around me.
Not that I mean to complain. I took the cup deliberately, I am
content to drink it, and rather look forward with hope than backward with regret. There are, nevertheless, weak as well as trying
moments, and, not having the constitutional placidity of my Uncle
Toby, I fear that I have been caught swearing more than once. It
might be some comfort to a less benevolent ambassador that his
young and reckless *attachés* have not a sound constitution among
them. Not one of them is equal to half the fatigue which I endure,
and often after the departure of a messenger there is a general
occultation of the minor luminaries. Lord Napier left us two days
ago with views of marriage for the benefit of a prettyish and clever
daughter of Lady Julia Lockwood's. It was to relieve the dulness
of copying a long despatch that he laid down his pen and stepped
across the street to propose.

A very interesting correspondence began when Lady Canning left for England in the summer of 1845.

So far all goes well [he wrote 17 Aug.] and I have great hopes
of getting through all my labours soon, and having in prospect all
that I can presume to expect for so rotten an empire as this. I am
working like a mole—a beaver—an ant—a horse in a mill—a *devil*
—to secure the good within reach. The weather is still intensely
hot, and we are as dry as tinder. But never mind, please God we
shall have rain as well as other good things. You will be glad to
know that the sultan is coming out handsomely. . . . We all jog

on well together—Layard, and Alison, and all.   You are never forgotten by any of us.

P.S.—If this finds you at Paris contrive to let Reshid Pasha
know in confidence that, though silent, I have never lost sight of
his interests, and that I trust the present change will soon make
an opening for him.   But he must be very quiet for the present,
and prepare to be very prudent in future.   Find out what he now is,
and what he thinks, and let me know, but *not* by the French post.

5 Sept.—I have got the *Church Firman* at last, and am to have
the Persian answer in a few days.   The commission, too, is drawing
to a close, and old Shekib is to be off the same day for Syria, where
things are looking better, and where Rose is quite enchanted with
the new settlement, or rather the end of the old one.   All this has
a third-volume air, and yet I have fears of being kept here till
towards Christmas. . . .

Woe is me!   There are moments when I am sadly puzzled in
speculating on what is to come out of so many steamers, and railroads, and printing-presses, and daguerreotypes.   Its *first* effect is
diffusion, and all diffusion is weakness; but under the scattered
materials there is, perhaps, a fertilizing principle, which may in
time be the parent of a rich crop of social blessings, resulting in a
vast extension of human happiness.   But to realize this hope, there
must be no premature disturbance of the heart's education; the
quiet domestic moralities interwoven with our earliest affections
must not be frightened away, like Thames salmon, by the rush of
steam and gas; the Bible must go forth with the engine; and
every choice assortment of Manchester stuffs must have an honest
John Bunyan to distribute them.

27 Oct.—The *beginning of April* must be the *extreme* limit of my
patience, and this is more than a fair allowance for all that I have
it at heart to do, or that can possibly be done at present.   The
nine points, which I have carefully written down on a small scrap
of paper, may be accomplished sooner, and if so what is to keep
me here?   I have already scratched out the one which seemed but a
few days ago the most difficult of all.   It stands thus on my memorandum : ~~Recall of Reshid.~~   Who knows whether I may not be
equally fortunate with the other eight, especially as two of them may
be fairly united into one?   Already I think one may be considered
as good as scratched out.   I mean *Persia*.   Pisani has just written
on A'li Efendi's authority, " La décision sera satisfaisante; je puis
l'annoncer."—I have also strong reason to believe that *certain
Marbles*, to which you know I attach great interest, will be given
me before ten days are out.   That will erase another notch from
my stick. . . .   The change of policy is now complete, and the
Sultan and his ministers vie with each other in shewing me confidence, and, as far as Turkish natures allow, making me amends

for past vexations and disappointments. This is doubly gratifying, as it confirms my *trust in principles*, and awakens in my heart that feeling of gratitude to Providence which is at once a source of the purest joy and an incentive to further exertion in the right path. Help me with your prayers and sweeten sweetness itself by making part of it your own work. . . . I reckon on Reshid being here about Christmas, and before he arrives I must have a thorough understanding with him, the more easily as what you said to him and caused him to say will serve as an excellent preface. . . . Supposing all to go right, a few weeks after Reshid's return will enable me to lay a foundation which may harden and consolidate during my visit to England and be fit for a superstructure of worthy proportions afterwards. If God be so pleased!

Candili, 21 *Nov.* 1845.—Think of that! and such a morning of brightness, and green sunny banks, strewed all over with daisies and glittering yellow flowers! It would be spring, if I had not found the turf, where we ate poor Layard's strawberries, sprinkled over with autumnal leaves. Mounted on my fat donkey, with the tallest of the two Slavonians at my side, I sauntered, if one can saunter on four legs, over to the steep wood of firs beneath the signal house and thence, from a thousand shady nooks, and as many sunbright knolls, I looked up and down the deep-blue, boat-mottled Bosphorus at half the lovely spots we have so often visited —Shehidler crowning them all—and I felt more solitary than words can express—why I need not tell you. Alas! that there should be so many beautiful objects without, and so much loneliness within! Yet I am far more happy here than in town, where I can neither breathe nor look about me, nor please myself with gazing on the waters which look up at me from between the castles, and as they glide along seem willing to bear my thoughts to those who are absent.

To his Brother, 2 Dec.

Is it possible, my dear William, that *you* can complain of *me* for not writing? At all events you have written, and here am I coming to write. But, alas! my will is puzzled by the rub of not knowing what to say. You don't care a farthing—now do you? —about Turkish reforms, and Pashas and Efendis and such kinds of things and persons? On the contrary, you have scarcely even pity for poor Tom, whose food has been of such like gear for the greater part, off and on, of half a century. Never mind; I am told you would like to know a little more of my goings on and so you shall. I must begin, however, by observing that my goings on are often very much like standings still. At this moment, for instance, though I have long wished to be amongst you all once more, and to rejoin my more especial belongings, it is to no purpose that I spur with both heels, use horse language, and vip, and vip, and vip ; the old hack will have its own way, sometimes with a start, then with a kick, not always unaccompanied with a plunge that bespatters one with mud, and not unfrequently with a dead stop. Not so with the mails and steamers. On they go, whizzing and whisking their paddles, or rattling their legs, and snorting out loads of paper—instructions, reports, remarks, notes, letters, journals, reviews, petitions, and Heaven knows what besides. In comes the never-ceasing drift, under the doors, through the windows, down the chimneys—there is no possibility of keeping it out. I shovel it, attachés shovel it, the dragomans shovel it, but the heap never disappears, and all we can do by shovelling together is to save ourselves from being choked by the accumulation. Where it all comes from and what it's all about is sometimes a puzzle to me as well as to you ; but you may be sure that it is more pleasant to read about it than to deal with. The humanity department is perhaps the most intelligible, but it is also the most troublesome. I assist in turning wicked functionaries into good ones, griping extortioners into pleasing collectors, bigoted Musulmans into easy latitudinarians, decapitated renegades into smiling churchgoers, highway robbers into domestic attendants, and the whole tribe of torturers and executioners into so many obliging sinecurists. Sometimes an ill-favoured Vezir, who growls and snarls at having the half-gnawed bone kicked from under his nose, might be taught by a sound bastinadoing to walk more steadily in the right path, but individuals are protected under the new constitution in their lives, fortunes, and honour (which lies throughout the East in the soles of the feet). And if it were not for an occasional massacre by the troops and the wholesale system of plunder in the provinces, there would be nothing to remind us of the good old times, when Turks did as they liked, and Christians were grateful for the use of their skins. One great object I long had at heart was to get hold of the sultan ; and, if appearances may be trusted, I *have* him ; another was to turn out a sort of old tory, peculating, suspicious, deceitful junto, and that too is done. Then war was to be prevented and friendship established along 700 miles of Turco-Kurdo-Persian frontier. I won't answer for the *friendship*, but war is prevented, and the foundations of a great work of peace and improvement among the barbarous tribes is laid in the mutual, though somewhat reluctant, consent of the growling parties. Allow me next to present to your reverence the Protestant Church established under the Sultan's firman on Sion's rock. Though it cost three years to get that firman, it will take three thousand to " rail off its seal," or at least as many as Shylock told you in the old school at Hackney that it would take to rail the seal off another bond. I will not trouble you with commercial matters, but we have had some tough questions to manage in that department, and I am happy to say that they are all either settled or on the eve of settlement, or so arranged as to give us all we require, till the conclusive agreements

shall be made. Our new Embassy house, or palace as it is called
here, is rising rapidly above the ashes of the old one, and I have
extorted a few thousand pounds from the Porte for the purchase of
a row of Turkish houses, the removal of which will open the garden
on one entire side to a fine terrace-view of Constantinople and its
Golden Horn. When you come to preach in our chapel, instead
of the young person of 72 who now does duty there, you will be
able to appreciate this acquisition. In the meantime it will interest
you more to know—though it is still an awful secret—that I have
obtained a promise of the famous Halicarnassus Marbles—the
remnants of the Mausoleum—which have been for centuries en-
cased in the walls of a Turkish fortress, and which I hope to have
on their way to England in a very few weeks.[1] More than this, I
have an agent at work among the mounds of Nineveh, and a letter
received from him this morning announces the discovery of a
marble chamber full of cuneiform inscriptions—now by Major
Rawlinson's ingenuity interpretable—and of an immense adjoining
edifice, apparently a palace, which he is endeavouring to penetrate
by cutting trenches through the mound, and which tradition assigns
to Ashur, the lieutenant, or more properly speaking, I suppose, the
whipper-in, of Nimrod!!—I tremble, while I inform you of these
incomplete acquisitions, lest any feeling or appearance of premature
confidence should indispose the genii and set them at work to defeat me. One is never so inclined to superstition as when some
favourite project is advancing gradually, and all but reaching its
final accomplishment. "'Twixt cup and lip The foot may slip;
And those who think They needs must win, When near the brink
May tumble in."—Thus have I tried, like a good younger brother,
to give you some idea of the butterflies which it is my vocation to
hunt. They are the more important to me because we have not
the social resources of Paris or London at our command. Yet in
a party of ten who dined with me yesterday, there was a traveller
from New South Wales, another well acquainted with America,
and Sir William Harris, our ambassador to the Christian King of
Ethiopia and the Nimrod of Southern Africa. After dinner we
broke off into chess, whist, and music, to which two of the guests
contributed on the piano, one on the violin, and a fourth on the
flute, and all admirable players. The day before, I had dined with
the Austrian minister, under whose hospitable roof the diplomatic
body with a fair sprinkling of the more amiable sex was collected.
In the morning I had been at a conference with the Russian
minister and the Reis Efendi, mounted on my good horse *Gazil*,
a brown wicked arched-necked beast with a magnificent black tail,
preceded by two kavasses (what *can* they be ?) on white and skittish
hacks, and followed by my faithful grooms Joseph and Henry.
To-morrow, with the blessing of Heaven, I hope to get into the

---

[1] See the following chapter.

country once more for a few days. In order to do this I must change continents; for my country house, which, to speak the truth, is but a box, looks down from the top of a steep Asiatic hill upon the Bosphorus. A ride of forty minutes takes me to the water's edge, where I find my pretty caïque with its three pair of oars, and the men, a Greek and two Turks, dressed in full white Dutchman-like drawers, with gauze shirts, and naked breasts and arms, and red waistcoats picked out with delicate black embroidery. Ten minutes suffice to convey me, without the help of a bull, across the most lovely of river-like waters, and at the landing-place opposite—a village market with an admirable *hummum* and the minaret of a mosque hard by—I bestride a punchy, serious, good-humoured, and not talkative donkey, with a glorious pair of long, flexible, hairy ears; and step after step, picking his way, never looking behind him, or betraying the slightest disrespect, he finds his way to the top of the steep declivity, where fifty more of his tiny jogging paces on level ground take me to the rural door. If it be night, and clear, I have all the host of heaven for lamps and flambeaux; if it be day, there is a noble view up the Bosphorus, and another rich and noble view down the Bosphorus. . . . These strange particulars, my dear William, may serve to bring me nearer to your mind's eye, and to afford you a glimpse of the sort of patched harlequin life that I am leading. But if in my ardour to meet your wishes I have allowed any diplomatic cat to escape from its bag, you must put a string round its neck and keep it close to you whether by your fireside or in the pulpit.

A few more extracts from the correspondence will complete the narrative of work at the Porte in 1846. Canning was labouring assiduously to bring his various negotiations to a close, but the progress was slow, and one obstacle after another delayed his departure.

To his Wife, 6 Feb.

I made a great exertion yesterday to get through the Persian business for your sake, and indeed for my own too. We had a conference here—Reshid and Titov and the interpreters. I dined them all. And what would you have said to see five pipes puffing away in your drawing-room? What a profanation! But the public service, you know, required it, and the consequence was that we got through our task completely. We broke up at half-past ten, and I was in bed at eleven. Now we have only to get all the papers put into their respective phraseologies, to pack them up, and to send them off that the Persians may do the same, and the Plenipos. sign and seal merrily at Erzerum. By the way, Reshid has promised me a *nishan* for Curzon, and if I can get him a "*Lion and Sun*" from Persia, I do not see what should keep him from being knighted and sporting "Sir Robert" till he gets his peerage in the course of nature. . . . The Turks have been much vexed by a speech of M. Guizot's about Syria. It is indeed but too much of a piece with much that has come of late from the same quarter. Everything is on the point of settling; and there is an evident determination to throw all into confusion for French purposes. Heaven knows what instructions the next messenger may bring me. Meanwhile I stand firm, and I keep the Porte steady.

5 *March.*—As for my political affairs—they are all moving on towards their conclusion, but their mode of progression is by *short hops* after long intervals of repose or *sedentary* agitation. Even the incomparable Reshid is either not perfect himself or is embarrassed by stupid colleagues. Between ourselves I suspect that *all* colleagues are so. If I can but settle all handsomely, secure my antiquities, leave Reshid to travel gently with his Sultan, and turn my back upon as quiet an empire as we have at this moment, after two or three measures of internal improvement shall have been adopted, I shall be satisfied, and forget all past and present vexations in self-content and the prospect of seeing you once more. In the meantime we are passing rather a dull existence, a long spell of wet bad weather, succeeded by a spell of fine cold ditto, very changeable, as you know. But, to be just, yesterday was a glorious exception, and I sallied forth with all my cavalry, seven horses from the stable, without the coachies, to pay visits to departing pashas who had called upon me. I made the grand tour of Constantinople and passed in returning for the first time over the new bridge—a very creditable construction. Wellesley went with me to see Suleyman Pasha, who goes ambassador to Paris. I found his more than octogenarian predecessor—old Khusruf—closeted with him, and I had some capital sport with the two, the old bird being by far the most alive of the two.

Think of my having five Armenian women closeted with me this morning—relations of poor persecuted devils excommunicated by the patriarch for *Gospel* opinions &c. You will recognize in this the work of the American missionaries. So it is, and my position is most embarrassing; but I am doing my best to rescue the persecuted in their civil interests and domestic relations without giving too much offence and exciting disobedience to just authority. A young lady of seventeen was the spokesman, and she delivered her English first through a yashmak and then, in her zeal, with uncovered lips. It is lucky for ambassadors that they are husbands and papas as well as elderly gentlemen.

18 *April.*—I made a *tremendous* speech [1] at the dinner given three days ago to a prince of Hesse-Darmstadt who has been here. He is a general in the Russian service and brother-in-law to the

[1] See the Library Edition, ii. 157.

Czar's eldest son. The Sultan dined us at Beylerbey, but did not appear himself. I did not mean to give a toast, but was egged on, and so made the best of it—and nothing could equal the joy and compliments of the Turks. Mark, too, that Titov shook me by the hand. . . . Sarim is here—the beast—he came sneaking up, and I was barely civil. He is already trying to insinuate venom against Reshid.

4 *May.*—Though I am not yet quite free I am dropping my shackles one after the other. . . . The Persian negotiation is still the main, if not the only, difficulty. I have, however, taken leave of the Sultan, who was graciousness itself. He thanked me for my services to his empire, was satisfied of my devotion to his interests, regretted my absence, and longed for my return. What more could the fondness of a lover have suggested? The audience was a private one, and Reshid, by accident, was my interpreter.

Canning did not escape from the Porte till the end of July, and he left with an unpleasant feeling that a reaction might be expected. His old enemy Riza Pasha had been recalled to office. " I fear that I have stayed too long," he wrote to his wife, 20 July; " Riza is in office again, not very high, but still in office—Minister of Commerce in place of Sarim. It looks as if Reshid had been very weak—or worse. I have had suspicions for some days, and wormed the thing out, but too late to prevent. It may be less disastrous than I apprehend in the first moment, and I have my assurances to hope so; but I am sick of assurances, and believe nothing." In this disconsolate mood ended his fourth mission to the Porte—a mission fraught with great results and marked throughout by a disinterested ambition to save Turkey for her own sake and raise her to a worthy place among European Powers.

―――――

CHAPTER XIV.

NINEVEH AND THE MAUSOLEUM.

1846.

EVERYONE has heard of the discoveries of Layard and Newton, of the palace of Nimrud and the colossal tomb of Mausolus; but few are aware that but for the liberality and public spirit of Sir Stratford Canning these discoveries might

never have borne fruit and the British Museum might have
been deprived of some of its chief treasures. It was not
merely that without the ambassador's influence the *firmans* or
necessary permits, by which alone excavations, purchases of
land, and exportations of antiquities could take place, might
not have been obtained ; but that it was Canning's own enterprize and money that rescued the first fruits of the Mausoleum and enabled Layard to begin his famous work at
Nineveh. Without being an archaeologist, the Elchi was an
ardent classical scholar of a good old type that we miss now-
adays, and everything connected with ancient history excited
his keenest interest. In the midst of pressing political duties,
we shall see how his mind wandered away with enthusiasm to
the labours of his agents at Mosil and Halicarnassus.

Mr. Austen Henry Layard had arrived at Constantinople
in 1842, after a rough experience of travel in the frontier lands
between Turkey and Persia. Canning was not slow to perceive
the abilities of the explorer, and employed him in more than
one tour of observation in the disturbed provinces of the
Ottoman Empire, and Layard's reports on the state of affairs
in Servia and Albania were scarcely less useful to his employer than his knowledge of the provinces in which the
labours of the Turco-Persian Boundary Commission were
centred. The ambassador would have willingly seen so intelligent and industrious an assistant enrolled among his
attachés ; indeed so earnest were his recommendations that
the Foreign Office went near to reproaching him with importunity ; and it was certainly no fault of his that Layard did
not obtain his first step in diplomacy at the Embassy at the
Porte in 1845. Failing in this, and deeply interested in the
traveller's reports of promising mounds, suggestive of buried
cities, in Mesopotamia, Canning resolved to attempt an exploration of the sites thus indicated, and despatched him in
October 1845 with such funds as he could afford to risk. He
gave him a salary at the rate of 200*l.* a year, and 120*l.* to
begin his digging. It was not much, but the expenses of the
Embassy left little margin for a speculation of this kind, and
the sum was enough to enable Layard to establish the truth
of his conjectures and to draw the attention of the Government to the importance of his discoveries. The explorer was
" to inform Sir Stratford Canning of his operations and to give
him a full account of any objects worthy of curiosity which
he might see or discover ; to abstain carefully from meddling

Q

with anything of a political or religious character ; to avoid confidential or frequent intercourse with missionaries, whatever might be their country or religion ; to shew respect and deference to the Turkish authorities and to lose no opportunity of cultivating their goodwill ; to maintain the character of a traveller fond of antiquities, of picturesque scenery, and of Asiatic manners ; not to leave without communication ; and to do his best to obtain permission on the spot for the removal of the objects discovered " &c. He was furnished with letters of recommendation, and in May 1846 he was sent a firman or Grand Vezirial letter authorizing him to excavate and export sculptures.

Such was the unambitious commencement of perhaps the most astonishing and important series of discoveries which any Englishman has conducted since the days when Belzoni explored the Tombs of the Kings at Thebes. In 1846, moved thereto by Canning's letters and Layard's reports, the Trustees of the British Museum took over the work which the ambassador had begun, and thenceforward Assyrian antiquities poured in an avalanche upon the astounded officials of Bloomsbury.

The excavations at Budrum, the ancient Halicarnassus, were even more the special delight of the ambassador than those at Nimrud. It had long been known that the Castle of St. Peter at Budrum was built by the Knights of St. John with the stones of the Mausoleum which Queen Artemisia constructed in B.C. 353-1 in memory of her husband Mausolus with such loving magnificence that it was numbered among the Seven Wonders of the World. Portions of the ancient sculptures had been detected in the masonry of the fortress, and Canning resolved to rescue these noble remains of the school of Scopas from the risk of Turkish demolition. In June 1844 Charles Alison, the Oriental secretary, was sent on a mission to Syria, and was instructed to call on his way at Budrum and report on the extent and condition of the remains of the Mausoleum which were visible in the walls of the fortress ; and the Elchi told him that he was prepared to find the necessary sum for transferring them to the protection of the British Museum. Alison's report, albeit not that of a specialist, was convincing as to the importance of the sculptures, and the ambassador redoubled his exertions to induce the Porte to grant him permission to remove them. It was not however till 1846 that he triumphed over Turkish procrastination and had the satisfaction of learning, not only that he had leave to extract the marbles from the walls in which

they were embedded, but that the Sultan, in sign of his high
regard, was graciously pleased to make them a personal gift
to the ambassador himself. Any ordinary present would have
been respectfully declined, but these monuments of Greek art
were too precious to be lost for a scruple, and they would
enrich, not the Elchi, but the British nation. The gift was
accordingly accepted with gratitude, and Alison was again
sent out to complete his task by superintending the removal
of the antiquities. The work was successfully accomplished
at a cost of three or four hundred pounds, and twelve out of
the seventeen slabs of the frieze of the Order, representing
combats of Greeks and Amazons, executed in the finest Parian
marble, which now adorn the walls of the British Museum,
are the fruits of these operations.

We read something of the history of these discoveries in a
letter to his wife, 3 January, 1846 :—

I see little of anyone out of the house, and the town is duller
than ever. On Christmas day I collected all the English bachelors
I could think of, and we had a merry party of fourteen. On New
Year's day I collected all the employés of the embassy from
Cumberbatch down to the two students. Wellesley was too ill to
make his appearance, and that reduced us to twenty-one. Old
Bennet said grace, and we drank the Queen's health standing, both
which ceremonies reminded one of earlier and better days. I have
not yet undertaken the diplomats, but must soon, and I meditate
a Turkish dinner to Reshid and some of his friends. . . .

I have at last surmounted all my difficulties about the Marbles
at Budrum. The letters are prepared, a Turkish engineer appointed,
and Alison sets off with them and him and one of Smith's masons
the day after to-morrow to secure the whole prize—thirteen inesti-
mable blocks of marble, sculptured by the four greatest artists of
the best days of Greece, mentioned in Herodotus and immortalized
by the sentiment to which they owed their creation no less than
by the genius which shaped them into perfection. Oh! if they
should stick in the wall! Oh! if they should break in coming out
of it! Oh! if they should founder on the way to England! Think
of my venturing all at my own expense! Think of the Sultan
saying that he won't hear of my paying a sou! Indeed, my own
Artemisia, I shall be much disappointed if the new Ministry and
the Corn Laws be not thrown into the shade by these celebrated
marbles, which it has cost me nearly three years of patient perseverance to obtain. But this is not all. Layard is making very
important discoveries in Mesopotamia. He has sent me the outline
of a most beautiful piece of sculpture representing warriors in active
fight, and chariots and horses with splendid trappings, all of great
antiquity and superior in workmanship to anything discovered by

M. Botta. The French are jealous to an extreme, and the wicked Pasha of Mosil under their influence is trying to counteract us. But I have a scheme, which I think will defeat them and secure us all we want for ourselves, and much more for the benefit of the world at large. Major Rawlinson writes me from Baghdad in high admiration and offers to send up a steamer in the spring to secure whatever Layard may have succeeded in getting out. I am quite proud of my public spirit in the cause of antiquity and fine art. But I must not ruin either you or the children ; and I propose to call in the aid of Government—whether Whig or Tory—to accomplish what may easily prove beyond my reach. Now you must be tired, dead tired of all this, and perhaps you think me crazy for caring so much about such trifles, but they are trifles for which colleges, universities, and nations would take each other by the ears, and, as Major Rawlinson tells me, the inscriptions are likely to throw much light upon Scripture history, particularly on our old friend *Tiglath-pileser.*

Part of Canning's letter to Sir Robert Peel (18 April, 1846) in support of Layard's excavations is here quoted. He perceived that the enterprize was too important to be neglected, and that larger means than his own would be needed to carry it out successfully, and he appealed without hesitation to the Prime Minister :—

While you are providing at so great a personal sacrifice for the ages to come, allow me to claim another of your moments on behalf of those which have preceded us.

M. Botta's success at Nineveh has induced me to adventure in the same lottery, and my ticket has turned up a prize. On the banks of the Tigris not far from Mosil there is a gigantic mound called *Nimrud.* My agent has succeeded in opening it here and there, and his labours have been rewarded by the discovery of many interesting sculptures and a world of inscriptions. If the excavation keeps its promise to the end there is much reason to hope that Montagu House will beat the Louvre hollow.

Although the operations have hitherto proceeded at my personal expense, and without any formal permission from this Government, I look forward to the time when you will think it worth while to step in and carry off the prize on behalf of the Museum. In cherishing this hope I may not, perhaps, have the fear of Exchequer sufficiently before my eyes, but however the Chancellor may demur I feel confident that the representative of a learned university will open his bosom largely to the claims of *Nimrud.* The expense would be small in comparison with the object, which promises results of the highest historical interest :—

tenuis non gloria, si quem
Numina laeva sinunt auditque vocatus Apollo.

The appeal was not made in vain, and the Trustees of the
Museum recognized so fully and gratefully Canning's share in
the great work that they consulted him in every step they
took and submitted the instructions they were sending to
Layard for the ambassador's advice. The Sultan having made
him a personal gift of the antiquities, Canning generously
presented all the results of his own excavation to the nation,
and only consented to the repayment of his advances (as also
in the case of the Budrum sculptures) from a sense of duty to
his family. Of his agent he always wrote with the warmest
appreciation, and Sir Henry Layard long afterwards enjoyed
the advantage of his employer's friendship and support.

The Mausoleum frieze had been safely shipped for England
at the beginning of the year. Canning announced his triumph
(19 Feb.) to his old friend Sir R. H. Inglis, one of the Trustees of the Museum in great exultation :—

Did you ever hear of one Stratford Canning, formerly a member,
if not of Grillion's, at least of parliament ?

Did you ever, as member for the University of Oxford, hear of
Queen Artemisia—not Artemisia, the friend of Xerxes, but Artemisia the inconsolable widow of Mausolus ?

My reason for asking is simply this. The above-mentioned
gentleman has lately broken into a Turkish fortress, and carried off
some dozen blocks of marble exhibiting reliefs of men and horses
fighting, not like Trojans, but true Greeks ; and these—the remains
of the original Mausoleum or seventh wonder of the world—he
proposes to present to the Museum, of which you are a venerable
and honoured Trustee—that is, to the British nation. Observe that
the marbles were stuck into the walls of the fortress of Budrum,
the ancient Halicarnassus—three or four outside, the rest within—
and that the latter, though known to exist, have been invisible to
all but Turkish jailors and artillerymen for ages. My *right* of
possession was obtained from the Sultan, who has made them a
personal gift to me ; the *de facto* possession derives from the
studied and determined exertions of a party of people, headed by
Mr. Alison, an Oriental savant here, whom I sent down to secure
and embark them. The valuables are now on their way to Malta
in H.M. ship *Siren.* They occupy sixteen cases in all, weighing
about twenty tons. I have only seen very imperfect sketches of
them, but if you wish to know more of their merits, you may look
into Clarke and Anacharsis, Pliny, and Vitruvius. The height of
the figures cannot be more than two feet and a half, though the
depth of the marble is about three, and the length varies from
about the same to six. It took me three years of patience and
occasional exertions to get them, and the operation of extracting,

lowering, and embarking them occupied many days. The operation was completed without a single accident, either to the men or
to the marbles. Time, however, though slow, has not been idle, and
some of the figures are consequently the worse for wear, though
not so much so as the artists who made them, or the originals
whom they represent.

It need hardly be said that the Trustees tendered their
" best and warmest thanks " for the liberality with which
Canning had presented the Mausoleum frieze to the nation.
Mr. Forshall, the secretary of the Museum, wrote with enthusiasm of the " Canning Marbles " ; but it is characteristic of
the ambassador's loyalty to the Sultan that he requested that
Abdu-l-Mejid's name should have the post of honour in the
official description of the monument. Accordingly the visitor
to the Mausoleum room in the British Museum now reads
beneath the frieze :—" Given by Sultan Abdul Medjid to
Viscount Stratford de Redcliffe, by whom it was presented to
the Trustees of the British Museum, 1846."

Canning's connexion with Halicarnassus did not end here.
In 1852 Sir Charles (then Mr.) Newton went to the Levant
as vice-consul at Mitylene, with a special view to further excavations in Ionia and the Greek islands. His preliminary
visit to Constantinople was more than an act of official
homage ; he knew both the zeal of the ambassador in the
cause of archaeological research and his unique power to
obtain the needful concessions from the Porte. The firmans
were readily promised, and Mr. Newton began the series of
tours of observation and excavation which he has described in
his authoritative *History of Discoveries at Halicarnassus,
Cnidus, and Branchidae* (1862), and in his eminently graphic
and interesting *Travels and Discoveries in the Levant* (1865).
Throughout these journeys of exploration Lord Stratford's
influence was at work to facilitate the labours of the archaeologist, and in 1854–5 Mr. Newton prosecuted an independent
series of excavations at Calymnos, with funds advanced by the
ambassador, which yielded very valuable results in inscriptions
and other antiquities of an interesting period. It was during
his researches in the Levant that Mr. Newton completed the
work which had been begun at Budrum, by his discovery—
not of fragments built into later masonry, but of the buried
Mausoleum itself, with the colossal statue of the king whom
it enshrined. Before, however, he had embarked on this
gigantic work, he made a discovery at the fortress of Budrum

itself. He observed, jutting out from the walls which Alison believed he had ransacked, but on the outside, some boldly carved lions which obviously belonged to the same period as the frieze which had been previously removed in 1846. How they had come to be overlooked when the frieze within the fortress was being removed is hard to understand; but of course there was now but one course open—to write immediately to Lord Stratford and beg for a firman to extract them. After agonies of suspense, during which the lions were almost kidnapped by the Turks, the firman arrived, and the noble beasts now repose in the British Museum.

We have anticipated the course of events in relating the capture of the Budrum lions by Lord Stratford's lasso, because this was his last important service to archaeology, and fitly concludes the subject. In future, for some years, we have to do with wars and rumours of wars; and though it was in the midst of the intricate negotiations which preceded the Crimean expedition that the ambassador found time to interest himself in Mr. Newton's discoveries at Calymnos, and to despatch the firman to Budrum, readers are not always capable of such divided attention, and the calm victories of archaeology would but interrupt a narrative which centres at Balaklava and Sevastopol. It is well, however, that the world should understand how much it owes to Canning's zeal in the cause of art, and that when it commemorates the signal services of Sir Henry Layard and Sir Charles Newton it may also give due honour to the statesman who was in a large degree the cause of their success.

CHAPTER XV.

THE REFUGEES.

1847–50.

A YEAR of rest and well-employed idleness, if such an expression may be allowed, followed upon five years of arduous labour. After so much vexatious toil and so many disappointments in the progress of his Turkish pupils, Canning was well pleased for a while to do nothing. The interval of leisure was soon over, and in the autumn of 1847 he was preparing for his return to Stambol. The journey was not, however, to be hurried or direct. There were signs in the political condition of Europe which caused uneasiness to Lord John Russell's cabinet : the first mutterings were already audible of the storm which was to burst in 1848 ; and it was considered desirable that a tried diplomatist should visit the principal Courts of Central Europe and sound their views upon the alarming prospect which lay before them. The envoy selected for this delicate and responsible task was Sir Stratford Canning.

On the eve of his departure for what he believed to be " the last act of his Oriental drama " he was delayed by a new complication. The scene of one of his early missions required his presence. Switzerland was then torn in two by a religious contest. For several years the Catholic question had been assuming formidable proportions in some of the cantons, and after long and careful consideration the Federal Diet, for reasons which were recognized as sound by the majority of the Swiss, had resolved upon the expulsion of the Jesuits from the cantons. In some parts, however, the Catholics preponderated, and here a strenuous resistance was offered to the edict. In the autumn of 1846 this opposition took definite form in the Sonderbund, a league comprizing the Seven Cantons of Lucerne, Uri, Schwyz, Unterwalden, Freiburg, Zug, and Valais. After several fruitless attempts at reconciliation, the Diet in July 1847 proclaimed the Sonderbund as an illegal combination—an infraction of the Federal constitution of 1815—and insisted on the expulsion of the Jesuits. Civil war ensued ; in September the Council at Bern authorized military preparations, and the troops were ordered to dissolve the league and occupy the disaffected cantons. The Five Powers who at Vienna had guaranteed the Federal Pact of 1815 hastened to concert plans of mediation. Some were inclined to translate their protective function into a right of marching troops into the disturbed districts, but against armed intervention Palmerston stood firm. Austria and France naturally favoured the Catholics, England the Protestants. All five at length agreed upon an identic note offering their collective mediation, to be presented both to the Diet and the Sonderbund by representatives of the several guaranteeing Powers.

Canning's old connexion with Switzerland, and the share he had taken in 1814-15 in drawing up the Federal constitution, naturally marked him out as the man for this mission. He had never lost his interest in the cantons which had once given him so much trouble; and the circumstance that his old friend David Morier was minister at Bern from 1831 to 1846 had enabled the former to keep up his information and acquaintances. In spite of the difficulties of the task, and the inclement season of the year, he was glad to feel that he might be of use to a country for which he entertained a genuine affection. "It is a work of much trouble and difficulty," he wrote to his brother, "but it is also a work of peace, and therefore I do not hesitate to obey." The main object of the mission, however, was frustrated by the time he had reached Paris at the end of November. Mediation implies two parties to be reconciled : but the Five Powers, proceeding in their cautious diplomatic manner, had not reckoned upon the celerity and thoroughness which the Federal army displayed ; and by the time the identic note was ready there were no combatants wherewith to mediate. The troops of the Diet marched into Freiburg, defeated the forces of the Sonderbund, entered Lucerne, and brought the whole of the Seven Cantons to submission in November 1847 ; and Lord Palmerston of course instructed Canning to hold back the note, since mediation had now no ground whereon to stand. The ambassador was nevertheless to continue his journey to Bern, to "make himself acquainted with the general posture of affairs in Switzerland, and . . . the sentiments and intentions of the leading men of the various political parties," and also to urge moderation upon the Federals, to counsel the Diet "to use its victory with temperance," and to warn it of the risk of armed intervention on the part of those Powers which had already viewed its course with disfavour.

On arriving at Bern, Canning found that Palmerston's forebodings were in a fair way to be realized. The Provisional Governments which had taken the place of the Sonderbund leaders in the subdued cantons had entered upon a course of wholesale imprisonment and confiscation. The counsels, however, of the English ambassador had some effect in moderating the vengeance of the successful party, and his voice had a considerable share in preventing the occupation of Neuchâtel by the federal troops. This canton had asserted its neutrality during the war, and the King of Prussia, who

was its hereditary sovereign, had sanctioned its policy. The
Diet acted on the principle that he who was not with it was
against it, and would have marched its men into Neuchâtel,
at the risk of bringing Prussia into the field, had not Canning
succeeded in inducing both parties to agree to a fine to be
paid for over-scrupulous neutrality.

By the end of December things were becoming settled.
Sir Stratford remained at Bern till the latter part of January,
and then returned by way of Paris, where he reported that he
found the King and Guizot jubilantly confident of their hold
on the people; yet only a fortnight elapsed before the royal
family had to fly to England from the Parisian mob! The
ambassador was satisfied with what he had accomplished;
and indeed, considering the thinly-veiled antagonism of the
four other Powers, it was no light success to have left Switzerland pacified on the lines laid down by the British Government—the expulsion of the Jesuits, the dissolution of the
Sonderbund, and the restoration of the Federal Pact. Palmerston wrote: "You have been able to do much good and
to prevent much mischief."

Canning arrived in London on 8 February, 1848. The close
of the month was full of gloomy forecasts of the coming storms.
On the 26th the news arrived of the flight of Louis Philippe.
That evening at Lady Palmerston's reception all faces were
troubled and melancholy. No one knew what had become of
the fugitives, but as the days passed, one by one the French
princes and ministers appeared in England, and anxiety now
turned upon Germany, where the riots were becoming so
violent that it seemed doubtful whether the ambassador could
take his family with him in his progress through Europe.
Lady Canning, however, decided that her duty took her with
her husband, especially as the Mission to the Porte was "only
for a very short time," and on 17 March the whole party
embarked for Brussels.

MEMOIRS. My last act before I embarked was one of respect to
the royal exiles at Claremont. The visit, I knew, would not be pleasing
to Lord Palmerston, who had given way to a strong feeling of resentment against Louis Philippe; but the King had always behaved
very graciously to me, and I wished him not to think that his misfortune had clouded my memory. I was received first by Queen
Amélie. Her manner and countenance were in keeping with her
well-known character. She was grave, but not depressed; resigned,
but not regretful. In talking of the late occurrences she displayed

an unassuming manliness of tone which made me think that in her
husband's place she might perhaps have reversed the fortunes of
her family. The King meanwhile was writing in a separate apartment. As soon as he had finished his letters I was admitted to his
presence. He had every appearance of health—cheerful features
and lively spirits. If any regret or anxiety weighed upon his mind,
there was no trace of it on his face or in his demeanour. One
might have thought that together with his crown and robes he had
thrown off all the cares of life. I took the liberty to remind him
of the fortifications round Paris, which he had rather boastingly
explained to me at the Tuileries, and also of the consultation, held
by his order some time before, with the view of providing against
any case of riots and barricades. How was it possible to think of
such things at such a moment? was his only reply. I said no
more, but could not help thinking that the outbreak which had
dethroned him and sent his whole family adrift was just the very
moment for turning precaution to account. Both he and the Queen
extolled in warm and affectionate terms the conduct of their son,
the Duc de Nemours. I had previously seen M. Guizot and
Madame Lieven after their arrival in London. They had travelled
in the same train from Paris without knowing it. The former told
me that late on the night preceding the King's departure in disguise
he had left the palace fully persuaded that on his return next
morning he should find the insurrection quelled. Marshal Bugeaud
was on horseback waiting for orders to attack the barricades.
Molé, Odillon Barrot, and another were with his Majesty. Before
giving the decisive word one of them proposed that a parley should
be first attempted, and Louis Philippe assented. The experiment
was made ; the reply was a threat to fire, the consequence a loss
of time irreparable and conclusive. Early next morning, probably
after learning this unhappy *dénouement*, M. Guizot was on his
way to the legislative hall, when he met M. Piscatory, not long
before French minister at Athens. Persuaded by that gentleman
that it would be useless, and indeed dangerous, for him to appear
in the assembly, he turned aside with much reluctance, and took
refuge in his friend's house until the means of escape could be
provided.

Looking back from a distance of forty years it is difficult
to realize the consternation with which all Europe regarded
the upheaval of society which marked the famous year of
revolutions. One capital after another became a prey to bands
of students, soldiers, or mere rabble, who paraded the streets
and extorted constitutions from trembling kings. It needed
some courage to pursue a journey, accompanied by ladies,
from one disturbed centre to another, and the news which
greeted the ambassador on his arrival at Brussels was calcu-

lated to arrest his further progress.   Berlin, he learnt, was a
scene of massacre and anarchy ; at Vienna the students had
stormed the council chamber and bearded Metternich himself.
" Forty years," said the old man, when he had listened to
their demands, " forty years have I served my country ; I
have never yielded to an insurrection, nor will I yield now."
One of the archdukes sprang to his feet and said, " But we
must."   Metternich merely bowed and left the room ; he was
soon a disguised fugitive bound for England, the only country
where such storms broke harmlessly.   On the 21st the news
from Berlin was more reassuring, and Canning resolved to
proceed ; but at Aix-la-Chapelle tidings came of more bloodshed and the flight of the Prince of Prussia.   At Hanover he
dined with the old King, who seemed in great alarm, and
nothing was thought or talked of but the revolutions.   The
blind Crown Prince was the most cheerful member of the
royal family ; when the storm was at its highest, he said,
sunshine was sometimes nearest.   At Brunswick the national
flag was waving from every window ; but on arriving at Berlin
the ambassador was surprized at the stillness of the city.   It
seemed almost deserted, save where a dozen burghers, enve-
loped in heavy cloaks, but shivering with cold, and heartily
tired of carrying muskets and swords, relieved guard with
white-gloved students, who seemed exceeding pleased to be
released from their posts.   The old Prussian Guard was
invisible, and *Burschen* marched before the Schloss.   On the
29th the ambassador had an audience of King Frederick
William, who had not seen him for twenty years, but greeted
him almost affectionately with the words " Oh, que je suis
content de revoir ces traits que je connais si bien ! "   Dining
thrice with the King at Potsdam, Canning was as much
impressed by his simple kindness as struck with his weakness
and indecision.

The 22nd of April found them at Vienna, where Lord and
Lady Ponsonby entertained them hospitably, and they saw
for almost the last time the old Court etiquette, and the quaint
livery of the footmen whose duty it was to run beside the
ambassador's carriage and stand behind his chair at dinner.
On 2 May the English travellers witnessed an *émeute* of the
students.   The mob went straight to Count Fieguelmont's
house, which the ambassador's party had just left, and compelled him to come on to the balcony and address them, after
which they went quietly home.   The next day the streets

were again in the hands of the students, who stormed the
Prime Minister's house and office, and Fieguelmont promised
to resign. The National Guard made no movement and the
Prime Minister and his family fled the city.

Early in May, Canning, accompanied only by Lord Au-
gustus Loftus, who had travelled with him from England and
acted as his private secretary, paid a visit to the King of
Bavaria at Munich ; but the 22nd found the whole party reunited at Trieste, and ready to embark on board the *Antelope*
for Athens and Constantinople. Trieste was at that moment
in consternation, for Lombardy and Venice had risen, the
King of Sardinia had espoused the cause of the Italians, and
on that very morning his fleet had come in sight. The ambassador could not leave until he had assured himself of the
safety of British interests in the Adriatic. The Austrian fleet
was in the harbour, and not at all anxious to sally out again ;
but fortunately three British men-of-war were drawn up outside, and the *Antelope* joined them. The people on shore
were hard at work erecting earthworks, and preparing for
attack, but the governor was in low spirits, and nobody seemed
able to give orders. The *Antelope*, with the ambassador's
party on board, was then despatched to communicate with the
Sardinian fleet, which presented a handsome line of five
frigates, five steamers, four brigs, and three schooners ; and
the sensations of the travellers may be imagined as they
approached this formidable array and made the agreeable
discovery that the guns were all manned and run out, and
the tompions removed. No catastrophe, however, ensued ; the
English were assured that Trieste was in no danger, and
nothing worse than a blockade was intended ; so leaving the
three British vessels as an additional security, Sir Stratford
proceeded on his way to Patras and the Gulf of Lepanto,
crossed the Isthmus of Corinth, and, taking ship again at
Callimachi, arrived at the Peiraeus.

Greece had from the first been a main object of Canning's
mission. The King of the Hellenes was on very unpleasant
terms with his subjects, and both the king and the Hellenes
in general were in perpetual discord with their neighbours
the Turks, who, to do them justice, deserved better treatment.
How to bring King Otho and his subjects to reason was the
problem, and the solution did not appear hopeful even to the
most sanguine. Palmerston considered the Bavarian an impracticable prince, and only instructed Canning to try what

he could do with him because, as he said, if anyone could
bring about a change for the better it was the man who
had always taken so warm an interest in the formation and
maintenance of the Greek State. The ambassador himself
expected little good to come of the attempt, nor was he
deceived. Otho was, as Lord Palmerston feared, impracticable, and the ambassador left Athens on 19 June with little
or nothing accomplished in the way of good, beyond presenting the King with a memorandum of warning and advice
couched in terms stronger than even Sir Edmund Lyons
could have expected. It took fourteen years more to get rid
of King Otho, and during the whole period Greece was a
thorn in the side of Europe.

Canning's fifth residence at Constantinople was marked
by a new phase in his relations with foreign Powers. His
first mission had been a long struggle with France, in which
at the close he had Russia on his side. In the second and
third, England, France, and Russia were united on the main
question, the pacification of Greece ; and in the fourth, though
occasional points of divergence arose, the three Powers were
on the whole sufficiently friendly to one another to allow him
to devote his chief energies to the internal reform of the
Ottoman Empire. In the fifth period, 1848–52, we see the
beginning of that coalition of the Western Powers against
Russia upon which the seal was set in the Crimean war. He
now found himself for the first time in acute antagonism to
Russia, and in his defence of Turkey in the matters of the
Danubian Principalities and of the Hungarian refugees we
find a foretaste of the resolute policy which ended at Sevastopol. In former years he, like almost every English statesman, had watched the policy of the Czars with suspicion, but
it so chanced that he was absent from Constantinople on the
occasions when Russia made her most dangerous advances,
in the war which terminated in the disastrous Treaty of
Adrianople, and in the no less menacing alliance which was
signalized by the compromising Treaty of Hunkiar Iskelesi.
Accident had hitherto placed him in the position of coöperation with Russia rather than of opposition ; and only in 1848
did that new condition of compulsory hostility begin which
marked the concluding years of his mission at the Porte.

The ambassador had fortunately returned to his post just
in time. The revolutionary wave broke upon the Danubian
provinces in the very month of his arrival. A popular rising

took place at Bucharest on 23 June ; the troops refused to act ; and the Hospodar conceded to the insurgents their demands of universal suffrage and the eligibility of all Wallachians to the princely office. Had this involved nothing more than an expedition of Turkish troops very little trouble would have ensued ; but Russia claimed under the Treaty of Adrianople the right to maintain order in the Danubian Principalities, and the immediate consequence of the Bucharest rising was a proposal for joint occupation by Russian and Turkish troops. There was more in this than met the eye. The differences between Austria and Hungary were watched by the Czar with anxiety, and there could be little doubt, as the event proved, that the entrance of Russian troops into the principalities would be but the preliminary step to a vigorous support of Austria. If Turkey were thus to be made a base for military operations in other countries, the Porte's neutrality would be compromised, and a dangerous precedent created.

In this strait the Turkish ministers, according to their wont, appealed for advice to Canning. He urged them not to treat the Wallachians as rebels, but to regard them merely as constitutional reformers, and to inquire into their demands and grievances ; and while he recommended the despatch of a special commissioner, he counselled a careful avoidance of military occupation, lest an ominous example should be set for Russia to follow. The Turks accepted half the advice and rejected the rest. They sent Suleyman Pasha to investigate the Wallachian demands, but they also despatched an army across the Danube, though not immediately to Bucharest. The natural result was that 4,000 Russians entered Moldavia. As the protector of oppressed Christianity against the barbarous Mohammedan, the Czar had no intention of allowing Turkey to act by herself in the Danube provinces, which he regarded as a close preserve, over which he and the Sultan had alone the right of shooting, with the proviso that the latter must never enjoy his sport without the accompaniment of the Russian gun. Turkey had already admitted far too much, though not the whole, of this doctrine in the Treaty of Adrianople and in the preamble to the firman which accorded the principalities their privileges. The Russian occupation evidently had the Porte's consent. The difficulty of the situation was aggravated by the totally divergent views of the two occupying Powers. Turkey, moved by the strenuous counsels of the British ambassador, was for mild measures, amnesty to the " reformers," liberal amendments in the constitution, and the speedy removal of the Russian troops. The Czar, on the other hand, imperiously demanded a severe repression of the " revolution," punishment of the " rebels," repudiation of free institutions, and a prolonged joint occupation in the interests of order. It was the old contest between the principles of the Holy Alliance and the liberal policy of George Canning.

Sir Stratford, true to his principles, strove to keep the Porte steady on the lines of moderation and reform. Some extracts from his correspondence with Lord Palmerston will explain his attitude : —

4 *Sept.*—I find it not a little puzzling to keep a steady line of march between the Porte and Russia, to keep the peace and to respect the treaties on one side and on the other to sustain the Porte's courage and to lay a foundation for real improvement in Wallachia.

At present Russia seems more disposed to force the Porte into measures of severity than to join with her in adopting those of improvement. If the Porte be pressed too hard, it is not impossible that she may appeal to the spectators. I would not put myself forward without necessity, but were the necessity to arise I could hardly err in trying by discreet and sensible means to rescue her from the humiliation of being forced to turn tail on her principles of benevolence and improvement. I am authorized to rely upon the concurrence of the Internuncio and of the French minister in such a contingency.

As winter approached, the situation in Wallachia did not improve. The Turkish commissioner was bodily threatened, and was forced to disperse the people by a charge of horse ; 12,000 Turks, marching into Bucharest, against Canning's advice, were fired upon, and retaliated with customary brutality. Russia talked of at least two years' occupation and had fully 30,000 men in the provinces. The Czar's attitude had been materially stiffened by a series of repulses at the Porte. He had proposed a close alliance with the Sultan, and had been put off with civil phrases. He had recommended a formal joint occupation of the Principalities, and the Turks had objected ; civil measures, not military, and a programme of reforms, had their preference. Russia urged vigorous concerted action ; Turkey replied that she could manage her own subjects unaided, and intended to manage them gently. Russia insisted on the Wallachians being punished as rebels; Turkey stoutly refused. In all this the Czar perceived rightly the influence of one man, and it was then that the personal dread of the British ambassador, which afterwards formed so prominent a motive in his conduct, first took strong hold of him.

If he knew what was passing between the Porte and its chief adviser at the time, he must have felt indeed that it had come to a personal duel. The Turks, in mortal fear of the Russian advance, were pressing for a defensive alliance with England at the very moment when Russia was seeking to bind the Porte to herself in the same way. Reshid and Rif'at Pasha had several interviews with Canning on this subject, and though the ambassador could not commit his Government to a definite opinion, and was bound to state objections, it is clear that the project met with his personal approval. Lord Palmerston's reply to the overture was friendly but inconclusive. It was not advisable to rouse the jealousy of the Eastern Powers by a decided step of this nature. At the same time no pains were to be spared to keep Turkey firm in the English interest.

During the winter of 1848-9 the relations between Russia and Turkey became still more strained. The Czar took upon himself to disarm the Wallachians without the Sultan's leave, and in all his acts and communications Nicholas assumed a perfect equality with the sovereign of Turkey in all that concerned the Danubian provinces. In January, when Wallachia was completely restored to tranquillity, Russia proposed a seven years' occupation of the Principalities and the signature of a Convention reviving those exclusive pretensions which it was the special object of the Treaty of 1841 to destroy. A further complication arose when the Porte was required to permit the Russian troops to pass into Transylvania for the purpose of crushing the Hungarian insurgents, and when Russia furnished Servia with 10,000 muskets for no other purpose than to stir up fresh strife. It is needless to say that all these proposals and proceedings were met by Canning's energetic resistance. The Convention was eluded and the entrance into Transylvania prohibited; yet the Russians marched against the Hungarians in defiance of the Porte, and were punished by a severe defeat at the hands of General Bem. The situation became daily more critical. The Turks, said Canning, must be "prepared for the worst," and England

R

must finally make up her mind ; "the time has come for adopting a definite and decisive course of policy with respect to this country viewed as to its relations with Russia. . . . A timely and effective demonstration of support, especially if it were concerted with France, might be expected to deter the Russian Cabinet from proceeding to extreme measures, or, should it fall short in that respect, to save the Porte from being overwhelmed in a single and unequal struggle." He evidently anticipated war, and hoped to enlist the forces of England and France on the Turkish side. For some time his eyes had been fixed on the Mediterranean squadron. Reshid, in evident anxiety, had asked about its actual position in November, and in February, when the Turks were arming for the expected struggle, and Russia was imperiously insisting on the proposed Convention, the ambassador went so far as to give the Grand Vezir a hint as to the possible approach of the fleet. He supported this in a vigorous despatch to Lord Palmerston, in which, whilst urging that no further concessions could possibly be granted to the overweening arrogance of Russia, he said :—

It requires no spirit of prophecy to foresee whither an unchecked excursion over a field so fertile in pretexts and opportunities for aggression will ultimately lead—no effort of intelligence to perceive that if the independence and integrity of this Empire have any value in the eyes of Europe for the sake of European interests, any weight in the scale of British policy, . . . the moment is arrived when general understandings, general representations, and general assurances must be followed up with distinct agreements, positive declarations, and pledges, not to be mistaken, of sympathy and eventual support.

Lord Palmerston did not feel that the time had actually come for a naval demonstration ; but he powerfully supported Canning's policy in a communication to Baron Brunov. Reshid, who took no step without consulting his English adviser, declared he would resign sooner than give way to Russia, and firmly stood out against the Convention. The Czar, temporarily repulsed by the Hungarians, and therefore unable to evacuate his base of operations in the Principalities, decided on a fresh effort. He despatched General Grabbe with an autograph letter to the Sultan and instructions to bring the Porte to terms, and in this the envoy so far succeeded that he extorted from the Turks, not indeed the disputed Convention, but an " Act " which conceded most of the Russian demands.

Canning had striven against the Act in vain. Without material support from the fleet, his influence could not avail against the heavy pressure of the Czar. He consoled himself with the reflection that the end " might have been worse," and took care that the Turks should not be deluded into a sense of security by the apparent termination of the dispute. The armies and fleets of the Porte continued their preparations for defence. In urging these precautions Canning shewed his usual foresight ; but even he can scarcely have anticipated the crisis which was about to occur. Events were at hand which forced the British Government into a totally different attitude from that indicated in the foregoing letter. Within five months England and France found themselves apparently on the verge of war with Russia, not for a matter of territorial aggrandizement, nor even for the balance of power, but for a cause far more generous than any national interest, the cause of humanity.

From the early spring there had been indications of a coming dispute between the Sultan and the two Imperial Governments of Vienna and St. Petersburg on the subject of insurgents who might take refuge in Turkish territory. By Article XVIII. of the Treaty of Belgrade the Porte was bound to " punish " such " evil-doers, and discontented and rebellious subjects [of Austria], as also robbers and brigands," as might seek an asylum in the Ottoman dominions. Under Article II. of the Treaty of Kaynarji, Russia could demand the extradition or the expulsion of refugees from Turkey, and *vice versâ*. Russia, however, had in former times disregarded her part of the mutual obligation, and the dispute was likely to turn chiefly upon the stipulation in the Treaty of Belgrade, where, it must be noted, there was no mention of extradition but only of " punishment." The question was sure to arise : Did the Hungarian insurgents, a nation in arms, come under the terms of Article XVIII. ? The Porte and its English adviser, though somewhat doubtful of the literal interpretation, held that in spirit the " punishment of evil-doers " applied only to ordinary offenders in time of peace, and could not be so stretched as to compromise the Hungarian patriots. Canning saw sufficient reason to believe that this view of the article might be sustained, and felt sure that the general sense of England would be in its favour. He counselled the Porte at all hazards to adopt a humane and generous policy, and to refuse to surrender those who might throw themselves

R 2

upon its compassion. The best course would be to let the
refugees pass immediately through and out of its territory;
but if this could not be effected, let the Sultan shield them
from certain death. They should be disarmed, and made to
understand that their safety depended on their good conduct;
but they should not be given up to their enemies.

The occasion for exercising this humane resolution soon
arose. On 14 August seventy-six fugitive Hungarians and
Poles landed at Constantinople; they were immediately scattered about in places where they were least likely to attract
notice. The Hungarian agent applied to Canning for assistance in procuring passports for sending them home. This, of
course, the ambassador of a neutral power could not do, nor
would the Turks take the responsibility; so he advised that
the fugitives should be suffered quietly to remain in Turkey.
The Internuncio of Austria at once demanded their extradition, and the Russian envoy followed suit. A week or so
later occurred a fresh invasion of refugees, and these of the
first rank. The short-lived triumph of the Hungarians, over
which Canning and Reshid had secretly rejoiced, was over,
and Görgei's forced surrender to the Russian commander was
followed by a general flight of the patriots. Kossuth, Bem,
Dembinski, and some fourscore less renowned civilians and
officers had crossed the Turkish frontier and were now at
Vidin. The presence of the leaders of the insurrectionary
armies, and of Kossuth himself, the mainspring of the national
movement, safe in Turkey, was intolerable to the two empires.
The Internuncio and M. Titov urgently insisted on their extradition. Canning, supported by General Aupick, his French
colleague, counselled unfaltering resistance. On 30 August
the Council of the Porte decided that they could not give up the
fugitives without dishonour. A Note, revised by the British
ambassador, was sent to the Austrian and Russian representatives, and the Porte stood firm to its duty.

On 4 Sept. the residents in the Embassy house at Therapia
were spectators of an ominous scene. An Austrian steamer
entered the Bosphorus, and, pausing before the Russian
Embassy at Buyukderé, saluted and hoisted Russian colours
at the fore; she then steamed on to the Golden Horn. Soon
afterwards Sir Stratford Canning received a message and
departed instantly for Pera. On the 17th the vessel was
observed returning the way she had come. She had brought
Prince Michael Radzivil with an ultimatum from the Czar,

and she was carrying the Prince and his ultimatum, discomfited and rejected, back to his master.

The Emperor had not minced words with his brother of Turkey. The war, he announced, was over, and the extradition of the rebels must imperatively ensue. He demanded a categorical answer, yes or no. The further relations of the two Empires, he wrote, would depend on that answer; and meanwhile the escape of a single Hungarian or Pole would be regarded as a declaration of war.

This was the news that had summoned Canning to the Porte. What passed between him and the Turkish ministers was not committed to writing, but its tenor may be guessed from the result. The ambassador, with all the impressive solemnity which he knew so well how to use, bade the Porte take courage, be true to the everlasting principles of honour and humanity, be true to its own independence and dignity, and boldly refuse to obey the Czar's command. And when he counselled unqualified resistance, the Turkish ministers knew that he was prepared to support them in the right course with the whole strength of Great Britain. He ventured even in writing to assert, and General Aupick coincided, that in case of war resulting from this resistance, it was certainly to be presumed that England and France would not leave the Porte unassisted. He had no authority to pledge the arms of England, and of course he left the Government the opportunity of repudiation; but the case was desperate, and he knew that Palmerston at the Foreign Office was not the man to desert him or to flinch from a resolute policy. To his chief he justified his action thus :—

If I had suspended my support for a moment, the Porte, I have no doubt, would have given way, and on almost any question but one involving such obvious considerations of humanity, honour, and permanent policy, I might have been inclined while left to myself to counsel a less dangerous course in spite of reason and right. As it is, I felt that there was no alternative unattended with loss of credit and character, to say nothing of the unfortunate and highly distinguished men awaiting their doom at Vidin, Zamoiski among others. The dishonour would have been *ours*, for everyone knows that even Reshid himself, with all his spirit and humanity, would not withstand the torrent without us. . . . I am sure that you will feel the importance of coming to the rescue as far and as fast as you can.

Hence he counselled a firm resistance, and the Porte, em-

boldened by his fearlessness, and even to some degree inspired
by his own high spirit, straightened itself up and defied the
Czar.   Thus it came to pass that the Porte stood firm; the
two embassies pulled down their flags 17 September, and
Prince Radzivil retired in angry amazement.

So far the victory was with Canning and his French ally,
but they both knew it was but the skirmish of outposts which
precedes the general engagement.   A terrible interval of six
weeks' suspense must be endured before they could learn
whether their bold policy would be countenanced by their
respective Governments.   Meanwhile Russian troops might
cross the Balkan; the Sevastopol fleet, which had long offered
unpleasant possibilities to the Turkish imagination, might
sail into the Bosphorus and bombard Constantinople; the
Ottoman Empire in Europe might be disabled before the
Western Powers could interfere.   All these thoughts passed
through Canning's mind as he paced his room at Therapia
and cast an anxious glance at the narrow gap between the
bordering hills through which he could see the billows of the
Euxine.   To wait was ever painful to his energetic nature;
but to wait then, with such issues at stake, must have been
torture.   Some relief, however, came to him in the first week
of October.   Admiral Sir William Parker, who had been
apprized by him (17 Sept.) of the possible need of his fleet at
the Dardanelles, grasped the situation in a moment, and made
all sail for the Archipelago.   Like the ambassador, he acted
on his own discretion; but there was nothing very unusual
in a cruise in the waters of the Levant, and the Turks were
not, of course, to take it as a demonstration on the part
of the British Government.   Nevertheless there was joy in
Stambol when, on 3 Oct., a frigate carrying the reassuring
white ensign made its appearance in the Golden Horn.   It
might mean nothing, but there was that in the face of the
Great Elchi which boded victory.   The frigate had brought
him information that Sir William Parker was on the watch.

Still three anxious weeks had to be gone through before
the decision of the English Cabinet could be known at
Therapia.   Not a day was lost by the vigorous mind that
ruled the Foreign Office.   The decision of the Cabinet was
taken immediately, and hardly was it pronounced when a
messenger was off with a note to Canning.   Palmerston hoped
to relieve him from his anxious position a day or two sooner
by sending a Queen's Messenger overland by Vienna; and, in

case the first should meet with an accident, he presently
despatched a second officer, whose name was renowned wherever hounds were running.   His orders were stringent : the
messenger was " not to spare himself, nor others."   How the
late Lieut.-Colonel (then Captain) Charles Townley interpreted
this instruction may be seen in his own narrative, published
anonymously in Major Byng Hall's *The Queen's Messenger.*
Let it suffice here to say that this royal messenger left Belgrade on 20 Oct. ; rode unrelieved the whole 820 miles to Constantinople, accompanied by a gallant Tartar guide ; spent
three days and nights in the saddle without cessation, in spite
of the reopening of an old musket wound ; and finally reached
Constantinople 26 Oct., thirty-three hours before the Austrian
despatches, which had passed him at Belgrade.

Thank God [he wrote], we had no other trouble but tired and
jaded horses to contend with, and at half-past five on Friday
morning I entered the old ruined gateway of Constantinople, traversed its narrow and tortuous streets, and, crossing the Golden
Horn in a caïque, reached the English Embassy at Pera (26 Oct.),
having been just five days and eleven hours in traversing on horseback 820 miles, having the whole of that time to contend with wind,
mud, and rain, besides two heavyish falls, which, if they broke no
bones, certainly did me no good.   I felt a certain pride in hearing
that it was considered the quickest journey ever performed in the
winter, and that the best Tartars in the service of the Porte took
six days during fine summer weather.   I can claim credit for
obstinacy, at least, if for no higher quality.

As one reads his quiet business-like narrative of a feat of
true British pluck one thinks of the legendary ride from
Ghent to Aix :—

Not a word to each other : we kept the great pace
Neck by neck, stride by stride, never changing our place . . .
And there was my Roland to bear the whole weight
Of the news which alone could save Aix from her fate.

It was a brave deed, and the Foreign Office did not forget it.
Lord Palmerston referred to it in the House of Commons, and
Captain Townley's ride became famous.

The despatch informed Canning that—

The Cabinet has to-day [2 Oct.] decided to give an affirmative
answer to the application for moral and material support which the
Turkish ambassador by order of his Government has presented to
us.   We are therefore going to enter immediately into communication with the Government of France in order to settle the course of

proceeding, assuming what we cannot doubt, namely, that the French Government is willing and prepared to coöperate with us. What we mean to propose is that the two Governments should make friendly and courteous representations at Vienna and Petersburg to induce the Imperial Governments to desist from their demands, urging that the Sultan is not bound by treaty to do what is asked of him, and that to do so would be dishonourable and disgraceful. We mean to propose at the same time that the two Mediterranean squadrons should proceed at once to the Dardanelles with orders to go up to the Bosphorus if invited to do so by the Sultan, either to defend Constantinople from attack, or to give him the moral support which their presence would afford.

It is easy to imagine the intense satisfaction with which the news was received at Constantinople. " The cause of honour and humanity has been vindicated," wrote Canning in proud delight, and the Sultan and his ministers were not behindhand in their expressions of gratitude. Abdu-l-Mejid sent a special aide-de-camp to the Embassy to tender his Majesty's thanks to the Queen and to signify his unfeigned pleasure at the outburst of sympathy which had sprung from the whole British nation. Indeed it was this unanimous sentiment, which re-echoed in every quarter of England, that carried the day. At the end of October the British fleet, soon to be followed by the French, appeared off the Dardanelles, and on 1 Nov. it entered within the Outer Castles ; but it may be doubted whether even this demonstration would have sufficed to shake the two Emperors' resolve if they had not been aware that the feeling of the nation was enthusiastically enlisted in the cause of the refugees. That being known, there was nothing for it but to fight or to retreat. On 7 Nov. Canning informed Lord Palmerston that Russia and Austria had withdrawn their demand for extradition, in deference, said M. Titov, to the pronounced expression of public feeling in England. The two Imperial Governments were disposed to throw the blame of the crisis upon the zeal of their agents, and to back out of the position at all hazards.

The danger, however, was not entirely over, though the main issue had been triumphantly decided. There was still the question as to what was to be done with the refugees, and diplomatic relations were not yet renewed by the offended Powers. The outstanding difference between the Porte and the two Imperial Governments related to the surveillance of the refugees. The greater number of the Hungarian rank

and file, 3,300 in all, had already accepted the Austrian amnesty and returned to their homes; but for the leaders there
was no pardon, and the difficulty was how to dispose of them.
The Porte removed them to Shumla, and thence to Brusa and
Kutahia in Asia Minor; but Austria insisted on a strict guard
being kept over them, and even stipulated for a surveillance
by Austrian officers. There were also rumours of a plot to
assassinate Kossuth and the other chiefs, and this was said to
be countenanced at Vienna. It thus became necessary not
only to guard the refugees in the interests of Austria—a precaution to which the Porte had weakly consented—but to
protect them against possible mischief at the hands of their
enemies. Their condition under these circumstances was not
agreeable. Turkish restraint involved hardships, and Kossuth
and his friends complained bitterly of their treatment, and
seemed to have forgotten the generosity with which the Porte
had exposed itself to imminent peril in order to save their
necks. To Canning, however, as the real cause of their
safety, they shewed a becoming spirit of gratitude. He had
restored their wives and children to them, and the little
Kossuths, among others, had been cared for at the Embassy.
Their father wrote in touching terms, 28 June:—

> I have my children again, and the happiness of seeing them out
> of the reach of my poor country's oppressors is still more heightened
> by the presence of my dearest sister, who so generously undertook
> to accompany them.
> They all find not enough words to praise the benevolent kindness
> they met with at your Excellency's house. Myself and my wife we
> are entirely penetrated of gratitude, and we will never cease to pray
> to God that He may bless your noble lady, and you, sir, for the
> consolation you afforded to our parental feelings.

Whatever consideration they received, whatever mitigation
of the hard conditions demanded by Austria, and only too
likely to be conceded by the timidity of the Porte, they owed
to the Great Elchi. Russia had retired from the discussion,
having less interest in the Hungarians. M. Titov resumed
his diplomatic relations at the close of December, and the
squadrons left the Archipelago; but Austria was still intrac-
table. On 5 Feb., 1850, she demanded that the refugees should
be kept under surveillance for twelve years; the term was
then reduced to five years; but Canning would not countenance any term at all. The Sultan, he said, must be trusted
to decide the proper time for their release. Palmerston also

felt strongly on this subject. "It is scarcely less derogatory
to the Sultan," wrote the Foreign Secretary, "to be jailor for
Austria than to be purveyor to the Austrian executioners."
At last the Emperor gave way and resumed diplomatic relations early in April. The next object of the British ambassador was to induce the Porte to liberate the captives, for
such they were, as soon as possible. He was authorized to
draw upon public funds for their assistance; the American
minister volunteered to ship them to the United States, but
still the Porte trembled lest she should offend the Viennese
Court. In Jan. 1851, however, with Austria's permission, the
embarkation began. The Porte was liberal in its provision
for the exiles, and gave them money, which was supplemented
by grants from the British embassy and from public subscrip-
tion; yet their future must have been a pitiful prospect, in a
strange land, and with small means of earning a livelihood.
All the summer the migration continued, till there remained
only the leaders, against whom the Government at Vienna
still hardened its heart. At last, after repeated efforts and a
personal application to the Sultan, Canning obtained his royal
word that Kossuth and the rest should be released on 1 Sept.
The promise was redeemed, and the refugees who for two
years had kept four empires in suspense finally disappeared
from the political horizon.

Canning's conduct throughout these trying negotiations
obtained the hearty admiration of his Government, and never
was he so popular with the whole people of England. Palmerston wrote, 5 Jan., "I can easily conceive that you must
as you say be overwhelmed with work, but you are doing your
work right well, and the consciousness of that must make the
labour less oppressive than it otherwise would be." And
again, 23 March, "I was very glad to have an opportunity in
debate of doing justice to your management of the important
matters you have had to deal with." Many private friends
also wrote to the ambassador in enthusiastic praise of his bold
defence of the refugees, and while he was recognized as the
true champion of the honourable principle he had successfully sustained, the Porte obtained its share of popular sympathy for the generosity and highmindedness it had displayed
in the affair. They were, indeed, as Palmerston said, "frightened at their own courage," but they were not frightened out
of it.

CHAPTER XVI.

ENGLAND AND TURKEY.

1849–52.

AMIDST such pressing emergencies it would have been but natural that the internal improvements upon which Canning laid so much stress should be neglected. That was not his way, however ; and, far from forgetting reform in the heat of conflict, his policy was to claim reform as the reward of his support. Whenever a Turkish minister came with an appeal for England's interference, Canning told him that aid would be given when aid was earned ; Turkey must make herself worthy of encouragement if the queen's influence was to be used in her favour. If a private audience took place with the Sultan, the ambassador did not shrink from speaking similar home-truths. His Majesty must deserve the friendship of England by acts of reform and toleration. The price of British intervention at the crisis of the refugee question was a forward step by Turkey towards European civilization.

On his arrival at Constantinople in 1848, the ambassador's first act had been to restore Reshid and his friends to power. Promises of future reforms thereafter abounded ; even Riza expressed his regret at having formerly opposed Canning's policy ; Rif'at engaged to do his best to improve the condition of the Christian rayas ; but the actual moment was always deemed unfavourable for any definite innovation, and so the months slipped by, and nothing was done. Nobody denied the validity of the argument, that the best way of preserving the integrity of the Empire and gaining the respect and support of foreign Powers was to remove every grievance that might occasion rebellion among the Rayas, every injustice that might invite foreign intervention, every barbarity that hindered the cordial sympathy of the Porte's Western Allies. The justice and reasonableness of all this were frankly granted ; but the time, said the Turks, was not propitious—perhaps presently something might be done. The Grand Vezir found himself thwarted in the council ; and the Sultan, alternately terrified by Russia and alarmed at symptoms of discontent among his more fanatical

Muslim subjects, had not the courage of his real convictions. In Sept. 1848 indeed Reshid despatched a circular to the provincial governors enjoining justice and mercy, and condemning oppression and extortion, and at the same time gave practical effect to his teaching by the release of some Nestorians who had been unjustly imprisoned. The circular and the release gave great satisfaction to the British ambassador, but a larger measure was needed to heal the wounds of Turkey. In Dec. 1848 a Commission sat at the Porte to take into consideration the various proposals which Canning had brought forward for the improvement of the internal administration. The experiment was tried of purifying the local councils by placing them under an approved president sent from the capital. Little, however, was effected; the Sultan was timorous; and the troubles in Wallachia occupied every mind to the exclusion of constitutional changes. Moreover the plan of an alliance with England had not been encouraged by the British Government, and the Porte was the less disposed to gratify the wishes of the English ambassador.

Canning's steady statesmanship during the disputes with Russia gradually effaced this feeling of chagrin, and the Turks once more began to draw closer to England. After an official audience of the Sultan in the spring of 1849, the Elchi was summoned to his Majesty's apartment for a private conference. Reshid, the only other person present, acted as interpreter. In the same breath the ambassador counselled a sturdy resistance to the Russian demands in Wallachia, and an energetic persistence in reform, despite the cloudy aspect of external politics. The Sultan replied that the Porte would always look to England for sympathy and help in the time of trouble. As we know, the Porte did not look in vain, and it was natural that the prompt support rendered by the Western Powers on the refugee question should revive the scheme of a defensive alliance, either with England and France or with the former alone. At the close of 1849 definite proposals were made by the Turkish Government, and in order to win Palmerston over to their plan, they agreed that if the alliance were formed England should be the sole arbiter as to whether or not a case for joint action had at any time arisen. Canning did not conceal his approval of the idea; he thought " the principle and objects of the alliance unexceptionable " and believed it would " emancipate the Porte and its ministers from the pressure of that baneful

influence which fascinates their spirits and cripples them in
every attempt at progress and independence." In recommending the Turkish proposals to Lord Palmerston he urged
warmly : " We are now called upon to choose between a more
determined and systematic support of this empire, with its
attendant inconveniences, risks, and sacrifices, or a tacit acquiescence in the Porte's habitual submission to the superior
fortunes and calculating energies of a neighbour whose moral
ascendency would prove more injurious in its consequences to
Europe than even its territorial aggrandizement at the expense
of Turkey." The Porte, he said, must either sink or swim ;
she could no longer *float*.

Charmed with the ambassador's reception of the scheme,
the Sultan held out an agreeable prospect of reform, without
which, it was remarked, the alliance would be impossible.
Internal improvements, a thorough revision of the defences
of the empire, and a systematic encouragement of commerce
were the chief points to be pressed, and Abdu-l-Mejid agreed
most graciously to the programme, only remarking that some
changes might be effected at once, but others would require
time and opportunity. The leading internal reforms advocated
by the Elchi were (1) the abolition of the capitation tax
levied on Christians, and their admission into the army ; (2)
Christian evidence to be allowed in the law courts ; (3) more
Christians to be elected to local councils ; (4) the revenue to
be collected in a more equitable manner. There was also a
hint, but no more, as to the suppression of the slave trade.
The whole programme was by order of the Sultan laid before
the Council.

Here apparently this promising movement ended. The
alliance was probably postponed in deference to Russia. The
programme remained " before the Council." At an audience
on 5 June, Canning taxed the Sultan with forgetting his engagements : the Russian panic was over, he observed, and
nothing now hindered the tranquil and orderly execution of
the reforms sketched at the earlier conference. " The truth
is," explained the official despatch describing the audience,
" that little or no practical advancement accompanies the
repeated professions of the Government. The few very
limited measures brought forward by Reshid Pasha in concurrence with me encounter the most vexatious difficulties
either in the Council or elsewhere. Time of immense value
is wasted in idle discussion or timid hesitation, and, in spite

of flattering addresses and the panegyrics of hired newspapers, there is more danger of losing what has been gained
than of realizing what is professed."

Yet something was accomplished before the ambassador
departed on leave in 1852. In November 1850 a firman
was issued according the same privileges to Protestants as to
Greeks and Catholics in Turkey. The Protestants, who previously had had no *locus standi* in the Turkish State, were
now formally and distinctly recognized as a separate body ;
they were instructed to elect an agent to represent their interests, and their religious rights and temporal concerns were
to be secure from molestation. Canning declared that the
firman granted all the protection that the Protestant rayas
could pretend to, and he looked forward to the steady
development of the now legally recognized community as a
valuable counterpoise to Graeco-Russ and Gallo-Catholic influences. Mixed courts of criminal judicature were to be
established, and the state of the Turkish prisons came under
review. Another important concession was the enactment
that from August 1850 no negro slaves were to be embarked
on Turkish vessels. The white slave traffic was still undisturbed ; but the Sultan regarded it as "a shameful and
barbarous practice," and "hoped before long to abolish the
infamous trade within his dominions." All these reforms, however, were only extorted by continual pressure. The reactionary party was strong both in the Council and in the
country. Too rapid and vigorous reforms would very probably bring about a revolution, and there were signs that
the Sultan's bigoted brother Abdu-l-Aziz would be a formidable candidate for the throne. Russia was ever on the watch,
lest Turkey should become too civilized to justify her interference. Reshid, Canning's chief hope, was an object of
jealousy both to the inferior ministers and to the Sultan.
Reforms cost money, and the Turkish treasury was just then
in sore straits, and salaries were reduced in every department.
To make roads, build batteries, remove venal officials, and
reform the taxation would necessitate a foreign loan, and
usury is against the Mohammedan law. Canning perceived
that to press the Porte further would only lead to his own
disfavour and Reshid's retirement. Even Palmerston had
become hopeless, and had warned Reshid (24 November, 1850)
that he foresaw that the Turkish empire was "doomed to
fall by the timidity and weakness and irresolution of its

sovereign and of his ministers, and it is evident that we shall
ere long have to consider what other arrangement can be set
up in its place ; " and Canning had at last admitted that " the
great game of improvement is altogether up for the present,
and though I shall do my best to promote the adoption of
separate measures, it is impossible for me to conceal that the
main object of my stay here is all but gone." He therefore
paused and resolved to give the Government time to recover
itself. He noted as a good sign the novel circumstance that
the Sultan assisted in person at a Greek wedding, standing
throughout the service, because " he had vowed never to sit
when prayers were addressed to God," and positively eating
Christian food cooked by Christian hands. No Sultan had
ever done so before, and Canning hoped the best from so
tolerant a precedent. Before leaving Constantinople in June
1852, " perhaps never to return," he once more essayed to
rouse the Sultan to active measures, and was assured in return
that his Majesty would bestir himself. Nevertheless the
Elchi left in sadness ; he had attempted so much, and had
attained comparatively so little, and he knew that his departure would be the signal for a return to the old order of things
against which he had striven with all his might for ten
laborious years. Yet he left Turkey the better for his work,
his seed had not all fallen on stony ground, and little harvests
of good fruit were springing up in more than one quarter of
the Ottoman territory. Moreover he had steered the vessel
of state safely through a tempestuous voyage ; the storms of
1848 had threatened to break over Turkey, and it was mainly
his own hand that had averted shipwreck. He left the country
tranquil and at peace with her neighbours. No alarms from
without menaced the State he had taken under his protection.
There had been a dispute between France and Russia relating
to the Holy Places at Jerusalem, but this appeared to have
come to an amicable settlement. On the eve of his departure,
which was believed to be final, he was entertained at a great
dinner given in his honour by the British subjects, and nothing could exceed their enthusiasm at his achievements or
their regret at his loss. Addresses poured in from the Armenian Protestants, the Greeks, the American missionaries,
the merchants of Smyrna and Constantinople, and the Elchi
knew that his labours were appreciated.

Before his departure Canning had received an overture
which pointed to a complete change in his sphere of work.

In 1851 the Earl of Derby (then Lord Stanley) invited him to join his Cabinet, should he be summoned by the Queen to form one, as Secretary for Foreign Affairs, and the conditional offer was accepted.   In the following year the opportunity of carrying out this intention presented itself; but, to everyone's surprize, Canning was left out of the ministry and Lord Malmesbury found himself dignified by the office which had been marked out by the popular voice for the Great Elchi.   It was rumoured that Russia objected to a strong man at the head of our Foreign Office, and Baron Brunov remarked openly that Canning's appointment if true was " une plaisanterie," and more, " une mauvaise plaisanterie."   The ambassador's share in the protection of the Hungarian and Polish refugees was certainly not calculated to recommend him to the autocratic Courts, and this circumstance, taken together with the arguments of those who dreaded the effects of Canning's imperious will both in the Cabinet and at the Office, may have induced the Premier to reconsider the offer. It was a severe disappointment, and when Lord Derby thereupon offered him a peerage, " on the score of long and able public service," he was on the point of refusing it, and only consented to become Viscount Stratford de Redcliffe on the understanding that the title was the reward of past services, and was in no degree a compensation for the Prime Minister's change of mind.[1]

Another disappointment occurred about the same time. The Paris Embassy fell vacant, and Lord Granville, on the plea of urgency and party politics, appointed Henry Wellesley, the second Lord Cowley.   After forty-five years of diplomatic service, mainly spent at a spot peculiarly distasteful to him, Canning was entitled to the blue ribbon among embassies ; and as he was no party man, but had been appointed to various missions by both of the great political parties, Lord Granville's plea of diverging feelings upon home subjects was unavailing.   It was a little galling to see one of his own assistants—the same Wellesley who had served under him at the Porte in 1846—raised to the dignity of ambassador at Paris, while his old chief remained buried at Stambol ; and according to the Dowager Lady Cowley no one was more surprized at the injustice than the fortunate diplomatist himself.

[1] The correspondence on the subject of the Foreign Office and the peerage is printed in the library edition, ii. 220–225.

Stratford de R.

Engraved by G. T. Stodart, from a drawing by George Richmond, R.A. 1853

Events, however, were gradually forming into shape which must have made the Great Elchi feel that there were compensations for the loss of Paris and the Foreign Office. Had he been appointed to either, who was there in the whole roll of diplomacy that could take his place when the storm that was gathering burst in all its fury upon the Porte ? Hardly had he been away six months when there arose a universal cry for Lord Stratford to return and protect his ancient ward. Ministers bowed to the necessity. Probably neither Lord Aberdeen nor the Foreign Secretary, Lord John Russell, was personally eager to restore a man whom they could not understand and of whom they were half afraid ; but no one else could manage the Turks, and Lord Stratford, who had resigned his embassy in January 1853, was begged to resume it and start with as little delay as possible for the scene of action.

CHAPTER XVII.

THE RETURN OF THE ELCHI.

FEBRUARY—APRIL 1853.

LORD STRATFORD's conduct of the negotiations which preceded the Crimean war will probably stand as the cornerstone of his career. Seldom, indeed, has diplomacy enjoyed so wide and pregnant an occasion for the exercise of its powers as was then presented. From April to December 1853 the British Embassy at Constantinople was the depositary of a series of proposals, emanating from various sources, for the settlement of the dispute between Russia and the Porte. France, England, and Austria had each in turn its own special nostrum to heal the rupture. The four representatives at Vienna ran an eager race against the four ambassadors at Pera for the prize of solving the problem. Never, even in the history of diplomacy, was there such a bewildering succession of rival schemes, often crossing each other in the swift exchange of royal and imperial messengers ; never was so much ink and paper lavished upon a simple issue—never, said Lord Stratford, with happy disregard of Homeric conditions, since the Siege of Troy. Through all

s

this tangled web two men alone held the ends of the skein ; two men knew exactly what they wanted, and resolutely kept to "the Question." Governments and ambassadors at St. James's, Paris, and Vienna might try their hands at notes, conventions, and declarations, which seemed to them to meet the exigencies of the case ; but these two men instantly detected the flaw and reverted to "the Question." One of them was the Emperor Nicholas, who, after a quarter of a century of moderation, had resolved to win for himself a predominating ascendency over Turkey ; the other was Viscount Stratford de Redcliffe, who already possessed the very influence that was coveted by the Czar, and who had no intention of allowing English prestige to be outshone by Russia.

The diplomatic transactions of this momentous epoch fall naturally into three principal divisions. The first consists of the direct negotiation at Constantinople between Russia and Turkey through Prince Menshikov between March and May 1853, and concludes with the exchange of notes between Count Nesselrode and Reshid Pasha and the passage of the Pruth by the Russian troops. The second period is that of neither war nor peace, when Four Powers exhausted their ingenuity in devising remedies for the crisis; and it ends with the formal ultimatum of the Porte to the Russian general in the Principalities in October, and the ensuing advance of the allied squadrons into the Hellespont. The third includes the months during which Turkey waged war with Russia unaided, save by the mere presence of the fleets, and concludes when the affair of Sinope and the avenging entrance of the allied squadrons into the Black Sea rendered all hopes of an accommodation futile. War was not declared till March 1854, but the advance into the Euxine at the beginning of January practically decided the question.

Everyone has read in the fascinating pages of Mr. Kinglake's first volume how the peace of Europe was disturbed on account of a door-key, a silver star, and the mending of a dilapidated dome. The historian of the British Expedition to the Crimea has written with becoming gravity of the religious sentiment associated with these apparently trivial objects, but it requires all the impressive seriousness which he possesses to conceal the smile over the follies of poor humanity which lurks behind his narrative of the dispute about the Holy Places at Jerusalem. There was an old quarrel between the rival Greek and Latin Churches, as to which of them had

certain, to us perhaps inappreciable, rights and privileges in
the sanctuaries of the Holy Land, and despite the impartial
police of the Turks many a sanguinary struggle had taken
place at Easter between the fanatics on the very site of the
sacred mysteries which both denominations revered. France
and Russia espoused the rival causes of their respective
Churches—France from her policy of predominant influence
in Syria, Russia partly from genuine religious fanaticism,
partly because she dreaded the weakening of her position as
would-be protector of the Orthodox Church in the east,
which it was her constant ambition to establish. In January
1842 the claims of the two parties to repair the cupola of the
Holy Sepulchre came before the Porte, and Sir Stratford
Canning, with his usual good sense, advised the Turks to
repair it themselves. The question reappeared from time to
time, and in 1850–2 attained alarming proportions. M. de
Lavalette, the French ambassador, carried his remonstrances
to the point of menace, and a rupture seemed imminent. The
wise conciliation of the Ottoman Government, however, calmed
the hostile passions of the claimants, and in March 1852 Canning was able to report to Lord Malmesbury what he believed
to be " the termination of the ill-advised and long-pending
question of the Syrian Sanctuaries." During his absence in
England, however, the dispute entered upon a new phase.
Russia, dissatisfied with the arrangement proffered by Turkey,
resolved to send a special embassy to the Porte, and Prince
Menshikov was entrusted with the task of settling the pending
difficulties as to the Holy Places and obtaining satisfactory
guarantees for the future. It was upon these guarantees
that the problem of peace or war turned.

There was seemingly little in this mission to rouse the
suspicions of the English Cabinet. Russia had given explicit
assurances that Prince Menshikov was instructed merely to
obtain a satisfactory settlement of the Jerusalem dispute, that
he had no ulterior aims, and that his intentions were purely
pacific. The question of a special Convention, nominally to
guarantee the rights and privileges of the Greek Church
throughout the Ottoman dominion, really to establish Russian
ascendency in Turkey, which formed part, and the essential
part, of the Prince's instructions, was not so much as hinted
at in the communications of the Czar's government with
England. There were rumours, however, of armed preparations in the south of Russia, and these, coupled with troubles

in Montenegro and the consequent despatch of Count Leiningen to Constantinople with an Austrian ultimatum, were
enough to make the British Government anxious to have
Lord Stratford back at his post. He had resigned his embassy in January, and had fully made up his mind that he
had seen the last of the old place of exile; but, under the circumstances, he did not feel himself justified in resisting the
request of Lord Aberdeen and Lord John Russell that he
would resume his duties at the Porte.

Accordingly on 25 February, 1853, he received his instructions. It is an open secret that they were drawn up by his
own hand. They are published in the official *Correspondence
concerning the rights and privileges of the Latin and Greek
Churches in Turkey*, 1854 (No. 94, 8vo ed., pp. 83–6). "At
this critical period of the fate of the Ottoman empire" he
was commanded by the Queen to return to his embassy "for
a special purpose and charged with special instructions." He
was to counsel prudence to the Porte and forbearance on the
part of France and Russia. He was to neutralize by England's
moral influences the alarming contingencies opened up by the
demands of the two Powers and the "dictatorial if not
menacing attitude they had assumed." On his way out he was
to pause at Paris and Vienna. At Paris he was to dwell upon
the identical interests of England and France in the East, to
further their "cordial coöperation in maintaining the integrity
and independence of the Turkish Empire," and to point out the
fatal embarrassment to which that Empire would be exposed
if unduly pressed by the French Government on the question
of the Holy Places. At Vienna he was to express the pleasure
of her Majesty's Government at Austria's assurance that her
friendly disposition towards the Porte remained unchanged
and her conservative policy in the East would be strictly ad-
hered to. The Sultan was to be assured of the friendly feelings
of England, as proved by the return of an envoy so well disposed as Lord Stratford, and at the same time to be warned
of the gravity of the situation which had hastened that return.
He was left unfettered by special instructions for the settlement of the Holy Places dispute; his own judgment and
discretion might be trusted to guide him. The Porte was to
be told that she had to thank her own maladministration and
the accumulated grievances of foreign nations for the menacing
tone now adopted towards her by certain Powers; that a
general revolt of her Christian subjects might ensue; and the

Sultan and his ministers were to be convinced "that the crisis
is one which requires the utmost prudence on their part, and
confidence in the sincerity and soundness of the advice they
will receive from you, to resolve it favourably for their future
peace and independence." He was to counsel reforms in the
administration of Turkey, by which alone could the sympathy
of the British nation be preserved.

"It remains," concluded the Foreign Secretary, "only for
me to say that in the event, which her Majesty's Government
earnestly hope may not arise, of imminent danger to the
existence of the Turkish Government, your Excellency will
in such case despatch a messenger to Malta, requesting the
Admiral to hold himself in readiness, but you will not direct
him to approach the Dardanelles without positive instructions
from her Majesty's Government."

He started at once for Paris, accompanied by Mr. Alison,
Mr. Layard (then member for Aylesbury), Lord Pevensey
(now Earl of Sheffield), and Count Pisani. They remained at
the French capital, intent upon gaining every possible insight
into the policy of the Emperor, until the 17th. His impressions of Louis Napoleon and the French policy are expressed
in the following memorandum of a conversation which took
place on 10 March :—

He began by expressing his satisfaction at finding that there was
nothing to prevent the two Governments from acting together in
the East, and that both agreed in wishing to uphold the Ottoman
Empire. He seemed to think that Austria had treated the Porte
rather sharply in the late transactions at Constantinople, and he
made some inquiries respecting what I understood to have been
settled about the Turkish claims in the *Bocche di Cattaro*. He
spoke of the Holy Places, and threw the blame of engaging in that
question on the *parti prêtre* of the Montalembert school and the
Legislative Assembly. He desired nothing better than to finish
the affair. He was not disposed to make difficulties so long as his
honour was uncompromised ; and he would not object to the maintenance of the Sultan's firman, supposing France to retain what
had been previously accorded. He talked of Egypt as having been
an object of some difference between the two Governments. He
understood that we only wanted the railway for our communications with India, and he had declared his mind to those who
seemed to forget that England, not France, possessed extensive
territories in that country. He said that he had no wish to make
the Mediterranean a *French* lake—to use a well-known expression—
but that he should like to see it made an *European* one. He did
not explain the meaning of this phrase. If he meant that the shores

of the Mediterranean should be exclusively in the hands of Christendom, the dream is rather colossal. Syria came next into consideration. I recommended a strict adherence to existing arrangements. He acquiesced, like a man who knew little of the subject. He shewed some curiosity respecting the Sultan's character, nothing that implied belief in the probability of Turkish regeneration. The Emperor then touched upon several topics unconnected with the East. . . .

The impression left upon my mind by the conversation thus recorded is that Louis Napoleon, meaning to be well with us, at least for the present, is ready to act politically in concert with England at Constantinople; but it remains to be seen whether he looks to the restoration of Turkish power, or merely to the consequences of its decay, preparing to avail himself of them hereafter in the interest of France. As it appears, moreover, that the maintenance of his own personal position is the mainspring of his policy, he is not likely to adopt without necessity any change of institutions calculated to give room for the play of influences adverse to his Government, nor can he be expected to abstain from any attempt required in his judgment by the circumstances of the time to consolidate his power or to avert any danger that may threaten its continuance. It may, therefore, be doubted whether his coöperation even in the East can be accepted by us without some shades of caution; nor would it apparently be safe to rely upon his goodwill, unable as her Majesty's Government must be to remove all causes of difference with him, unless our means of defence be improved.

While at Paris, Lord Stratford received ominous news from Constantinople. Matters had apparently become so menacing there that the chargé d'affaires, Colonel Rose (afterwards Lord Strathnairn), had taken the grave step of summoning the Mediterranean squadron to Vourla Bay. Vice-Admiral Dundas refused to move without express orders from the Government, and his refusal was approved. The French, however, were more adventurous, and hastily despatched their fleet to the Gulf of Salamis: a movement which had considerable influence upon the question of peace or war. Lord Clarendon's opinion is given with sufficient clearness in the following letter (23 March) to Lord Stratford:—

Rose acted hastily in sending for the fleet, and Admiral Dundas very discreetly in not quitting Malta without orders from home. The French Government have come to a precipitate decision in ordering their fleet to sail, but it will not go further than Salamis. Why it goes at all they are rather puzzled to say. After all the solemn and personal assurances given to us by the Emperor of

Russia, it would have been utterly unjustifiable on our part to
doubt his word, and we do therefore believe that the independence
and integrity of the Turkish Empire are not endangered by the
mission of Prince Menshikov.

It is certainly unfortunate that you should not have been on the
spot when he arrived. Your experience and position might have
kept matters in a right direction, and prevented both Russian and
Turkish ebullitions, from which mischief is still to be apprehended.
You know what importance Russians attach to rank, and that
Prince Menshikov is therefore not likely to have paid much attention to the chargés d'affaires who represented England and France
at this critical moment of Turkish affairs. I am sure under the
grave circumstances of the case you will not lose an unnecessary
moment in getting to Constantinople.

Admiral Dundas despatched a steamer immediately there to inform Colonel Rose that the fleet *would not come*.

Leaving Paris on 17 March, the Embassy entered upon a
journey which was a series of mishaps: trains did not fit,
railroads were blocked with snow, and it took nearly a week
to get to Vienna. Here, after interviews with the Emperor
and Count Buol, the ambassador was able to report that the
views of the Austrian Government in reference to Turkey appeared to coincide with those of her Majesty's Cabinet; that
the Emperor was not acquainted with any ulterior object for
Prince Menshikov's mission beyond the settlement of the
Holy Places question; and that, except in regard to the
enthusiastic reception accorded to Kossuth and Mazzini and
other " rebels " in England, the feelings of Austria to Great
Britain were friendly. On the way to Trieste the party was
again snowed up; but at length (4 April) Lord Stratford was
able to write to his wife from the Sea of Marmora :—

We started from Trieste on Wednesday at 11 A.M., we entered
the Archipelago on Saturday night, and we passed the Dardanelles
this (Monday) morning at an early hour. Stephen Pisani is on
board. He has been giving me all the news, and if things have
remained at Constantinople as he left them more than a week ago
there will be no lack of difficulty. The Russian demands and ac-
companying demonstrations seem to mean the acquirement once
for all of a preponderating influence with all the Greeks in their
train, or some act of territorial encroachment by way of substitute.
The Turks are alarmed, the Greeks excited, the Sultan *as usual*,
and his ministers fluctuating between their fears and better feelings. . . . I also learn that the Grand Vezir, though negotiating
secretly with Prince Menshikov, intends to wait for my arrival
before taking a decision. If he can stick to this resolution, I leave

you to guess with what feelings of interest the appearance of H.M.S. *Fury* will be hailed to-morrow morning from both sides of the Golden Horn. The prospect is more than enough to make one nervous; but there is hope to be derived from the best of books, and possibly a pebble from the brook by the wayside may be found once more the most effectual weapon against an armed colossus. My pebble is the simple truth, but I must stoop to pick it up where the heavens lie reflected on smooth, flowing water. Do you understand my metaphors?

Tuesday evening, my own study in the Palace.

How strange! and without you? It cannot be, yet so it is. We got into port soon after daylight. A glorious morning—the domes and minarets towering above the mist and over each the crescent glittering in sunlit gold. I dressed and went on deck. Soon the old faces began to appear—Hardy, Black, Hanson, Skene, &c. &c. &c. Then came what would have brought your hands to your ears—a row of saluting reverberated by a thousand echoes. The colonel came on board, attachés also—Hughes radiant, Smythe lambent— a new, uncouth cub. After a time Old Duz Oghlu appeared, not a smile or a wrinkle the less. He kissed my hand, he inquired after you, he assured me of the sultan's regard. . . . At 11 we landed, under a salute from the *Tiger*, at Tophana on the place d'armes; a crowd of English, Ionians, and Maltese were collected there. They received me with three shouts, which brought tears into my eyes and made my horse very skittish! The horse, richly caparisoned, had been sent to me by Rif'at with a dozen kavasses, and up the hill we went, followed by a long train and through ranks of people greeting the old ambassador. We reached the palace in due course; I dismissed my friends with a speech, the pattern of brevity, and here I am, Heaven help me!

" On the morning of the 5th of April, 1853," says Mr. Kinglake,[1] " the Sultan and all his ministers learned that a vessel of war was coming up the Propontis, and they knew who it was that was on board. Long before noon the voyage and the turmoil of the reception were over, and except that a corvette under the English flag lay at anchor in the Golden Horn, there was no seeming change in the outward world. Yet all was changed. Lord Stratford de Redcliffe had entered once more the palace of the British Embassy. The event spread a sense of safety, but also a sense of awe. It seemed to bring with it confusion to the enemies of Turkey, but austere reproof for past errors at home, and punishment where punishment was due, and an enforcement of hard toils and

---

[1] *Invasion of the Crimea*, i. 128.

painful sacrifices of many kinds, and a long farewell to repose. It was the angry return of a king whose realm had been suffered to fall into a danger."

CHAPTER XVIII.

PRINCE MENSHIKOV'S MISSION.

APRIL—MAY, 1853.

THE ambassador had his suspicions of what had been going on in his absence. He was of course in possession of all the correspondence of the Embassy, and was aware from Colonel Rose's reports to the Government that Prince Menshikov had mooted much more serious matters than the custody of a key at a Sanctuary; that he had suggested a Turko-Russian defensive alliance, whereby a fleet and 400,000 of the Czar's troops would be at the service of the Porte to help her against any Western Power; and that he had demanded secretly " an addition to the Treaty of Kaynarji, whereby the Greek Church should be placed entirely under Russian protection, without reference to Turkey, which was to be the equivalent for the proffered aid above mentioned. Prince Menshikov had stated that the greatest secrecy must be maintained relative to this proposition, and that, should Turkey allow it to be made known to England, he and his Mission would instantly quit Constantinople." So the Grand Vezir told Colonel Rose (1 April), and his Highness added that " nothing whatever should be added to the Treaty of Kaynarji; that he would ask to retire from office rather than agree to either of the two propositions made by Prince Menshikov, which would be fatal to Turkey."

A peculiar inconvenience of the Russian demands was the mixture of the reasonable with the inadmissible. Russia was within her right in her claims about the Holy Places, but the granting of these just claims was to be comprized in a document having the force of a treaty and including certain guarantees for the future which, though introduced *à propos* of the Holy Places, had a much wider application than the Sanctuaries in Palestine : the trick was ingenious, and, as

Lord Stratford remarked, " Jacob's voice and Esau's hand
were never more skilfully combined." The issue of firmans
according or confirming certain privileges in the Holy Places
presented no special difficulty, if France could be induced to
accept a compromise ; but a general guarantee of the rights
and privileges of the Greek Church in Turkey, conveyed *to
Russia alone* among the Great Powers in a formal treaty,
meant nothing less than endowing the Czar with the right to
interfere in almost any matter relating to the twelve or thirteen
thousand members of the Greek Church who were subjects
of the Porte ; in other words, it meant the surrender of the
Eastern Question. Lord Stratford perceived the complication
instantly, and cut the knot with characteristic sagacity. In
the interview which he had with the Grand Vezir and Rif'at
Pasha, the Foreign Secretary, on the day after his landing,
he said, " Endeavour to keep the affair of the Holy Places
separate from the ulterior proposals, whatever they may be, of
Russia. The course which you appear to have taken under
the former head was probably the best ; and I am glad to find
that there is a fair prospect of its success to the satisfaction
of France as well as of Russia. Whenever Prince Menshikov
comes forward with further propositions, you are at perfect
liberty to decline entering into negotiation without a full statement of their nature, extent, and reasons. Should he ground
them on any existing treaty, it would be equally incumbent
on him to afford a full explanatory statement in the first instance. Should they be found on examination to carry with
them that degree of influence over the Christian subjects of
the Porte in favour of a foreign Power, which might eventually prove dangerous or seriously inconvenient to the exercise of the Sultan's legitimate authority, his Majesty's ministers
cannot be denied the right of declining them, which would
not prevent the removal, by direct sovereign authority, of any
existing abuse, or the more strict execution by the Porte
itself of any treaty engagement affording to Russia a fair
ground of remonstrance."

What Lord Stratford thus sketched out was precisely
what happened. The Holy Places dispute was satisfactorily
arranged ; the " ulterior proposals " were refused ; and the
privileges and rights of the Christians were guaranteed " by
direct sovereign authority," not by an instrument addressed
exclusively to Russia.

We need not enter into the details of the negotiation re-

specting the Holy Places. This was not the critical part of
the affair, and Russia has acknowledged that the British
ambassador contributed to the happy termination of this misunderstanding. In point of fact, he brought the French and
Russian representatives together, and a brief discussion face
to face in the Elchi's presence sufficed to remove all remaining points of difference (22 April). "I thought," he wrote,
"it was time for me to adopt a more prominent part in
reconciling the adverse parties." He was more than equal
to the task. "Being by nature so grave and stately as to
be able to refrain from a smile without effort and even without design, he prevented the vain and presumptuous Russian
from seeing the minuteness and inanity of the things which
he was gaining by his violent attempt at diplomacy. For
the Greek Patriarch to be authorized to watch the mending of a dilapidated roof, for the Greek votaries to have the
first hour of the day at a tomb, and finally for the doorkeeper of a church to be always a Greek, though without any
right of keeping out his opponents—these things might be
trifles, but awarded to All the Russias through the stately
mediation of the English ambassador, they seemed to gain in
size and majesty, and for the moment, perhaps, the sensations
of the Prince were nearly the same as though he were receiving the surrender of a province or the engagements of a great
alliance. On the other hand, Lord Stratford was unfailing in
his deference to the motives of action which he had classed
under the head of ' French feelings of honour ' ; and if M. de
la Cour was set on fire by the thought that at the Tomb of
the Virgin, or anywhere else, the Greek priests were to perform
their daily worship before the hour appointed for the services
of the Church which looked to France for support, Lord
Stratford was there to explain, in his grand quiet way, that
the priority proposed to be given to the Greeks was a priority
resulting from the habit of early prayer which obtained in
oriental churches, and not from their claim to have prece-
dence over the species of monk which was protected by
Frenchmen. At length he addressed the two ambassadors ;
he solemnly expressed his hope that they would come to an
adjustment. His words brought calm. In obedience, as it
were, to the order of Nature, the lesser minds gave way to the
greater, and the contention between the Churches for the
shrines of Palestine was closed. The manner in which the
Sultan should guarantee this apportionment of the shrines

was still left open, but in all other respects the question of the
Holy Places was settled." [1]

With the ulterior proposals, however, it was otherwise.
At first the Turkish Foreign Secretary was afraid to reveal
the full extent of Prince Menshikov's demands to the Elchi.
No doubt Rif'at stood in wholesome dread of the ambassador's
lash, with which he had long been intimately acquainted;
but the chief reason for his reticence was the menacing tone
adopted by the Russian envoy. By degrees, however, under
the protecting influence which now emanated from the British
Palace, the Turkish ministers revealed the full details of the
Russian project. On 11 April Lord Stratford was able to
transmit the substance of it to his Government. He was also
in personal communication with Prince Menshikov, and, as
Mr. Kinglake says, he " did not fail to deal with him tenderly;
and for several days the Prince had the satisfaction of imagining that the imperious and overbearing Englishman of whom
they were always talking at St. Petersburg was become very
gentle in his presence. The two ambassadors, without being
yet in negotiation, began to talk with one another of the
matters which were bringing the peace of the world into
danger. They spoke of the Holy Places. Far from seeming
to be hard or scornful in regard to that matter, Lord Stratford was full of deference to a cause which, whether it was
founded on error or on truth, was still the honest heart's
desire of fifty millions of pious men. . . . Where he could do
so with justice, he admitted the fairness of the Russian
claims." [2]   Naturally the Prince's tone became " considerably
softened " under this soothing influence; they even touched
upon the "ulterior demands," and Menshikov "sought to
attenuate their extent and effect; but I drew a clear line of
distinction," reported the Englishman, " between the confirmation of special points already stipulated by treaty and
an extension of influence having the virtual force of a protectorate to be exercised exclusively by a single foreign Power
over the most important and numerous class of the Sultan's
tributary subjects. We both avoided entering into a discussion, which might have proved irritating, on this question;
and I was glad to learn from Prince Menshikov that, notwithstanding the great importance attached to it by his
Government, there was no danger of any hostile aggression
as the result of its failure, but at most an estrangement

[1] Kinglake, *Invasion of the Crimea*, i. 144-5.   [2] *Ibid.* i. 133.

between the two Courts, and perhaps, though it was not so
said, an interruption of diplomatic relations.''

On 19 April Prince Menshikov addressed to Rif'at Pasha
a second Note, in which, after some offensive remarks about
the duplicity of his predecessors, the bad faith of the Turkish
ministers, and their want of respect towards the Emperor of
Russia, he proceeded to formulate the demands of his Court,
which culminated in the peremptory insistence of a *Sened*
or Convention to guarantee the strict *status quo* of the privileges of the Catholic Graeco-Russian Eastern Church. '' The
Ottoman Cabinet,'' concluded this remarkable document, '' will
be good enough also to weigh in its wisdom the gravity of the
offence that has been committed'' in comparison with the
moderation of the demands now made for reparation and
guarantee ; and upon its response would depend the '' devoirs
ultérieurs '' which the ambassador might have to fulfil.

On 21 April Rif'at Pasha communicated this Note to the
British ambassador, informing him at the same time that the
Russian had that morning sent to inquire whether the firmans
for the Holy Places were being drawn up, whether the Sened
was drafted, and also whether Rif'at Pasha was empowered to
enter into negotiation respecting the treaty to be concluded
between the two Powers. The same afternoon a messenger
again arrived at the Porte from Prince Menshikov and stated
to the Grand Vezir and the Foreign Secretary that he was
directed by his master '' to apprize them that the Prince was
not at all satisfied with the answer brought to him by his
dragoman that morning, and he conceived some suspicion that
the Porte was doing a thing, very objectionable in his opinion,
which is to consult and act upon the advice of the British
ambassador, and that they had better abstain from doing so
in future.'' The Grand Vezir is reported to have replied that
the Porte had no occasion to ask advice of anyone, as the
question was perfectly clear; but at the same time he thought
'' no one could prevent their shewing regard and respect to
one who on every occasion evinced so much good-will and
friendly dispositions towards the Porte, and who takes so much
interest in the promotion and welfare of this country.'' Lord
Stratford was indeed shewing his interest unmistakably, and
his efforts for a peaceful arrangement were untiring. He told
his wife :—

25 *April.*—I am well, thank God ! but my brain is half on fire,
and my fingers worn down to the quick. I get up at five ; I work

the livelong day and I fall asleep before I reach my bed. . . .
Affairs are getting on. The Holy Places question is virtually
settled, and I had the good luck to bring the two ambassadors
together in the nick of time. But we are not yet out of the wood.
Russia wants what the Porte cannot give, and it remains to be seen
whether Menshikov will be satisfied with what I may conscientiously advise the Turks to give him. You will be glad to know
that I am so far on good terms with all the world. So at least it
seems. I hope they will be satisfied in England.

27 *April*.—Dundas was as right about the squadron as Rose was
wrong. But Scotchmen, you know, are always right—except by the
way when they tie me down about the use of the steamer here
without necessity or propriety. . . . Well we have got over our
Holy Places leisurely but surely. The Porte is thankful. I have
also had the luck to receive from the Russian an assurance that he
surrenders the worst feature of a very ugly sort of treaty which he
wants the Sultan to adopt. Enough, however, remains, and there
are strange contradictory appearances afloat, so that I can only say
that, on the whole, there is less to fear than to hope. It seems certain that the Greeks are generally excited and sanguine, and also
that the young men of the Russian Embassy are out of humour
with their chief, who was yesterday unwell and in bed. Don't be
alarmed, but people will have it that there is to be a rising or a
massacre, or both. Without believing a word of it, I have engaged
the Porte to take quiet precautions, in the fashion of our poor lost
Duke, to keep the peace at Easter, which takes place for the Greeks
next Sunday. Massacres, like ends of the world, never happen when
they are expected and talked of.

The next stage in the Menshikov crisis occurred on 5 May.
The Note of 19 April had at least the merit of containing just
demands for the redress of real grievances; for the Holy
Places affair was not settled till three days after its appearance. The Note and Project of 5 May had no such advantage.
Lord Stratford had removed the grievances connected with
the sanctuaries out of the range of discussion, and the Czar's
ambassador found himself obliged to create a grievance out
of nothing. It was of course his own fault that he now found
himself standing upon empty air; he had allowed the real
ground of remonstrance, the Holy Places dispute, to slip
from under his feet, and now he had to find fresh ground,
where none was, whereon to base his more serious requisition.
The Czar had probably by this time found out his mistake in
sending a swashbuckler to play with a master of fence; he had
hoped no doubt that the Prince would carry all before him in
the absence of the ambassador, or that failing this happy end

he would by his blundering menaces so outrage the dignity of
the Porte and the British Embassy that both would lose their
tempers.   Instead of this the Turkish ministers and their
English adviser maintained the same cool, wary, and courteous
bearing towards the Prince-Governor of Finland from first to
last.   They were never off their guard, but on the other hand
they abstained from the slightest provocation.   This prudent
self-restraint, however, had an effect which might have been
foreseen.   There is such a thing as being too polite to a heated
adversary, and the Turkish policy proved an example of this
truth.   The Czar, irritated beyond endurance by the unvary-
ing reasonableness of his opponent—for he saw but one hand
and heard but one voice throughout the negotiations at Constantinople—lost his own self-control at the wrong moment.
Had he commanded violence at the beginning, Prince Menshikov might perhaps have carried the Turkish lines by a *coup
de main* before the Elchi's arrival.   But that moment was
past ; the real grievances had been repaired.   Nevertheless
Nicholas selected this particular stage of the business to
deliver more than usually peremptory orders to his representative, and Prince Menshikov, who must now have perceived
clearly his blunder, was forced to send in the Note of 5 May.
In this composition he acknowledges the receipt of the firmans granting all the original Russian demands concerning
the Holy Places, but " having obtained so far no response to
the third and most important point, which requires guarantees
for the future, and having received the command to redouble
his pressure in order to come to the immediate decision of the
question which forms the chief object of the Emperor's solicitude, the ambassador finds himself under compulsion at once
to address the Foreign Secretary and formulate his demands
in the final limits of his instructions."   He gave the Porte
five days to decide, and threatened painful consequences in
case of further delay.   Enclosed with the Note was a *Projet
de Convention*, which contained the old demand of Russia on
behalf of the Greek Church, with the same effect of giving
Russia the right of interference in the internal affairs of the
Ottoman Empire.   The Czar's ambassador changed the form
of his requisition more than once, but from the first to the
last Note the main point remained in all its unpleasant con-
spicuousness.   The bases laid down by the Prince were :
(1) that the Orthodox religion, its clergy and property, should
enjoy in future without diminution under the aegis of the

Sultan the privileges and immunities which had been assured
to them *ab antiquo*, and should share in any advantages
granted to other Christian religions ; (2) that the new Holy
Places Firman should have the force of a formal engagement
with the Russian Government ; and (3) that the points thus
summarized should form the subject of a *Sened* which should
attest the mutual confidence of the two Governments.

At this point in the proceedings Lord Stratford visited
the Grand Vezir at his country house on the Bosphorus. He
found Rif'at and the Seraskier already there in debate. The
Elchi urged them "to open a door for negotiation" in their
reply to the Prince, and strongly recommended that, if the
guarantee could not be granted, " a substitute for it should be
found in a frank and comprehensive exercise of the Sultan's
authority in the promulgation of a firman securing both the
spiritual and temporal privileges of all the Porte's tributary
subjects, and by way of further security communicated
officially to the five Great Powers of Christendom." The Grand
Vezir asked whether the eventual approach of the English
squadron could be relied on. It was a pregnant question,
and shewed which way the Turkish mind was moving. " I
replied," said Lord Stratford, " that I considered the position
in its present stage to be one of a moral character, and consequently that its difficulties or hazards, whatever they might
be, should be rather met by acts of a similar description than
by demonstrations calculated to increase alarm and provoke
resentment."

The ambassador was not to be drawn on faster than he
judged wise. He would communicate what he had to say
about the fleet in his own way and at his own time ; not at a
hurried meeting by night at a minister's country house, but
at a solemn audience in the Sultan's palace. There on 9 May
Lord Stratford in his most impressive tones informed Abdu-l-
Mejid that in case of danger he "was instructed to request
the commander of her Majesty's forces in the Mediterranean
to hold his squadron in readiness." He had not communicated this to the ministers, because he wished them to make
their decision without bias from without. They had already
made up their minds. They had adopted Lord Stratford's
suggestions, and on 10 May Rif'at Pasha addressed Prince
Menshikov in a conciliatory Note, which, in substance, was
the work of the British ambassador. He agreed to negotiate
upon any points still left undetermined in regard to a church

and hospital in Jerusalem, assured the Russian envoy of the
Sultan's intention to maintain and confirm in perpetuity the
privileges of his Christian subjects, hinting at an Imperial
document to this effect ; but he held it " contrary to international rights that one government should conclude a treaty
with another on a dangerous matter affecting not only those
things on which her independence is grounded, but, as is well
known, her independence itself in its very foundations."

On the following day the Prince replied. His letter expressed
his painful surprise at the distrust of the Porte, and gave it
three more days to reflect before he considered his mission at an
end and the diplomatic relations of the two Courts interrupted,
with all the consequences. The Russian was not idle in the
interval. He knocked at every door where the slightest chance
existed of gaining a vote, he wrote to Reshid, he employed
secret agents to work upon Rif'at, he even waited upon the
Grand Vezir, and finally he forced his way into the presence
of the Sultan himself, without previous consultation with the
ministers. Abdu-l-Mejid, who ought not to have received
him, had at least the wisdom to refer him back to his
ministers ; but the Grand Vezir, rightly indignant at this
breach of official etiquette, resigned (13 May). A reconstruction of the Government ensued, in which the offices were
shuffled rather in favour of the anti-Russian party; Lord
Stratford's old ally Reshid went to the Foreign Office; and the
outlook for Prince Menshikov had certainly not brightened.

The new ministry could not be expected to take up the
threads of so momentous a question in an hour, and Reshid
requested a few days—five or six—in order to prepare the
Porte's reply to the Prince's last Note. Without a moment's
reflection the Russian ambassador declared his official relations with the Porte to be broken (15 May). This precipitate
step was of a piece with all his conduct. Like his Imperial
master, he was always putting himself in the wrong. Just as
Nicholas had gone out of his way to assure the world that he
wanted nothing of the Porte but the settlement of the Palestine
dispute, and then made a totally distinct and unwarrantable
demand the ground of a quarrel with Turkey ; just as his
envoy had chosen, though perhaps not wholly of his own
accord, the precise moment, when the Porte had removed
every reasonable grievance, to put forth an ultimatum based
upon no recognized right or precedent : so once more did the
luckless would-be diplomatist break off his relations with the

T

Porte at the very instant when every dictate of courtesy required a short period of delay to be accorded to a new ministry.
And to make his position if possible more absurd than in
nature it was, he coupled his declaration of the snapping of
all diplomatic relations with a hint that he was still to be
found at Constantinople for a brief while. He apparently expected the Sultan and his ministers to come to him on bended
knees and tell him they were sorry. To complete the mal-
adroitness of his whole mission, at the moment when the
Great Council had decided by a majority of forty-two to three
to adhere to a Note granting all that Russia demanded, save
the " engagement with force of treaty," the Prince sent in a
final letter which left no further alternative. He announced,
in phrases which were to say the least unusual as addressed
to a free government, the termination of his mission ; threatened various consequences ; and stated that the refusal of a
guarantee would compel the Russian Government " to seek
one in its own might," and that any injury to the *status quo*
of the Orthodox Church would be taken as an act of hostility
to Russia and would " impose upon his Majesty the obligation of having recourse to measures which, in his constant
solicitude for the stability of the Ottoman Empire and in his
sincere friendship for the Sultan, and that which he had professed for his august father, the Emperor has always had it
at heart to avoid."

As soon as he had heard of this " decisive Note " Lord Stratford took an important step. He assembled the three other
representatives of the Great Powers at his house, and laid the
situation before them. By this act he placed the Eastern
Question on the sure and safe ground of European control,
and did all that lay in his power to prevent the possibility of
separate and interested interference. The four representatives
were entirely of one mind on the subject of the Prince's last
Note ; and M. Klezl, the Austrian chargé d'affaires, was requested to call upon the Russian ambassador, and, while
expressing the regret of the four at his decision, to discover
whether he would consent to receive the as yet undelivered
Note of the Porte through a private channel. To this the
Prince replied that he had no objection to receiving the Note
(which was accordingly sent), but that he was going off that
night (20 May) unless the Porte surrendered to his demands
in full. It then appeared that, like a bashful youth, this extraordinary diplomatist did not know when to take his leave.

After having twice declared that there was no longer a Russian Embassy at the Porte, he had sent a last Note to be shewn to, but not left with, Reshid Pasha. What was to be gained by this document, which reiterated the most objectionable parts of the preceding Notes, it is hard to see. The four representatives, who met again at the British Embassy, could not see any improvement, and communicated their opinion to the Porte that, " in a matter which touched so closely upon the freedom of action and the sovereignty of the Sultan, Reshid Pasha was the best judge of the line to be pursued"; in other words, they supported the Turkish construction of the document.

Reshid had already determined to resist the Russian demands in their last form. The claim to protect the Greek Church was obviously inadmissible ; "it was not the amputation of a limb, but the infusion of poison into the system" which had to be averted. The Prince had asked him to say a plain Yes or No, and No had been said.

Accordingly on 21 May Prince Menshikov's " untoward negotiations," to use Lord Stratford's words, came to an end; the Russian arms were taken down from the palace of the embassy, and the Prince-Governor of Finland steamed up the Bosphorus for Odessa. On 31 May Count Nesselrode addressed an arrogant letter to Reshid Pasha, approving Prince Menshikov's proceedings, and demanding the Porte's acceptance *sans variation* of the Prince's last Note, in default of which the Russian troops would cross the frontier, not to make war, but to obtain material guarantees for the satisfaction of the Czar's demands. To this Reshid, under Lord Stratford's guidance, made a temperate and reasonable reply on 16 June. Meanwhile, on 7 June, at the Elchi's instance, the Sultan had issued a Hatti-Sherif promulgating a new firman in confirmation of all the existing privileges of his Christian subjects, and thus taking the last breath of wind out of the Russian sails. So ended the first act of the drama which afterwards shifted its scene to the Crimea.

On 29 May the Elchi wrote to his wife :—

Exactly on this day four centuries ago did Mohammed II., Mohammed Ghazi, batter down the walls of Constantinople, turn St. Sophia into a mosque, and cut off one of the serpents' heads in the hippodrome with his battle-axe. Twelve days more will bring us to the same anniversary, Old Style, and who can say what may happen between this and then? . . . The Turkish squadron is coming up to take position in advance of Buyukderé Bay, and all sorts of rumours and alarms are afloat. . . . I left Pera this morning impromptu to see Reshid, whom it was important I should see without delay. I found him in excellent spirits, and more like himself in better days than I have seen him for a long time. . . . Reshid assured me that he does not wish to be Grand Vezir again —at least just now—and he speaks as if he were convinced that he had taken the right side in opposing the Russian demands. He has been working very hard for some days. The firmans renewing and confirming all the Christian and even Jewish religious privileges are prepared, and I put in two good sentences into them this morning, having had the drafts of them communicated to me privately for that purpose. I hope other privileges will follow, and then I shall feel as if I was doing some good.

I rejoice to have been absent during the Leiningen triumph. Instinct told me to keep away. In settling the Jerusalem question I have been of some use. I would have settled the other, but it could not be. The Russians were determined to have the whole, and it was necessary to prevent them. The consequences of their defeat may certainly be very serious, but it was my duty to support the Turks in withstanding them, and *there* I have succeeded. On the point at issue there can hardly be two opinions; but the fear of perturbation will cause many a sigh in England, and there are those who will be inclined to wish me at old Nick because I would not keep the peace by giving way to the *new* one. All now depends upon our Cabinet at home. Will they look the crisis fairly in the face and be wise enough as well as great enough, now that it has unavoidably occurred, to meet it fairly and settle it for ever ? *Shilly-shally* will spoil all. France, it seems, has come to a stout resolution; should Russia invade, the Emperor will come to the rescue. Such is the private message conveyed yesterday to Reshid. We shall see. Even I, who am behind the curtains, as it were, was half mystified at one time. How bad it must be when Austria and Prussia are with us ! So at least it would seem judging from the language of their representatives here. Even many of the better educated Greeks see through the Russian gauze. . . .

I found a letter from Calvert at the Dardanelles saying that the Russian merchants there had received official notice from here to wind up their affairs. This looks *very* bad. Yet there are contradictory symptoms, too, and it is almost impossible to come to a steady conclusion. The Russians in the confidence of their power play with us. They mumble their prey to make easier eating of it. ' Oh ! for one blast &c.,' or rather, as I should say,

> Oh ! for one glance from Chatham's eye
> To make our vile misgivings fly ;
> Oh ! for one cheer like that which broke
> From English hearts when Canning spoke !

What had been accomplished in the six busy weeks which had elapsed between the arrival of the formidable Elchi and the day when Prince Menshikov was sent in confusion to Odessa may be summed up in a few words.   In seventeen days Lord Stratford had terminated the ostensible object of the Menshikov mission by inducing the Porte to grant the firmans about the Holy Places.   For three weeks more he did everything in his power to keep the Porte in a conciliatory mood towards the Russian ambassador, with the result that Turkey came out of the long conflict with an indisputable air of being in the right, while Russia had so mismanaged the weapons she possessed that she appeared solely in the light of a wanton aggressor.   The one thing neither he nor the Turks would grant was a Russian protectorate over the Greek Church.   The Turks had made up their minds upon that point before he came upon the scene; but even if they had been undecided, it would have been his duty, in view of what was, and, it is hoped, still is the English policy on the Eastern Question, to bring them to the very decision at which they had arrived unaided.

CHAPTER XIX.

THE TOILS OF DIPLOMACY.

June—October 1853.

When Prince Menshikov had flown to Odessa to compose his ruffled plumage the statesmen of Europe began to play what must have appeared to impartial spectators a curious and complicated game, whereof the exact name and rules were apparently not understood, at least by the players.   There were four corners to this game: one was Paris, another London, a third Vienna, and the fourth Constantinople; indeed Berlin considered itself a fifth, but this was presumption.   The object was to throw a ball—which they called by various names, as Note, Project, Declaration, Convention—from Constantinople to the goal at St. Petersburg.   But the most extraordinary accidents happened on the way.   Sometimes the ball, after being thrown from corner to corner, got hopelessly lost.   Sometimes, after much careful preparation, it never

started on its way at all. But most often two balls were pro-
jected from opposite corners at the same instant, and meeting
in mid-air broke each other in pieces. About a dozen of these
missiles were flying about Europe in the summer of 1853,
and the strangest part of the performance was, that each was
so timed as to arrive at its destination (if it did not burst
on the way) exactly at the moment when another missile
had been sent off. One only reached the Petersburg goal in
safety, and that was found to contain some explosive matter,
and was hastily dropped by the players.

It is not our wish to ridicule the efforts of the many wise
and eminent men who devoted their anxious minds to the
attempt to pacify the Czar of Russia. Their intentions, for
the most part, were honest and right, and the reason they
failed was perhaps chiefly because their aim was by nature
unattainable; the Czar was not to be appeased. Nevertheless
it cannot be denied that the old saying " in the multitude of
counsellors there is wisdom " was hardly justified in this
instance; and it would be hard to discover in the history of
diplomacy a more painful example of good intentions egre-
giously, we had almost said ludicrously, foiled by their own
superabundance. Every Great Power, as represented by its
Foreign Secretary, was laudably eager to have its share in
the work of healing, and managed its contribution so skilfully
that it was certain to be neutralized by some other prescription.
A scheme is hatched at Vienna; nobody owns it, so it is
fathered upon the French ambassador. All the Powers
discuss it—and then it vanishes. No one can say what has
happened to it, but it never is heard of again. But the in-
cubation of Vienna is inexhaustible: a second chick is instantly
produced, shewn round, approved, and sent to Turkey. It
penetrates the Seraglio precincts, receives the Sultan's assent,
and then, like its predecessor, is unaccountably mislaid.
Seeing that Austrian broods do not thrive in Turkish air,
other Powers set their wits to work, and, as though in order to
insure failure, and oblivious of the space-destroying telegraph,
they elaborate their plans separately, unknown to each other,
and with curious disregard of the real point at issue. So we
find M. Drouyn de Lhuys full of his own scheme in June,
while Lord Clarendon is simultaneously despatching his rival
project to Constantinople, where it arrives just as Lord
Stratford's own plan is leaving for Vienna, where this is
received at the very moment when M. Drouyn de Lhuys'

Note, after emendation, has been formally adopted by the Great Powers. And this famous Franco-Austrian project, known as the Vienna Note—which spoilt Lord Stratford's plan, which spoilt Lord Clarendon's Convention, which spoilt the first French draft, and so on, like the celebrated house that Jack built—was found on examination to surrender the very point it was intended to guard!

So everything began over again, with very similar results. Austria strove to mend the breach without hurting the sensibility of Russia. France approved various pacific measures, and meanwhile pressed on the machinery of war. England agreed to everything that anybody proposed, and so anxiously strove for peace that she made war a certainty. Note, Convention, and Declaration crossed and recrossed from London to Paris, from Constantinople to Vienna, and back again, to no purpose; and meanwhile ships of war were doing their own work and rendering all the peaceful instruments of diplomacy vain and of no account. Eleven different solutions of the problem of peace with honour were exhibited between June and December, and all failed to avert war.

The first, or Austrian "fusion" plan was communicated to Reshid Pasha, the Turkish Secretary for Foreign Affairs, towards the end of June. This was an improvisation of Count Buol's, the Austrian Foreign Minister, and Lord Stratford had received no instructions from his Government how to deal with it. He anticipated little success from any attempt to unite views so divergent as those contained in the Menshikov and Reshid notes of 20 May, especially since the former, and afterwards Count Nesselrode, had made it perfectly clear that they would not "hear of the slightest variation in the terms." Nevertheless, the Elchi saw the advantage of setting diplomacy to work to gain time, if not to heal the breach. " I think it right," he wrote to Lord Clarendon, " to catch at any chance of peace which is not attended with a sacrifice of principle or a loss of time," and he forthwith assembled his colleagues of Austria, France, and Russia at his house. There the four agreed to a memorandum recommending Count Buol's plan to the Porte; and by this simple expedient the exclusive mediation of Austria was skilfully quashed and the " fusion " scheme was offered to the Sultan with the joint weight and authority of the Four Powers. It is worth remembering that the idea of placing the Eastern Question of 1853 before a jury of the Great Powers was Lord Stratford's. He had called together

the ambassadors in May to deal with Prince Menshikov's
demands; and now he repeated the measure. From the
meeting at his house on 24 June dates the collective action
of Europe which, properly directed, might have averted the
misery and futility of the Crimean War. The Porte itself
greatly preferred such collective action, and this preference
was a weapon in the armoury of peace.

At this time two circumstances occurred to delay negotiations. On 7 July news arrived that the Russians had crossed
the Pruth four days before. Hardly was this known when
Mustafa, the Grand Vezir, and Reshid Pasha were suddenly
dismissed from office. This was believed to signalize the
triumph of the war party in the ministry. Lord Stratford
went straight to the Sultan on the 9th, and, on being informed
that purely personal causes had led to the removal of the two
leading ministers, advised his Majesty to allow no secondary
considerations to deprive him of valuable counsellors at so
critical a moment. Abdu-l-Mejid restored the ministers on
the spot. Extracts from the ambassador's letters to Lady
Stratford and to Lord Clarendon, and a report from Stephen
Pisani, the dragoman, shew clearly enough how the Turks
relied upon their English adviser at every step. Unprepared
as they were, time was of urgent consequence ; he therefore
bade them not resist the Czar's armies, but protest ; and they
obeyed.

To his Wife, 9 July.

The Russians are actually in the Provinces, and we must try to
get them out without yielding the point in dispute. How is that
to be done without war, and war on a large scale ? I tremble to
think of it, and yet know not how, except by miracle, it is to be
avoided. At all events let people make up their minds, and equal
Russia in foresight and consistency. I have written oceans, public
and private—that is private to Lord Clarendon. Now is the time
for decision—one more attempt if possible at negotiation, and then
war.

We have had a sudden change of ministry again—the Grand
Vezir and Reshid out in a moment. I went bang down to the
Padishah and put them in again. But it is sad work at such a
crisis. The Sultan accuses his ministers of pestering him with
their petty jealousies and personal interests. They accuse him of
weakness and duplicity.

To Lord Clarendon, 9 July.

Whatever may be hoped from negotiations ought, I submit, to
be tried at once and brought to a point. Delay will prove most

fatal to Turkey if prolonged beyond a very few weeks, and I confess my own impression to be that if the next attempt at negotiation
fails, there will be no room for half measures. If the object be, as
I presume, to get the Russians out of the Principalities without
surrendering the main point in dispute, it is difficult to conceive
how that object can have a chance of being accomplished without
hard knocks on a large scale, or some counter-occupation which
will be equivalent to a partial dismemberment of the empire. . . .
Surely it is time to come to a decision which may give consistency,
ensemble, and energy to our proceedings. I am as much for peace
as any man ; but if the object at stake is to be maintained, as I
think it ought, there should be a limit to attempts which can only
prove nugatory in the end and turn to the benefit of uncompromising
Russia.

From Stephen Pisani, 10 July.

Reshid Pasha is much pleased with the Protest as amended by
your lordship. It will be read in the Council which is to be held
to-morrow at the Porte, and subsequently submitted to the Sultan's
sanction. As soon as his Majesty's pleasure will be given to it,
Reshid Pasha will lose no time in communicating it officially to
the representatives of the Four Powers parties to the treaty of 1841.

Reshid Pasha is preparing a Note to be addressed to the Russian
government—I mean a fusion of Prince Menshikov's last Note, and
that privately communicated by the Porte to the latter. He hopes
to get it ready by to-morrow, when he will submit it to your
Excellency's consideration.

Although, according to Pisani's report, Reshid was busy
with the proposed " fusion " Note, it was clear that something
different was required now that the Russians had actually
invaded Turkey. On 18 June Lord Clarendon had advised
a protest against so unjustifiable an act, should the occupation
of the Principalities really take place; and on 9 July Lord
Stratford reported that a union of the Austrian "fusion"
with such a protest would probably be found the preferable
course. " At the request of Reshid Pasha," he added, "I have
endeavoured to adapt to that plan the draft of a protest which
his Highness had originally prepared for the case which has
since occurred."

Lord Stratford lost no time in carrying out the new plan
of a Note combined with a Protest against the occupation.
On 15 July the Protest was printed. It contained the principal ideas of Lord Clarendon's instruction of 18 June, and
was agreed to by the four representatives assembled in council
16 July, at the British Palace. They agreed in advising the
Porte to send to Count Nesselrode, together with the Protest,

copies of the firmans confirming the privileges of the non-Musulman subjects of Turkey, and they offered to transmit the Porte's communication to Russia by way of Vienna, and to write to their colleagues at St. Petersburg on the subject. On 20 July they met again, this time in conference with Reshid Pasha, and a letter was adopted to be addressed by the latter to Count Nesselrode, in company with the Protest and the firmans. They were all despatched post-haste to Vienna on the same day, and followed on the 23rd by a supplementary Note or *Projet de Convention* guaranteeing the enjoyment of the spiritual privileges confirmed by the firmans and promising to accord in future to the Greek Church "such other privileges and immunities as it may hereafter please his Majesty to grant to any other sect whatever of his Christian subjects." A General Council on the 24th approved the whole of this arrangement, which was declared to be of the nature of an ultimatum on the part of Turkey. The most jealous scrutiny of these various documents can only elicit the fact that they contain all that the Porte could reasonably be expected to concede, and all that Russia had originally demanded in her communications with the Great Powers. The language of the protest, whilst dignified, was eminently conciliatory.

Lord Stratford's letter (23 July) to his colleague Lord Westmorland at Vienna, will shew the importance he attached to these proposals :—

The present batch is forwarded by an express, supplied by Reshid, and paid by "the Four." We are anxious that it should arrive without a moment's delay. If you really wish for peace, you must make the most of the present experiment. The Porte will hear of nothing else, and the war party is soon more likely to be in the ascendant than reduced to order. All the separate schemes have come to nought. Our own particular notion of a Convention was found no better than Buol's and Bourqueney's. We are now, I humbly conceive, on the right ground, and in the right direction. There must be firmness as well as conciliation.

Meanwhile diplomacy at Vienna was becoming impatient as the weeks passed and no satisfactory news arrived from Constantinople. Count Buol therefore proposed, on 24 July, a new Note based on a draft drawn up at Paris, and to this Lord Clarendon assented by telegraph on the 25th. Three days later this Vienna Note was agreed to. On that very evening arrived the despatches of the 20th, bringing the Turkish Ultimatum from Constantinople. The London telegraph wire had spoilt all, for the Vienna Note being adopted, it was not to be supposed that the Turkish plan would be entertained. Count Buol said that, after taking the Emperor's commands, he considered that Reshid's letter was calculated "à aigrir les débats plus qu'à les concilier," and he declined the responsibility of transmitting it to St. Petersburg. The Constantinople despatches would be considered as "non-avenues." Lord Westmorland telegraphed to the Foreign Office for instructions, and Lord Clarendon replied (30 July) that he was to suspend the Turkish Ultimatum.

The representatives at Vienna took upon themselves a grave responsibility in detaining what was, after all, the ultimatum of an independent Power to a State with which it was technically at war. Had the Note been sent on to Petersburg, whatever might have been the effect upon the excited mind of the Emperor Nicholas, at least this result would have been attained : Turkey would have appeared in the true light of offering the last olive-branch, and Russia would by her refusal have acknowledged that she wanted what no independent State could grant. Had the Four Powers, by their representatives at Vienna, been formally committed to this Note, its rejection by Russia would probably have been followed by a collective remonstrance and possibly a collective armed interference ; and the separate action of the Western Powers and their entrance into the Dardanelles in October would thus have been avoided. The whole position as against Russia would have been materially strengthened, and all Europe would have joined in united mediation on just grounds accepted by the aggrieved party. *Sed legatis aliter visum.* Austria and Prussia shrank from the prospect of extreme measures ; they wished nothing less than to be dragged into the approaching struggle. So the four representatives at Vienna threw away the opportunity for the collective action of Europe in deference to the selfish timidity of the German Powers. Pressed by Austria, they preferred to work upon a plan approved by Russia, the aggressor, than upon one recommended by Turkey the aggrieved; and still more, with professional jealousy, they preferred their own plan to anyone else's.

On 9 August a despatch from Vienna informed Lord Stratford of the suppression of the Turkish Ultimatum and the simultaneous transmission of the Austrian Note to Constantinople and Petersburg. Telegraphing to the Foreign

Secretary on 31 July, the British ambassador at Vienna said,
" J'enverrai vos ordres à Lord Stratford." The " ordres " in
question were dated 28 July, *before the Turkish Ultimatum
was known to Lord Clarendon*, and they commanded Lord
Westmorland to " inform Lord Stratford that her Majesty's
Government desire that this project [the Vienna Note] should
be adopted by the Porte, *if no other arrangement has been
already made*." As another arrangement *had* already been
made, it is open to argument whether Lord Westmorland
ought not to have arrested the transmission of the Vienna
Note. At all events Lord Stratford felt that it was necessary
to wait for despatches from London before he could officially
support this Note, of which, though he had seen it, he had
not even a copy. Unfair use has been made of the consequent
delay to shew that the ambassador did his best to counteract
the instructions of his Government ; but as those instructions
were addressed through a third person, subject to a condition
which had not been realized, it was clearly his duty to wait
till he should ascertain whether after being fully informed of
the nature of the Turkish proposal Lord Clarendon still ad-
hered to the Vienna note. In his own polished language he
" determined not to forego unnecessarily the prospect of acting with the advantage of your lordship's *deliberate* instructions." The word I have italicized marks the ambassador's
sense of the flurried character of Lord Clarendon's telegraphic
assent to the Vienna Note.

Two days later the *Caradoc* brought these " deliberate
instructions," which were to the effect that, while " entirely
approving " Lord Stratford's proceedings, the Government
agreed with Count Buol in setting them aside and substituting
the Vienna Note, on the ground that Russia had adopted the
mediation of Austria and that there was reason to believe
that the note in question would be acceptable to the Czar.
Until the arrival of the *Caradoc* Lord Stratford had maintained complete silence on the subject of the new Note. Now
he recommended it officially to the Porte, dwelt on " the
strong and earnest manner " in which the Austrian project
was supported by the British Government, and its similarity
in general tenor to Reshid's original Note to Menshikov,
and pressed the fact that the Emperor of Russia's acceptance
of the Note had already been telegraphed. Reshid listened
" with a very good grace," but took exception to certain
portions of the document, which he considered would have

the effect of creating a Russian protectorate over the Greek
Church in Turkey; a danger, remarked the ambassador in
his despatch, which "was carefully avoided in the *Projet de
Note* [ultimatum] drawn up here." In forwarding the pasha's
unofficial and personal comments Lord Stratford added: "My
own impression is that the amendments do not cover his
objections, but I have abstained from telling him so in order
to incur no risk of encouraging an opposition to a Note so
highly recommended."

On 14 August the Council of ministers held a stormy
meeting, and the majority seemed determined to have nothing
to say to the Vienna Note, with or without amendments. The
next day Reshid Pasha told the British ambassador that
there was no hope of obtaining a majority in the Council for
the acceptance of the Vienna Note, and that he could not
himself sign it without modification. He complained of the
inconsiderate manner in which the London Cabinet had
agreed to this compromising arrangement. It would have
been better for Turkey, he said, to have yielded at the first,
than after so much support from the Powers to be now un-
seasonably abandoned. In reply, the ambassador of England
"abstained from making any admissions calculated to encourage the Porte in its resistance." But as soon as it was
certain that the Note would not be accepted as it stood, Lord
Stratford began to search for a middle course. "Not being
authorized to use intimidating language," he told Lord Clarendon, "I felt myself free, indeed compelled by a sense of
duty, to suggest some form of decision which might present
the character of an acceptance, and yet leave room for such
an adjustment of terms as would completely secure the
Porte." His plan was "simply that the Porte should signify
its acceptance of the Note under its own construction of the
objectionable passages, and for securities rely on the assent
and sanction of the Four Powers." Mr. Alison was at the
Porte while the adjourned Council was sitting on the 17th,
and as soon as he had ascertained that the Note was going
to be thrown out, he offered this suggestion. It was not accepted. On the 18th Reshid shewed the Elchi the amendments and the arguments which he had drawn up and presented to the Council, and Lord Stratford was obliged to
conceal his appreciation of the good grounds which the
Turkish minister had brought forward to justify resistance.
The Elchi himself had not anticipated so much sound reason.

to distrust the Note. A painful scene ensued. The Pasha kissed the ambassador's hand and implored him with tears not to "forsake his country in the midst of such dangers and distresses." Lord Stratford made one more attempt to procure at least a conditional acceptance of the unmodified Note, but on 20 August the Grand Council of sixty members decided that it could only be adopted with certain specified amendments.

There is no need to describe the Turkish modifications of the Vienna Note. They were regretted by the Four Powers, (though the French Government, not unnaturally, admitted that they were improvements upon the original draft) ; but all united in urging the Czar to accept them, as being really too trivial to be worth a quarrel. There are times when fate seems to put folly in the minds of the wise ; otherwise how could the statesmen of four Great Powers describe as trivial the very differences upon which the whole dispute rested ? Lord Stratford told Lord Clarendon that, although he had " scrupulously abstained from expressing any private opinion on the merits of Count Buol's Note, while it was under the consideration of the Porte," he could not help confessing to his lordship that the amendments were in his opinion necessary, unless a full right of interference over twelve million subjects of Turkey were to be granted to Russia. The point in dispute was clear enough to him, and it was equally clear to the Court at St. Petersburg. The Four Governments, however, continued innocently blind, until the Czar rejected the Turkish amendments on 7 September, and soon afterwards the famous " Russian analysis of the Three Modifications introduced by the Ottoman Porte into the Vienna Note" was let out of the diplomatic bag, and all the world was immediately aware that Lord Stratford and the Turks were right, and the Four Powers wrong, in their interpretation of that "highly recommended" document. Lord Clarendon hastily dropped the Note with as much the air of having burnt his fingers as a statesman can be expected to reveal.

What would have been the result of the acceptance of the Vienna Note by the Porte is thus summarized by the Russian Foreign Office in its ingenuous *Diplomatic Study*: " The triumph of Russia, who in fact was winning the day over the resistance of the maritime Powers, and saw her position in the East strengthened by a solemn covenant concluded with the participation of all Europe ; the exhaustion of Turkey, forced to a gratuitous display of her military forces, which completed the ruin of her finances, to leave her after all at the same point; lastly, a complete check to the personal influence of the Ambassador, which in his patriotism he identified with that of his Government."[1] Truly, a Daniel come to judgment! Every act of Lord Stratford's finds its perfect justification in the candid avowals of this remarkable work. There are, as it were, tears in its eyes as it laments the imprudence of Russia in insisting upon precise definitions of her rights in Turkey : " In face of the incurable mistrust of which we were the object, it was better to leave a certain vagueness around these delicate questions. It was always in our power to interpret them in accordance with our views, which were perfectly proper." Of course ; but propriety varies according to latitude and longitude.

That the Vienna Note was inadmissible was now evident ; and it seems scarcely worth while to ask whether Lord Stratford did all in his official power to procure the acceptance by the Turks of a proposal which was afterwards proved to be delusive. That he saw the dangerous features of the Note, at least in part, is obvious, and equally obvious that his private influence could not be wielded in favour of a plan which he could not approve. But the despatches shew that he used his official power to the full in support of the instructions of his Government, and that he " scrupulously abstained " from letting his personal opinions transpire. More could not be expected. It is absolutely false to insinuate that his private converse with the Turkish ministers contradicted his official acts. It has been surmised that in such a case " silence gave consent " : but the papers of the time prove clearly that the Turks required no consent, silent or spoken, to make them resist the Note.

It was natural that the ambassador should feel annoyed at the suppression of his own plan of pacification, and he wrote in some irritation to Lord Clarendon and to Lady Stratford :—

To Lord Clarendon, 20 Aug.

The last stage of the business has proved more irksome than any that preceded it. The formal approbation of my conduct does not make up for the rejection of the plan transmitted from here, which I had sent home in full reliance on its usefulness and with

[1] *Diplomatic Study on the Crimean War,* i. 211.

the conviction that within its circle everything was placed on its proper footing. I have not even the consolation of thinking that it gave way to a more successful invention.

I was not aware till after the arrival here of the latter that a regular Conference was established at Vienna. My impression was that the occasional meetings of the Four were similar to those which have been held here, neither more formal nor more authorized. . . .

I hope you will feel yourself at liberty to approve and second the suggestions of the Porte. It is impossible not to fear that the Emperor of Russia's acceptance of the Note *telle quelle* may have raised an additional difficulty. The Porte is to all appearance ready for anything.

To his Wife, Saturday night—Sunday morning, 20-1 *Aug.*

I am more than ever to be pitied. It is literally out of my power to write twenty lines to you. I wrote or otherwise laboured in public matters the whole of yesterday, and I have sat up writing all night. The subjects, too, are disagreeable and will give much annoyance in Downing Street and still more at Argyll House. The Porte will not accept the Vienna Note without amendments, and the Turks are altogether on their high horse. Who can wonder after all that has happened ? Our joint labours were thrown overboard in the beginning of the month, and they think it hard to be so used. They have better motives, however, for following their present course. The Note proposed to them was not safe, and I think they have no less justly than courageously held their own. As the Emperor Nicholas had accepted, the shock may be *awful,* and it is difficult to say what will be the end of it.

To his Wife, 31 *Aug.*

I have read the Queen's Speech and I have skimmed over the speeches of her Majesty's lieges in the H. of C. They have both made a very uncomfortable impression upon me. Politically they make me fear that an abstract idea of peace has carried the day over every other consideration, that the Turks will be left to themselves, and that Russia will finally come back with a flood tide. Personally they seem to foreshadow an evil end to my embassy. . . . Alas! alas! Such a triumph to be so thrown away ! and why ? Because the affairs of this country are not honestly looked in the face—because they are made subordinate to party politics and other interests elsewhere—because people think small while they talk big—and finally because we make an idol of the aggressor and offer him incense when he ought to have smoke of another kind. Do not infer from this that your ancient is a chimaera breathing fire and flame. He is neither for peace nor for war. He is for the Question—for its settlement—its settlement on fair and durable grounds. If we are mistaken about the Question, if it has been exaggerated and has not the importance we have hitherto attached to it—let that be made clear—I will be the first to recant and to recommend the best piece of tinkering that diplomacy can offer. If, on the contrary, we are really in presence of the great Eastern Question, if it knocks at our door, stands on tiptoe and looks in at our window, it may be an ugly and frightful object, but we must look it in the face and deal with it as men and statesmen ought to do. Clarendon writes in private good-humouredly and kindly, and his despatches are all more or less approving ; but our Constantinople plan of arrangement has been *overlaid* ; my notions have not been followed up ; and the Turks are treated with levity, not to say disrespect. The consequence of all this is that their pride is up and that they are so circumstanced with their army and subjects as to find it almost equally dangerous to give in or to resist. In short what I wrote to the Office several weeks ago may easily be realized : "The extreme desire of peace, if care be not taken, may bring on the danger of war." I know not what to think of it ; but a very small slip in Downing Street, or rather at Argyll House, on the receipt of my last despatches may cause a world of mischief. The die is, however, probably cast by this time, and we shall see. . . . The Turks, I think, are bent on *war, unless their amendments are accepted*, and I fear they cannot help themselves with respect to their army and nation, now thoroughly roused though hitherto well-behaved. The poor Sultan! I have much to say, but, alas ! no time.

The Czar's total rejection of the Turkish amendments was officially known at Constantinople on 25 September, and the original Note was again recommended to the Porte. Lord Stratford himself joined anxiously in this step, and urged the Turkish ministers to accept the unmodified Note under a guarantee of the Four Powers. He implored Reshid to adopt this plan, but in vain ; the popular spirit was roused, and neither Sultan nor Minister dared stand against it. On the following day the Great Council of the Empire, mustering 172 members, unanimously resolved that the unmodified Vienna Note could not be accepted on any terms, " even if accompanied by a guarantee of the Four Powers," and that war was inevitable. On 4 Oct. a notification was despatched through Omar Pasha to Prince Gorchakov, summoning him to evacuate the Principalities within fifteen days ; a negative reply would be regarded as a declaration of war. The Russian commander replied on 10 Oct. that he had " no authority to treat of peace or war or evacuation of the Principalities," and this evasive but practically negative answer was accepted by

Reshid Pasha as the "beginning of war." The negative reply reached him on the 10th or 11th, and from that date, in theory at least, a state of open war existed. Fearing that Russia might immediately attack the capital with her fleet, the Turks urged the French and English ambassadors to bring up their squadrons to protect the Sultan. But before we enter upon the naval phase, a few extracts from the private correspondence may be quoted in illustration of the period between the amending of the Vienna Note and the summoning of the squadrons.

To his Wife, 1 Oct.

We have narrowly escaped a sanguinary revolution, and we have escaped it only to go *full tilt* into war. The Sultan and General Council have resolved upon war, and the Russians will soon be summoned to march out of the provinces, preparatory to hostilities if they don't, as they won't, comply.

This is an awful prospect—as near as it is awful. I have done what I could to avert it, but circumstances swollen by mismanagement have carried all before them. My only satisfaction is that I admonished in time and that I have kept the even march which I resolved on keeping from the commencement. . . . I shall be asked to bring up the squadrons, and feel embarrassed beforehand. . . . God bless you and the children! Have a kind, pitying thought for poor papa, who knows little of this charming Bosphorus except the spray dashed against his windows and the smoke from twenty steamers brought morning and evening into his room.

To W. Canning, 9 Oct.

Here is Sunday but no Sabbath. I wish you could see the litter of papers in my room. I am literally up to my neck in them and there are puzzling questions to be decided, and all on my own responsibility. Four months since Menchikov went away, and not only just as we were, but worse. In fact, we are on the very verge of war, and only waiting for actual hostilities. Nobody, I suppose, is to blame on this side of the Danube, certainly not the poor Turks, who have done, and are still doing, wonders, that is to say, in their way, and yet not quite in their way, for they have acted with singular prudence and good order. The head and front of the offence is that man who has been humbugging Europe, and perhaps at times even duping himself, for the last quarter of a century. He, and he alone, is the original cause—there have been accessories since—of a mischief which nothing short of a miracle can now prevent, and which sooner or later will probably drag within its vortex the greater part of the civilized world. I have done my best for peace—in *propria persona* where I could with honour and conviction—as *an agent* when I did not like the manner of proceeding; but I have also stuck close to *the Question*, and we now have ample proof from Russia herself that the Turks were right in mistrusting the Vienna Note, and that there *is a question* worth contending for, as is admitted even by Mr. Reeve, the *Times* writer, who is now here and who dined with me yesterday. When I induced the Sultan not to declare war when the Russians entered the Principalities I did so not only for peace, but for the question also, meaning and thoroughly expecting that the "Allies" would coöperate with vigour to settle the dispute. On one side there was a strong man with a bad cause; on the other a weak man with a good one. I leave others to say which of the two has been flattered and which repressed. If the quarrel had occurred in any street of London, it would probably have been otherwise. Be that as it may, the storm is coming on and it is more easy to see the beginning than the end of it.

CHAPTER XX.

THE SUMMONS TO THE FLEET.

October–December 1853.

THE question of bringing up the squadrons had long been a subject of anxious thought to Lord Stratford. He knew all the risks attending the appearance of the Allied fleets in the Bosphorus; so long as war was not declared, he was aware that the passage of the Dardanelles would be regarded as a violation of the Treaty of 1841, by which foreign ships of war are excluded from the Straits in time of peace, and he was therefore careful not to bring on the crisis by a precipitate appeal to the Admiral. It will be remembered that he left England for the East armed with no further powers than to request the Admiral at Malta to hold himself in readiness for sea. This power was augmented on 2 June when the Western Governments took the first united step towards war by ordering the fleets to Besika Bay, where they were to await the ambassador's further instructions. It might be urged that the movement formed part of their ordinary cruising, but all Europe knew that they had gone to succour the Porte, and that their advance was a direct reply to the Ultimatum and departure of Prince Menchikov. Still, so long as the fleets remained outside the Castles of the Dardanelles Russia had

no treaty right to protest ; and Lord Stratford, whilst rejoicing
in what he hoped was a sign of a manly policy, resolved that
outside they should remain so long as he could keep them
there.

The spirit of the Turks needed no rousing then. Even
Lord Stratford found them " out of hand," and the Sheykh-
el-Islam had declared that he would sooner break his seal
than affix it to such a document as the Vienna Note. Reshid
told M. de la Cour that the persistence of the Western Courts
in recommending humiliating concessions to the Porte would
end in throwing Turkey into the arms of Russia ; to which
the French ambassador replied that in such a case France
would look to a close alliance with Austria and Prussia and
would leave England and Turkey in the lurch. The high
tone of the Porte found a ready echo in the voices of the
theological students and professors, Softas and Ulema, who
rose in open mutiny, angrily protesting against concessions to
the infidels. Such movements are not unusual among the
fanatical scholars of the East, and there is no reason to
suppose that the insurrection was a device of the ministers to
force the hands of the Western ambassadors. It had, however, that effect ; for M. de la Cour, with all the Frenchman's
vivacity, drew a harrowing picture to his Government of a
coming massacre of his countrymen, and M. Drouyn de Lhuys
hastened to the rescue. It is amazing to read in his own
words that Lord Clarendon, in concert of course with Lord
Aberdeen, was induced by the representations of a foreign
government, based upon a single telegraphic report, to take
the serious step of ordering the advance of the squadron
through the Dardanelles without waiting for Lord Stratford's
despatches. A few days' delay would have shewn that there
was no danger to foreigners at Constantinople and that Lord
Stratford himself had quelled the disturbance and provided
for the safety of the British colony without summoning the
fleet. He had only brought up a couple of steamers to protect
English subjects, and the French had done the same; no
more formidable preparations were needed. An insurrection,
the mere rumour of which had sufficed to frighten the Secretary of State into a panic, had been witnessed, met, and
quelled without discomposure by the calm mind that watched
over the Embassy at the Porte. The strong man, loth to put
forth his strength, imposes peace by the mere ascendency of
his dauntless will. The weakling, in his dread of blows, cries

out for weapons which he cannot sheathe.   In this vivid
contrast the Elchi stands forth superbly.

The immediate effect of Lord Clarendon's ill-starred decision was a remonstrance from Baron Brunov, the Russian
ambassador, who declared that the instruction to the fleet was
a breach of treaty.   To this the Foreign Minister replied that
the Porte had " ceased to be at peace from the moment when
the first Russian soldier entered the Danubian Principalities,"
and added that the whole fleet was to go up to Constantinople.
The sinister impression created at St. Petersburg by this correspondence forms an important link in the chain of circumstances that made towards war ; but the singular part of the
transaction is that at the place most concerned in the advance
of the fleets Lord Clarendon's precipitate instruction had no
effect at all.   The mischief was done at St. Petersburg, but
there was one at Constantinople who was determined that he
would have no hand in it.   Lord Stratford received the order
to call up the fleet with characteristic coolness and sagacity.
His reply shewed a delicate tinge of sarcasm. He was " deeply
sensible " of the Government's " interest in the preservation of
British lives and property at Constantinople, under the impressions derived from M. de la Cour's telegraphic despatch,"
and especially of " that part of these instructions [of 23
September] which authorizes me to *consider the presence* of
her Majesty's squadron here, *if I thought proper to require it,*
as intended to embrace the protection of the Sultan also in
case of need."   Lord Clarendon had said nothing of the
nature of the words which I have italicized : " Your Excellency is instructed to send for the British fleet to Constantinople " was his order.   But Lord Stratford was determined
not to understand it in its plain sense and his despatch very
quietly went on : " Fortunately there is no necessity whatever
for calling up the squadron on either account. . . . I am still
of opinion that assistance thus limited [to two or three
steamers] would have answered every purpose. . . . I
wished to save her Majesty's Government from any embarrassments likely to accrue from a premature passage of the Dardanelles."   The despatch from which these sentences are taken
was written on 6 October, and for a fortnight longer Lord
Stratford resisted every attempt to force on a hasty appeal to
the Admirals.   Had the order been obeyed, it might plausibly
have been argued that the Treaty of 1841 had been violated.
But it was not obeyed ; the situation at the Porte remained in

the same state as it had been ever since Lord Clarendon's despatch of 2 June; and the fleets were summoned, for a quite different reason, after the Turks had declared themselves to be at overt war with the Czar.

That reason was simply that the Porte, after giving Prince Gorchakov fifteen days to arrange for the evacuation of the Danubian provinces, feared that Russia would not wait the time, but would make a sudden descent, possibly upon the Bosphorus, and place the capital in jeopardy; and the Sultan accordingly requested the protecting presence of the fleets, which he knew was provided for in the ambassadors' instructions. The request was made on the 8th, but twelve days passed before Lord Stratford issued the momentous order to the Admiral. In the interval, Prince Gorchakov's reply to the Turkish notice to quit had removed the last doubt as to whether the two Powers were at war or peace, and the Treaty of 1841 formed, therefore, no obstacle to the entrance of the squadrons. The Sevastopol fleet was also said to be under weigh. Accordingly on 20 October the ambassadors of England and France summoned the squadrons, and on the 22nd they entered the Hellespont.

In announcing this important step to his Government Lord Stratford made it clear that it was based upon his "original instructions"—i.e. to protect the Sultan. With reference to the order of 23 September he added: "The juncture for which the last ones were framed has long since ceased to have any existence in fact." There was no longer any risk of a revolution. For nearly eight months he had held those original instructions; for four months he had possessed complete authority over the fleet; France had tried vainly to hurry him, and his own Government had rashly yielded to the imprudent counsels of Paris; but Lord Stratford had stood unmoved till the time came when he could bring up the fleet with no breach of international engagements. He would have preferred to hold out yet a little longer, but the Turks were anxious, and the French ambassador was becoming unmanageable. "I have almost risked a quarrel," he wrote to Lord Clarendon, "by holding out so long."

The entrance of the squadrons caused no break in the negotiations for peace. At the very moment when his summons was speeding to the Admiral, Lord Stratford was communicating (21 October) to London and Vienna his "Note and Declaration," which he believed the Porte would accept, and which once more accorded to Russia all and more than all that she had any right to ask. At the same time he obtained with great difficulty the consent of the Turkish Government to a postponement of hostilities for ten days. The message which procured this postponement is characteristic; it was addressed to Reshid Pasha (20 Oct.) through Stephen Pisani :—

Tell Reshid Pasha that I have fresh letters from London just come in, and he *must* prepare to stop hostilities for the moment. There is no avoiding it. He will lose all—France and England, too—if war is precipitated. I also shall be materially injured. Steamers *must* go off *to-day, coûte que coûte*, with orders to Omar Pasha and to the commanders in Asia not to stir an inch without further orders. We—the four or the two—will bear the Porte out in this. Say all this to him *immediately*. I am waiting for the others, who are not come yet. As soon as we have talked, I will write again or go myself to the Pasha at Balta Liman, where you will stay for the present.

His Note was accepted at Paris and London. Lord Clarendon earnestly entreated that *anything* coming from Lord Stratford might be " favourably considered " at Vienna. But in spite of the arguments of the English and French Governments, the Note and Declaration were thrown over by Austria, on the ground that a treaty of peace, and not a Note, was required, now that war was declared. Thus for the second time Austria destroyed the chance of a collective pressure upon the Czar.

Lord Stratford, however, was not surprized at the failure. He wrote disconsolately to his wife, 22 October :—

I have made another effort for peace—one which made three months ago might, I verily believe, have succeeded, in so far as anything tolerable for the Turks can succeed with the Czar. But it will only serve to figure in the Blue Book. War is a decree of the Fates, and we shall surely have it. Therefore I have written urging the necessity of looking to the means of success at once on a large scale. Help the Turks we must, and the more decidedly we do it the better for ourselves in the end. . . .

I wrote my requisition to the Admiral to bring in the squadrons on the anniversary of the battle of Navarino.

25 *Oct.*—The squadrons have entered the Dardanelles, but our portion is not yet arrived. The winds have been and still are strong from the north.

You tell me to make another attempt for peace. I have done so, and with the greatest difficulty obtained a suspension of hos-

tilities—the last—for ten days. My *forlorn hope* was accepted in
London and at Paris, and I put the whole into shape, so that the
Porte most evidently could, and Russia ought to, accept it. But I
am convinced that Russia never would accept it, and that Austria
would not join in pressing it. On the whole, I am satisfied that
nothing can now avert the war, which in fact exists, though
hostilities are not yet known to have begun.

No sooner was one proposal rejected than another was
made. Indeed, at the moment that Lord Stratford's Note
and Declaration were travelling to Vienna, a new *Projet de
Note*, based upon his suggestion of a revised edition of the
Vienna Note, was being despatched from Downing Street.
We must at least give Lord Clarendon credit for industry if
we are obliged to regret his want of resolution. The Elchi
and the Foreign Secretary had been working at the same
idea—Lord Stratford had suggested it on 28 September—and
the results took final shape almost on the same day. Not to
be behindhand with a specific remedy, Count Buol was at the
moment sketching, and the English Foreign Minister was
amiable enough to aid him in preparing, a Collective Note of
the Four Powers, which, together with a Protocol of an important explanatory meeting of the four representatives at Vienna,
was despatched on 5 December to Constantinople.

But many things had happened at Stambol before the
Collective Note arrived on 17 December. The Austrian
Internuncio, after endeavouring once more to obtain the
acceptance of the original Vienna Note, was again ordered
to approach the Porte on peaceful aims intent. Russia had
informed Austria of her willingness to treat, and the Internuncio was accordingly to assure the Turkish Government of
the conciliatory desires of the Emperor Nicholas, as explained
at the meeting at Olmütz, and the just and reasonable character of his demands on behalf of the Greek Church. Lord
Clarendon did not see the matter in this light. The recent
manifesto of the Czar, the appointment of a Russian governor
in the Principalities, the threats of Prince Gorchakov to
the Sultan's subjects did not, in his opinion, breathe an air
of conciliation. So thought the Porte when the Note was
laid before it on 24 November. Moreover, war was now
briskly going on, and this did not look conciliatory. Alison
reported to Lady Stratford, 25 Nov. :—

H.E. himself is very well off, but we have nothing but our
ardour for peace to keep us warm. I suppose it will come about.

The Turks in the meantime are fighting like tigers. In the last engagement in Asia they threw away their muskets and attacked the Russians with their knives, making no prisoners. They say that if we are not expeditious there will be no Russians left to make peace with. The great embarrassment is the number of peacemakers. Lord Cl. sends a very reasonable project, and before we have half beaten it into the heads of the Turks, the Frenchman abandons us to advocate an Austrian project newly arrived. With the greatest respect for Cabinets, all this is very foolish and playing into the hands of the Turks. When everyone else is dead I intend to write an Oriental romance, to be called "Les Mille et une Notes."

This was no exaggeration. When Austria failed, Prussia ventured to rush in with a proposal of her own. To make confusion worse confounded the French ambassador stepped forward with a new plan. And on the top of all this, with the Collective Note gradually being built up at Vienna, Lord Clarendon's Project of 24 October arrived at Constantinople with instructions that it should be submitted to the Porte with the concurrence of France, and if possible of Austria and Prussia. The despatch of course went on the supposition that hostilities had not yet broken out, and that therefore no treaty of peace was requisite. Reshid Pasha admitted that two months earlier the Clarendon Note would have been accepted by the Porte with satisfaction, but it was different now that hostilities had broken out. Lord Stratford used every means to recommend the Note. He conscientiously approved it, as far as it went, as a tolerable compromise. He personally visited Reshid and urged its acceptance. He drew up a vigorous argument in favour of it. On 14 November, the evening when the Council was to meet to discuss the subject, he went to Reshid's house and remained with him till the very moment that he left to join his colleagues at the Council. "I omitted," he wrote, "nothing which my instructions, my recollections, or my reflection could support, in order to make an impression on his mind. I lament to say that all my efforts were unavailing, and that I could obtain nothing beyond a promise that my arguments should be faithfully repeated to the Council before he expressed any opinion of his own. I might accompany him, he said, to the Council, and make my own statement to the assembled ministers; or, if I thought that he was an obstacle to the acceptance of my proposals, he was ready to give in his resignation."

Some extracts from the correspondence illustrate this anxious November :—

To his Wife, 14 *Nov.*

I am still labouring for peace, but all alone—a thorough forlorn hope. Our present offer would undoubtedly have been accepted two months ago. But now the case is altered wholly, at least to those who see and feel as Turks see and feel, not unnaturally too. I tell them that in all cases there is a wish and an opinion, passion and judgment. I sympathize with the wish, but judgment whispers that they had better accept. Still they have to answer to their army and nation—the former victorious, the latter enthusiastic to a degree. It is very difficult; and the present offer, founded on my suggestion, but not carried out as I meant, yet tolerable, and enough for conscience. The fleets are at anchor in full [view] and others coming. We shall have a magnificent squadron. Thank Graham if you see him. Poor De la Cour is recalled. He does not like it, but bears it well.

19 *Nov.*—No peace as yet, and I grieve to say that Reshid is as hot upon war as the most military of his colleagues. There is much to excuse, to explain, and to justify this; but I lament it in the conviction that, all things considered, peace is really best for the Porte on the terms which now appear to be within its reach. I have been exerting myself to the utmost under this conviction, but hitherto with no success. Reshid has declared, however, that two months ago the same propositions would have been accepted with satisfaction. Do not forget that they are founded on my suggestion.

It was becoming daily more and more difficult to keep down the warlike spirit of the Turks. For six months, ever since Prince Menshikov's departure, the British ambassador had pressed upon the home Government the unfairness and danger of delaying the settlement of the dispute. Turkey could not bear the financial strain of long-continued preparations for war, and the military zeal of her people, once kindled by the signs and pomps of war, was not easily to be repressed. Every week had added to these dangers, and rendered the Porte less disposed to accept any proposal which seemed to carry the smallest concession to Russia. So far indeed they had had the best of the campaign, and it must be remembered that the idea that there can be only one end to a Russo-Turkish war is quite a modern notion. From the days when Peter the Great was surrounded by the Ottomans on the banks of the Pruth, and unfortunately let out, the superiority of the Russian troops had never been proved. The campaigns of

1809-12 were marked by no extraordinary successes on either side, though Russia was probably winning when peace was made at Bucharest. The triumph at Adrianople was a piece of daring impudence on the part of Diebitsch, and, had the smallness of his force been known, it would have ended in his total discomfiture. There are people now who argue, apparently with reason, that in the last war the Turks were really a match for their adversaries; that Plevna would never have fallen but for bribes, and that then it fell to the attack of little Rumania, not to the onslaught of Russia. It is at all events certain that the Turks themselves in 1853 were by no means oppressed with a sense of inferiority. They were eager for war, and hopeful of success. Soldiers were pouring in from distant provinces; Egypt was furnishing a contingent, and there seemed every probability of an enthusiastic response to the Manifesto of the Khalif of the Mohammedan world. Besides, whatever the ambassadors might say, were not the armaments of the two greatest maritime Powers of the world now lying at anchor above the capital? Was it to be believed that the fleets had come there for nothing, that they would not fight, and that England and France, in spite of big words, would fire no shot but paper notes, and projects instead of projectiles? Is there any wonder that the Turks felt like fighting, and fighting in company?

Lord Stratford had long seen this feeling growing, and was powerless to repress it. There might have been time had his July scheme been adopted at Vienna, but now matters had reached such a pass that it was extremely doubtful whether any proposal for terms would be listened to by the Porte. Concession to Russia might mean revolution at Stambol. Yet it was essential if possible to place Turkey in the position of acquiescence in the wishes of the powers, so that there should be no doubt that Russia was the real obstacle to peace. To effect this object, almost unattainable as it appeared, became Lord Stratford's intense desire. His calm and statesmanlike survey of the situation is nowhere better expressed than in the following despatch to Lord Clarendon (24 Nov.):—

Moderation and firmness are the two principles of conduct which the Porte has been most assiduously advised to maintain in the course of her differences with Russia. She has exhibited the former to a striking degree from the time of Prince Menshikov's Ultimatum to the publication of her final manifesto. She has displayed the latter most particularly in rejecting the Note of Vienna

without modifications, and in collecting her means of defence with
an amount of energy, good order, and perseverance, not easily sur-
passed.

The great test of her moderation was the course pursued by her
Government when a Russian army crossed her frontier and insult-
ingly occupied the Principalities. A respectful protest and a confiding appeal to Europe were her substitutes for a declaration of
war. But half her duty would have been neglected if, while she
gave time for negotiation, she had not provided for the contingency
of its failure by preparing the means of an efficient armed resistance against Russia. The Allies might well have complained if the
Sultan had betrayed a weak indifference to his own cause, and
thrown the whole burden of its vindication on their shoulders.

The Ottoman ministers, in carrying out the policy prescribed to
them alike by interest and by duty, roused of necessity a strong
national feeling throughout the Empire, and at the same time a
general expectation that unusual sacrifices would be followed by
an adequate return. Among the Mohammedans, as your lordship
knows, patriotism is always more or less a religious sentiment, and
the Porte could hardly be expected to restrain the fanaticism of its
adherents without directing their zeal to some distinct object of
national desire. It was no longer thought enough to resist any
specific pretensions of Russia. The mortifying ascendency of that
Power was to be shaken off altogether, and the independence of
the Empire to be placed once for all on a level with that of its
neighbour. A concurrence of circumstances originating in the
presumption and duplicity of Russia appeared to favour this very
natural ambition, and the united sympathies of the Government,
the army, and the people, excited, no doubt, by the partisans of a
war policy, had only to be acted upon with spirit in order to repress
all dissensions in the Cabinet and to avert the danger, whatever may
have been its degree, of a popular outbreak. The personal antagonism of Reshid Pasha and the Seraskier no longer disturbs the
administration; the former has gained a large accession of popularity, and also of the Sultan's favour, and his Majesty, to all
appearance, has accepted frankly the decision of his people as
expressed with unanimity by the General Council some two months
ago.

If, then, it was true that circumstances for which the Porte is
not answerable have naturally brought on a state of things impart-
ing force, unity, and direction to a general sentiment laudable in
itself, and offering, when adopted by the Government, much advantage and convenience both to the Sultan and to his leading ministers, it is hardly surprizing that, with considerable armies on the
frontier, the squadrons of England and France on the Bosphorus,
a pervading enthusiam in their favour, and some unexpected successes in battle, the Sultan and his Cabinet should receive with
reluctance and dislike any proposition invested with the badge of

their old inferiority towards Russia, and calculated to disappoint the hopes of the nation, and, with the overthrow of their popularity, to expose them to the most serious embarrassments.   It may be alleged with truth, and I have striven to impress this truth in every form of language on their minds, that, however natural such sentiments may be, their indulgence on the present occasion is neither just, nor wise, nor humane, seeing that the original difference can now be settled on safe and honourable grounds, with every moral and political advantage on the Sultan's side, while an unnecessary continuance of hostilities would invite the most perilous hazards, the most exhausting sacrifices, a vast effusion of blood, and, more than possibly, the horrors of a general war.   Unfortunately the motives to forbearance are thrown into shade by the dazzling illusions of hope, and passion is in league with occasion to merge all fears of danger and all considerations of prudence in a wild though attractive speculation, difficult at best to realize, and of which even the accomplishment would not be unattended with formidable drawbacks.

I question whether Reshid himself is at all times entirely free from these delusive influences, though, to do justice both to him and to his colleagues, they still profess a willingness to seek no further advantage than a relinquishment of Russia's religious pretensions, and of the notes prepared to embody them.   In their hearts they may aspire to arrangements calculated to secure them from future disturbance, and they would gladly put forward claims to a new disposition in the Principalities, to the recognition of Circassian independence, and to the reimbursement of their military expenses.   But deference to the counsels of their Allies would prevail with them to forego such notions, and their cooler aspirations would, I think, be satisfied with a renewal in clear, comprehensive terms of the formal declarations and treaties already existing in favour of the Porte.   What they never cease to insist upon is a clear and unquestionable deliverance from Russian interference applied to spiritual matters.   They are persuaded that silence would be the best and safest form of accomplishing that purpose ; and they are now bent upon excluding every kind of note, however carefully expressed, as liable to offend their own people and to afford a dangerous opening for what they presume to be the real designs of Russia.

This apprehension is, I fear, but too well justified by the late proceedings of the Russian Cabinet, and after so many sacrifices forced upon Turkey by that Power, it is but fair that the Porte should be secured from further molestation on the same score, not only virtually, but in a form and manner calculated to leave no room for mistakes upon the subject, either here or elsewhere.

Should the Emperor of Russia, acting in the spirit of his new manifesto, after giving the lie publicly to his neighbour, and supporting by force of arms his usurpation in the Principalities, decline a form of arrangement accepted by the Porte and recommended by her Allies, your lordship would probably agree with the Ottoman ministers in thinking that a wider region would then be opened for diplomatic views as well as for military operations. Most sincerely do I deprecate the occurrence of any such case, and no exertion will be wanting on my part, under the guidance of your lordship's instructions, to dissuade the Porte from wantonly bringing on a necessity of the kind. But should it so happen that Russia herself continues to be the obstacle to a pacific arrangement, the interests of international security, no less than those of Turkish independence, will probably be found to require exertions and remedies little short of those which the more sanguine Mohammedans already contemplate.

There was a singular fatality about the negotiations that preceded the Crimean war; it seemed as though the best conceived and all but executed plans were doomed to failure just when all appeared to be going right. Diplomacy was on the point of attaining its well-earned triumph when a catastrophe, for which it was not responsible, reduced its laurels to ashes.

To understand how this happened it is necessary to consider the position of the Allied squadrons. They were anchored in the Bosphorus and offered a complete bulwark between the Sevastopol fleet and Constantinople. But the coasts of Turkey are extensive, and the Allies proposed to defend them in all parts from Russian invasion. The most pressing danger was naturally on the Turkish shores of the Black Sea, and the obvious course was to send at least part of the squadrons out into the Euxine to reconnoitre. But here that disastrous duality, which England had afterwards such cause to rue, began to shew its baneful influence. Any movement of the Allied fleets required the assent of two ambassadors and two admirals. The new French ambassador, General Baraguay d'Hilliers, who succeeded M. de la Cour, supported the French admiral, Hamelin, in his objections to the Black Sea trip. The British fleet could not issue out alone, lest the concert of the two Powers should be disturbed; and Lord Stratford began to experience something of the embarrassment from which Lord Raglan afterwards suffered so acutely. Lord Clarendon " regretted extremely " the refusal of the French admiral, and acknowledged that it was impossible to send out the English ships alone.

It happened that towards the close of November eleven Turkish light vessels of war were lying at anchor in the harbour of Sinope. On the 30th six Russian ships of the line entered, anchored, destroyed the entire Turkish squadron, massacred 4,000 men, and presently sailed away. The importance of the action lay, not in its barbarity or wantonness, but in the fact that it was done in the face of the Allied fleets, and after Russia had been officially informed that they were there to protect Turkish territory from attack. The Turkish ships had been sunk, not on the high seas, or when engaged in any hostile act, but when peaceably anchored in a Turkish port. Lord Clarendon could only look upon it as a challenge; "it was not," he wrote to St. Petersburg, "the Turkish squadron alone that was deliberately attacked in the harbour of Sinope." To prevent the recurrence of such disasters, the admirals were ordered to take "complete command" of the Black Sea and to "require and if necessary compel" Russian ships of war to return to their ports. "We have undertaken to defend the territory of the Sultan from aggression, and that engagement must be fulfilled."

When matters had reached this point, Notes and Conventions cut but a sorry figure. The Collective Note from Vienna reached Constantinople on 16 December, one day after Reshid had received the final *Projet* of Lord Stratford and the other three ambassadors at the Porte. They all agreed that it must be held back, as calculated to do more harm than good at the present juncture.

The private correspondence of December describes the strange state of affairs at Constantinople—the arrival of pacificatory Notes, side by side with the movements of ships of war, and another rising of the fanatical classes of the population, subdued, like the first, by the Elchi's presence of mind.

To Lord Clarendon, 17 Dec.

The Vienna Note arrived *yesterday*, and we all agree that its presentation must at least be suspended. It would mar all if presented *now*; and should the plan adopted here and in the hands of Reshid Pasha since the *day before yesterday* fail of success, there will remain another string for our bow. Heaven grant that in some way or other we may get out of this mixed state of peace and war. It is far too painful and compromizing in every way.

The admirals appear to be anything but pleased with the prospect of a Black Sea cruise, and I question whether my military colleague would not side with them if he were left to himself. I feel most severely how responsible my position is, but with God's help I will shrink from nothing which my judgment carefully exercised imposes upon me.

To his Wife, 17 Dec.

There is no time to think of anything but the reigning question. I am still between peace and war—like Garrick between Tragedy and Comedy. The long continuance of such a state is very distressing to all concerned, and I long to get out of it—peaceably if possible with honour—but at all events anyhow. The Turks are beginning to listen once more to the voice of the charmer, and the General Council is clucking at this moment over an egg out of which may come peace or war, though probably, I hope, the former. I have likewise laid an egg, with the assistance of the three, and the ministers will have to sit upon it as soon as they get permission, if they *do* get it, from the General Council. If this egg is not addled in the hatching, it will, I trust, be approved in Downing Street—and possibly in the end at St. Petersburg. The case stands thus. Turco has obtained some *credit by land* but no *durable advantage* as yet, and at sea he has been cruelly unfortunate. It appears as if he would have peace now with a settlement, safe and honourable for him, on the old principle, improved in *form* and *result*; but then he must forego his ulterior hopes, magnificent, natural, and seducing—but illusive, because he cannot carry them out by himself, and his two seconds are not prepared to back him *so far* at present. If he accepts our fair proposals and Russia also accepts, he gets a prize equal to his first pretension, though not quite equal to his outlay. If he accepts and Russia refuses, the whole game is before him, and I shall myself entertain a sanguine hope of seeing Russia put into her proper place. But we must *all* fight for *that*—and stoutly, too. If the Porte refuses, there will be dudgeon at Paris and in London, and I fear the whole fabric of hope, pride, and resistance will sink into the slough of despond, and the Czar will be triumphant, to the humiliation of this empire and the final disturbance of every European interest. Now you have the whole of it—that is the cream.

The last night of 1853 witnessed the consummation of the Elchi's diplomatic labours for peace. In the face of every difficulty Lord Stratford had induced the Porte to agree to terms of arrangement. In spite of Sinope, and in spite of an ominous rising among the theological students, who were burning for the Holy War, his *Projet* was accepted on 31 December. Whatever might be the fate of this last plan, he remarked : " It will always be gratifying to remember that the injured and by no means unsuccessful party was the first to give proof of its pacific views, and to accede, with almost unlimited confidence, to the suggestion of its European Allies."

So ended the work of diplomacy. There is no need to describe minutely the plan thus accepted both by Turkey and

the Four Powers; its object was gained by the mere acceptance, and nothing could now stay the course of the European
war which began in the harbour of Sinope. Lord Clarendon
considered that the negotiation reflected " the highest credit
on his Excellency," and he conveyed " the entire approbation
of her Majesty's Government for the zeal and judgment "
which he had displayed. The Foreign Secretary considered
the Porte's reply " quite satisfactory." But the English and
French squadrons entered the Black Sea, Lord Clarendon's
stringent orders were put in force, the Czar's pride was irrevocably wounded, and diplomacy's work, at least at Constantinople, was at an end. For nine months many brains had
striven, with varied powers, for a peaceful settlement. None
had laboured harder than Lord Stratford to promote the
cause of honourable peace. He had succeeded so far that
he had placed the Turks in the right, and put Russia in the
ignoble position of a wanton aggressor. He had so guided
the Sultan that his Majesty had the sympathies of Europe.
The just demands of Russia had been granted by Imperial
firmans consolidating all the reasonable rights and privileges
of the Christians of Turkey. The numerous proposals of the
mediating Powers had been respectfully considered, and two
projects of reconciliation had received the Porte's assent. The
unjustifiable seizure of the Principalities had been met with
exemplary moderation. From April to December the Turks
had comported themselves with marvellous patience and judgment. The policy of patience had become more and more
difficult to sustain as the warlike spirit of a people, whose
name is famous in the annals of the battlefield, waxed fierce.
Yet even in their zeal, in their bitter wrath when the news of
Sinope came to their ears, the Turks still kept measure, and
ended the memorable year with an acceptance of a peaceful
settlement. During the long course of negotiation, of menace,
and of attack, there is no point where it can be said that the
Turks provoked the war or frustrated an honourable arrangement of the controversy. And this moderation and the
righteousness of their cause had drawn to them the respect
and sympathy of Europe, and had loosened the sword from
the scabbard in the West. Let full credit be theirs for a display of rare wisdom and self-control; but the chief honour
rests with the man who guided their steps, whose daily counsel
ruled their acts, whose measures for peace were at once just
and acceptable—the man they called the Great Elchi.

X

CHAPTER XXI.

THE EXPEDITION TO TURKEY.

1854.

THE new year dawned in a wreath of stormy clouds. Turkey indeed stood four-square, and had committed no false move, save the error of sending part of her fleet to Sinope, and thus precipitating the crisis which everyone knew to be inevitable. The Porte, with this solitary exception, had done as Lord Stratford would have it do, and the very last day of the old year had witnessed its adhesion to the scheme of pacification which the Elchi had drawn up. Thus Turkey entered upon 1854 with a serene consciousness of being in the right, and the even serener conviction that all Europe, west of Russia, approved her conduct. But unfortunately that which was Turkey's right was Russia's wrong. "The Question" still remained unsolved, and would so remain as long as the two nations existed. The Emperor still insisted upon the protectorate which he had so long disguised from the eyes of the other Powers, and the Sultan, whatever he might personally have been induced to concede, clearly perceived that to admit such a protectorate would cost him his throne; for he well knew that his brother Abdu-l-Aziz was ready to lead the war party. It was impossible that this antagonism between Turkey and Russia could be allowed to end in an isolated struggle between the two. Whatever might have been the termination of such a conflict, the Western nations at all events were not sufficiently convinced of the strength and resources of Turkey to permit her to wage the war unaided. They had distinctly given the Sultan to understand that he would enjoy their support, and they had backed their promise by the presence of their fleets in the Bosphorus. Even if a reconciliation had been possible after so warlike a demonstration, the meaning which Lord Clarendon naturally put upon the action at Sinope excluded the smallest hope of peace. Whether that affair was a designed challenge to the maritime Powers or not, their subsequent action in taking the command of the Euxine and threatening to drive all Russian vessels back into port constituted something nearly resembling

a declaration of war. It was obvious to everybody that Russia
had no alternative but either to accept the terms of the Four
Powers, or to break off diplomatic relations and wage war, at
least with the two Western nations.

The fleets went forth into the Black Sea in the first week
of January; but three months wore on before the declaration
of war issued from the Queen in Council on 28 March. The
interval was filled with abortive correspondence between the
several Courts, with which Lord Stratford had nothing to do.
He rested on his final scheme of pacification, accepted by
Turkey and the Four Powers, and from a seat of perfect equity,
and even of the maximum of concession, watched the progress
of events as Europe gradually roused herself to action.
Diplomacy had done its utmost; the last possible effort had
been made for peace, and all that remained was to wait and
watch. The Great Elchi was in the position of the man who
has wound up and regulated the clock, and now stands regarding the hands and listening to hear if it will strike the
right hour. To all Europe he was the centre of the situation.
Whether they blamed his policy or applauded it, there were
not two opinions as to his influence. The late Speaker, Mr.
Denison, afterwards Lord Ossington, only recorded the feeling of all the world when he wrote to Lady Stratford: "Probably in the history of diplomacy, such great events never
hinged on one man as have lately hinged on Lord Stratford.
If Turkey is called back to life, and set upon her legs, it will
be mainly his doing, and if all the Great Powers are bound
together in a confederacy to check the career of Russia, he will
have had a chief part in weaving the band which ties them
together. This will be a great work to have done, and will
set up a mark to be for ever remembered in the history of the
world."

But now the man at the wheel had made his last point, and
stood by, while the steering gear swung idly to and fro and
the rudder plashed uncertainly in the water. He had steered
as long as steering was possible, and so far as his part lay he
had avoided every rock and shoal in his course. His vessel,
whose figure-head was the Sublime Porte, but whose flag was
the Union Jack, still answered to her helm, but her course
now depended upon other craft, and the steersman stood
by, and waited for a signal. What he was thinking during
this period of inaction may be seen from a letter to his wife
(23 Jan.):—

x 2

The importance of the work in hand goes on increasing. It is like the cloud on the horizon, no bigger than a man's hand at first, but destined to cover the whole vault of heaven. I thank God that it has been my lot to bring about the last offer of peace, and in such terms as to satisfy Government and to be thought acceptable by Russia. You may depend upon it that without me that offer never would have been made. My own impression is that the Emperor of Russia will *not* accept. Judging by my own notions, I do not see how it is possible for him to accept under the circumstances in which he has so wantonly placed himself. But our proposals are based on his own declarations. I took care to place them on that ground, and I consented to as many of Baron Brück's modifications as I could in order to have his testimony in proof of our plan being in harmony with the Emperor's own declarations as stated by Austria. In this manner the Turk is placed in the position of one who is sure of gaining a ten thousand pound prize in the lottery, and who may get a million. You must admit that this looks comfortable for the Porte, and most assuredly is satisfactory in every sense to your *worse* half, who has been thrown upon the Eastern Question like a fish upon a volcanic shore. But the "*million*" cannot be gained without much exertion and strong reinforcements from the cardinal virtues. If we have war, as I expect, it will be a war of giants. We *must* not be losers. We cannot afford *that*; and we must make the sacrifices necessary for success, and obtain results equal to the sacrifices. For this we must gird up our loins, as they of old are recorded to have done, and the feeble hands must be held up when the battle fluctuates. I can fairly say that I have never seen the matter in any other light, and it was exactly because I foresaw the depth and extent of the contest that I was against having out the squadrons in the first instance, that I was for peace if attainable with safety and honour to the Porte, and endeavouring to obtain peace by confronting the danger at once and imposing on Russia the necessity of either giving way to European principles, clearly and stoutly asserted, or of throwing off the mask and picking up the gauntlet without further prevarication.

What might and ought to have been done more than six months ago is now at last in operation, but under circumstances which make arrangement far more difficult, and a war, more or less general, far more probable. How wonderful is Providence in all its dealings! How strangely have things been brought to this pass! How inconceivable that such an atom as myself should be made the rallying point in such a chaos! I told you from the first that I would have no armour, nothing but a pebble from the brook; that when intrigues multiplied, their crookedness should be shewn by contrast with my straight line of conduct, and that I would see nothing in myself but a weak and humble instrument of Providence. Do me justice. I have never sought this distinction;

my position here is an accident. I always thought that the great
struggle of the East would not be in my time, and that I was
destined only to fall in the ditch that others more fortunate in later
times might pass over with less difficulty. It seems to be otherwise ordained, and with Heaven's grace I accept my lot, and will
apply what little remains of me to reach the promised land. All
generous hearts will be with me. . . .

The Tritons came back yesterday, in spite of a steamer which
I sent out four or five days before to keep them in the Black Sea.
They are horribly afraid of losing their sails and their spars. I
wish well to both, but I want full protection for the Turkish flag
and territory, and not to risk, by sending out a small force, a dishonourable retreat before the Russians, many of whose ships we
know *not* to be at Sevastopol. In the course of to-day or to-morrow
I shall probably have to come to close quarters with them. I wish
Lyons had the command. We quarrelled at Athens. I do not
think we should quarrel here. His heart, if I mistake not, is in
unison—as I trust one other heart is—with that mighty heart
which throbs from John o' Groat's to the Land's End.

On 5 March the news reached Constantinople that the
troops were ordered out to Malta, *en route* for Turkey. The
order had been given on 16 February ; eleven days later Lord
Clarendon wrote to Count Nesselrode and required the evacuation of the Principalities by the Russian troops by 30 April
on penalty of war ; and on 18 March the Emperor Nicholas
declined to make any reply to this communication. War was
accordingly declared. In all these transactions France moved
more or less shoulder to shoulder with England.

To his Wife, 15 *April.*

It is almost sunset, and the despatches are already sent to the
messenger. Will you believe that I was up at half-past 4, and
have toiled incessantly ever since ? Yesterday arrived the first
detachment of the army, 2,000 in the *Himalaya*, a magnificent
steamer, a giant, which I would give the world to see, but cannot.
I have housed them in the Scutari barracks.

16 *April.* We have had to deal with some tough questions.
(1) Keeping Omar Pasha in order. He was for crossing the
Danube, and risking all with a self-confident spirit fraught with
danger to himself, the army, and the empire. I got Sir J. Bur-
goyne to visit him, thinking he was the man to influence him
without his perceiving it. The plan *seems* to have answered, for
the Pasha is quite an altered man. (2) The reform of the army in
Asia. Immense mischief had already been done under Mohammed
Ali's administration, and the wounds are still scarcely scarred over.

Guyon has done marvels, I really believe, and I have obtained his appointment as Chief of the Staff, which is much as being second in command. I have also obtained the recall, and hope to obtain the signal, if not the condign, punishment of two most naughty pashas—one now here, the other expected. Ahmed Pasha is the type and personification of cruelty, falsehood, and cowardice. He committed horrors in Africa several years ago, and was appointed without my knowledge. If it depends upon me, he shall commit no more cruelties. Much remains to be done for the army in general, and particularly for that in Asia. But without money, knowledge, or roads, and an abundance of nothing but snow, what can be done? (3) The irregulars, *Bashi-Bozuks*, as they are called; miscreants, as they ought to be called. No pen can write the crimes they have committed. If they were paid by Russia they could not serve her cause better. In Greece they have burnt countless villages, in Asia they caused the defeat of the regular troops. I have at last obtained a right good firman for their control and chastisement. They will be tried for every crime by a court-martial, and executed, when guilty, on the spot. Their leaders and the regular generals are made responsible. (4) The Greek insurrection—all very bad—not even spontaneous, but stirred up from Athens. The scoundrels sent by Otho across the frontier are as murderous as the wildest Turks, and they force the Rayas to join them by burning the villages and plundering everything. I have got as many *regular* troops to be sent to Epirus and Thessaly as can be spared. But troops are still wanted in Bulgaria; the garrison here is reduced; and money and means of transport were deficient in the outset. I applied to the admiral for steam, and he found a plausible excuse, no doubt agreeable to our friend at the *telegraph*, if you know where that is. (5) The undescribable conduct at Athens; for *Greece*? not a bit of it; for Emperor Nic. and no one else. Is he not the queen's uncle, or cousin, and has she not surrounded herself with Russians? If I had been free to act, that matter should have been settled six weeks ago. There is nothing for it but *force*, and the Allies must serve it out. They will in the end, but with speed and effect enough for the necessity, not. (6) The exclusion of the Greeks (Hellenic) from Turkey. The measure was not mine, but it is quite justifiable, I think, under such provocation, embarrassment, and danger. If the mischief be not stopped, it will compromise everything, and may prove fatal to our cause. I have done my best to soften the application of the excluding measure to *individuals*. . . . (7) The organization of Poles and other emigrants into a legion, or other kind of military body. The question lies with me, but I think it better to wait for Lord Raglan. It involves military considerations as well as political and party ones. Meanwhile I am besieged by the Zamoyskis, the Wysovkis, and a host of others, agreeing more in name than in fact. (8) Plans for getting up Wallachian and

Circassian resistance, which have introduced me to men of high
spirit and persevering characters, laudable for military boldness
and enduring patriotism. All these things are to be done, but the
difficulty lies in opportunity, mode of proceeding, and means of
carrying out. Austrian hesitations and financial deficiency are
sorely in the way. *Bakalum!* (9) Samos, where it has been
necessary for me to take part in changing the governor, feeding
the destitute, and providing against an attack from Greece. . . .
There are lots of other questions in daily course respecting the
fleet, the troops, the commissaries, the finances, &c. In short, my
life is become an almost unbroken series of labours, vexations, and
anxieties. But Providence is merciful—far more than I deserve—
and, in spite of toils and privations, your venerable partner sleeps
like a top, eats like an ogre, drinks like a fish, and walks and talks
very considerably more than King Charles is reported to have done
half an hour after the consummation of his martyrdom.

No news from the fleet. What can the Admiral be about?
Perhaps he is getting up a surprise. Who knows? Something
grand—the conflagration of Odessa; the scouring of the coasts of
Circassia; the explosion of Sevastopol? Well, Lyons is with him,
and I don't despair.

No news from Omar. He is getting strength at Shumla, and
will probably bide the grand attack there. Meanwhile I hear
rumours of a fresh encounter at Kalafat. If so, the Russians have
probably attempted another and more formidable passage of the
Danube. Paskievich is expected.

I am writing in *your* bedroom at a small table close by the
fireplace window. About an hour ago I was interrupted by a
solemn knock at the door. I had scarcely uttered "Come in," when
Alison appeared with an open letter in his hand. 'What's the
matter?" "Read, and you'll see." I read and saw that 3,000
Greeks had landed near Salonica and threatened to open insurrection on a new scene. They have chosen their place of landing
well, and may give much trouble. I sent Etienne Pisani with the
news in all haste to Reshid, inquiring whether they could send
troops and steamers at once to the place of attack—close by our
old friend Mount Athos. It is of consequence, you know, to stop
such things at once, if possible. Before Pisani had left me, I learnt
that an A.D.C. of the D. of Cambridge had arrived. Where was
he to go to? What was to be done with the horses?—thirty in
all, though not the Duke's entirely. No room here—so, off to the
barracks at Scutari—and off they went. Another knock. What
now? Brigadier Adams with General Sir De Lacy Evans! Shew
them into the drawing-room and I'll come. Anon, and I was
smartened and appeared. Behold, not only the brace of Generals,
but their respective staffs—a room-full! To escape bewilderment
I flew straight at my General—Sir De Lacy—held out my hand,
and we were fast friends at once. The conference ended, I made

acquaintance with the junior red-coats, and found Percy Herbert—looking very infirm—and Captain Gordon, a son, I believe, of the Premier's. Squeezing of hands, rapid commonplaces, and mutual *attendrissement* ensued. To-morrow I am to dine fourteen of them, including the two Generals—and then to Brück's ball for the Emperor's marriage. A fresh chasm. Since the last sentence I have had some polite small talk with two officers—an interesting conversation with a French consul from Erzerum, a solemn conference with two Commissaries, and a stand-up interview with the Captain of the *Banshee*—my only naval officer—who has special orders not to move to the *west*. I mention all these particulars that you may have a notion of the life I lead, and cease to wonder at the *occasional* shortness of my letters. Think, too, that only half the army is yet arrived, and that the campaign is still to begin.

No army, perhaps, ever went forth worse equipped for war than the expedition to the Crimea. For months Lord Stratford had warned the Government that if there should be war, they must be prepared for war on a grand scale; but they took no heed. It was not easy to move the torpidity of men who were under a spell of fifty years of peace. So the troops poured into Turkey, and depended upon Turkey for nearly all their wants. The difficulties began even before they arrived; barracks had to be found for them. Hardly had the first transport come in view when a universal cry for coal arose, and it was the English ambassador who had, if not to dig it, at least to arrange with the Porte (and with the French chargé d'affaires, who was very punctilious as to who should have the *entrée* to the mine), that some one should use the shovel. And so it went on. It was all very well for the Government to express unbounded confidence in the ambassador, and for Lord Clarendon to give him *carte blanche*; but the admirals apparently possessed the faculty of refusal, and it was in Lord Stratford's opinion largely owing to their unwillingness to convey the Turkish troops to Volo and Prevesa that the Greek rebellion was not immediately strangled. While the ambassador was pressing forward vigorous and effective measures, he was perpetually met by the irresolution of the naval commanders, and the evil did not disappear until the fleet came under the energetic control of Sir Edmund Lyons. With the home Government Lord Stratford experienced the same difficulty in making them understand the essential conditions of the struggle in which they were engaged. " My conviction," he wrote on 7 April to Lord

Clarendon, " is that, cost what it will, this awful contest must
be carried through to a triumphant issue if it be in Hercules
and the strong shoulder to keep the waggon moving : and
hence I conclude that the most decided, vigorous, and comprehensive measures in the outset are likely to prove the
most economical in the end, and also—what I can never lose
sight of—the most humane." But the Government never
grasped this fact till the horrors of a Crimean winter taught
them its truth, and meanwhile they trusted to their ambassador to do all those things which they ought to have done.
Not only did they seem wholly unable to calculate the means
required to attain the end in view, but they appeared to be
groping in dim uncertainty as to the nature of the end itself.
Lord Stratford was under no illusion as to this ; he knew well
enough what the struggle was for, and how it ought to end ;
and in a letter (12 June) to Lord Clarendon, written some
little time after the Allied forces had arrived in Turkey, he set
forth his views with unmistakable precision. The letter is
worth quoting in its entirety, and may be compared with
advantage with the provisions ultimately established by the
Treaty of Paris :—

I may venture to congratulate you on something like progress
in our vast affair. Greece brought successfully to book—Austria all
but in line with us, Prussia neutralized, if not enlisted, the Turks
well prepared at Shumla, and shewing nobly at Silistria, the Allied
armies taking up their ground on the scene of action, the conclusion
of a loan in fair prospect, and no symptoms of mistrust between
France and England—these, taken together, are surely just grounds
of hope and confidence for the future. Not that I presume to
expect an early termination of the war, even if Austria should
coöperate heartily with us. Without her active assistance Turkey
and its two Allies may fairly reckon on driving the Russians back.
But would that suffice to bring the Emperor to terms ? His character, his position towards Europe and his people, the interests at
stake, his great defensive resources, all seem to whisper, No! Then,
on our side, success must naturally bring with it an increase of
expectation and demand. People, with a press and a parliament
to plead for them, will not like to make sacrifices, going to the
quick, and then sit down quietly under a canopy of laurels to heal
their wounds and prepare for the chances of a fresh struggle. What
says our greatest man upon this subject ? I think I have read
somewhere in the Duke of Wellington's Spanish correspondence a
passage to this effect :—" Those who embark in plans of this kind "
(resistance to colossal power threatening the liberties of Europe)
" ought to understand that the sword, once drawn, cannot be

sheathed again, until their object is *completely attained.* They
must be prepared and even constrained to spare no sacrifice for the
success of their cause. In a struggle where *everything is at stake*
there is no comfort that must not be renounced, no risk that must
not be incurred."

If the words of our Cid were true in his day, are they less so
in ours? What signifies a *name*? We have to deal with a *thing*
—that most odious of things, the tyrannous will of one opposed to
the interests, the feelings, the convictions of millions. We have
undertaken to curb that will; but in order to curb it effectually, we
must do more than check its present outbreak, we must paralyze
its spring of action by bringing home to its inner sense a feeling of
permanent restraint—the "hither shalt thou come, and no further."

The Czar, in his agony, might exclaim—Well! I am defeated
by a combination of all Europe against me, but the combination is
formed of elements which do not easily unite a second time, and
the power of Russia is a natural growth, instinctively encroaching
and necessarily united. Clip it, and it shoots out with greater
vigour; stir the soil around it, and the very disturbance becomes
in due season a cause of its refreshment.

Now, what have we to do in answer to this very natural, but
dangerous, train of thought? The tree we have to deal with is of
the Upas kind; *Juniperi gravis umbra: nocent et frugibus umbrae.*
We cannot *girdle* it, if we would; but we may stunt it by *pollard-
ing,* and that operation is a mere question of power and occasion,
both, perhaps, beyond our reach, and certainly not to be attained
without a skilful, vigorous, persevering application of means to the
end. Our best exertions, however, may fall short of their object,
and in that case we must submit to necessity, and be content with
what we can get. But if we wish to avoid reproach, we must be
able to shew that no means of success have been neglected; that
morally and commercially, no less than materially, we have acted
up to the opportunities afforded by Providence in so wonderful a
manner.

Three mighty forces are those which I have named, and you
know better than I do how far they are already in play. Though
more despatch might possibly have been displayed, the fleets and
armies already called into action are admirable evidences of power,
good faith, and resolution. More, indeed, is likely to be wanted,
and judging from the "notes of preparation," *that* also will be
forthcoming in due season. The wear and tear of cruising and
campaigning is itself a heavy charge. Occasional reverses may
occur, advantages already obtained may have to be followed up, and
fresh enterprises may be necessary to insure success. Yet these
contingencies must be foreseen, and, if possible, provided for.

Greece is still but a "scotch'd" snake; Persia, with such a Shah,
may forget her neutrality; the Slavic race, from Servia to Monte-

negro, requires to be watched; the Sultan's Asiatic frontier is weakly defended; the *Bashi-Bozuks* are not yet restrained.

Add to all this that Circassia remains to be cleared, the Crimea to be disarmed, and something worthy of our name to be achieved in the Baltic.

The list, I confess, is formidable; but the object is great and beneficial. With justice and necessity for our companions we have no room for groundless regrets or premature fears. Back we cannot go. Our duties are all ahead, and, with a timely preparation of *means* and a just estimate of *ends*, we may be masters of the future.

What ends and *what* means? There's the rub.

To begin with the *ends*, what kind of Russia, what kind of Turkey, do we mean to have after the conclusion of peace? Is it the Russia of Catharine, the Russia of Alexander, or the Russia of Nicholas? Is it Russia founded on the *status quo ante*, or Russia separated from Turkey by a *cordon* of principalities, or states, no longer dependent upon her; or, finally, Russia, such as Russia was before she proclaimed without shame or disguise her appetite for territorial extension at the expense of every neighbour in turn, whether friend or foe?

There is little room for doubting which of these Russias would answer best to the interests of Europe, of commerce, and of humanity. The puzzle is not there, but in judging of the relation between means and end in each of the supposed cases.

The present combination vigorously carried out may suffice to procure not only diplomatic, but a certain degree of material, guarantee against further Russian aggression. It is manifest, however, that the Emperor Nicholas will never voluntarily yield either the one or the other. Position is to Russia what existence is to Turkey. The Russia of this day is, more or less, a result of national tendencies and national traditions ably directed by a Government which, partly sympathizing and partly affecting to sympathize, employs them for the twofold purpose of dynastic despotism and political aggrandizement. This, Heaven knows! is formidable enough. But it is far from being all. The Power, thus raised on a million of soldiers trained to implicit obedience and selected from sixty millions of ignorant and fanatical slaves, is an ever-growing and ever-encroaching force—encroaching as much from inherent gravitation as from systematic policy. The strength of such a Power is the measure of our motives to resist it, multiplied by its character and the necessary consequences of its progress. Rome, of old, extended its sway by conquest. But wherever its eagles flew the arts of civilization followed, or the conquerors themselves were softened by the refinements of those whom they subdued. The Russian bird of prey has no such commission. It turns, indeed, towards the sun, but the shadow of its wings is blighting, and moral desolation closes on its flight. The Russian soldier is not contented with marching in a strait waistcoat. His knapsack is

stuffed with spare ones for the accommodation of his foreign victims
—partizans or opponents, as it may chance to be.

What have we then to choose? Where is our alternative?
Look back! What says the past—the recent past? At Adrianople
the Emperor seemed to be satisfied for life. He was satisfied before
at Akkerman. But the Greek war was tempting; he stole a march
on his friends, and took another meal, solitary like the boa's, and
for a time tranquillizing. Then came the generous era. Forbearance, longanimity, protection, patronage, fraternal sympathy, and
Hunkiar Iskelesi. The Sultan gradually discovered that hugging
was pressure, and pressure coercion. He betrayed his alarm by an
occasional struggle, and then came the era of loving remonstrances,
imperious *aides-de-camp*, unpalatable Seneds, and smuggled occupations. The Porte was still feeble, and Russian influence continued to preponderate. The seeming moderation, which blinded
Europe, might therefore yet go on without danger of escape. But
the uneasiness excited at St. Petersburg by the Porte's independent
conduct regarding the Hungarian and Polish refugees assumed a
more alarming character when at one and the same time appeared
the question of the Holy Places and a crisis intimating that Turkey
must either sink into hopeless decrepitude or make a new start by
the enforcement and expansion of its reforming policy. Russian
susceptibility here found itself in presence of a danger and of a
temptation—the danger of losing a paramount influence, the temptation of a dismemberment. Hence the secret overtures to Sir
H. Seymour; hence, on their failure, the Menshikov requisition;
hence a determination to rule the roast in Turkey, either by a concerted division of the Empire, or through a recognized protection
at Constantinople, by way of substitute during another turn of
expectancy.

If this be true—and who can contradict it?—where, I repeat, is
our alternative? The Emperor will fight as obstinately for his
dictatorial position, his dominant influence here, as if the Turkish
Empire were already in pieces, and he were scrambling for his share
of the spoil. We cannot, then, hope to hasten peace and to staunch
the wounds of Europe by the moderation of our views. Take the
object, for which we have entered the lists, in its narrowest proportions—reduce it to the principle, which we cannot without an
overwhelming necessity surrender, and still we must see in Russia
a determined adversary, pledged, as the Emperor Nicholas has himself declared, to stake his last soldier and his last rouble in a cause,
as unjust and as idle as you please, but binding on all his sentiments, riveted by his prejudices, and sanctified by the workings of
a mistaken religious zeal.

The prospect, I admit, is neither agreeable nor encouraging.
But can we help it? Can we shrink from it? Does the responsibility rest with us? The answer must be negative. No other can
be given without a sacrifice of truth and justice.

Our *ends*, therefore, resolve themselves into one—an arrangement by which the integrity and independence of Turkey would be maintained under such material and diplomatic guarantees as are really indispensable for the purpose. Let a rigorous necessity be the limitation of our demands. Let a *minimum* of effective guarantee be the aim and goal of our exertions.

Now this must be measured with reference to our means. There is not so much difficulty in figuring the least that might suffice to bridle Russia, as in determining what aids are *required* and what *available* for reaching that minimum of security.

Take, for example, a settlement by which the course of the Danube would be free, the Principalities extended to the Black Sea, and released from Russian protection, Circassia restored to independence under the *suzeraineté* of the Porte, the Crimea established in a similar manner, the Black Sea opened to foreign ships of war, and Poland restored in the limits recognized by the Congress of Vienna. With these objects in view it would be most desirable, and indeed necessary, to have the material coöperation of Austria, and also to enrol a Polish Legion on national principles. But we may be sure that Austria would never look with favour on the latter measure, nor easily be led to contemplate conditions of peace so onerous to Russia.

Such being the case, if Austrian coöperation is indispensable, England and France would probably have to make up their minds to a guarantee such as Austria, consulting its own interests, would require. It may well be doubted whether Austria would extend its conditions of peace beyond the free navigation of the Danube, and possibly some improvement in the relations of the two Principalities with Russia and Turkey. The rest, according to her apprehension, would be mere *status quo* with the old diplomatic guarantees confirmed in clearer terms.

At the end of April Lord Raglan took up his residence at the Embassy while a house was being got ready for him at Scutari. The jealousies and intrigues which marked the greater part of the next two years began as soon as the French landed. An attempt was made to oust Omar Pasha from his post as commander-in-chief of the Turkish army, and it needed all the combined efforts of the English leaders to defeat the opposition of the Seraskier and Marshal St. Arnaud. A visit to Varna and Shumla, however, enabled Lord Raglan to convince Omar that the English were on his side, and this difficulty being overcome, the next question was the advance of the Allied forces to the support of the Turks on the Danube, and especially to the relief of Silistria, to which the French were strangely indifferent. On 23 May Lord Raglan informed the Elchi of his intention of sending the troops to

Varna, and intimated that the Turks would have to furnish
"large supplies of horses and mules for the carriage of
ammunition and provisions, as well as of waggons drawn
by buffaloes or bullocks," all of which must be immediately
afforded. Demands of this sort were coming in daily, and the
worst was that there was no system about them. The general
and his staff appeared quite unequal to drawing up a schedule
of their wants, and request after request dropped in, often
contradicting each other, and leading to nothing but confusion
and delay. "I wish," wrote the ambassador, "your people
would let me know *en bloc* whatever remains to be required
or done for the service of your army by the Porte and its
subalterns. I have asked for a conference with the whole
Cabinet, and M. Benedetti will accompany me. Our object
is to make them understand their duty with respect to the
Allied forces and to facilitate by an appropriate arrangement
the practical enforcement of their orders. By making the
general demand in common, giving in a statement of requisitions, and appointing agents to see that they are really and
properly complied with in the several departments, I should
hope to obviate in a great degree the inconveniences and disappointments which seem to have been hitherto experienced
by both armies, though not perhaps in equal proportions."

This was, of course, the right way to set to work, but the
"general demand" was never furnished, and "what remained"
to be required for the army proved to be incalculable.

At last Lord Raglan set out for the scene of operations,
but not without a severe struggle with the Turkish Divan,
who happened to be celebrating the annual fast of Ramazan,
and consequently were completely *hors de combat* for anything
like vigorous action.

To his Wife, 20 June.

Lord Raglan has just left me with his staff for Varna. He is
very amiable, and very stout-hearted. He will do his duty on the
field of battle as he did it at the Horse Guards. He acknowledged
with much kindness at parting my attentions to him, and the advantage which his health and spirits had derived from living here. I
think the army will move on very soon after his arrival at headquarters. The French also are on the move, but less forward. St.
Arnaud leaves in a few days. I have had terrible work with the
Turkish ministers and the Sultan to get the slightest result out of
them in Ramazan. I must gather up all my forces and make a
regular onslaught as soon as Bayram is over. Meanwhile I have

helped to get a Turkish regiment 3,000 strong, with cavalry and twenty pieces of artillery, attached to Lord Raglan's army. The French will have an *annexe* of the same kind. You may expect to hear of important operations very soon. The Turks continue to fight like dragons at Silistria, which holds out, but rather precariously.

22 *June*.—The tide has rolled on. The slopes of Hayder Pasha are no longer mottled over with the tents of our army, and in place of old Neptune-Dundas and nineteen sail of the line, French and English—we have Admiral Boxer, two transports, and a steamer. Other troops have yet to pass, and when they are all together there will be on the battle-ground about 25,000 English, 50,000 French, and 70,000 Turks, making in all not far from 150,000 men. The Russians have, at the utmost, about 180,000, of whom half, it is supposed, on this side of the Danube, about 30,000 more immediately within reach, and the remainder in reserve. Silistria makes a glorious stand. Some of our people have distinguished themselves favourably—above all, a young officer named Butler, who kept the Turks together in the most exposed battery when their officers left them. I had the good fortune to place a young engineer of great merit [Captain, now General Sir Lintorn Simmons] at Shumla months ago, and he has rendered immense services. He was here three days ago fresh from Silistria, and described to me what he had seen and *heard*, for the minié rifle balls whistled about his ears wildly. Lord Raglan must be at Varna by this time. St. Arnaud follows in two days. I gave the latter a grand dinner *below*, with *music*, last week. . . . His [Lord Raglan's] manners and character are the reverse of his name—attractive, gracious, tranquillizing. I am right glad to have seen so much of him. He left us with every appearance of being satisfied, and we are to be good correspondents in a quiet way. What is better, he had quite recruited his strength, and recovered his spirits, making me in that way the best possible return for hospitality and attention. The night before his departure I stayed with him and Napier till after midnight chatting of old times, comparing Spaniards with Turks, and ever placing the old hero of his youthful days in the foreground. He had seen the *king of men* at Busaco, stretched out in a furrow writing letters on finance, a few paces in front of his army arrayed in battle line against the French not 500 yards off! That is really great, thought I; not so much for the exposure to peril, as for the perfect command of thought under such circumstances.

25 *June*.—My position, as chief of the Embassy I mean, is in sundry respects awkward and uncomfortable for the present. I am placed between Western energy and Eastern impassiveness, between British downrightness and local trickery, a red-hot horse-shoe between the anvil and half a dozen sledge-hammers. I care not; such is my business just now; and I console myself by thinking of the illustrious Greek who served his native city as a scavenger, and

of the modern general who has recorded that the fate of a campaign will sometimes turn upon a string of twenty mules. What I cannot brook is the slightest appearance of mistrust, or the foisting of consular opinions over the embassy—both occasional results of the *clerkery* of the Foreign Office, and of a certain degree of incompleteness in its chief. Patience, which (you may dissent if you please) I possess at bottom under a very ruffled surface, is my anchoring ground.

CHAPTER XXII.

THE INVASION OF THE CRIMEA.

1854.

ENGLAND and France had gone forth to aid the Sultan in driving the Russians out of the Principalities. Austria had taken the invaders in the rear with an army of observation, and had summoned the Czar to withdraw. But at this moment two events occurred which achieved the object of the three Powers without engaging any of their armies. The celebrated fortress of Silistria was the key of the situation; until it had been reduced or masked no Russian army could venture upon an invasion of Turkey. General Paskievich accordingly laid siege to the fortress with extraordinary vigour in the middle of May. Perhaps with merely Ottoman commanders the garrison might have surrendered; but it happened that two young English officers, Butler and Nasmyth, had thrown themselves into the beleaguered city, and had inspired the defenders with a zeal and enthusiasm that no skill of Russian engineers could quench. Silistria was saved; the Czar's army drew off (June 23); and as if to shew that it was not only in siege works that the Turks were a match for their enemy, the Ottoman troops, headed by half a dozen British officers, followed the Russians over the Danube at Giurgevo, and thus achieved the object for which two nations had sent forth their armies and a third had begun to advance. By the second week of July the cause of war had been removed; the Russians were in retreat, and nothing remained but to make an honourable peace and ship the troops back to England and France.

It was hard for the Czar to be forced to hear that his

armies had been withstood, and even compelled to retreat, by
inferior bodies of Turks whose lack of numbers had been
counterbalanced by the skill and enthusiasm of a handful
of Englishmen.   Nicholas had made war out of jealousy of
England ; he could not brook the supremacy of English influence in Turkey, and this more than anything else had
prompted his reckless advance into the Principalities.   His
sensations may be imagined when he learnt that his troops
had been resisted and driven out of the provinces—not by the
Turks alone, for that to him was incredible—but by Turks
inspired to emulate their ancient warlike fame under the
guidance of a few young officers of that very England whose
position in Turkey was to him wormwood and gall.   It was
the last drop in a cup that was already filled to overflowing.

It was then that a new and perilous course was entered
upon.   The spirit of the English nation was roused, and
Louis Napoleon was fain to fan its zeal.   As early as February
the French ambassador had sounded the Porte about an attack
upon the Crimea, and the idea was soon taken up in other
quarters.   Indeed Lord Clarendon had contemplated the step
from the first.   On 28 June the Duke of Newcastle, Secretary
of War, wrote the famous letter, followed by the still more
celebrated despatch, which in Lord Raglan's opinion left him
no alternative but to invade the Crimea.   The opinion in
England was that, until the fortifications of Sevastopol were
destroyed, there would be no safe or honourable termination to the quarrel.   What England did not consider was
whether the expedition was competent and adequate for the
task.   This consideration was nominally left to the decision
of Lord Raglan, but in reality was already prejudged by the
letter and despatch of the Duke of Newcastle.   In spite of his
own better judgment, and influenced perhaps by the more
fiery spirits under his command, the General gave way, and
ordered, in concert with Marshal St. Arnaud, that shifting of
the scene of operations which was destined to involve both
countries in so many tribulations, and to cause the death of
one of the most high-minded of England's commanders.   On
15 July Lord Raglan communicated the Duke's letter to Lord
Stratford, and three days later sent him the final decision of
the Allied commanders, which had not been arrived at without
sore misgivings, especially among the French officers :—

Admiral Dundas and Sir Edmund Lyons, Admiral Hamelin and
Admiral Bruat came from Buljik this morning, and Marshal St.

Y

Arnaud and myself have had a conference with them, which lasted four hours and half.

It has been determined to attempt a landing in the Crimea and the attack of Sevastopol, and in order that our design should not be immediately known, it has been suggested that Odessa should be reported as the object of the Allied armies.

In accordance with this determination the fleets eventually set sail for the Crimea. Lord Stratford had of course no voice in the decision, but there can be no manner of doubt that he rejoiced in the thought of the destruction of Sevastopol. The thing he dreaded most of all was a "shortcoming" inadequate peace. Two months, however, passed before the Allies had landed at Old Fort, and the interval was rendered all the more painful by the mortality from cholera at Varna, and the daily more obvious insufficiency of the British arrangements for transport and commissariat. At last the expedition was off, reports came in of a reconnaissance by the fleet, then of a landing, and finally one day near the end of September the ambassador came into the room where his family was assembled—and all who saw him say that the expression of his pale face can never be forgotten. He held a letter in his hand; it told of deadly fighting on the Alma. "We attacked," wrote Lord Raglan, "we attacked and carried a most formidable position yesterday, and we drove the enemy clean off it, notwithstanding the large force of infantry and artillery by which it was occupied. I never recollect to have been under so heavy a cannonade except at Waterloo, and many of the guns were of heavy calibre."

Two letters from Sir E. Lyons and Lord Raglan, relating to the flank march, are interesting, not merely as shewing the high spirit in which the leaders embarked upon the siege, but especially because there is in them no trace of hesitation about the much-disputed question of attacking Sevastopol from the south side :—

From Sir E. Lyons, "Agamemnon," Balaklava Harbour,
28 September.

A splendid flank march of Lord Raglan's, *steering by compass through a dense wood*, has put us in possession of this convenient little port, in which the *Agamemnon* looks like a Leviathan, but what is more to the purpose is that it affords us the means of landing the siege guns and all other wants of the army with safety and certainty.

Lord Raglan is in high health and spirits, and we have a

month's fine weather before us, which will, I trust, be productive
of events that may make many a true and honest heart leap for
joy.

Be assured of one thing. If ever a leader deserved success
Lord Raglan does. He has never thrown up his cap and cried
"*Sevastopol for ever*," as the poor Marshal has done, but never
has he by speech, or manner, or manner of acting, put it in the
power of mortal man to say that he has flinched from or regretted
the *yes* he calmly but decidedly enunciated at the Conference at
Varna when St. Arnaud put to the vote whether the expedition
should take place or not. The slightest symptom of vacillation on
his part would have been seized upon by the opponents of the
expedition, who were always on the watch, and would have been
well-nigh, if not altogether, fatal to it.

From Lord Raglan, Balaklava, 1 October.

We arrived here and took possession of this place on 26 September, after having performed a flank march, for which the enemy
were by no means prepared, with perfect success, and thereby
secured a new base and a beautiful little harbour where the *Agamemnon* rides protected from every wind. This is an immense
advantage, particularly as it was found that the mouth of the Bel-
bek was under the enemy's fire, and could not be used as a place
of disembarkation for our guns, stores, &c.

We shall now be enabled to attack the south side of Sevastopol.
Our troops are investing it, and are barely without the range of the
guns of the place. Indeed some of them have fired over the heads
of Sir George Cathcart's division.

We are busily occupied in landing our siege train, and have
already got a good many heavy guns up the heights, and we shall
open our attack at the earliest moment possible.

Lord Raglan had hardly settled down to the siege when
he found himself in need of reinforcements. He had already
discovered that, if anything had to be done in Turkey, the
Great Elchi alone could do it ; and in reference to the measures
which had been taken to facilitate the transhipment of the
troops to the Crimea, the Commander-in-Chief had listened to
fervid eulogies from Sir George Brown on the ambassador's
" zealous coöperation and the happy effect of his influence
over the Turkish Government." Accordingly to Lord Stratford he applied for more Ottoman troops. The result exceeded
his highest expectations. In two or three days, the reinforcements, to the number of some 4,000 men, were reported as
ready, and though the usual delay, which disgraced all our
transport arrangements during the early months of the Crimean

war, kept the men in the Bosphorus a day or two longer than
was necessary, they arrived at Balaklava in less than a week
from the date on which Lord Raglan's application was received.
The following letter (13 October) will shew the warm appreciation of the ambassador's services by the Commander-in-
Chief :—

Your exertions have indeed been most prompt and successful,
and I thank you most warmly for them.

Thirteen hundred Turks landed this morning at Balaklava, and
the *Trent* has since arrived with at least as many more, and the
third vessel is expected with equal or greater numbers. The *Himalaya* and *Simla* were despatched on the 11th as mentioned in my
letter of that day, and the *Victoria* goes down to-night. I hope all
these will return full. The more Turks we can get the better the
chance of Balaklava not being attacked, and we shall give them
every opportunity of entrenching themselves.

I shall always recollect with the most grateful feelings that we
owe this timely reinforcement to you. You must have worked hard
to have introduced so much activity into the Turkish authorities.

We have made good progress the last two days, with very little
serious interruption from the enemy. In two or three days it is
hoped that the Allied armies will be able to open a very powerful
fire upon Sevastopol.

More Turkish troops arrived two days later, " a fine body
of men," wrote Lord Raglan, " and in the most efficient state.
. . . I must repeat my grateful acknowledgments to you for
having so promptly and effectually provided me with so respectable a reinforcement ; the six battalions amount to 4,400
men." And again (19 October) : " I cannot say how much I
feel the exertions you have made for us. They have been
eminently successful, which is a marvel, considering the slug-
gards you have to deal with. But you know them, and
what would have been impossible for another was practicable
with you. St. Arnaud used to say, ' Le Sultan c'est Lord
Stratford.' " Once more (24 October) : " I shall be delighted
to receive the battalions from Volo. I am sure I am indebted
to you for the despatch of the ships to fetch them as well as
for the troops themselves."

The heavy losses of our troops at the Alma and Balaklava
entailed fresh and onerous duties at Constantinople. It had
been presumed that ample accommodation had been provided
for the sick and wounded at the hospital at Scutari, on the
Asiatic shore of the Bosphorus, immediately opposite Pera ;
but when the transports laden with maimed and fevered

soldiers began to arrive in an apparently interminable succession, it was soon discovered that there was neither accommodation nor medical and nursing staff, nor furniture and
stores at all adequate to the sudden and severe strain. The
worst sufferings of the wounded were endured on board the
transports, where no sort of provision seems to have been
made for the care of the sick ; but there was also mismanagement at Scutari. The long interval of peace had lulled the
Medical Department into a torpor no less profound than that
which in other branches of our military establishments be-
numbed every faculty save that of fighting ; and the situation
was aggravated by the circumstance that, like persons in a
state of intoxication, the sleepy officials refused to admit that
anything was wrong. There is no jealousy like that of departments ; and to have appealed to the Foreign Office for aid
which should have come from the War Office would, in the
eyes of the medical and commissariat staff, have been a worse
crime than letting the patients die for want of such assistance.
To the authorities at Scutari the last person in the world to
ask for help was the ambassador, not because he could not
help, but because he belonged to a different department. The
red tape was of the wrong sort.

At this early stage of the war the work of providing for
the necessities of the hospitals depended almost wholly on
the British Embassy ; and, though it was manifestly impossible, with a small staff, and in face of the opposition of the
medical authorities, to put matters in perfect trim, yet on
24 October the Elchi was able to record considerable progress.
" Encouraged by your approval," he wrote, 24 October, to
Lord Raglan, " I have made another visit to the hospitals and
barracks at Scutari. According to my notions there is room
for improvement ; but things were in much better order than
at first, though many new sufferers had just come in. I was
assured that the medical attendance was no longer deficient ;
and that medicines were so abundant as to make the offers of
a respectable chymist here superfluous. At the suggestion of
the Duke of Newcastle, Lord Clarendon has authorized me to
supply any additional wants, and I shall have much satisfaction in acting on the instruction."

Miss Nightingale happily arrived with a brigade of forty
nurses on 4 November, and thenceforward, so long as she
continued her devoted work, it was almost impossible for
anyone to be of use to the hospital unless at Miss Nightingale's

initiative. Like many other admirable commanders, including
Lord Stratford himself, she did not like colleagues. After
she came he did his best to help her. Of course he could not
personally visit the hospitals as often as he would have wished.
All his influence was freely and powerfully given in behalf of
the sufferers and those who came to help them, but it was
given in vigorous strokes of the pen, while the personal
superintendence was left, and safely left, in the hands of the
ambassadress, aided by such men as Lord William Paulet,
General Storks, Major Gordon, and Admiral Grey. Whatever
difficulties were experienced in carrying out the constant
demands for more accommodation and supplies were due
mainly to the English authorities. The Sultan was ready
enough to give up his palaces and barracks to the wounded,
and to order his ministers to collect supplies and stores ;
but it must be remembered that the Sultan and the Elchi
and the markets were on one shore of the Bosphorus, and
most of the hospitals were on the other side, whilst between
them reigned one Admiral Boxer, in command of the transport service—a gallant old seaman, by all accounts, but
wholly incapable of organizing the troublesome and intricate
duties of his important department. Nor was this altogether
his fault. He was under-manned, and the supply of steam
vessels under his control was so inadequate that he could not
furnish one to ply across for the service of the hospitals.
In spite of these obstacles, however, the Bosphorus teemed
with zealous helpers, and more nurses arrived, rather to Miss
Nightingale's dismay. Miss Stanley, sister of the Dean (then
a canon of Canterbury), appeared at the end of December,
accompanied by forty-six nurses and sisters—a number, said
Miss Nightingale, "which exceeds my worst anticipations."
It seems that there was not accommodation at Scutari for
more than six additional nurses, and there was an imminent
prospect of the newcomers being sent home discomfited.
This appeared so monstrous, at a moment when fifteen
hundred sick were just arriving from Balaklava, that the
ambassador resolved to do all in his power to utilize their
services. The Turkish cavalry barrack at Kulali, near Candili, on the Asiatic shore of the Bosphorus, was obtained from
the Sultan, and placed under the sole authority of Lady
Stratford ; and hither Miss Stanley and her assistants were
transported from the two houses within the embassy grounds
at Therapia which had been placed at their disposal. Miss

Stanley was appointed superintendent, and Lady Stratford
spent a great part of her time in attending to the necessities
of the hospital, and among her assistants none were more
active than an engineer officer, Major Gordon, who devoted
his energies unceasingly to the improvement of the accommodation and comforts of the sick and wounded. In a very
short time everything was in working order and managed not
only on principles of benevolence towards the patients, but of
economy towards the Government. General Storks, who
succeeded Lord William Paulet in command of the Bosphorus, and made himself very useful to the hospitals, wrote
that "the cheapest of the four hospitals is Kulali," and Dr.
Hall, the Surgeon-General to the Forces, placed it on record
that "both Lord and Lady Stratford de Redcliffe have taken
great interest in the military hospitals at Scutari, and from
all the accounts I receive her ladyship may well be proud of
the one at Kulali that is under her own immediate protection." The hospital remained actively employed till December,
but Miss Stanley's delicate health compelled her to return to
England in April, when her place was taken by Miss Hutton.
The good work at Kulali was rivalled by the separate officers'
hospital at Scutari, the requisites for which were entirely
provided by friends from England. Lady Canning superin-
tended the selection of nurses, in constant correspondence
with Lady Stratford; and the Queen took a special interest
in this benevolent work.

Meanwhile, ignorant of much that was being done, and
only too well informed of what had been left undone, the
philanthropic soul of England was ablaze with indignation at
the state of the hospitals at Scutari. The newspapers had
got hold of the subject, and in their hands it was not likely
to grow less. The *Times* took the lead in the onslaught upon
the authorities, and the country, following the *Times*, wept
and gnashed its teeth at sufferings and cruelties which were
half imaginary, and when strictly true were the consequence
of an inexperience which was rapidly disappearing in face of
actual duty. Real good, however, came out of the excited tumult
thus stirred up in England. Whether the hospitals were in as
bad a state as was reported or not, it was a fine spirit of devotion
that took so many English ladies out to the Bosphorus to
face the horrors of a hospital at the seat of war; and it was
good to see men of fashion and indolence, natives rather of
Bond Street than Aldershot, leaving their pleasures to go

forth and minister to the wants of their wounded countrymen. Their task was not always smooth ; and at first they had to face a good deal of official prejudice. As an instance of this it may be useful to recall what happened to two zealous and devoted gentlemen who sought out Admiral Boxer in his office at Tophana, in order to beseech him to improve the steam communications between the city and the hospitals on the Asiatic side of the Bosphorus. The Admiral sat in an inner office, where he could hear the communications which the young men were holding with his clerk, and when they came suddenly face to face with the blunt old sailor, he was prepared for them. " I see who *you* are," said he ; " you're two d——d sympathizers. I'll tell you who *I* am—I'm ' Bloody Old Boxer ' ! " The sturdy seaman who rejoiced in this *sobriquet*, however, had in the end to admit the necessity of improvement, and no one worked harder than he did afterwards in reorganizing the harbour of Balaclava, where he ended his life worthily toiling for the good of the troops. The example of the ladies and men of fashion who came out to help the sick was not thrown away. A good principle was then established which has borne fruit ever since ; and a movement which began in what was little better than a " scare " has since expanded into a well-organized and invaluable branch of the service.

CHAPTER XXIII.

THE SIEGE OF SEVASTOPOL.

1854-55.

MEANWHILE the army was beginning to feel the hardships of a Crimean winter. Writing on 16 November, a week after the battle of Inkerman, Lord Raglan described the terrific storm of the 14th :—

When I wrote to you on the 12th instant I mentioned, I believe, that the weather was very bad and boisterous. It so continued the following day, but after nightfall on the 13th the rain ceased and the wind went down, and it remained fine until after 5 on the morning of the 14th, when suddenly a tempest arose such as I had never before witnessed.

The tents in our several camps were blown down almost without exception. The sick and well were prostrate in the mud, and a scene of misery ensued of which the reality was perhaps beyond the power of description. The roads were rendered nearly impassable, and single horsemen in many cases found it impossible to make headway, and several horses were blown down with their riders on them. Fires could not be lighted, and the men were consequently unable to cook their food. . . .

You will see that our loss in shipping is immense; it is equally great in provisions, forage, warm clothing, ammunition, and warlike stores.

The Commissary-General writes to Mr. Smith at Constantinople to send up without loss of time provisions, corn, and forage, and by the same opportunity I have directed Captain Wetherall, of the Quartermaster-General's Department, to proceed there for the purpose of purchasing warm clothing, and many other things that our soldiers want; and I earnestly solicit your powerful assistance, which I am sure will be readily and cordially given, in the fulfilment of his instructions. If you could lend him one of your dragomans it would materially facilitate his operations, which at this inclement season are of vital importance to the efficiency, and I might say the very existence, of our troops.

When this news came in, the ambassador laid siege to the Porte and strove to hasten the despatch of supplies. It was hard work. He had written some time before to Sir E. Lyons (20 June) that his "solicitations to the Porte for necessary arrangements were sadly embarrassed by the never-ceasing slowness, ignorance, and prejudice of the Turks; there is no getting them out of the old ruts, and I lose my patience in fruitless efforts to make them worthy of our assistance." Still, the situation was urgent, and the bazars were scoured for warm clothing for the destitute troops before Sevastopol; the ambassador compelled the Turkish ministers, of whom Reshid Pasha was now once more the head, to help their utmost, and provided the necessary authority for levying requisitions upon the markets of Brusa, Smyrna, and other places. Whatever could be procured, we may be sure, " by hook or by crook," was sent off to the army as promptly as the transport service permitted; and an " urgent and peremptory " despatch to Admiral Boxer on the subject had some effect in hastening his usually deliberate movements; but the Turks had generally to find the vessels as well as the stores. All the exertions of the ambassador and his small staff could not make amends for the short-sighted follies of the home authorities, the inadequacy of the transport and commissariat departments, and the criminal frauds of the contractors.

So the year 1854 came to an end amid troubles and calamities—doubts and anxieties in the trenches, sickness and destitution in the tents. England was palpitating with sympathy and indignation, but her hearty aid was long in reaching the sufferers, and many of her gifts went astray and never served the end to which they were so anxiously and lovingly destined. A violent public feeling was rising against incompetent officialism, and like most popular sentiment overshot its mark. Everyone concerned in the war came in for his share in the general vituperation, and the newspapers daily slew reputations that had been won on hard-fought battlefields. Lord Stratford, despite his incessant toil and not a little disagreeable opposition and criticism, continued sanguine and firm. The deeds of Alma, Balaklava, and Inkerman recalled, he said, his young days, when Trafalgar and Waterloo were the words in all men's mouths. He was proud of his country's arms, and confident that, in spite of every obstacle from man and the elements, the good cause would triumph in the end.

The first month of 1855 found every department of government, and not least the Embassy at Constantinople, absorbed in the effort to remedy the effects of unpreparedness which had plunged the army in the Crimea into that state of sickness and depression and starvation which roused the indignation of the whole people of England. The two chief difficulties that hindered the proper provisioning and clothing of the men were the crowded and disorganized state of the little harbour of Balaklava, and the total effacement of all roads by the frost, snow, rain, and constant deluge of mud. On 6 January Lord Stratford wrote to the Commander-in-Chief, apologizing for what might appear as an officious interference, but strongly urging the employment of a body of labourers, which he offered to send at once from Constantinople, to make passable roads from the harbour to the camps, and also calling his attention in urgent but very friendly terms to the disorder that was still reigning at Balaklava. In the same letter he remarked that every officer he had seen, both French and English, believed that Sevastopol might be taken by assault without further delay, and that reports were gaining ground of the discontent of both armies at the hesitation of their generals. A tone of gloomy anticipation of failure had indeed taken the place of that cheerful spirit which had hitherto characterized the predictions of the soldiers, and

there was a general belief that a fatal mistake had been
made in not attacking the fortress from the north side immediately after the victory of the Alma.

The arrival of an engineer, soon followed by English
navvies, for the construction of a railway from Balaklava to
the camps, did not interfere with Lord Stratford's plan of
sending labourers from Constantinople. Lord Raglan thankfully accepted the suggestion, and, though there was some
delay in consequence of the men at first refusing to go to
a place which by all accounts seemed to be little better than
a pest-hole, a thousand navvies were soon despatched and did
excellent service. All through January there was unabated
activity at the Embassy on behalf of the troops. The correspondence about procuring, shipping, conveying, and unlading
supplies of food and clothing was uninterrupted. The deficiencies of our transport service had to be supplied with such
assistance as the Turks could render; the deficiency of stores,
by what could be purchased in the markets of Turkey; and
for both these purposes the authority and constant vigilance
of the Elchi were unceasingly exerted. More houses had to
be obtained for the wounded, and before the month was out,
the Sultan had parted with every available accommodation,
including several of his palaces and private apartments.
Just when it seemed impossible to discover a single empty
house or stable, a requisition came from the Duke of Newcastle for the ambassador to find accommodation for 2,000
horses; and somehow or other it was done. Hardly was this
feat accomplished when the Sardinian contingent, which had
gallantly come to the assistance of the Allies, required a
depôt, and, of course, it was to Lord Stratford, and not to
Baron Tecco, their own representative, that they looked for
the satisfaction of their needs. Telegraphs were to be established, and the British ambassador was the only person to
procure the necessary firmans and vezirial letters. Even the
Turkish forces could not obtain the stores and other supplies
of which they stood in great need without his mediation.
Demand after demand was made from England and from headquarters for every conceivable kind of assistance; and it is
very noteworthy, in reading through the unpublished despatches, how frequently the requirements of Lord Clarendon
or the Duke of Newcastle had already been successfully
anticipated by the Queen's representative at Constantinople.
But in spite of all the energy displayed by the Embassy, and

also (when they awoke to the necessity) by the home authorities, such evils as had taken root at the seat of war were not to be speedily remedied. The report at the beginning of February was still far from encouraging, though not bad enough to justify the gloomy despair which marked every one of Lord Clarendon's letters to the ambassador at this period, and, indeed, almost throughout the war.

Lord Stratford was soon able to judge the state of affairs with his own eyes. In one of the few autobiographical fragments which he wrote concerning the period of the Crimean War, he describes his first visit to the scene of operations :—

MEMOIRS.   I went twice to the Crimea, the first time at Lord Raglan's request, the second under instructions from home. If ever the characters of a thorough gentleman and gallant soldier were contained in one person Lord Raglan was the man. Companion in arms and friend of Wellington, heir of that great commander's military principles, he was naturally chosen to conduct the war against Russia in concert with our allies the French. More than a generation had passed away from the time of the battle of Waterloo to that in which he went forth at the head of our Crimean expedition. Vast changes had taken place in the interval. I will not say that England had declined from her warlike spirit, that, to use a well-known expression—

> " Longoque togae tranquillior usu
> Dedidicit jam pace ducem."—Lucan, *Civ. Bell.* i. 130.

But certain it is that her habits of military practice had been entirely interrupted, except in India, and that new ideas, at least in degree, had sprung up with regard to the instruments of warfare, the comfort of the soldier, and the duty of the officer. These causes of increased difficulty in the conduct of a campaign were magnified by the critical activity of the press, the livelier sensibilities of the public, and other circumstances peculiar to the scene of operations.

The spring was advancing in the second year of the war when I received Lord Raglan's invitation. I embarked without any unnecessary delay in the steamer *Caradoc*, commanded by Captain Derriman, and landed after an easy passage in the narrow but picturesque harbour of Balaklava, which was then crowded with our shipping. Lord Raglan paid us the compliment of a visit, and I rode up to headquarters, the ladies remaining on board. The wretched state of the roads, which had been a principal source of suffering in winter, no longer existed. I had sent up a thousand hired labourers from Constantinople as soon as I was at liberty to do so, and, what was more to the purpose, a number of navvies had recently arrived from England. In other respects as well as in this the pressure of unforeseen difficulties had ceased ; but the operations against Sevastopol made no marked progress, and plans of attack on other more distant points were suspended by considerations which did not originate on our side. Lord Raglan proposed that I should take part in the councils which were held between the respective commanders, but I thought it prudent to decline an honour that would convey with it a certain degree of responsibility and no adequate usefulness. He told me that it had been agreed in council to send an expedition to Kerch, but that his French colleague a few hours later had receded from the agreement ; during my short visit Canrobert changed his mind about three times.[1] A day or two after my arrival a review of the French army took place. It was a very pleasing sight. The troops appeared to be in excellent condition, and their gay, well-ordered step in marching was prettily set off by the vivandières, who, in smart costumes at each end of the lines, kept pace with the soldiers. I was so near their general that we could hold converse with each other while the march went on. So good an opportunity of saying a word in Lord Raglan's sense was not to be lost. I expressed my admiration of the gallant bearing and spirited movement of the troops with a hint in conclusion that it was a pity to delay their active employment against the enemy. The general replied in his own language : " Ah ! monsieur l'ambassadeur, les conséquences d'un insuccès dans la guerre sont très graves." " Sans doute, monsieur le général," I rejoined, at some little risk of causing displeasure ; " mais il me paraît que le plus grand des insuccès c'est de ne rien faire."

No one seemed to apprehend an attack. The siege operations continued, but they were directed against the outward forts, particularly the Mamelon, and until they were reduced Sevastopol could not be assailed with effect. Lord Raglan and his staff occupied a house at no great distance from the French headquarters, and a room was kindly allotted to me within its precincts. One evening after dark we heard firing on the French line. The moon was up, horses were ordered, and I joined the party from mere curiosity. We rode to a point known as the White House, and a little beyond fell in with General Canrobert. We were on high ground, and in a valley below an action was going on between a portion of his troops and a Russian detachment. We could not see them, but we were near enough to hear their shouts and to perceive the flashes of their muskets. Shells were at the same time careering in the air in our direction, but from too great a distance to reach us. Messages came in from time to time, and the general, taking me into a little hut, allowed me to see them. I do not remember which party got the better of the other. The engagement in fact

[1] It is only fair to add that recent publications have traced Canrobert's vacillations to the direct interference of Louis Napoleon.

was of little consequence, except to those who were personally concerned in it.

All that I have related above took place in the months of April–May, 1855. I went at the beginning of May to Eupatoria with Sir Edmund Lyons, and on board the ship which carried his flag. Eupatoria was then in possession of a Turkish division commanded by Omar Pasha. I was received at the landing by the Pasha and his numerous party, dressed out in full uniform. Their finery made me feel ashamed of my plain clothes, which I had no means of changing, especially when I was called upon to mount a fidgety charger accoutred in the Eastern fashion. Nor was the feeling of awkwardness diminished when I had to pass a saluting battery with my hat in hand, and an air of undisturbed serenity.

The troops were drawn out in line along the ramparts of the town, and observing that their persons were considerably exposed to missiles in that position, I was told, in reply to my inquiry, that they were expected neither to duck nor to swerve however near the enemy's shot might come. This puts me in mind of what I had been told by a veteran admiral many years before. His story was that serving at a battery in Corsica, when the French were defending that island, he saw Lord Nelson come up and plant his telescope towards a redoubt from which the French were firing. His lordship, being asked what the enemy were about, replied, "You will hardly believe it, but those fellows duck when the shot pass over their heads." I knew, said my admiral, what he meant, for heads at our battery had gone down under fire just before. I kept silence, he added, till a fresh volley came, and Nelson had ducked in company with the rest of us. Then I thought my time had come, and I said, "You see, my lord, the bravest are not exempt from the common instinct." Whether the Turks, as fatalists, were or were not expected to be more than men, it is certain that they kept possession of Eupatoria to the end of the war.

As for myself and party, we returned to Constantinople with the satisfaction of having witnessed a most interesting scene, and being entitled to entertain a reasonable hope of final success. There were other elements in this feeling of satisfaction. We left the army in health and relieved from all unusual privations, with an absence of any apparent differences between the respective commanders, and a most cordial understanding between the land and sea services in our own part of the expedition.

Lord George Paget, in his interesting *Crimean Journal*, has recorded an amusing incident of the ambassador's visit. Lord Raglan, it appears, on riding down to welcome his Excellency, had ordered the Guards to form a guard of honour. But here an unforeseen difficulty arose. By the "privileges of the Guards" those distinguished regiments could not present arms to anyone below the royal rank; and

so Lord Stratford had to wait an hour or more on board ship
till the Highlanders could be hurried up to do him honour!
Lord George describes the sensation made by the ambassador
and the party of ladies as they rode round the position at
Balaklava up to the Crow's Nest, and again when the Elchi
and the Commander-in-Chief made a stately progress by
water, followed by their suites, round the vessels which were
destined for the first expedition to Kerch. Lord George
Paget had a special reason for remembering the occasion,
for the visitors included his beautiful wife, who had been
the guest of Lady Stratford ever since she had arrived in
Turkey. From a complete stranger she soon became almost
one of the family, and during those long months of anxiety
it was to her that the ambassador owed the chief pleasure of
his brief moments of relaxation. There was a perpetual
stream of people passing to and fro between Constantinople
and the seat of war, and, whether they were strangers or
acquaintances, Lord and Lady Stratford considered them as
their natural guests and shewed them every possible kindness
and hospitality.

Extracts from two letters to Lord Clarendon relating to
this visit to the Crimea may be introduced here :—

28 *April.*—Alas ! there is but one thing of which I can give you
a positive assurance—namely, that if Lord Raglan's opinion had
prevailed, or rather if his colleague had kept *to the agreement*, the
assault would be in progress at this very moment under my eyes.
You will have from better authority than mine an explanation of
the circumstances to which I allude. They present a melancholy
picture of the difficulties with which our noble army has to deal.
It has the weakness of inadequate numbers, not always to be overcome even by heroic valour, and it is condemned to witness a want
of energy and steadiness of purpose which might serve to paralyze
the efficiency of any amount of numbers.

It is quite true that one ought to be on the spot in order to conceive the extent of the operations, and the difficulties of the ground.
Siege, there is none. Two parties are engaged in fighting with each
other by means of advanced trenches and earthwork batteries, one
of them having the advantage of a town and arsenal behind it with
stationary defences in aid of the advancing attack. I have read
enough in my small compass to know that an enemy under such
circumstances must necessarily have the advantage. What I find
most general, as matter of opinion, is that the place might have
been taken at first, and would have been if common sense had not
been overruled by the suggestions of science. All that I hear of
Lord Raglan's decision and firmness is greatly to his credit; but

with so many delicate considerations, I will not say to warp his
judgment, but to arrest execution, the engineering on one side and
French colleagues on the other, there is little room for surprise that
the "poor cat in the adage" should come so often into play. Another general impression is that the Russian outworks can be carried,
though the success would only, in the first instance, afford an
opportunity, which, however, is indispensable, of knowing whether
the possession of them would enable the Allies to get into the
fortress. . . .

Canrobert, who has just been here to call on me, says that on
the 10th of May the reinforcements will be here, amounting, as he
declares, to 70,000 men, including the Sardinians, and that no time
will then be lost in taking a decisive measure against the enemy's
fortifications. He speaks in the highest terms of the English army.
I told him in confidence that almost all the officers I had seen
were for an immediate attack. He said he was aware of it as to
the inferior officers of both armies, but that fifteen out of twenty of
the superior officers were for waiting for reinforcements.

21 May.—I rejoice that you approved of my visit to the Crimea.
To me it was a most interesting excursion; and I agree with you
in hoping that it may have been of some comfort, if not of any use,
to Lord Raglan. In common with the generality of our officers he
reckoned more upon Vienna than I have been accustomed to do.
My language on that subject was not agreeable to him; but he was
glad to shew me over the ground, to perceive that I comprehended
his difficulties, appreciated his improvements, and knew where the
causes of inaction principally lay. His noble bearing, his cheerfulness, his courage and consideration for others, are the brilliant
points of his character; but time will tell upon the best, and his
disposition does not inspire that energy which is so necessary to
make all the departments draw well together. In Gordon Cum-
ming's book of African field-sports there is a description of a Cape
waggon with its span of twenty oxen stuck fast in the channel of a
river, and extricated only when all the waggoners cracked their
long whips at the same moment and kept them going. I thought
of it when I was on the plateau, and wished that some one else had
thought of it sooner. The effects of the first imbroglio have not
entirely vanished; but the appearance of health and cheerfulness
among the troops gratified me much, and all that related to their
diet, clothing, and condition in the hospitals was either quite satisfactory or in a way to become so. Traces of pigheadedness and
confusion still, I believe, linger about the Commissariat, and the
fever, which has shaken sundry of its younger members, has spared
with singular perverseness the grey veteran at its head. Old
Boxer, who was out of his element here, has performed miracles at
Balaklava, where, however, I understand that, since the arrival of
the Sardinians, the shipping has become more crowded than ever.
A fire or an attack there might be attended with awful conse-

quences. Our three principal difficulties now may be referred to the over-caution of our mercurial colleagues, to the backwardness of our land-transport service, and the deficiencies of our steam conveyance. These drags upon our activity may occasion other difficulties by affording time for Russian reinforcements to arrive, by exposing our troops to the hot season, and by keeping such numbers together at a time and in a place where water may become scarce.

It is exactly because our difficulties are so great that we stand in need of a clear field and an unclogged use of our energies. We cannot afford to go on manœuvring for ever in a jungle. We ought by this time to know whether we can rely on France, whether Austria will go to war for us, whether our own people mean as much as they pretend. My creed as to these matters may be stated in few words : I believe in the spirit, resolution, and resources of the United Kingdom ; I believe that Austria is with us up to the verge of war and not beyond ; I believe that we may count upon the French Emperor ; I believe that, without the belligerent co-operation of Austria, the two great maritime Powers together may bring Russia to terms ; and I am furthermore persuaded that, if we do not accomplish that purpose, and put the seal on our success by obtaining material as well as diplomatic guarantees, we shall have to pass through years of bitter unavailing repentance.

No doubt we have hazards to incur as well as sacrifices to make. But would not a patched-up peace have also its hazards and its sacrifices ? Surely the answer is " yes "—with this difference, that in one case even failure would leave us the resource of unstained, unquestioned honour, while in the other, success itself would consign us to the weakness of conscious shame.

Among the causes for dissatisfaction which weighed upon Lord Stratford's mind, none perhaps was more keenly felt than the excessive disparity between the two armies of the Allies. It galled his national pride to see the French outnumbering the British troops in the proportion of at least four to one. Not only was the disparity injurious to the success of the siege, inasmuch as our men were numerically incapable of working and holding the wide extent of front which was allotted to them, without undue and consequently injurious physical strain ; but the comparative insignificance of the British army brought the credit and prestige of England so low that her commanders found themselves compelled to give way to the superior influence of the French, even when there was no doubt that the latter were in the wrong. The effects of this disparity were felt as much in the Embassy as at headquarters. M. Benedetti, the French chargé d'affaires, who presided over the Legation pending the arrival of M.

z

Baraguay d'Hilliers' successor, was unwearying in his efforts
to counteract Lord Stratford's influence in every possible or
impossible way; he plotted to bring about the fall of Omar
Pasha, the generalissimo of the Ottoman forces, because the
latter enjoyed to a certain extent the confidence of the British
ambassador; and it was largely owing to this sinister influence
that Omar was not on his way to the relief of Kars long before
he actually departed.   Soon after Lord Stratford's return
from the Crimea these plots bore fruit in the sudden resignation of the generalissimo, and it needed all the Elchi's personal influence to smooth the pasha's ruffled plumes.

A favourite scheme of the ambassador was the reinforcement of the small army of England in the Crimea
by a Contingent of twenty thousand efficient Turks, paid,
clothed and fed at the cost of England and officered by
Englishmen.   A somewhat similar plan had been already
tried.   An energetic, if somewhat hasty, officer had scoured
both European and Asiatic Turkey in search of those irregulars (or Bashi-Bozuks—a word which means merely soldiers
of no particular uniform, "ragtag and bobtail"), who were
known, from his name, as "Beatson's Horse."   It was not,
however, part of the Turkish Contingent; but belonged to an
earlier period, and was in the pay of the Turkish and not the
English Government.   It was only in September 1855, after
an unfortunate misunderstanding, which was followed by
Beatson's retirement and a subsequent trial at law, that this
body of cavalry was transferred to Shumla, where the Turkish
Contingent, under the command of General Vivian, was there
mustered under orders to proceed to Eupatoria.   This new
corps of 20,000 men, after being reviewed with no small feeling of pride and satisfaction by the ambassador who had
prompted and carried out its formation, departed for the seat
of war; but its arrival, owing to the progress of the peace
negotiations, was not destined to exercise any material effect
upon the enemy.   Several months before the Contingent
received its marching orders, a great assault upon Sevastopol
had been attempted and had failed; and this disaster had
been followed on 28 June by the death of Lord Raglan.   Not
long after this the Elchi again visited the Crimea.   It was
the month of August, and the visitor little suspected how near
was the final triumph for which all were so eagerly longing.
The account of this second excursion is given in the last fragment of autobiography which will be quoted.

MEMOIRS.   The object of my second visit to the Crimea was
to invest several of our officers with the Order of the Bath.   Little
more than three months had passed since the first.   Lord Raglan
had died in the interval, and the chief command had devolved upon
General Simpson.   No action of decided consequence had taken
place in the field since the days of Balaklava and Inkerman.   The
siege operations were still going on against the outward forts, but
the town and arsenal of Sevastopol were not yet bombarded, and
the attack on the defences of the harbour under the special command of Sir E. Lyons had been more distinguished by the habitual
bravery of our seamen than by any decisive result.   The *Caradoc*
did not return to its former anchorage at Balaklava, but took up a
position nearer to Sevastopol and the Allied squadrons.   There was
some inconvenience in this, the distance from headquarters being
considerable and to be traversed only on horseback.   Consequently
I saw more of our naval than of our military commanders, particularly Sir Edmund Lyons and Admiral Houston Stewart, the former
a man of active mind, eager for distinction, and striving incessantly
by thought and deed to carry out the object of the day, the latter
an officer of merit, never lagging in the performance of duty, and a
most agreeable companion.   The Sardinians with judicious foresight were now taking part in the war.   They had thrown in their
lot with the belligerent Allies, and their contingent, commanded by
General La Marmora, was encamped eastward beyond Sir Colin
Campbell's position at and near Balaklava.   The Russians not long
before had made an advance on that side [Battle of the Chernaya,
16 Aug.] with a certain display of force, but being effectively
opposed, their plan, whatever it was, had ended in their retreat.
The attempt had been followed by a state of inaction on that side
of the lines, which was put to trial one day in my presence.   I accompanied the French commander on a visit to the Sardinian
quarters, and on our ride thither we halted on open ground in front
of a steep declivity garnished half way up with a strong Russian
battery.   Our party was numerous.   The officers composing it
were in uniform, and Pélissier himself wore a white African burnous,
which fluttered with every motion of his horse, and offered a
tempting mark for gunners in the opposite fort.   Not a shot, however, was fired, and after stopping some little while without the
slightest molestation we went on to the Sardinian encampment,
where we found an abundance of good cheer, and a most enjoyable
repose.

   The ceremony, for which I was sent to the Crimea, took place
under canvas at the British headquarters.   Such arrangements as
a camp could afford to express the dignity of the occasion were
carefully prepared.   It was my business to sit in a sort of extem-
porized state-chair, to make three or four little speeches suggested
severally by the merits of the intended knights, and finally to lay
my sword upon the shoulders of each when invested with the star

and riband of the Order.   The commanders-in-chief of both armies
and their respective staffs assisted.   We were all within hearing of
the guns which almost continually announced the progress of the
siege and suggested solemn thoughts.   Sir Edmund Lyons was
singular in receiving a second Grand Cross, the civil decoration
having been already conferred upon him.

The secret of the assault was well kept.   Hardly had Lord
Stratford left the Crimea when Sevastopol fell (8 September).
The ambassador's joy at the great news, however, was clouded
by the fear that the Allies would be satisfied with this success,
instead of following it up, and bringing Russia to her knees.
He foresaw a temporary "shortcoming" peace, which would
only leave the struggle to be fought over again.   In this dread
he wrote to Lord Clarendon (13 Sept.) :—

To judge from the first remarks or questions of my German
colleagues, you will be earnestly solicited to make peace now that
the great arsenal of the Black Sea has fallen.   It may sound hard-
hearted, and it is certainly against my private feelings and wishes,
to express the thought, but nevertheless I do think that for our
own national honour and European interest we have still more
exertions to make before we can satisfactorily return the sword to
its scabbard.

In *justice* the Russians have no indulgence to expect from us.
Having reduced the Russia of *accumulated power*, we have to
guard against the Russia of *prospective growth*.   This, I imagine,
might be effected by interposing a barrier of independent neutrals
along the whole frontier.   The Principalities are already better
than independent.   The remaining part of the line seems to offer
more difficulty as to the arrangement in peace than to acquisition
in war.

This, on the side of Georgia, would open a noble field for British
valour and energy *next year*, after the ground shall have been tried
by Omar Pasha *this autumn*, and the results, if successful, would
be in their character *compensatory* as to our military credit in
Europe, and highly influential as to our political power in Asia.

It may be presumed that Russia is not yet quite prepared to
accept such terms of peace.   But Russia must be losing her self-
confidence from day to day, and in a nation of superstitious slaves,
when devotion is puzzled, and fear of authority relaxed, to say
nothing of pressure on trade and property, the spirit of resistance
declines rapidly, and the moral preparation for peace on any terms
makes progress in proportion.   A bold advance from Eupatoria, or
some other well-selected point, would probably be attended with
success beyond our expectation ; but to produce its full effect the
Russians ought not to be allowed time for looking about them and
recovering their breath.

I abstain from pushing the speculation further, and I have already betrayed my conviction that enough is done or in progress even now to secure a *complete* satisfaction on the *Four Points*;[1] but surely our title to more solid guarantees and a more perfect settlement grows naturally out of a larger amount of hazard, sacrifice, and success on our side. It can hardly be denied that in such matters a heavy responsibility attaches to unseasonable moderation. It may justly be said that the duty of Governments, who have required so much of their subjects, is to take care that the profits of the sickle shall be equal to the labours of the plough.

The opinions of those on the spot, however, went for little in the Peace negotiations. Just when our army was in splendid health and spirits, when the defects of transport and commissariat had been overcome, when 20,000 sturdy Turks had been enrolled and disciplined by Englishmen to swell the muster roll of our forces, when Russia was all but on her knees; just then the golden opportunity was let slip, the armies were suffered to lie inactive, while diplomatists were gulled into negotiations for a false peace, which left Russia almost untouched, instead of making any further encroachments not only in Europe but above all in Asia impossible so long as treaties have force. But the peace had not yet been signed, and in the autumn of 1855 there was still hope that England might prevent such a disaster as a surrender of all that she had striven for.

CHAPTER XXIV.

THE SURRENDER OF KARS.

1855.

As Lord Stratford de Redcliffe, one day towards the close of the eventful year 1855, sat before his desk, strewn with despatches, reports, orders, requisitions, and all the other

[1] The Four Points upon which the negotiations (which had never been entirely abandoned) for peace were founded were: 1. The abolition of the Russian protectorate over the Danubian Principalities; 2. The freedom of the Danube and its embouchures; 3. The neutralization of the Black Sea and closing of the straits to ships of war; 4. The confirmation of the rights and immunities of the Christian subjects of the Porte without injury to the Sultan's dignity and independence.

material of an immense official correspondence during a great war, a letter was brought to him which carried back his thoughts to the very beginning of his career at Constantinople. It was signed, " Your ancien secrétaire perpetuel, D. R. Morier," and it announced the death of the old ambassador, Sir Robert Adair, under whose benevolent sway they had both won their first experiences of diplomatic work in Turkey nearly half a century before. " My dear Canning," wrote Morier, " you must let me still address you by that old familiar name, while, like Pharaoh's chief butler, ' I do remember my faults this day,' and no longer delay to fulfil the promise I made some months ago to our dear old Chief of times past, now in his grave. He was very, very aged, and well he might be at ninety-two—but although failing both in sight and hearing, and in the memory of recent trifles, his *heart's memory* was as retentive as ever, and of you he never spoke without the most warm expressions of affection and sincerest regard, making me promise that whenever I wrote to you I would not fail to convey them to you with the special assurance of these his unaltered sentiments." The younger man— and he was but one year short of seventy—was deeply moved by this message from the old master who had taught him diplomacy in 1809. " It has touched my heart," he said, " and brought tears into my eyes."

As he read the words, his mind wandered back to those early days at Stambol, when life was in its morning glow, and the world lay before him like a country to be explored. He had seen much of that world in the forty-seven years which had passed since then. To use, as he would have done, the words of his favourite author, *multum ille et terris jactatus et alto*. On the very spot where he and Adair had held converse together he could now stand and contemplate the work of a life already long. He remembered the Treaty of Bucharest, his first, and in his own eyes always his greatest, triumph. He thought of the brilliant throng at Vienna, and the sudden shock, like the boom of a distant gun, when the news came that the " Enemy of Europe " was again at large. His thoughts quickly sped from the tidings of Waterloo, which blazed forth like a beacon fire in the midst of " rustic diplomacy " in Switzerland, to that lonely island in the Atlantic where the mighty Enemy had breathed his last, while the man who had successfully opposed him in the East was enduring the rude experiences of a mission in the Western

world. Then memories of the Greek struggle for liberty
crowded upon his mind ; he fought his battles o'er again with
the Porte, recalled the tragedy of Navarino, and the final
founding of the State of Greece ; and there was sadness in
the thought, for the kingdom had not realized his hopes. He
had laboured to create a nation, but so far neither he nor any
one else had been able to teach it how to live.

With the recollection of the War of Independence came
memories of the first step in its aid—his mission to Petersburg—and then his rejection by that second " Enemy of
Europe " whose armies had but lately been worsted in open
field and stubborn forts by the men of the West. Nicholas
Paulovich, Emperor of All the Russias, had fought his long
duel with the Elchi, and was dead ; and there on the littered
table lay one of his last letters—a despatch to Lord Stratford
himself, thanking him for his kindness to the Russian
prisoners. So the old rivalry ended in a gracious act. There
was no hardness in his mind as the memory of Nicholas
arose. The Czar he had detested ; for the man he had no
feeling but pity. Besides, the Czar had lived to see his armies
thrice hurled back by the very English who had so long
excited his jealousy and hatred ; and it was no part of the
Elchi's nature to triumph over the fallen. In his hour of
crowning glory, moreover, there was much to make him grave.
It was true that he had met and faced the great Eastern Question, that he had upheld the right when all others flinched,
and with a clear conscience had seen our soldiers go forth to
maintain the cause of justice. But much remained. Turkey
had been sustained for awhile in her corner of Europe, but if
she was to keep her place as Warden of the Marches over-
against Russia, she must look to herself. It was of no
avail to pour forth English blood and treasure for people who
would not help themselves, but who, by oppression and bad
government, almost made their protectors ashamed to shield
them. The one great aim of his later years in the East had
been to raise up a new Turkey, a State worthy to be defended,
a moral as well as a material barrier to the encroachments of
Russia. His consistent plan had been to remove all disabilities of race and creed, to make the Christian subjects of the
Sultan in every way the equals of their Mohammedan neighbours, and to infuse into every department of the administration such a proportion of Christian and educated influence
that the old corrupt system of government should become

impossible. The task was Herculean, well-nigh hopeless; yet more had been accomplished than those acquainted with the East could have expected. Reform after reform had been enacted, and the main difficulty that remained was to insist that they should be rigidly enforced. The Turks as a body were not to be trusted to do this; there was always a party of reaction and bigotry which was sure to check the moderate efforts of the reformers. Effective supervision could only be exerted by the personal influence of a European; and as the Great Elchi meditated on the long years of his work in Turkey he could not but see reason to distrust the future.

There were grounds for these misgivings. Several circumstances had combined to diminish the prestige of England and the popularity of her representative. The first and most important of these was the position which France had attained in Turkey and at Downing Street. Ever since 1840, when England rescued the Ottoman Empire from the hands of Mohammed Ali, in direct opposition to the policy of France, British counsels had been almost supreme at the Porte. Turkey was convinced that England was her truest friend, and with this conviction, and such a man as the Elchi to enforce it, the task of asserting English influence at Constantinople had been comparatively easy. Lord Stratford had enjoyed a scarcely interrupted reign for many years, not indeed unopposed by the Turks and uncontested by the other embassies, but on the whole the opposition had been unavailing and the contest had left him unshaken in his power.

The Crimean War brought about a change in this position. The immense numerical preponderance of the French army, their taking of the Malakov and the consequent withdrawal of the Russians from the south side of Sevastopol, and the insidious skill of their latest representative at the Porte, had materially strengthened the ascendency of France in Turkey. The Ottoman ministers were now almost disposed to think that, after all, France might be their best ally; or if they did not go so far as this, they were at least fully alive to the advantages which must accrue to Turkey by playing upon the jealousies of the rivals. Lord Stratford could easily have held his own, had he been adequately supported by the Government at home; but unfortunately Lord Clarendon was under the spell of Louis Napoleon, and much more ready to take the part of the French than of the Elchi, whose resignation he would gladly have accepted. Deserted by the Foreign Secretary, Lord Stratford found himself contending at the odds of one against three instead of even numbers. From the beginning of the war the unequal duel never ceased. Publicly, indeed, the forms of courtesy were observed, and in private there was even a good-humoured cordiality between the two embassies; but officially there was undying suspicion beneath the polished surface. As an instance of the intrigues which were carried on in 1855 we may revert to Lord Stratford's first visit to the Crimea. Hardly had his back been turned, when the French representative succeeded in inducing the ever-complaisant Sultan to recall from exile his brother-in-law Mohammed Ali. This man had murdered one of his Christian concubines, and had consequently been denied admission to the British Embassy on the ground that "the Queen's ambassador cannot receive a cowardly assassin." Such was the man whom the French smuggled back to Constantinople during Lord Stratford's brief absence in the Crimea. In reply to his indignant remonstrance, the frightened Sultan gave his word that Mohammed Ali should not be reinstated in office. Nevertheless, on the ambassador's return from his second visit to the Crimea in August he found the delinquent, at the instigation of the French, comfortably installed in the office of Kapudan Pasha, or High Admiral. This was too much for mortal endurance, and Lord Stratford approached the Sultan with a memorandum couched in words such as no sovereign, one would think, had ever before been forced to hear. Indeed Abdu-l-Mejid would not listen to it, and something of the nature of a "scene" ensued—the angry Sultan calling for his secretary, and the Elchi standing before him with the terrible indictment in his hand.

The jealousy of the French and the disaffection of some of the Turkish ministers were not the only blows aimed at the Elchi's sway. The people of England themselves were now turning against one who had not long before been their idol. There was no more popular man in Europe than Sir Stratford Canning in 1849, when he made the Sultan protect the Hungarian refugees; and his triumph over Menshikov had sustained his reputation. But a change had now come over the popular sentiment. There was a considerable section of the Radicals who disapproved of the war, and could not rid themselves of the false impression that the ambassador was its cause. During the troubles of the winter of 1854–5 England had become frantic against everyone in authority, and even the Elchi was not spared. The attack soon collapsed, but there is an old saying about the adhesive property of mud, and the imperfect recollection of even false charges is apt to tinge so unstable an element as public opinion. Towards the close of 1855 a fresh charge was preferred, which gathered to itself all the rancour that had remained over from previous assaults. In November the fortress of Kars, in Armenia, which had been gallantly defended by the Turks for about four months, under the direction of European officers, among whom General Kmety, General Williams, Baron Schwarzenberg, Major Lake, and Lieutenant (now Sir Christopher) Teesdale were the most active, was starved into surrender; and the good people at home, prompted by malicious journalists, jumped to the conclusion that Kars fell because Lord Stratford would not try to relieve it.

The story of Kars is soon told. On 15 August, 1854, Colonel Williams arrived at Constantinople on his way to his post as Commissioner to the Turkish Army of Asia. The office was analogous to that of Colonel Simmons in the Turkish Army of Europe; he was to advise and report, but he held no command. There had been nothing but pleasant relations between him and the ambassador during the dozen years of their official connexion. Lord Stratford had himself selected Williams for the Persian Boundary Commission in 1842, and had employed him in that work ever since. On the Colonel's return to Constantinople on his way to Erzerum nothing occurred to alter his grateful sentiments. On the 23rd August the Elchi wrote to Lord Raglan in friendly terms about Williams, and urged both the British Commander-in-Chief and the Turkish ministers to take vigorous measures for the strengthening and reorganizing of the Army of Asia. On 23 September he wrote to Williams, who was then on his way to Erzerum, " It gave me much pleasure to find that you had got so far on your journey with so much success. . . . I am anxious to receive your first reports from the army." On 1 October Williams's reports came in, and Lord Stratford immediately urged his various requisitions upon the Grand Vezir, upon Reshid, and upon the Seraskier or War Minister. In reply, these officials enumerated a large quantity of supplies which had, they said, been ordered and partly sent to Erzerum. More reports arrived from Williams on 14 October, and concerning these the Elchi wrote to Lord Raglan on the same day, "I rejoice that a sensible and dispassionate professional man should be on the spot to report the exact state of things. I propose to act vigorously on all his recommendations." The Porte manifested no opposition; everything was promised; supplies were ordered; corrupt officers were recalled and put under arrest. How far these promises and orders were genuine is another matter; but it was not easy to pursue a consignment of goods through Asia Minor, and the ambassador naturally could not be expected to trace the course and fate of every load or case that was supposed to have arrived at Kars or Erzerum. So far as he knew, everything was in course of preparation; the progress was slow, as progress is wont to be in Turkey, and the Turks were really at their wits' end to provide the necessary supplies and transport; but there was nothing to cause suspicion of foul play, and as the winter was setting in, when the Russians would be compelled to postpone all military operations, there was every hope that the provisions and stores would arrive at their destination in ample time for the necessities of the army.

Williams was apparently as well pleased with the ambassador as the latter was with him. Writing on 7 October, the Commissioner referred to his lordship's "most welcome letter," and agreed with the opinions therein expressed. In this strain he continued to correspond throughout October and November. He made no complaints about the manner in which he was treated by the Embassy. His letters are full of reports of the bad state of the army, and he apparently entertained, and certainly expressed, no doubt that Lord Stratford was taking all possible steps to have the evils remedied. The aspect of these letters, scored along the margins with the ambassador's pencil, shews that each separate suggestion or complaint was carefully noted for immediate reference to the Porte. On 27 November, writing to Lord Stratford, Williams records with satisfaction the arrival of provisions at Kars and the punishment of military Pashas, both of which must, as he knew, be the consequences of the steps taken by Lord Stratford, acting on his own reports. But on the very next day after this amicable communication, Williams wrote to Lord Clarendon to complain of the total neglect with which he had been treated by her Majesty's ambassador at the Porte. So sudden a *volte-face* requires explanation. It is also strange that having informed Lord Clarendon at that date of his charge against the ambassador, he did not see fit to communicate his complaint to Lord Stratford himself till 8 December, and it was not till ten days later that the ambassador was put in possession of the accusations which had apparently been growing in the Commissioner's mind ever since the beginning of October.

Lord Stratford received the communication with amazement. He was conscious of having spared no pains, of having neglected no method, opportunity, or argument, to goad the Turkish Government into action in the sense of Colonel Williams's recommendations, and this sudden assault from one for whom he entertained nothing but friendly feelings, and for whom he had been working hard, was to him simply incomprehensible. The gravamen of the charge was that he had not written often enough to the Commissioner. He had, in fact, only written twice since the latter's departure from Constantinople. Lord Stratford had no leisure for writing about nothing, and up to December there was little that he could communicate bearing upon Williams's recommendations. The Porte was considering them; the Porte was gradually pushing forward preparations for sending supplies; the Porte was thinking about making Williams a Ferik, &c.: such would have been the sum of his despatches, had he written them. There was so much other work to be done for the army in the Crimea, for the hospitals, and other pressing affairs, in the winter of 1854, that the ambassador necessarily found himself unable to spare time for merely formal communications. Had there been anything worth telling he would have told it. So he wrote to Lord Raglan on the day on which he received Williams's denunciatory despatch. "He has misunderstood my silence," he said, "which was simply this: I was unwilling to write long histories until I could state distinctly that all my recommendations were either executed or in course of being so. You know what people I have to deal with, and will understand the rest." This was the true explanation, and Lord Stratford's silence had nothing to do with personal feeling of any kind. Nevertheless, Lord Clarendon's despatch of 11 January amounted to a severe condemnation of the ambassador's silence, and elevated Colonel (or, as he then became, Brigadier-General) Williams into the position of a forlorn martyr deprived of the support of his "natural protector," the ambassador at the Porte.

Here the incident appeared to have terminated. There has never, I believe, been any pretence that, after the corre-

spondence which took place in November and December 1854,
Lord Stratford neglected in any way the interests of General
Williams and the armies at Erzerum and Kars. The Blue-
Book on *Military Affairs in Asiatic Turkey*, with its 400
despatches and numerous enclosures, contains abundant evidence of the zeal and perseverance with which the Elchi
pressed the Turkish Government to reinforce and provision
its army in Asia, and, from the papers of the Embassy now
before me, I could add a mass of supplementary evidence of
his untiring activity in its cause. He wrote thirty-two official
despatches to Williams between January and November 1855.
He communicated weekly, sometimes daily, with the Ottoman
ministers in support of the Commissioner's requisitions. He
never ceased to impress upon them, and upon the authorities
appointed to command in Asia, the necessity of complete
reliance upon Williams's advice. If little was accomplished,
it was partly due to the exhausted resources of the Porte, and
partly the result of the evil influence of the Seraskier, who
was the same Riza Pasha who had made a point of opposing
Lord Stratford throughout his career. Fortunately, in June
Riza was dismissed, and his successor, Mohammed Rushdi,
was a decided improvement. The Elchi's first communication with the new minister related to the urgent necessity of
succouring Kars, whither General Williams had at length
repaired from Erzerum.

As the reports of the advance of the Russians upon Kars
gained strength, the Turks began at last to take serious
measures. On 27 June they proposed that the Turkish Contingent, then mustering under General Vivian, and part of
Beatson's Horse, should be ordered to relieve Kars by making
a diversion from Redoutkalé and Kutais, so as to take the
Russians in the rear. In a few days the details of this scheme
were fully arranged. General Mansfield, who had lately been
attached to the Embassy as Lord Stratford's military adviser,
spent many hours in consultation with the Turkish ministers
on every branch of the subject, and sanguine hopes of success
were entertained by all who were professionally able to estimate the chances of the proposed expedition. The British
Government, however, interposed, and positively prohibited
the transfer of the Turkish Contingent to Asia. It was fully
determined in Downing Street and Pall Mall that Kars should
be relieved by way of Trebizond, and that the relief should be
executed by Turkish troops alone. The preference for the

Trebizond route, which was known to be extremely difficult in autumn, was not shared by anyone out of London.

What was to be done next? There was a talk of detaching some of the English from before Sevastopol, but their numbers hardly admitted of diminution, and it was thought that if they were further reduced they would be really little better than a brigade of the French army. The French, who did not care about Kars, would not dream of leaving the scene of their coming glory. The only alternative was to send Omar Pasha with Turkish troops from the Crimea. Omar himself, as soon as he learnt the critical condition of Kars, strongly urged this measure; but he was met with decided opposition from the English and French Commanders-in-Chief, and the latter especially would not hear of any reduction of the forces in the Crimea. Louis Napoleon still shewed himself "insensible to the consequences of any serious disaster in Asia," and his opinion had more than its due weight in the camps before Sevastopol. The difficulty was at last met by proposing to supply the place of the troops under Omar Pasha by the now completed Turkish Contingent. Then came a further obstacle. Were Omar's men to be taken from the Turks before Sevastopol or from those at Eupatoria? And so the negotiation wore on, to the disgust both of the Elchi and the Turks themselves, who were at last thoroughly in earnest. Finally Omar managed to satisfy the Home governments and the Commanders-in-Chief, and set off for the Circassian coast with the object of operating upon the rear of the Russians. This was not arranged till September, and the time was then running very short if anything was to be done for Kars. There were delays in land transport, and other obstacles, and Omar had not advanced far on his road through Mingrelia when General Williams suddenly surrendered on 23 November, and, with most of the other officers, became a prisoner of war.

This is not the place to discuss the various causes which contributed to the fall of Kars, the apathy and cowardice of Selim Pasha, the commander at Erzerum, and the possibility of provisioning the town from the stores which were known to exist, not only at Erzerum, but at a day's march from the beleaguered fortress itself. What concerns us is merely how far the relief of Kars was hindered or promoted at Constantinople; and enough has been said to shew, and a perusal of the Blue Book will confirm the statement, that not only was Lord Stratford perseveringly zealous in his endeavours to get provisions and reinforcements sent out, but even the Turkish Government itself, as soon as Riza had been replaced by a new Seraskier, was honestly active in the same direction, and was foiled to a large extent by the objections of the British Government to the first plan of relief, and by the obstacles thrown in the way of the second plan by the commanders in the Crimea and by the French Government. So far as Lord Stratford was concerned, there never had been a time, from the day Williams set out to that on which Kars fell, when he had not done his utmost for the Commissioner and the Army of Asia.

The news of the surrender of Kars caused immense excitement in England. The people, naturally moved by a story of brave resistance to privations and more than one stirring feat of arms, could not show enough sympathy for the defenders of Kars. Sympathy for the distressed is seldom complete without indignation against the cause of distress, and popular indignation is not choice in the selection of a victim. So, after a year had elapsed, the old tale of the unanswered despatches was dragged to light; dates were forgotten; 1854 was confounded with 1855, and Kars with Erzerum; and in the excitement of the moment the remarkable theory was advanced, in effect, that because Lord Stratford neglected to reply to certain letters of Colonel Williams at Erzerum in October and November 1854 he was responsible for the fall of Kars in November 1855.

Stated thus plainly, the charge appears in its naked absurdity; but it was far from seeming absurd to the excited populace in the early months of 1856. As soon as he heard the first rumour of the attack Lord Stratford telegraphed to Lord Clarendon to beg that every word he had written on the subject might be laid before Parliament: "I have no fear of my countrymen," he wrote, "when they have the means of judging fairly before them," and the Blue Book on the *Military Affairs in Asiatic Turkey* was the result. As soon as the documents had been published, sane men regretted the temporary infatuation which had possessed them. But meanwhile the hero and the victim had received their respective meed. Williams returned triumphant and a pensioned baronet, while Whiteside gave notice of a motion in the House of Commons. The Blue Book was out before the motion came on for debate (1 May), and the result was a triumph for the Government. Whiteside's vituperation of

Lord Stratford was forgotten when Palmerston, with all his manly straightforward vigour, dwelt upon the long and honourable career of the Great Elchi, his many services to his country, and his fair unspotted fame, and demonstrated in unanswerable terms the absurdity of the charge brought against him. He fairly carried the House with him; they turned away from the petty detail of unanswered despatches to the great facts of Lord Stratford's career, and the motion was triumphantly defeated by a majority of 127. Lord Malmesbury, who had a corresponding motion in the House of Lords, hastily withdrew it, to the disappointment of the Duke of Newcastle, the Earl of Harrowby, Lord Glenelg, and others, who had looked forward to a field-day in defence of their friend. The Elchi's name was safe.

CHAPTER XXV.

THE CHARTER OF REFORM.

1856-58.

In the preceding chapters the centre of interest has been seen to shift itself from Constantinople to the seat of war, and the work of diplomacy has been overshadowed by the stern business of battle. We are now to witness another and much more violent change of scene: the crisis was no longer to be met by steady firmness at the Porte or by gallant deeds of arms in the Crimea; Lord Stratford's great influence and the zeal and courage of the armies were alike superseded, from no defect of their own, but in consequence of treachery in high places. For the fall of the south side of Sevastopol was followed by an event perhaps unparalleled in history. In 1854 two great nations bound themselves together by a solemn treaty to withstand by force of arms the encroachments of Russia; in 1855, one of those great nations betrayed the other in presence of the enemy. To treat separately for peace was expressly prohibited by the treaty of alliance : yet at the close of 1855 the Emperor of the French was in secret communication with the son-in-law of the Russian Chancellor, and the purport was treasonable to England. Satisfied with the

half-successes of the siege, Louis Napoleon was now as anxious
for peace as he had formerly been eager for military glory.
All the plans for the coming campaign were thrown over, and,
after a while, the secret negotiations bore fruit in Russia's
acceptance of an Ultimatum. Plenipotentiaries were summoned to Paris, where Lord Clarendon soon discovered that
England stood alone, and that peace was not so much offered
as, in the words of Brunov, thrust down the jaws of Russia.

When Lord Stratford learned the terms of the Treaty of
Paris, his first words were, "I would rather have cut off my
right hand than have signed that treaty." It was hard to see
all the hard-won triumphs of his diplomacy of 1853 utterly
abandoned in 1856. His own notions as to what it should
have comprized have already been outlined in former extracts
from the correspondence, but the two following letters to Lord
Clarendon, one written before the negotiations at Paris, the
other after their conclusion, will complete as far as it is needful the statement of his views :—

3 *Feb.*—I was glad to learn that you are to go to Paris. Your
labours there will no doubt be attended with vexation and risk, but
proportioned thereto will be the credit of success, or the consolation
of failure. It gratified me to observe that your opinion and mine,
let me add, of the peace agrees with the general impressions of the
country. The attempt was a necessity under the circumstances,
and a continuance of the war, if such be the will of Heaven, might
atone for the loss of an occasion which, however advantageous in
the main points, would leave much to desire. Nicholas's Russia
is to all appearance on its knees. The Russia of nature is still in
its growth, shorn of its most forward branches, but capable of
shooting into greater luxuriance at no distant period. Against this
latter Russia I should like to see due precautions taken, and I
know nothing better than a barrier of neutral or independent States
prolonged between the two empires in Europe and Asia.

As for the Crimea, I know not what could be done with it if
severed from Russia. Restored without its fleet and fortifications,
laid open to a free commercial intercourse, and placed under the
surveillance of consular dragons, I conceive that it would offer the
maximum of advantage to us and our allies.

I have already troubled you with my notions about the Dniester
as a frontier, and the means of raising a title to it. My impression
is, that you would be fully justified in demanding it in lieu of a
pecuniary indemnity so justly due to the Allies, and more especially
to the Porte itself.

I may be wrong, but it seems to me that without further success
in the war, you would only do a high act of justice in reviving the

A A

Duchy of Warsaw, which was created by Europe, for European purposes, out of the spoils wrested from France by the alliance of that day, and in establishing the independence of Circassia, which the Porte had no more right to cede than Russia to receive.

A'li Pasha will try to make the fourth point of the Treaty as loose as possible, and yet there is little prospect of keeping the Porte steady to the execution of the measures which are necessarily to be founded on the arrangement now in progress, unless some kind of supervision be retained, which surely may be done without violating any principles of justice, on the grounds of our assistance to the Empire, and the proposed guarantee of the Empire's integrity.

If the integrity of the Sultan's dominions be formally secured, there is but too much reason to fear that the Porte will give way to its natural indolence, and leave the firman of reform, now almost completed, a lifeless paper, valuable only as a record of sound principles.

15 *April.*—It was kind of you to make a point of sending me the Treaty so soon, and it may gratify you to know that I was enabled, by your promptitude in sending it, to share my early knowledge with Thouvenel and Prokesch. The present ministry, whatever A'li may tell you, is so French as to be contented with any treaty which pleased the Emperor. The Sultan, too, who was never enamoured of the war, is delighted at peace without reference to the terms of the Treaty. Elsewhere, as would seem to be the case in England, another campaign would have been preferred, and when the terms of peace are known, it is not impossible that a feeling of positive dissatisfaction may be got up here, whatever may be the case in more polished parts of the world.

It does seem hard, I confess, that with all but 60,000 rank and file in the Crimea, nearly 400 sail ready for the Baltic, no lack of financial means, our commerce undistressed, the wishes of the nation steady, and our soldiers and sailors with few exceptions eager only for fresh trials of strength, we should have got under the harrow of a gratuitous necessity, and found ourselves inextricably committed to an act of voluntary abnegation. As you have done me the honour to sympathize with my *wishes*, I cannot doubt that you have done all which you thought practicable in reason and prudence to obtain a more complete settlement. Few men can do more than see things from their own point of view. Looking from mine, which officially, and perhaps naturally too, affords a more limited horizon, I fancy that the die was cast in the very commencement, and that if of the pipers concerned we are the least well paid, it is because we were then content, from necessity or indifference, to play second fiddle to our Imperial ally.

But I am wrong to take up your time with idle speculations. Long before this can reach you, the measure of British opinion will have been shewn in all its length and breadth; nor should I

be at all surprized if, after a good grumble, the press and the public
were to resign themselves quietly to the blandishments of peace
and reserve the dregs of their bile for audit-day.

Here the peace gives rise to many anxious thoughts.   How are
the Sultan's reforms to be carried through—the Allied troops all
gone, and no power of foreign interference reserved ?   How is the
country to be kept quiet, if hopes and fears, equally excited in
adverse quarters, have to find their own level ?   What means shall
we possess of allaying the discordant elements, if our credit is to
decline and our influence to be overlaid by the persevering artifices
of a jealous and artful ally ?   How can we hope to supply the usefulness derivable from our command of the Contingent and Irregulars if they are to be given up ?—In short, when I hear the politicians of the country remark that the troubles of Europe with respect
to this Empire are only beginning, I know not how to reply.

Lord Stratford was still full of the object which he had
always had at heart—to reform Turkey from within, and at
the same time to provide such external surveillance that it
should not be possible for the native indolence of the official
classes to make the reforms of no effect.   A letter to Lord
Clarendon (3 June) pointedly refers to the necessity for such
supervision and enforcement, if reforms were to have any
real effect :—

What did Lord J. Russell write to me on leaving Vienna ?   I
forget the words ; they amounted to this : All that can be done for
the rayas in *principles* and *measures* may be said to be accomplished.   Now for the *enforcement*—turn in that direction and
complete your work.

I ask for nothing better, not only as regards the rayas, but the
improvement of the Empire generally, if possible, so as to restore it
on sound principles of humane and civilized government.   How is
it to be done ? there's " the question," ay, and " the rub."   Three
levers are requisite ; where are they to be found ?   First, the provincial authorities to act in a right spirit ; secondly, the power of
the Government duly exerted for their appointment and direction ;
thirdly, *a force from without* to keep up a steady animating
pressure on the Government.

The last, I am persuaded, can alone constitute—if even *that*
can—a durable and efficient *principe moteur.*

What shall it be ?   England alone—the Alliance—or Europe ?
One of them it must be.   *Which*, is the question.   I should prefer
the first, as more single-minded, steady, and trusted.   But France
would insist upon having her moiety, and *she* often works by
means and works for ends which would not suit us.   While the
war goes on, however, there is nothing better, as far as I know, and

a thorough understanding between the Governments, expressed in common instructions, might perhaps give a uniform direction to the process.

So long as Lord Stratford was on the spot, there was no lack of *a force from without* to carry reforms into practice ; but it was necessary to look forward to the time when Turkey should be deprived of his counsels.   To guard against future backslidings two things were vital.   One was to confirm, corroborate, and so to speak codify, all the reforms which had been wrung from the Porte since the decree of Gulhané in 1839 ; the other was to provide an external engine for their enforcement.   The Elchi was busy with the former of these two points before the opening of the negotiations at Paris.   It was extremely important that the details should be settled by the Sultan himself before Russia had the opportunity of putting in her oar.   To effect this the ambassador set to work with all his might, and the result was the crown of all his many efforts for the regeneration of Turkey, the famous *Hatti-Humayun* of 21 February, 1856.   In this Imperial proclamation the Sultan announced his desire of renewing and enlarging the numerous improvements which had been introduced into his institutions with a view to making them worthy of the place which his Empire held among civilized nations; he was anxious, he said, to assure the happiness of his people, "who in my sight are all equal, and equally dear to me"; and with this object he first confirmed the former guarantees of the Hatti-Sherif of Gulhané to all his subjects, without distinction of class or religion, for their security in person, property, and honour ; and at the same time renewed all the privileges and spiritual immunities granted *ab antiquo*, and subsequently to Christian and other non-Musulman communities established in Turkey.   The proclamation went on to enumerate various ecclesiastical privileges, guaranteed the free exercise of its religious rites and the control of its sacred and educational buildings to each and every sect ; and announced in bold terms that "Every distinction or designation tending to make any class whatever of the subjects of my Empire inferior to another class on account of their religion, language, or race, shall be for ever effaced. . . . As all forms of religion are and shall be freely professed in my dominions, no subject of my Empire shall be hindered in the exercise of the religion which he professes nor shall be in any way annoyed on that account.   No one shall be compelled to change his religion." The eligibility of all Turkish subjects, without distinction, to public offices; their admission to the civil and military schools; the acceptance of sworn evidence according to the oaths of the several sects in courts of justice; the reference of all inter-religious causes to Mixed Tribunals; the reform of the penitentiary and disciplinary systems; the absolute equality of taxation among the different classes of the population without distinction of creed; the abolition of the system of farming the taxes; and various other reforms tending to the repression of corruption, extortion, and mal- versation, and the equal encouragement of good citizenship without prejudice of class or creed, were all promised in this great Charter. Lord Stratford's hand is traceable in every line; these were his reforms, either already carried, or often pressed upon the Porte; this was the culminating moment in his career, and the seal to all his labours on behalf of just and equal government in Turkey.

It was a signal triumph to have extorted such a pro- gramme of reform from a Mohammedan sovereign, in face of the hostility of the vast majority of his Muslim subjects, despite the opposition of most of the men in office, and not- withstanding the indifference, if not contempt, manifested by the European Powers for all dreams of Turkish regeneration. The ambassador himself was astonished: "Considering that of the five persons who joined me," he wrote, "in drawing up the Charter, two were Mohammedans, two Roman Catholics, and one a member of the Greek Church, its acceptance was little short of a miracle. I confess that I had no previous ex- pectation whatever of overcoming the prejudices of such col- leagues in negotiation, and particularly of those who professed the Musulman belief." No one but Lord Stratford could have won such a victory. But, like the Alma, like Inkerman, it was a victory that required to be followed up; and just at the crowning point, when the whole position of Turkish bigotry and exclusiveness and corruption had been carried by the Elchi's impetuous charge, the Powers of Europe combined to refuse him and his successors the means of securing for ever the advantages he had won. The Hatti-Humayun was indeed part of the Treaty of Paris; it was formally recognized in Art. IX. But it needed more than recognition—it needed enforcement. This was the point upon which Lord Stratford had never ceased to insist. But the Treaty of Paris, while recognizing the importance of the measure, specially enacted that the recognition of the Hatt did not entitle any of the Powers, collectively or severally, to interfere in the internal affairs of the Ottoman Empire. The qualification abrogated whatever effect the recognition might have had.

The great Charter of Reform of 1856 was the climax of Lord Stratford's career. In it he had at last accomplished what his friend Reshid had attempted at Gulhané in 1839. Reshid's effort was premature, and for many years the Elchi's life was one long struggle to overcome the reaction which had ensued. Then one by one the degrading distinctions of creed and nationality had been effaced from the Ottoman institutions; one by one the rights and privileges of the Christians had been secured; and finally the Hatti-Humayun had recapitulated, confirmed, and enlarged all that had gone before. Whatever might hinder the execution of its provisions, the Great Elchi could view with satisfaction the accomplishment of his desire.

His mission in the East was nearly ended. As soon as the Treaty of Paris was signed, he asked for leave of absence. After four years of incessant toil he felt the need of repose. The Government begged him to stay so long as the various details of the peace arrangements required his supervision, and one thing after another delayed him till the following year. He left at last in December 1857, in a depressed frame of mind, due partly to ill-health and partly to political considerations. The betrayal of England at Paris had naturally affected her prestige in the East. The French cared nothing for Turkish reform, and what weighed most heavily upon his mind was the fear that their influence might make the Hatti-Humayun a dead letter. He felt very keenly the pusillanimity of his own Government, who had made him a victim to their deference to France. But with all this to discourage, there was much to inspire hope and confidence. He was satisfied that the work he had accomplished was the right work for Turkey and for England, and he was not conscious of any material loss of his personal influence for carrying on that work. "To be the victim," he wrote to his brother, "of so much trickery and dupery and charlatanism is no small trial; but I have faith in principles, as working out their own justification, and fix my thoughts steadily on that coming day when the Peace of Paris will be felt in its miserable consequences."

If the years succeeding the war had seen his labours aggra-

vated by intrigue at the Porte, by want of support at home, by
partisan writers, and by all the personal hostility that a strong
uncompromising character is apt to arouse ; on the other
hand they had witnessed such an approximation between the
East and West as few who knew Turkey in the earlier decades of the century could have imagined possible. The
barriers between Muslim and Christian, Turk and Frank,
were breaking down.   The year had opened with a sign of
the changes that were taking place : the Elchi had received a
congratulatory New Year's letter from "Abd-el-Kadir, the
Champion of the Faith," in which the noble old chief said, "We
have not forgotten the day on which we met your Excellency at
Therapia ; that was a fête day for us."   Two years before, a
Mohammedan General had been decorated with the Christian
Cross of the Bath.   In 1856 a still more novel and imposing
ceremony took place at Constantinople.   Sultan Abdu-l-Mejid
was invested by Lord Stratford, as the Queen's representative,
with the most exclusive order of knighthood in the world.   Assisted by the King of Arms, the Elchi made his Majesty a
Knight of the Garter.   Did the Sultan know what the stately
ambassador was saying, as he placed the George and Riband
round his neck?   "*Taeniam hanc gestato, imagine Sancti
Georgii Martyris et Militis Christi insignitam, cujus aemula-
tione accensus, per adversos simul prosperosque casus feraris
invictus, donec tam animi quam corporis hostibus fractis, non
solum palmam pugnae terrestris, sed et aeternae victoriae coro-
nam reportes.*"   When a Sultan submits to be enjoined to
emulate the career of a Martyr and Soldier of Christ, who
shall say that the fanaticism of Islam is inextinguishable?

Other signs there were that the work of the Great Elchi
had not been in vain ; that his efforts to draw East and West
together, so that perchance the East might be saved by the
West, had not been fruitless.   Let us picture him as he stood,
bareheaded, surrounded by his staff, in full uniform, at the
gate of the Embassy in Pera one evening in February 1856.
Over his head coloured lamps traced the linked names of
"Victoria" and "Abdu-l-Mejid" in lines of fire across the
court, lighting up the arms of the Grenadiers, Highlanders,
the Horse and Foot Artillery, who formed the guard of
honour.   In front, a troop of English Lancers clashed up to
the gate escorting a carriage wherein was seated the Commander of the Faithful himself, "Sultan of Sultans, Lord of
the Two Seas and the Two Continents, Abdu-l-Mejid Khan,

son of Mahmud." As the Grand Turk alighted, an electric
wire communicated the fact to the British fleet, and the
Golden Horn forthwith rang out with salvos of cannon, while
the band in the court played "God save the Queen." For
the first time in the history of Turkey a Sultan was the guest
of a Christian ambassador. Lady Stratford was giving a *bal
costumé*, and the Sultan had honoured it with his presence.
Never at Pera was a more gorgeous sight witnessed. The
dress uniforms of the English, French, and Sardinian officers
were matched and outshone by the rich costumes and jewelled
arms of the Armenians, Persians, Kurds, Greeks, Turks, and
Albanians who crowded the rooms, by the robes of the
Greek Patriarch, the Armenian Archbishop, and the Jewish
High Priest. Abdu-l-Mejid took in the sight with the wonder-
ing enjoyment of a child; and as he redescended the staircase, which was lined with Lancers and Light Dragoons,
many of whom wore the Balaklava clasp, he might have
fancied that he had changed places with his predecessor,
Harun er-Rashid, and lost himself in the enchanted palaces of
the Thousand and One Nights. The Sultan was delighted with
his "first ball;" and it must have been a proud moment for
Lord Stratford, when, in the presence of all his colleagues, he
walked hand in hand with the Grand Signior through the files
of British soldiers, to the amazement of all beholders. Whose
was the triumph that day, when the bars which fenced about
the seclusion of the greatest Musulman sovereign were
loosed, and Christian and Turk met on equal terms? In the
midst of opposition and dejection, of despair of doing good,
of sad forebodings for the future, this hour of triumph shone
forth like the flash of a beacon at sea, telling the storm-tossed
mariner of firm ground and a haven near at hand. Whatever still remained to be done, the Great Elchi knew that this
was certain: the distinctions of class and race and creed had
been publicly done away with in Turkey, and it was he who
had worked the miracle.

.   .   .   .

The Elchi arrived in London (Dec. 1857) at a time when the
popular sentiment about him had veered round again, and the
papers were, as he said, "braying panegyrics." Lord Palmerston welcomed him cordially; Clarendon was civil; and the past
was not discussed. A very few weeks had elapsed since the

Ambassador's return, however, when a circumstance occurred which altered all his plans. He had at first no intention of resigning his embassy ; on the contrary, he had left Constantinople with the expressed intention of returning, and this expectation was alluded to in the Sultan's parting speech. But on 20 February Lord Palmerston's Government was turned out on Milner Gibson's amendment relating to the neglect of the Government to reply to Count Walewski's despatch, complaining of the asylum given in England to conspirators like the then notorious Orsini. Lord Stratford could not conceal a certain sense of humour when he learnt the cause of the defeat : " I confess," he remarked to a friend, " that it interests me to hear of a Government being dissolved on account of unanswered despatches ; " for he remembered the Kars dispute and the censure passed upon him by the same Foreign Secretary who had now been dismissed for the same fault. But his prevailing feeling was that of sympathy for Palmerston, whose loyalty to the Elchi during the attacks of recent years had confirmed his old admiration for a manful English statesman, once connected, too, by political ties with the party of his illustrious kinsman, George Canning. In a generous impulse he resolved to shew his personal respect for the defeated minister by declining to hold office under his successors, and accordingly as soon as Lord Derby's administration had taken possession of their posts, he sent in his resignation to the Foreign Office. On 28 February Lord Malmesbury informed him that he had sent the resignation to the Queen, adding " I don't know how to replace you," and by 3 March Her Majesty's acceptance was known.

There can be little doubt that, in spite of a pleasant sense of unwonted freedom, Lord Stratford had no sooner resigned his post than he began to regret it. He had become so accustomed to diplomatic work that he did not quite know how to exist without it. Disliking Constantinople as he had done all his life, so many years had been passed there, so much both of happiness and trouble, of triumph and failure, had been experienced in those palaces on the shores of the Bosphorus, that all his chief interests and all the salient epochs of his life seemed to be indissolubly linked with Stambol. Lady Stratford moreover was warmly attached to the spot where she had spent so many years. It was not unnatural that the Elchi should desire to end his connexion with the Sultan in a more ceremonious manner than his recent

parting, and it was speedily arranged that after an interval of
rest Lord Stratford should go back to the Porte to take a
formal leave of the Sultan, and "wind-up" the affairs of his
mission.   He naturally considered that the expressed wish of
the Government that he should return for a while to the
Porte temporarily suspended his resignation ; in his view he
was practically ambassador until he had gone out and taken
leave.   Any business that might call for special attention
during the interval would be, according to this view, entrusted
to him ; for by "winding up" he meant quite as much the
conclusion of pending affairs of a political kind as his own
personal business.   The Government, however, viewed the
arrangement differently ; they considered his embassy closed,
his services no longer available, and his return to Constantinople purely a compliment to himself and to the Sultan.
Accordingly, as the aspirations of Montenegro were just then
assuming a critical aspect, they appointed a new ambassador
who was to go out with all possible speed and undertake the
question.   Many people might say that it was a waste of
public money to send out a second ambassador when Lord
Stratford was in any case going, and had repeatedly given
proofs of his readiness to start almost at a day's notice on
important service without considering personal convenience ;
and it must certainly have appeared odd that a difficult
problem in Turkey should have been given to a comparatively
new man when the old and trusted adviser of the Sultan was
at hand ; but most amazing of all is it to read that the
appointment was made without a hint to Lord Stratford, and
that the diplomatist chosen to succeed him was one who was
notorious for holding diametrically opposite views on almost
every subject, and who had already had disagreements with
him during the negotiations concerning the Principalities in
the preceding year.   The cause of reform in Turkey, the
cause for which he had striven for so many years, began
its downward course when the Turks began to understand
the altered character of the British embassy under Sir Henry
Bulwer.

In spite of his wonder and indignation at the appointment, Lord Stratford did not relinquish the plan of returning
to take leave of the Sultan.   On 4 September, 1858, accompanied by his family and suite, he left London for Marseilles,
where H.M.S. *Curaçoa* awaited him.   The stately vessel lent
an added dignity to this final leave-taking.

Once more the Elchi revisited the scene of so many toils
and triumphs; once again he paced the Palace at Pera; but
his time was short, and he came only to depart again, for
ever. All the stately ceremony with which he was welcomed
by Sultan and ministers, all the grateful devotion of the many
whom he had rescued from oppression, all the hearty loyalty
of the British subjects whose champion he had stood for half
a century, could not reconcile him to the mournful nature of
his task. For he knew that he was assisting at the obsequies
of his hopes. His long struggle for reform in the Ottoman
Empire was at an end, and in the character of his successor
he believed he could trace the antithesis of all he had striven
for and the abandonment of all that he had won. The very
respect with which he was received had a melancholy side; it
was the last time that he would witness that reverence which
he had conquered by his own firm will and lofty purpose.
With some such thoughts the ambassador entered his ten-oar
caïque at Tophana, and crossed the waters of the Golden
Horn. The Ottoman carriages of state were awaiting him; a
guard of honour presented arms as he alighted at the official
residence of the Grand Vezir; and A'li Pasha himself,
attended by the Master of the Ceremonies, came forth to
receive him at the entrance of his saloon. A'li, despite his
French proclivities, was moved as he welcomed the old and
staunch friend of his country. He told the Elchi how his
departure was deplored, and how gratefully and unreservedly
his great services to the Ottoman State were recognized and
applauded. The interview was cordial; but in the midst of
the Grand Vezir's courtesies, Lord Stratford remembered the
affection of his old friend Reshid, and felt that in his newly
made grave lay buried whatever hope might have remained for
the future of Turkey.

Three days later the scene changed to the Sultan's palace,
and once more the Elchi stood before his imperial pupil. As
he delivered the letter addressed to " Sir, my Brother," and
signed *regiâ manu* " Victoria R.," the ambassador failed not
to dwell on the theme which was ever uppermost in his mind.
He spoke of the great measures that had illumined his
Majesty's reign, he touched on his own share in them, and
he begged for a firm assurance that the course of reform
which had begun so auspiciously should not be stayed when
he was no longer there to see and warn. The Sultan's reply
was brief: he was very glad, he said, to see again one who

had so largely contributed to drawing closer the links that
bound his Empire and Great Britain together; reforms were
being attended to;—he repeated, he was glad to see him.
Abdu-l-Mejid had begun to be but the shadow of his former
self. Intemperance was already too evidently undermining
his weakly constitution. Yet he was still capable of real
emotion, and his countenance evinced the deep feeling with
which he now took leave for ever of his old counsellor and
friend. Three years later he died.

The return of the great ambassador roused the warm
enthusiasm of the British colony. The merchants of Constantinople gathered together, and presented him with an
address, in which they testified their "heartfelt pleasure" at
seeing him once more among them, though only for a little
while, and assured him of their undying "personal regard
and esteem," and the "lively remembrance we shall ever
retain of the constant and efficient protection of our various
nterests during the long course of years in which they have
been under your lordship's care and vigilance;" they prayed
for his health and happiness; they spoke of how the poor
would never cease to lament the loss of Lady Stratford's
untiring benevolence; and they begged the Elchi not to
forget the country which he had so greatly benefited. Other
voices were then lifted up in praise and honour, and none
came more sweetly to the ear of the departing statesman
than the memorial of the American missionaries, in which
they recited the many reforms which he had brought into
Turkey, and especially the abolition of executions for apostasy, the recognition of the Protestant community, the open
sale of the Bible in the Turkish bazars, and the building of
the first Protestant church in Jerusalem; and added, "We
love to consider your lordship's influence as one of the important providential means by which God has been pleased
to carry on His work. . . . You have been guided wisely by
Him whose cause you have served." The Armenian Protestants were not behind their American brothers in their tribute
to the ambassador's noble work in their behalf, and their
memorial is touching in its humble thankfulness :—

It is with unfeigned regret that we have heard that your lordship is now taking leave of our country, probably for the last time.
On an occasion to us so mournful we find it difficult to give utterance to the true feelings of our hearts.

Our minds go back to the past, and we see everywhere memorials

of your lordship's humane and benevolent endeavours to ameliorate
the condition of the downcast and suffering in this our land.

We can testify that your lordship's benevolent exertions have
not been confined to the narrow limits of race or sect, but have
been freely extended to all who stood in need of your aid, whether
Mohammedan, Jew, or Christian. But especially, as Protestants,
are we now forcibly reminded of all your lordship's kind offices in
our behalf, when men bearing the Christian name, through ignorance of our real motives, became our persecutors. By your
lordship's favourable representations of us before the Sultan's
Government, we were recognised as loyal subjects, and the same
civil rights conceded to us as are enjoyed by the other Christian
communities in Turkey. Although few in number and of little
political influence, through your gracious interposition we are a
fully recognised community in Turkey, having our own chosen
representative at the Porte, and our members scattered over the
whole country, enjoying for the most part freedom to worship God
according to our own consciences and His most holy Word.

In the name of the five or six thousand Protestants scattered
over every part of Asiatic Turkey, we desire this day to render to
your lordship our most sincere and hearty thanks. The prayers
and best wishes of a grateful people will follow you from these
shores wherever you go. The memory of what you have done will
never be effaced from our hearts, and our children and our children's
children, to the latest generation, shall mention your name with
veneration, gratitude, and love.

On 19 October a great assembly of merchants and other
British residents met together on the brow of the hill of
Pera, where a noble site had been given by the Sultan at the
Elchi's request for the foundation of a Memorial Church—a
monument at once of the brave Englishmen who had fallen
in the late war, and of the progress of religious freedom
which had made the erection of an Anglican church, hard by
a mosque, a possibility in a Mohammedan country. And
now the foundation-stone was to be laid; and who could
worthily lay it but the venerable statesman who had spent
his life in the defence of liberty of conscience and the protection of oppressed Christianity? So Lord Stratford stood
forth before the multitude, and, before he took the trowel in
his hand, spoke solemn last words to the people. He dwelt
on the wonderful achievements of the past; on the changes
which had made such a ceremony possible in Turkey; on
the character of the war which had called forth such energies
and ended in such a crowning triumph as the Charter of Reform; and he bade them consider how henceforward every

Christian who sailed to the Golden Horn would see the
Memorial Church commanding the slope of the hill, and
would think of the victory of free religious worship, while he
remembered the successes of the battle-field, and the deeds
of those who had fallen in the fight over there to the eastward
amid the Crimean hills.

The parting followed soon. The people whom he had
succoured and protected crowded down to the landing-place
to see the Great Elchi take his last farewell of the scene of
his many labours. He stood on the steamer's poop, calm and
collected, no sign of the mental strain upon his unruffled
features, stately and courteous as an English gentleman alone
knows how to be. At last the farewells were said, the ship of
war moved off with a stately grace, as though conscious of the
honourable burden she conveyed, and many eyes were strained
to see the last of that commanding presence which had been
the centre of their world for the greater part of the century.
The Great Elchi would never again stand guard over the Bosphorus.

EPILOGUE.

1858–1880.

With many men the end of work is the close of life; few
really hard workers abandon their profession or business till
it has begun to forsake them; and in most cases the loss of
the familiar desk or well-known office has something of the
sharpness of a mortal blow. A hale old man too often
becomes an infirm invalid when there is nothing left to call
forth the energy which kept him in health; and with the
cessation of the necessity, the capability of effort often disappears. And so the Seventh Age is reached, which, if protracted beyond the common span, is apt to realize the word of
the Psalmist, and is but labour and sorrow, till we pass away.

The old age of Lord Stratford de Redcliffe was very different: it was a shining example of what faith and hope in
the best things, and a bright, intellectual activity may do to
preserve the fire and energy of youth to a period long beyond
the lives of most of the strongest men. In 1858 his diplomatic work was done, but he had not retired from his labours

out of any feeling of impaired powers. Mentally and physically he was still as capable of conducting the affairs of any embassy as he had been twenty years before; yet he had passed the traditional limit, and had all but completed his seventy-second year when he bade his last farewell to Constantinople. So far from being " labour and sorrow," the last twenty years of his life were the happiest of all. The loss of the accustomed occupation brought with it no corresponding diminution in the capacity for work or in the interest in all that was going forward in the world. Compulsory routine gave place to voluntary tasks; for his mind was of that active sort to which idleness is impossible and vigorous exercise is recreation.

Not all at once, however, did he arrive at this sense of peace and contentment. The disappointments that had marred the closing years of his mission were scars too deep for aught but time to obliterate. The healing work began at Rome, where he wintered after his farewell journey to the East. There, in the midst of an intellectual circle, courted by the most distinguished members of foreign society, many of whom he had met in former days, surrounded by objects of the deepest interest to a mind well stored in the archives of classical antiquity, and a spectator of the beginning of that movement of " Italia Irredenta " which has since developed into such happy results, the vexations of the immediate past were gradually forgotten, and their real insignificance was measured.

There is a passage in the Lives of the Lords Strangford which fitly expresses the part that the Great Elchi was to play in public life after his retirement from an official career. Lord Strangford—the same Percy Smythe who had been an attaché at Constantinople during the Crimean War—wrote to his wife in 1862 : " I want Lord Stratford de Redcliffe to feel that his position in foreign politics is that which was held by the Great Duke in war, and by Lyndhurst in law, and that he is not only able, but bound, before it is too late, to survey the world from his height, and to speak of the future with impartial utterance, like Moses from Mount Pisgah." Unfortunately the want of oratorical powers affected him almost as much in the Lords as it had done thirty years before in the Commons; but he never neglected the duty of speaking, and few great foreign questions came before the House without drawing from him some of those wise and spirited counsels which, from their brevity and rare occurrence, and their unmistakable stamp of profound experience, carried with them the weight which belonged to "the genuine and naturally selected Nestor of foreign politics." Disclaiming all party ties, Lord Stratford was able to speak impartially out of the depths of his long acquaintance with the springs of foreign policy, and to confront boldly the inevitable issues of varying combinations. There was, it is true, little in his delivery to persuade, and much in his policy to alarm the timid, yet there was that in his words which commanded attention and respect from all parties in the House, for they carried with them a sense of right and reason. His voice was always raised in the cause of freedom against oppression and for the weak against the strong.

He had not long returned to England in 1859 when he rose to call the attention of the Peers to the state of Italian affairs, and protested against the cautious neutrality which had induced the calamities of the war. The speech contained an eloquent appeal for the maintenance and enforcement of the treaties of 1815 : "Notwithstanding the wounds inflicted on them as a body of international right," he said, " far from being cast aside as a whole or being extinguished in public estimation, they are still the title-deeds of many an extensive territory, securities for Sardinian unity, no less than for Austrian incumbency ; and, what is more than being barriers against encroachment and confusion, they are the living records and guards of those achievements in civilization which have made the abolition of slavery a part and parcel of the law of Europe, and have consecrated the world of waters, whether flowing through separated States or expanding in boundless ocean, to the uses of an unfettered and almost unquestioned navigation. My Lords, there is a vitality even in their amputated limbs ; there is something judicial even in their submission to violence. The stroke which blasted the independence of Cracow, that last refuge and monument of Polish nationality, invested its memory with a sacred character, and the feeble protest issued on its behalf in a whisper from London and Paris now comes back in peals of thunder on the alarmed conscience."

Other speeches were in his own special province ; as when in May 1861 he moved to get the French troops out of Syria, and maintained that the chief cause of the disturbances in the Lebanon was the general misgovernment of the Ottoman Em-

pire, and especially the neglect to enforce the provisions of the
Charter of Reform. In 1864 he spoke against the cession of
the Ionian Islands, and in favour of Denmark; in 1867 on the
insurrection in Candia, and in 1870 on massacres by Greek
brigands. The Poles always had his warm support. On home
affairs he spoke rarely, yet his earnest protest against the exclusion of the Jews from the privileges of the Oaths Bill is
worth recording.

Outside the House of Lords his influence was felt in public
affairs, especially in those connected with the East. Like
Palmerston, he had always opposed the Suez Canal, which
he set down as a French stratagem ; but he was a warm sup-
porter of the Euphrates route to India, and its chief promoter,
General Chesney, was in constant communication with him
in every stage of that long-struggling but still unrealized en-
terprise. He was a vigorous leader in the cause of the unhappy Circassians when they were exiled by Russia in 1864 ;
and at almost the same moment he was adding his voice to
the protests which were raised by the Evangelical Alliance
against the neglect of the interests and even of the bare protection of the missionaries in Turkey.

In 1869 an honour, wholly unexpected and unsolicited,
came to Lord Stratford. As years rolled on, his great services
stood out from the shadows of past politics bright and conspicuous ; and it was remembered that of all who had served
England in those years of trial he alone had been left without
adequate reward. Mr. Gladstone's generous admiration for
intellect and character, as apart from politics, was conspicuous
in his offer of the Garter to a peer who had never been a
partisan. " Two garters are now available," he wrote to
Lord Stratford; " after your long career of distinguished
public service, allow me to place one of them at your disposal.
. . . It is scarcely necessary that I should add that much as
the Government might feel the honour and advantage of your
support, this note is written neither with the expectation nor
with the desire to modify your position of perfect political
independence." As Lord Ellenborough said, it was a valuable
example of the " recognition of services rendered, not to a
party, but to the State."

Of his private life it is difficult to give any adequate
picture. When he returned to England it was to settle down
in the old house in Grosvenor Square, which had been his
ever since 1829, but which, owing to his constant absences

on diplomatic service, he had seldom occupied. Though he had been so much abroad, his love for England had remained just as strong; all other places, however lovely, were indifferent to him in comparison to his own country—the country he loved so passionately—and this house in London was his _home_, to which he always came back with pleasure. Here he found himself, after a time, the centre of a large circle of friends. Many of the old ones had indeed passed away, yet the youthful buoyancy of his spirit and the charm of his manner and conversation drew to him a new generation, who soon loved him as well and appreciated him as much as those who had gone. Instead of commanding homage as a right, he seemed to be surprised that anyone should take the trouble to come and see him; and he laid himself out to interest his visitors with a courteous grace that had its own peculiar fascination. It was said by one who knew him well, " I always entered his presence as that of a great man; I always left it loving the _man_ more each time."

Released from the vexations and the contentions of his official post, his character lost those elements of austerity and peremptoriness which were no longer fostered by circumstances. In earlier years the idealist's visions of "the Good, the Beautiful, and the True " were too often marred by some passing disturbance which called up the fighting spirit of the man and rudely startled the poet from his dream. In latter years there was no such disturbing force. Outward events indeed would move him deeply; he would rise to righteous indignation at a tale of wrong, at a base or selfish or false action; and the cowardice of governments or the meanness of a policy would ever arouse that fiery wrath which was among Lord Stratford's titles to our respect. But these were no longer personal causes; he was not himself concerned, more than any other Englishman; and his passion, being abstract and impersonal, was no interruption to the poetry of his nature. We must not forget that throughout his long life no pressure of work, no load of responsibility, could ever make him forego the poetry which was the delight of his leisure. Most men, worthy of the name, feel the need of some mode of expressing their inmost thoughts and emotions which shall not have the blunt directness of open speech. Some find utterance in music, some in the painter's art, or the wide expressiveness of sculpture. But to others the forms of verse are the natural exponents of their inward nature, and they can say in metre what nothing could induce them to reveal in prose. Lord Stratford's was one of these minds, and his poetry is no artificial product of the fancy, but the natural expression of himself.

In *Shadows of the Past* (1866) we see some of the best of his earlier verse, and amid much that is indifferent to modern criticism, we find many beautiful lines. His old age, however, was the flowering time of his poetry. The faculty of expression seemed to develop, and the old metres were cast away in favour of more fervid and dramatic forms. This is especially notable in *Jubilee in Fatherland*, an ode on the triumph of United Germany in 1871, which burns with a fire and a spirit that, in a more than octogenarian, is amazing, and which won such admiration in Germany that a German translation was made at the special request of some leading men. Carlyle wrote of it:—

I received with great pleasure the vigorous and brilliant piece of verse in honour of the Germans, whom I also, as you know, much honour. There is a fine old tone of classicality in these stanzas, a sound withal as of ringing steel, and the sentiment throughout has the great merit of being at once cordial, emphatic, and just.

A theme which was frequently in his thoughts was suggested by Shakspere's line, "Reverence is the angel of the world." An essay on the ennobling influence of reverence upon mankind lay at the time of his death unfinished on his table. The subject was one on which he was well qualified to speak; for of all his qualities, reverence was one of the most striking: reverence for established institutions, reverence for national engagements, for the sanctities of home and honour, and above all for the Source and Object of all reverence. Firm in his own faith, he was very tolerant of those who differed from him; but as the growing scepticism of the age forced itself upon his observation, he desired to leave on record his own steadfast belief in the God of his fathers—that faith that had stood by him in his active public life and had never failed him either in youth or age. The record was to be the brief statement of his own practical thoughts on religion, a humble testimony which, whilst leaving no doubt as to his own views, might, perhaps, be helpful to others of less assured faith than himself. The titles of the two small volumes speak for themselves: *Why am I a Christian?* (1873) and *The Greatest of Miracles* (1876). "I am most struck,"

says Dean Stanley, after reading the former, " with the amount
of matter which you have been able to place within so small
a compass. I trust that the world may be better for seeing
that the result of your long experience is so firm a faith, and
that the Church may be the better also for seeing that so firm
a faith can be combined with so large and deep an insight
into the great truths which all Christians hold or ought to
hold alike."

The testimony of one who belonged to a different order of
mind from Dean Stanley may also be quoted.

24 Dec. 1875.

My dear and long-known Friend,— How could you suppose that
I should feel otherwise than honoured and delighted by such a
mark of your esteem and affection ?   I accept it with gratitude and
joy.   Right glad am I to see such a clear stout handwriting as
yours, in an age that has passed the " threescore years and ten "—
but still more to learn that, though the body may wax infirm, the
heart has not grown cold.   Somehow or other the love of Christ
keeps people very young and fresh, however old they may be.   God
be with you and yours, in time and in eternity.

Yours ever truly,
SHAFTESBURY.

The last years of his life were spent on the borders of his
favourite Kentish country. He had always loved the neighbourhood of Tunbridge Wells, where he had met and won his
wife, and in 1873 he bought a house at Frant which was
gradually enlarged to the present extent of Frant Court.
Here he finally retired in 1878, never again to move. Hither
people came to see and consult him about the struggle then
going on in Turkey and the reopening of the Eastern Question. Few letters to the *Times* have produced a greater
impression upon sensible people than the temperate survey
of the " Bulgarian Atrocity " question which the ex-Ambassador contributed to its columns in 1876. Letters of con-
gratulation and applause arrived from all parts of England
and all ranks of society. From 1875 to 1880 the menacing
aspect of the Eastern Question drew forth repeated comments,
criticisms, precedents, and warnings, from the pen of the
veteran statesman who had himself steered the Turkish ship
of state through so many storms. There was an impression
that in his old age he had changed his views and deserted his
old *protégé* ; but the impression was due to a misconception
of his earlier attitude towards the Ottoman Empire. He had

never been a Turcophil, as people supposed ; but had always looked forward to the creation of a belt of practically auto-nomous Christian states, under the suzerainty of the Sultan, as the surest barrier against Russian aggression. He would have welcomed the formation of a Christian empire in the place of Turkey if he could have discovered any Eastern Christians fit to rule it. Failing this, he believed that the supreme authority of the Sultan was essential to counteract the influence of Russia in the Christian provinces, and he hoped for a regenerate Turkey worthy to take a place among civilized nations. To deny that he was disappointed with the course of events in the later history of Turkey would be un-true : the reckless extravagance of Abdu-l-Aziz, and the consequent financial catastrophe ; the failure of the European States to enforce those reforms which he knew to be the only palliative for the increasing decay of the Ottoman Empire ; the want of union and moral courage in the Powers which permitted such an outrage as the Russian war of 1877—all these were sore subjects of reflection. But disappointment did not alter his long and firmly established views on the duty of England in the East, and on the only method of saving the Turks from themselves. These papers on the Eastern Question [1] written at the age of ninety—indeed the last was composed in the summer of 1880, when its author had passed the meridian of his ninety-fourth year—only con-firm, explain, and amplify what he had frequently urged in his despatches, and laid impressively before the Sultan, forty years before.

Deep as was his interest in Eastern affairs during these latter years, they formed but one of the many subjects that occupied his ever-vigorous mind. It is seldom that men retain in extreme age so marvellous a receptive, one might say ac-quisitive, power. In whatever company he found himself, whether of statesman, scholar, or plain working man, he had always something to ask and something to learn.

To the last his enthusiasm for heroic deeds remained fresh and warm as a boy's. Tears would come to his eyes as he read the news of some gallant act or heroic rescue. So was it when he was told the story of how the colours of the 24th were saved out of the carnage of Isandlana by the devo-tion of two young officers. It was a deed to rouse the envious

---

[1] They were republished under the title of *The Eastern Question*, with a preface by Dean Stanley (Murray, 1881).

admiration of every man, but in no one did it awake a more responsive cord of sympathy than in Lord Stratford. Many who had perhaps almost forgotten that the great Ambassador still survived were startled one morning as they opened the *Times* to hear what was well named "the sound of a trumpet, signed S. de R." It was the dismal story of Isandlana told in vigorous verse ; and then came the deed which had called forth the poem :—

Far, far away, at fearful risk, a nobler charge was moved,
And those in trust right well achieved what more than valour
　　proved ;
Both still were young, and firm in minds that ne'er from duty
　　roved.

Quick, quick, they mount the bridled steeds ; while near each loyal
　　breast,
The colours lie, from ill secured, as in a miser's chest.
What could in haste be done they did ; to faith they gave the rest.

In fast succession forth they passed, along the straggling host ;
On, gallant youths ! ye may not heed the peril or the cost.
Oh ! speed them, Heaven ; direct their course ; what shame if such
　　were lost !

A stare of silent brief surprise, and then a deafening yell,
As if the imprisoned souls below had burst the bonds of hell ;
On dashed the dauntless riders still ; who dared to cross them fell.

Soon clear of foemen, side by side, athwart the pathless wild
Conveyers of a precious charge, by capture ne'er defiled,
On, boldly on, they stretched with speed, by youthful hope beguiled.

Alike through pools of rotten marsh, o'er beds of flint they rode ;
They crossed the dell, they scaled the hill, they shunned the lone
　　abode,
Nor ceased to urge the foaming beasts their weary limbs bestrode.

At length the frontier stream appears ; hurrah ! what need of more ?
Oh, fate ! They plunge, the waters flash, the rushing waters roar.
Unseated, wounded, all but drowned, they touch, they clasp the
　　shore.

A few brief hours of calm succeed, they share the joy of those
Who, purpose gained and danger past, from anxious toil repose ;
But nature sinks—too great the strain, and wounds are slow to
　　close.

One slept, nor woke again ; like him, too soon the other slept ;
And those who sought and found them dead, the colours near them
      kept ;
In pity—doubt not—stooped a while, and o'er the bodies wept.

Melvill and Coghill, honoured names ; ye need no verse of mine
To fix the record of your worth on memory's faithful shrine ;
To you a wreath that may not fade shall England's praise assign.

Ye crown the list of glorious acts which form our country's boast,
Ye rescued from the brink of shame what soldiers prize the most,
And reached by duty's path a life beyond the lives ye lost.

Perhaps one of the greatest pleasures that Lord Stratford
experienced at this time was that afforded him by the appreciation of his long services by the Queen, conveyed to him in
touching terms. The assurance that her Majesty, far removed as she is above prejudice and faction, felt " how true
and faithful " he had been " and how valuable," was, to a
mind like his, a far higher reward than pensions, decorations,
or titles. Such rewards the Queen well knows how to bestow,
and the consideration with which they are given causes them
to be doubly valued.

A fortnight before his death the son of his ancient comrade
David Morier, who had preceded him to the grave but a few
years, came to see his father's old chief. Sir Robert Morier
thus records his last visit : " His intellect was as clear, his
speech as incisive, his interest in poetry and politics as keen,
as when I last saw him three years ago. It was a beautiful
English summer afternoon ; a warm sun lit up his pale features
which fully retained their splendid outlines, and were entirely
wanting in the wrinkles or withered look of extreme old age.
I could not help thinking of the line—

    Slow sinks more lovely ere his race be run. . . .

He seemed some grand old Titan majestically sinking to his
rest in all his glory, as if he knew the Infinite was waiting to
receive him with all due honour."

It was very shortly after this visit that Lord Stratford's
strength began to fail ; a few days of weary restlessness, and
then, in the early morning of Saturday, 14 August, 1880,
beautiful in death as he had been in life, he passed, without
pain or struggle, to where " beyond these voices there is peace."

" Even now his presence seems to fill the room where he

lived and thought and wrote. Here the trifles and vexations of every-day life did not come; it seemed to be another, better, higher life that surrounded him and glorified all he touched. Truer views of men and events, calmer judgments, higher appreciation for a noble aim, even though it seemed to fail, in the least as in the greatest; with a scorn, or rather pity beyond all expression, for everything in a man or a nation that was mean, cruel, or self-seeking. Gathered round him in that room were the treasured relics of the past, each with its own story; the books he was so fond of, the prints of the men he most admired, silent companions of his exile for so many years; the little picture of Nelson, which had never left him since his earliest days; George Canning, his honoured master in public life; Pitt, Wellington, his country's heroes— all cared for to the very last. The table at which he wrote, and from which he could look out on the broad stretch of woodland crowning the heights of Eridge—look out, beyond, to the distant hills and to the sunset that he loved to watch— the sunset that always spoke to him—spoke clearer as each year passed on—of the unseen home above."

On the Saturday following he was laid to rest in the churchyard of Frant village, followed to the grave by many friends and mourned by his countrymen as few men, perhaps, have been mourned whose life survived so long the close of their public career.

"Yesterday," so spoke Dean Stanley in his sermon, "the greatest ambassador of our time was, after a life prolonged far beyond the natural limits of human existence, laid to rest in a little churchyard in the county of Sussex. Many are they who will be grateful to the end of their days that they had known his majestic character. No one could enter into his presence, either as he sat on what may truly be called his throne at Constantinople, or during the long years of his dignified retirement, without feeling that they had seen a king of men. No one could hear the name of Stratford Canning named throughout the far East without feeling that, so long as he retained his post, the honour of England was safe in his incorruptible integrity, in his magnificent liberality, in his unshaken firmness. No one could hear his influence spoken of by Christian or Musulman, Protestant or Catholic, Greek or Turk, without feeling that each man knew that he was a terror to evildoers which none could confront with impunity, a refuge for the desolate and oppressed which none could seek in vain. No one who had ever witnessed it could forget the boundless industry, the noble generosity, with which through all the chaos of the Crimean War he laboured for the sick and suffering soldiers, or defended those who went out to succour them. No one could mistake that in his energy, in his remonstrances, in his purity, the tottering fabric of the Eastern Empire, which for years he held in his mighty grasp, had at once the best bulwark against its ruin, the best guarantee against its evil deeds.

"Such an example did indeed lift us up from the base and sordid atmosphere of party strife and bitterness. Such an old age, with the fire of youth subdued but not extinct, with the experience of years giving ever fresh life to the memory of the past, was worthy of remembrance to every toiling sufferer. He had chosen that better part which neither falling empires, nor political rancour, nor worldly disappointment, nor ungrateful obliviousness could ever take from him."

.   .   .   .

Four years later, on 24 May, 1884, a statue was unveiled by Lord Granville in Westminster Abbey. The occasion was memorable ; for now, for the first time, was diplomacy honoured with a place among England's greatest sons, in the person of " one who had rendered the profession brilliant by his genius and invigorated it by the manliness of his character."

It was a national tribute, freely and publicly subscribed, to the memory of a great Englishman who had signally upheld the honour of his country at the post of danger.

The Poet Laureate wrote the epitaph :—

> Thou third great Canning, stand among our best
> And noblest, now thy long day's work has ceased,
> Here silent in our Minster of the West
> Who wert the voice of England in the East.

THE END

Spottiswoode & Co. Printers, New-street Square, London.

LIST OF THE WORKS OF STANLEY LANE-POOLE.

1. LIFE of EDWARD WILLIAM LANE, Translator of the 1001 Nights. 8vo. pp. 138. (Reprinted from Part VI. of Lane's Arabic Lexicon.) Williams & Norgate. 1877.

2, 3. The PEOPLE of TURKEY. By a Consul's Daughter. Edited by STANLEY LANE-POOLE. Two vols. 8vo. pp. xxxi, 288 ; x, 352. Murray. 1878.

4. LANE'S SELECTIONS from the KURAN. New Edition, with Introduction by STANLEY LANE-POOLE. 8vo. Frontispiece. Pp. cxii, 173, 2. Trübner's Oriental Series. 1879.

5. EGYPT. Illustrated. Fcp. 8vo. pp. xii, 200. Sampson Low. 1881.

6. The SPEECHES and TABLE-TALK of the PROPHET MOHAMMAD. 18mo. pp. lxiii, 196. Macmillan's Golden Treasury Series. 1882.

7. Le KORAN, sa POÉSIE et ses LOIS. 24mo. pp. vi, 112. Leroux' Bibl. Orient. Elzévirienne. 1882.

8. STUDIES in a MOSQUE. 8vo. pp. viii, 288. Allen. 1883.

9. ARABIAN SOCIETY in the MIDDLE AGES. Edited by STANLEY LANE-POOLE. 8vo. pp. xvi, 283. Chatto & Windus. 1883.

10. PICTURESQUE PALESTINE, SINAI, and EGYPT. Vol. IV. EGYPT. 4to. pp. 121-234. Illustrated. Virtue. 1883.

11. SOCIAL LIFE in EGYPT : a Description of the Country and its People. (Supplement to 'Picturesque Palestine.') 4to. Illustrated. Pp. vi, 138. Virtue. 1883.

12. SELECTIONS from the PROSE WRITINGS of JONATHAN SWIFT. With Portrait, Preface, and Notes. 8vo. pp. xxx, 284. Paul & Trench's Parchment Library. 1884.

13. NOTES for a BIBLIOGRAPHY of SWIFT. 8vo. pp. 36. Elliot Stock. 1884.

14. LETTERS and JOURNALS of JONATHAN SWIFT. With Commentary and Notes. 8vo. pp. xv, 292. Paul & Trench's Parchment Library. 1885.

15. The LIFE of GENERAL F. R. CHESNEY, R.A. By his Wife and Daughter. Edited, with Preface, by STANLEY LANE-POOLE. Portrait. 8vo. pp. xxiii, 279. Allen. 1885.

16. The ART of the SARACENS in EGYPT. Illustrated. 8vo. pp. xviii, 264. Published for Committee of Council on Education by Chapman & Hall. 1886.

17. The MOORS in SPAIN. Illustrated. 8vo. pp. xx, 285. Story of the Nations Series. Unwin. 1887.

18. TURKEY. Illustrated. 8vo. pp. xix, 373. Story of the Nations Series. Unwin. 1888.

19, 20. **The LIFE of the Rt. Hon. STRATFORD CANNING,**
VISCOUNT STRATFORD DE REDCLIFFE, K.G. From his
Memoirs and Papers. Three Portraits. Two vols. 8vo. pp. xxix,
519; xviii, 475. LIBRARY EDITION. Longmans. 1888.

21. POPULAR EDITION. Pp. xx, 377. Longmans. 1890.

22, 23. **THIRTY YEARS of COLONIAL GOVERNMENT.**
From the Papers of the Rt. Hon. Sir G. F. Bowen, G.C.M.G.
Portrait. Two vols. pp. viii, 460 ; viii, 467. Longmans. 1889.

24. **The BARBARY CORSAIRS.** Illustrated. 8vo. pp. xviii,
316. Story of the Nations Series. Unwin. 1890.

25. **CATALOGUE of the COLLECTION of ORIENTAL**
COINS belonging to Colonel C. SETON GUTHRIE, R.E.
Fasc. I. Pp. viii, 38. Five Autotype Plates. (And Large-
Paper Edition.) Austin. 1874.

26. **INTERNATIONAL NUMISMATA ORIENTALIA.**
Part II. COINS of the TURKUMANS. 4to. pp. xii, 44. Six
Plates. Trübner. 1875.

27, 28. **ESSAYS in ORIENTAL NUMISMATICS.** First
and Second Series. Plates. 8vo. Trübner. 1877.

29-38. **CATALOGUE of ORIENTAL COINS in the**
BRITISH MUSEUM. Printed for the Trustees. 8vo. 10 vols.
(Ouvrage couronné par l'Institut de France. 1881).

Vol.   I. EASTERN KHALEEFEHS. Pp. xx, 263. Eight Autotype Plates.
1875.
II. MOHAMMADAN DYNASTIES. Pp. xii, 279. Eight Autotype Plates.
1876.
III. TURKUMANS. Pp. xxvii, 305. Twelve Autotype Plates. 1877.
IV. EGYPT. Pp. xxx, 279. Eight Autotype Plates. 1879.
V. The MOORS and ARABIA. Pp. lii, 175. Seven Autotype Plates. 1880.
VI. The MONGOLS. Pp. lxxv, 300. Nine Autotype Plates. 1881.
VII. BUKHARA. Pp. xlviii, 131. Five Autotype Plates. 1882.
VIII. TURKS. Pp. li, 431. Twelve Autotype Plates. 1883.
IX. } ADDITIONS : 1875-1889. Two vols. Pp. 420, 460. Twenty Autotype
X. }   Plates, and General Index. 1889, 1890.

39, 40. **CATALOGUE of INDIAN COINS in the BRITISH**
MUSEUM. Printed for the Trustees. 8vo.

Vol. I. SULTANS of DEHLI. Pp. xliv, 199. Nine Autotype Plates. 1884.
II. MOHAMMADAN STATES. Pp. lxxx, 239. Twelve Autotype Plates. 1885.

41. **COINS and MEDALS** : their Place in History and Art. By
the Authors of the British Museum Official Catalogues. Edited
by STANLEY LANE-POOLE. Illustrated. 8vo. pp. x, 286. Elliot
Stock. 1885.

42. **The CABINET of ORIENTAL COINS at CHRIST**
CHURCH, OXFORD. 8vo. pp. 8. Virtue. 1886.

43. **CATALOGUE of the MOHAMMADAN COINS in**
the BODLEIAN LIBRARY, OXFORD. Pp. xvi. 55. Four
Plates. Clarendon Press. 1888.

44-6. **LANE'S ARABIC-ENGLISH LEXICONS.** Vols.
6-8. Imp. 4to. pp. xxxix, 2221-3000. Williams & Norgate.
1877-1890.

Printed in the United States
88672LV00003B/65/A